THE POLITICS OF HISTORY

The Politics of History

BY HOWARD ZINN

Beacon Press   Boston

A Note on the Contents:

The essay "Knowledge as a Form of Power" has appeared in the *Saturday
Review*. "History as Private Enterprise" appears in the Festschrift for
Herbert Marcuse, *The Critical Spirit,* edited by Kurt H. Wolff and Bar-
rington Moore, Jr., published by Beacon Press. "LaGuardia in the Jazz
Age" is drawn from various material in my book *LaGuardia in Congress,*
published by Cornell University Press and the American Historical Asso-
ciation, © 1958 by Howard Zinn, © 1959 by the American Historical
Association, used here by permission of Cornell University Press. "The
Limits of the New Deal" is the introductory essay in my book *New Deal
Thought,* copyright © 1966 by the Bobbs-Merrill Company, Inc., published by Bobbs-Merrill. "Abolitionists and the Tactics of Agitation" ap-
peared in the *Columbia University Forum*. The part of "Psychoanalyzing
the Dissenter: Two Cases" that deals with Lewis Feuer was a review in
The New Republic. "Vietnam: The Moral Equation" and "The Prisoners:
A Bit of Contemporary History" appeared as articles in *The Nation*. The
Hiroshima part of "Hiroshima and Royan" is an adaptation of an article
in the *Columbia University Forum*. "Freedom and Responsibility" is an
adaptation of an essay that appeared on page two of *The New York Times
Book Review*.

To, for, with
Roslyn

Acknowledgments

To the American Philosophical Society, the Louis Rabinowitz Foundation, and the Graduate School of Boston University for support during the various stages of writing this book. To Ernest Young, Marilyn Young, and Hilda Hein for critical readings of certain sections of the book. To all the Magraws for the peaceful beauty of the Cobbles, where I could finish my writing. To the librarians of Royan for their kindness. To Joan Agri, Marion Lee, and Judith Mandelbaum for invaluable assistance. To Jim Miller, for constant help and encouragement. To anonymous friends for anonymous spiritual support. To Myla and Jeff, for being themselves.

Contents

"Other historians relate facts to inform us of facts. You relate them to excite in our hearts an intense hatred of lying, ignorance, hypocrisy, superstition, tyranny; and the anger remains even after the memory of the facts has disappeared."

—DIDEROT, WRITING OF VOLTAIRE

Introduction

Sometime in 1968, newspapers recorded the death of America's leading entrepreneur of political buttons. He had always worn his own button which said: "I don't care who wins. My business is buttons."

The historian, by habit, is a passive reporter, studying the combatants of yesterday, while those of today clash outside his window. His preferences are usually private. His business is history.

He may ask philosophical questions about the past: do we find certain sequential patterns in history? or are historical events unique, disorderly? But he rarely sees himself as helpful in changing the pattern or affecting the disorder. He may believe that people through history have been caught in the grip of extra-human forces. Or he may see them as free agents shaping the world. But whether they are free or not, he himself is bound—by professional commitment—to tally but not to vote, to touch but not to feel. Or to feel, but not to act. At most, to act after hours, but not through his writing, in his job as a historian.

Out of this sense of the situation comes the question which underlies this book: in a world where children are still not safe from starvation or bombs, should not the historian thrust himself and his writing into history, on behalf of goals in which he deeply believes? Are we historians not humans first, and scholars because of that?

Recall Rousseau's accusation: "We have physicists, geometricians, chemists, astronomers, poets, musicians and painters in plenty, but we have no longer a citizen among us." Since the eighteenth century, that list of specialists has grown, to include sociologists, political scientists, psychologists, historians. The scholars multiply diligently, but with little passion. The passion I speak of

1

is the urgent desire for a better world. I will contend that it should overcome those professional rules which call, impossibly and callously, for neutrality.

My argument can be easily exaggerated (by me as well as by others), so let me say now what this book does and does not intend:

1. It does not aim to disengage history from the classical effort to be scientific, but rather to reaffirm the ancient humanist aims of the scientists (before military needs began to command so much of their talent), and to catch up with the new understanding in science about what "scientific" means. The physicist Werner Heisenberg put it this way: "Science no longer confronts nature as an objective observer, but sees itself as an actor in this interplay between man and nature.*

2. It does not argue for a uniform approach—mine or anyone's—to the writing of history, and certainly not for the banning of any kind of historical work, bland or controversial, pernicious or humane, whether written for pleasure or profit or social objectives. Its aim is, by encouragement and example, to stimulate a higher proportion of socially relevant, value-motivated, action-inducing historical work.

3. It certainly does not call for tampering with the facts—by distortion or concealment or invention. My point is not to approach historical data with preconceived answers, but with preconceived questions.** I assume accuracy is a prerequisite, but that history is not praiseworthy for having merely achieved that. Freud once said some people are always polishing their spectacles and never putting them on.

The Politics of History has two kinds of essays. The essays in the first and third sections are *about* the writing of history. They proceed from a discussion of the uses of knowledge in general to

---

* See the review essay on Karl Löwith by Heinz Lubasz in *History and Theory*, Vol. II, No. 2, 1962, where Lubasz also quotes Heisenberg as saying that "by its intervention science alters and refashions the object of investigation."

** Abraham Kaplan, although his main concern is methodological, discusses the role values play in the work of a behavioral scientist, and says: "Values make for bias, not when they dictate problems, but when they prejudge solutions." *The Conduct of Inquiry,* Chandler, 1964, p. 382.

historical consciousness in particular. In them, I try to argue for the notion of the historian as an actor, and this requires discussing many of the problems which fall, professionally speaking, within "the philosophy of history." Is history "determined" or are we free to make our own? Can the historian justifiably write as a participant-observer in the social struggles of our time? Does "history as an act" lead to distorting the truth? What is the role of causality in history, of explanation? Should we be "present-minded" or "past-minded"? Analytical or speculative? And what of straight narrative as opposed to theoretical history? What is history for, anyway, and what is the responsibility of the historian? One of these essays suggests some criteria for a radical history.

The middle part of the book—the essays *in* history—represents an attempt to begin to meet those criteria for a radical history. These essays do not have the usual connective tissue of standard historical works; they do not deal with a specific period, or with all periods, or with one problem of the American past. What ties each to the others is a common purpose—to participate a bit in the social combat of our time. Whether or not the essays actually fulfill this aim, I leave to the reader to judge. I have my own doubts. My chief hope is to provoke more historical writing which is consciously activist on behalf of the kind of world which history has not yet disclosed, but perhaps hinted at.

1

Knowledge as a form of power

Is it not time that we scholars began to earn our keep in this world? Thanks to a gullible public, we have been honored, flattered, even paid, for producing the largest number of inconsequential studies in the history of civilization: tens of thousands of articles, books, monographs; millions of term papers; enough lectures to deafen the gods. Like politicians, we have thrived on public innocence.

Occasionally, we emerge from the library stacks to sign a petition or deliver a speech, then return to produce even more of inconsequence. We are accustomed to keeping our social commitment extracurricular and our scholarly work safely neutral. We were quick to understand that awe and honor greet those who have flown off into space while people suffer on earth.

If this accusation seems harsh, read the titles of doctoral dissertations published in the past twenty years, and the pages of the leading scholarly journals for the same period, alongside the lists of war dead, the figures on per capita income in Latin America, the autobiography of Malcolm X. We publish while others perish.

The gap between the products of scholarly activity and the needs of a troubled world could be borne with some equanimity so long as the nation seemed to be solving its problems. And for most of our history, this seemed to be the case. We had a race question, but we "solved" it: by a war to end slavery, and by papering over the continued degradation of the black population with laws and rhetoric. Wealth was not distributed equitably; but the New Deal, and then war orders, kept that problem under control—or at least, out of sight. There was turmoil in the world, but we were always at the periphery; the European imperial powers did the nasty work while we nibbled at the edges of their empires (except in Latin America where our firm control was disguised by a fatherly sounding Monroe Doctrine, and the pose of a Good Neighbor).

None of those "solutions" is working anymore. The Black Power revolt, the festering of the cities beyond our control, the rebellion of students against the Vietnam war and the draft—all indicate that the United States has run out of time, space, and rhetoric. The liberal artifacts which represented our farthest reaches toward reform—the Fourteenth Amendment, New Deal welfare legislation, and the U.N. Charter—are not enough. Revolutionary changes are required in social policy.

The trouble is, we don't know how to make such a revolution. There is no precedent for it in an advanced industrial society where power and wealth are highly concentrated in government, corporations, and the military, while the rest of us have pieces of that fragmented power which political scientists are pleased to call "pluralism." We have voices, and even votes, but not the means— more crassly, the power—to turn either domestic or foreign policy in completely new directions.

That is why the knowledge industry (the universities, colleges, schools, representing directly fifty billions of the national spending each year) is so important. Knowledge is a form of power. True, force is the most direct form of power, and government has a monopoly of that (as Max Weber once pointed out). But in modern times, when social control rests on "the consent of the governed," force is kept in abeyance for emergencies, and everyday control is exercised by a set of rules, a fabric of values passed on from one generation to another by the priests and the teachers of the society. What we call the rise of democracy in the world means that force is replaced by deception (a blunt way of saying "education") as the chief method for keeping society as it is.

This makes knowledge important, because although it cannot confront force directly, it can counteract the deception that makes the government's force legitimate. And the knowledge industry, which directly reaches seven million young people in colleges and universities, thus becomes a vital and sensitive locus of power. That power can be used, as traditionally, to maintain the status quo, or (as is being demanded by the student rebels) to change it.

Those who command more obvious forms of power (political control and wealth) try also to commandeer knowledge. Industry entices some of the most agile minds for executive posts in business. Government lures others for more glamorous special jobs: physicists to work on H-bombs; biologists to work on what we might call for want of a better name, the field of communicable disease; chemists to work on nerve gas (like that which killed those six thousand sheep in Utah); political scientists to work on counter-insurgency warfare; historians to sit in a room in the White House and wait for a phone call to let them know when history is being made so they can record it. And sometimes one's field doesn't matter. War is interdisciplinary.

Most knowledge is not directly bought, however. It can also serve the purpose of social stability in another way—by being squandered on trivia. Thus, the university becomes a playpen in which the society invites its favored children to play—and gives them toys and prizes, to keep them out of trouble. For instance, we might note an article in the leading journal in political science not long ago, dealing with the effects of Hurricane Betsy on the mayoralty election in New Orleans. Or, a team of social psychologists (armed with a fat government grant) may move right into the ghetto (surely the scholar is getting relevant here) and discover two important facts from its extensive, sophisticated research: that black people in the ghetto are poor; and that they have family difficulties.

I am touching a sensitive nerve in the academy now: Am I trying to obliterate all scholarship except the immediately relevant? No—it is a matter of proportion. The erection of new skyscraper office buildings is not offensive in itself, but it becomes lamentable alongside the continued existence of ghetto slums. It was not wrong for the Association of Asian Studies at its 1969 meeting to discuss some problems of the Ming dynasty and a battery of similar remote topics, but *no* session of the dozens at the meeting dealt with Vietnam.

Aside from trivial or esoteric inquiry, knowledge is also dissipated on pretentious conceptualizing in the social sciences. A catch-phrase can become a stimulus for endless academic discussion, and for the proliferation of debates which go nowhere into the real world, only round and round in ever smaller circles of scholarly discourse. Schemes and models and systems are invented which have the air of profundity and which advance careers, but hardly anything else.

We should not be surprised then at the volatile demonstrations for black studies programs which began around 1967–68, or for the creation of new student-run courses based on radical critiques of American society. Students demanding relevance in scholarship began to be joined in 1968–69 by professors dissenting at the annual ceremonials called Scholarly Meetings: at the American Philosophical Association a resolution denouncing U. S. policy in Vietnam; at the American Political Science Association a new caucus making radical changes in the program; at the American Historical Association, a successful campaign removing the 1968 meeting from Chicago to protest Mayor Daley's hooliganism; at the Modern Language Association the election of a young radical English teacher to the presidential succession.

Still we remain troubled, because the new urgency to use our heads for good purposes gets tangled in a cluster of beliefs which are so stuck, fungus-like, to the scholar, that even the most activist of us cannot cleanly extricate ourselves. These beliefs are roughly expressed by the phrases "disinterested scholarship . . . dispassionate learning . . . objective study . . . scientific method"— all adding up to the fear that using our intelligence to further our moral ends is somehow improper. And so we mostly remain subservient to the beliefs of the profession although they violate our deepest feelings as human beings, although we suspect that the traditional neutrality of the scholar is a disservice to the very ideals we teach about as history, and a betrayal of the victims of an un-neutral world.

It may, therefore, be worthwhile to examine the arguments for "disinterested, neutral, scientific, objective" scholarship. If there is to be a revolution in the uses of knowledge to correspond to the revolution in society, it will have to begin by challenging the rules which sustain the wasting of knowledge. Let me cite a number of them, and argue briefly for new approaches.

Rule 1. *Carry on "disinterested scholarship."* (In one hour's reading I came across three such exhortations, using just that phrase: in a *New Republic* essay by Walter Lippmann; in the 1968 Columbia University commencement address of Richard Hofstadter; in an article by Daniel Bell, appearing, ironically, in a magazine called *The Public Interest.*) The call is naive, because there are powerful interests already at work in the academy, with varying degrees of self-consciousness.

There is the Establishment of political power and corporate wealth, whose interest is that the universities produce people who will fit into existing niches in the social structure rather than try to change the structure. We always knew our educational system "socialized" people, but we never worried about this because we assumed our social norms were worth perpetuating. Now, and rightly, we are beginning to doubt this. There is the interest of the educational bureaucracy in maintaining itself: its endowment, its buildings, its positions (both honorific and material), its steady growth along orthodox lines. These larger interests are internalized in the motivations of the scholar: promotion, tenure, higher salaries, prestige—all of which are best secured by innovating in prescribed directions.

All of these interests operate, not through any conspiratorial decision but through the mechanism of a well-oiled system, just as the irrationality of the economic system operates not through any devilish plot but through the mechanism of the profit motive and the market, and as the same kinds of political decisions reproduce themselves in Congress year after year.

No one *intends* exactly what happens. They just follow the normal rules of the game. Similarly with education; hence the need to challenge these rules which quietly lead the scholar toward trivia, pretentiousness, orotundity, and the production of objects: books, degrees, buildings, research projects, dead knowledge. (Emerson is still right: *"Things* are in the saddle, and ride mankind."*)

There is no question, then, of a "disinterested" community of scholars, only a question about what kinds of interests the scholars will serve. There are fundamental humanistic interests—above any particular class, party, nation, ideology—which I believe we should consciously serve. I assume this is what we mean when we speak (however we act) of fostering certain "values" in education.

The university and its scholars (teachers, students, researchers) should unashamedly declare that their interest is in eliminating war, poverty, race and national hatred, governmental restrictions on individual freedom, and in fostering a spirit of cooperation and concern in the generation growing up. They should *not* serve the interests of particular nations or parties or religions or political dogmas. Ironically, scholars have often served narrow governmental, military, or business interests, and yet withheld support from larger, transcendental values, on the ground that they needed to maintain neutrality.

Rule 2. *Be objective.* The myth of "objectivity" in teaching and scholarship is based on a common confusion. If to be objective is to be scrupulously careful about reporting accurately what one sees, then of course this is laudable. But accuracy is only a prerequisite. That a metalsmith uses reliable measuring instruments is a condition for doing good work, but does not answer the crucial question: will he now forge a sword or a plowshare with his instruments? That the metalsmith has determined in advance that he prefers a plowshare does not require him to distort his measurements. That the scholar has decided he prefers peace to war does not require him to distort his facts.

Too many scholars abjure a starting set of values because they fail to make the proper distinction between an ultimate set of values and the instruments needed to obtain them. The values may well be subjective (derived from human needs); but the instruments must be objective (accurate). Our values should determine the *questions* we ask in scholarly inquiry, but not the answers.

To be "objective" in writing history, for example, is as pointless as trying to draw a map which shows everything—or even samples of everything—on a piece of terrain. No map can show all the elements in that terrain, nor should it, if it is to serve efficiently a present purpose, to take us toward some goal. Therefore, different maps are constructed, depending on the aim of the mapmaker. Each map, including what is essential to its purpose, excluding the irrelevant, can be accused of "partiality." But it is exactly in being partial that it is most true to its particular present job.

A map fails us, not when it is untrue to the abstract universal of total inclusiveness, but when it is untrue to the only realm in which truth has meaning—some present human need, and what we must do to attain it. And so with a historical account. As Kierkegaard put it: "Truth exists only as the individual produces it in action."

Rule 3: *Stick to your discipline.* Specialization has become as absurdly extreme in the educational world as in the medical world. One no longer is a specialist in American Government, but in Congress, or the Presidency, or Pressure Groups: a historian is a "colonialist" or an "early national period" man. This is natural when education is divorced from the promotion of values. To work on a real problem (like how to eliminate poverty in a nation producing eight hundred billion dollars' worth of wealth each year), one would have to follow that problem across many disciplinary lines without qualm, dealing with historical materials, economic theories, political obstacles. Specialization ensures that one cannot follow a problem through from start to finish. It ensures the functioning in the academy of the system's dictum: divide and rule.

Another kind of scholarly segregation serves to keep those in the university from dealing with urgent social problems: that which divorces fact from theory. We learn the ideas of the great philosophers and poets in one part of our educational experience. In the other part, we prepare to take our place in the real occupational world. In political science, for instance, a political theorist discusses transcendental visions of the good society; someone else presents factual descriptions of present governments. But no one deals with both the *is* and the *ought;* if they did they would have to deal with how to get from here to there, from the present reality to the poetic vision. Note how little work is done in political science on the tactics of social change. Both student and teacher deal with theory and reality in separate courses; the compartmentalization safely neutralizes them.

Rule 4. *To be "scientific" requires neutrality.* This is a misconception of how science works, both in fact, and in purpose. Scientists *do* have values, but they decided on these so long ago that we have forgotten it; they aim to save human life, to extend human control over the environment for the happiness of men and women. This is the tacit assumption behind scientific work, and a physiologist would be astonished if someone suggested that he starts from a neutral position as regards life or death, health or sickness. Somehow the social scientists have not yet gotten around to accepting openly that their aim is to keep people alive, to equitably distribute the resources of the earth, to widen the areas of human freedom, and therefore to direct their efforts toward these ends.

The claim that social science is "different" because its instruments are tainted with subjectivity ignores discoveries in the hard sciences: that the very fact of observation distorts the measurement of the physicist, and what he sees depends on his position in space. The physical sciences do not talk about certainty any more, but rather about "probability"; and while the probabilities may be higher for them than in the social sciences, both fields are dealing with elusive data.

Rule 5. *A scholar must, in order to be "rational," avoid "emotionalism."* True, emotion can distort. But it can also enhance. If one of the functions of the scholar is accurate description, then it is impossible to describe a war both unemotionally and accurately at the same time. And if the special competence of the mind is in enabling us to perceive what is outside our own limited experience, that competence is furthered, that perception sharpened, by emotion. A large dose of "emotionalism" in the description of slavery would merely *begin* to convey accurately to a white college student what slavery was like for the black man.

Thus, exactly from the standpoint of what intellect is supposed to do for us—extend the boundaries of our understanding—the "cool, rational, unemotional" approach fails. For too long, white Americans were emotionally separated from what the Negro suffered in this country by cold, and therefore inadequate, historical description. War and violence, divested of their brutality by the prosaic quality of the printed page, became tolerable to the young. (True, the poem and the novel were read in the English classes; but these were neatly separated from the history and government classes.) Reason, to be accurate, must be supplemented by emotion, as Reinhold Niebuhr once reminded us.

Refusing, then, to let ourselves be bound by traditional notions of disinterestedness, objectivity, scientific procedure, rationality— what kinds of work can scholars do, in deliberate unneutral pursuit of a more livable world? Am I urging Orwellian control of scholarly activities? Not at all. I am, rather suggesting that scholars, on their own, reconsider the rules by which they have worked, and begin to turn their intellectual energies to the urgent problems of our time. The true task of education, Alfred North Whitehead cautioned, is to abjure stale knowledge. "Knowledge does not keep any better than fish," he said. We need to keep it alive, vital, potent.

Specifically, we might use our scholarly time and energy to sharpen the perceptions of the complacent by exposing those facts that any society tends to hide about itself: the facts about wealth and poverty; about tyranny in both communist and capitalist states; about lies told by politicians, by the mass media, by the church, by popular leaders. We need to expose fallacious logic, spurious analogies, deceptive slogans, and those intoxicating symbols and concepts which drive people to murder (the flag, communism, capitalism, freedom). We need to dig beneath the abstractions so that our fellow citizens can make judgments on the particular realities beneath political rhetoric. We need to expose inconsistencies and double standards. In short, we need to become the critics of the culture rather than its apologists and perpetuators.

We who are fortunate in having the resources of knowledge are especially equipped for such a task. Although obviously not remote from the pressures of business, military needs, and politics, we have just that margin of leeway, just that tradition of truth-telling (however violated in practice) which can allow us to become spokesmen for change.

This will require holding up before society forgotten visions, lost utopias, unfulfilled dreams—badly needed in this age of cynicism. Along with such visions, we will need specific schemes for accomplishing important purposes, which can then be laid before the groups that can use them. Let the economists work out a plan for free food, instead of advising the Federal Reserve Board on interest rates. Let the political scientists work out insurgency tactics for the poor, rather than counter-insurgency tactics for the military. Let the historians instruct us or inspire us, from the data of the past, rather than amusing us, boring us, or deceiving us. Let the scientists figure out and lay before the public plans on how to make autos safe, cities beautiful, air pure. Let all social scientists work on modes of change instead of merely describing the world that is, so that we can make the necessary revolutionary alterations with the least pain.

I am not sure what a revolution among scholars will look like, any more than I know what a revolution in the society will look like. I doubt that it will take the form of some great cataclysmic event. More likely, it will be a process, with periods of tumult and of quiet, in which we will, here and there, by ones and twos and tens, create pockets of concern inside old institutions, transforming them from within. There is no great day of reckoning to work toward. Rather, we must begin *now* to liberate those patches of ground on which we stand—in our classrooms, in our studies, in our writing—to "vote" for a new world (as Thoreau suggested) with our whole selves all the time, rather than in moments carefully selected by others.

Thus, we will be acting out the beliefs that always moved us as humans but rarely as scholars. To do that, we will need to defy the professional mythology which has kept us on the tracks of custom, our eyes averted (except for moments of charity) from the cruelty on all sides. We will be taking seriously for the first time the words of the great poets and philosophers whom we love to quote but not to emulate. We will be doing this, not in the interest of the rich and powerful, or in behalf of our own careers, but for those who have never had a chance to read poetry or study philosophy, who so far have had to strive alone just to stay warm in winter, to stay alive through the calls for war. Ultimately, we will be acting for ourselves and our children.

2

History as private enterprise

Let us turn now from scholars in general to historians in particular. For a long time, the historian has been embarrassed by his own humanity. Touched by the sight of poverty, horrified by war, revolted by racism, indignant at the strangling of dissent, he has nevertheless tried his best to keep his tie straight, his voice unruffled, and his emotions to himself. True, he has often slyly attuned his research to his feelings, but so slyly, and with such scholarly skill, that only close friends and investigators for congressional committees might suspect him of compassion.

Historians worry that a deep concern with current affairs may lead to twisting the truth about the past. And indeed, it may, under conditions which I will discuss below. But nonconcern results in another kind of distortion, in which the ore of history is beaten neither into plowshare nor sword, but is melted down and sold. For the historian is a specialist who makes his living by writing and teaching, and his need to maintain his position in the profession tends to pull him away from controversy (except the polite controversy of academic disputation) and out of trouble.*

The tension between human drives and professional mores leads many to a schizophrenic separation of scholarly work from

* The historian of the eighteenth and nineteenth century was not a professional, and so tended more often to write partisan history, although his very independence in wealth and stature in society (Henry Adams, George Bancroft) meant his partisanship was most often on behalf of national or upper class interests. In any case, his writing had the tang of life and combat so often missing in the professional historian. This is not to close out the occasional transcendence of narrow interest as by Richard Hildreth, who wrote in the early national period, "unbedaubed with patriotic rough" (as he described himself), while Bancroft wrote with nationalist fervor. Hildreth was relatively obscure, Bancroft immensely popular.

other activities; thus, research on Carolingian relations with the
Papacy is interrupted momentarily to sign a petition on civil
rights. Sometimes the separation is harder to maintain, and so
the specialist on Asia scrupulously stays away from teach-ins on
Vietnam, and seeks to keep his work unsullied by application to
the current situation. One overall result is that common American
phenomenon—the secret radical.

There is more than a fifty-fifty chance that the academic historian will lose what vital organs of social concern he has in the
process of acquiring a doctorate, where the primary requirement
of finding an untouched decade or person or topic almost assures
that several years of intense labor will end in some monstrous irrelevancy. And after that, the considerations of rank, tenure, and
salary, while not absolutely excluding either personal activism or
socially pertinent scholarship, tend to discourage either.

We find, of course, oddities of academic behavior: Henry Steele
Commager writing letters to the *Times* defending Communists;
Martin Duberman putting the nation's shame on stage; Staughton
Lynd flying to Hanoi. And to the rule of scholarly caution, the ex-
ceptions have been glorious:

Beard's *An Economic Interpretation of the Constitution* was
muckraking history, not because it splattered mud on past heroes,
but because it made several generations of readers worry about the
working of economic interest in the politics of their own time. The
senior Arthur Schlesinger, in an essay in *New Viewpoints in American History,* so flattened pretensions of "states' rights" that no
reader could hear that phrase again without smiling. DuBois'
Black Reconstruction was as close as a scholar could get to a
demonstration, in the deepest sense of that term, puncturing a long
and destructive innocence. Matthew Josephson's *The Robber Barons* and Henry David's *History of the Haymarket Affair* were un-
abashed in their sympathies. Walter Millis' *The Road to War* was
a deliberate and effective counter to romantic nonsense about the
First World War. Arthur Weinberg's *Manifest Destiny* quietly ex-
posed the hypocrisy of both conservatives and liberals in the ideal-
ization of American expansion. Richard Hofstadter's *The American Political Tradition* made us wonder about *now* by brilliantly
deflating the liberal heroes—Jefferson, Jackson, Wilson, the two
Roosevelts. And C. Vann Woodward gently reminded the nation.

in *The Strange Career of Jim Crow,* that racism might be deeply embedded, yet it could change its ways in remarkably short time. There are many others.

But with all this, the dominant mood in historical writing in the United States (look at the pages of the historical reviews) avoids direct confrontation of contemporary problems, apologizes for any sign of departure from "objectivity," spurns a liaison with social action. Introducing a recent collection of theoretical essays on American history,[1] historian Edward N. Saveth asserts that the social science approach to history "was confused" by "the teleology of presentism." (In the space of three pages, Saveth uses three variations of the word "confusion" to discuss the effect of presentism.)

What is presentism? It was defined by Carl Becker in 1912 as "the imperative command that knowledge shall serve purpose, and learning be applied to the solution of the problem of human life." Saveth, speaking for so many of his colleagues, shakes his head: "The fires surrounding the issues of reform and relativism had to be banked before the relationship between history and social science could come under objective scrutiny." [2]

They were not really fires, but only devilishly persistent sparks, struck by Charles Beard, James Harvey Robinson, and Carl Becker.* There was no need to "bank" them, only to smother them under thousands of volumes of "objective" trivia, which became the trade mark of academic history, revealed to fellow members of the profession in papers delivered at meetings, doctoral dissertations, and articles in professional journals.

In *Knowledge for What?,* Robert S. Lynd questioned the relevance of a detailed analysis of "The Shield Signal at Marathon" which appeared in the *American Historical Review* in 1937. He wondered if it was a "warranted expenditure of scientific energy." Twenty-six years later (in the issue of July 1965), the lead article in the *American Historical Review* is "William of Malmesbury's Robert of Gloucester: a Reevaluation of the *Historia Novella.*" In

---

* See James Harvey Robinson's *The New History,* MacMillan, 1912; Carl Becker's *Everyman His Own Historian,* Appleton-Century-Crofts, 1935. See also the discussion of Beard's activism in Richard Hofstadter, *The Progressive Historians: Turner, Beard, Parrington,* Knopf, 1968, especially pp. 170–181.

1959, we find historians at a meeting of the Southern Historical
Association (the same meeting which tabled a resolution asking
an immediate end to the practice of holding sessions at hotels that
barred Negroes) presenting long papers on "British Men of War
in Southern Waters, 1793–1802," "Textiles: A Period of Sturm
und Drang," and "Bampson of Bampson's Raiders."

As Professor Lynd put it long ago: "History, thus voyaging
forth with no pole star except the objective recovery of the past,
becomes a vast, wandering enterprise." And in its essence, I would
add, it is *private* enterprise.

This is not to deny that there are many excellent historical studies only one or two degrees removed from immediate applicability
to crucial social problems. The problem is in the proportion.
There is immense intellectual energy in the United States devoted
to inspecting the past, but only a tiny amount of this is deliberately
directed to the solution of vital problems: racism, poverty, war,
repression, loneliness, alienation, imprisonment. Where historical
research has been useful, it has often been by chance rather than
by design, in accord with a kind of trickle-down theory which
holds that if only you fill the libraries to bursting with enough
processed pulpwood, something useful will eventually reach a society desperate for understanding.

While scholars do have a vague, general desire to serve a social
purpose, the production of historical works is largely motivated
by profit (promotion, prestige, and even a bit of money) rather
than by use. This does not mean that useful knowledge is not produced (or that what is produced is not of excellent quality in its
own terms, as our society constructs excellent office buildings
while people live in rattraps). It does mean that this production is
incidental, more often than not. In a rich economy, not in some
significant degree directed toward social reform, waste is bound
to be huge, measured in lost opportunities and misdirected effort.

True, the writing of history is really a mixed economy, but an
inspection of the mixture shows that the social sector is only a
small proportion of the mass.* What I am suggesting is not a total-

---

* "In sheer bulk," John Higham points out in *The Reconstruction of
American History,* "the product equals or surpasses the historical literature of any modern nation." Harper (Torchbook edition), 1962, p. 10.

istic direction of scholarship but (leaving complete freedom and best wishes to all who want to analyze "The Shield Signal at Marathon" or "Bampson of Bampson's Raiders") an enlargement of the social sector by encouragement, persuasion, and demonstration.

I am not directing my criticism against those few histories which are works of art, which make no claim to illuminate a social problem, but instead capture the mood, the color, the reality of an age, an incident, or an individual, conveying pleasure and the warmth of genuine emotion. This needs no justification, for it is, after all, the ultimate purpose of social change to enlarge human happiness.

However, too much work in history is neither art nor science. It is sometimes defended as "pure research" like that of the mathematician, whose formulas have no knowable immediate use. But the pure scientist is working on data which open toward infinity in their possible future uses. This is not true of the historian working on a dead battle or an obscure figure. Also, the proportion of scientists working on "pure research" is quite small. The historian's situation is the reverse; the proportion working on applicable data is tiny. Only when the pendulum swings the other way will the historian be able justly to complain that pure research is being crowded out.

Enlarging the social sector of historiography requires, as a start, removing the shame from "subjectivity." Benedetto Croce undertook this, as far back as 1920, reacting against the strict claims of "scientific history": what von Ranke called history "as it actually was," and what Bury called "simply a science, no less and no more." Croce openly avowed that what he chose to investigate in the past was determined by "an interest in the life of the present" and that past facts must answer "to a present interest." [3] In America, James Harvey Robinson said: "The present has hitherto been the willing victim of the past; the time has now come when it should turn on the past and exploit it in the interest of advance." [4]

But this confession of concern for current problems made other scholars uneasy. Philosopher Arthur O. Lovejoy, for instance, said the aims of the historian must not be confused with those of the "social reformer," and that the more a historian based his research on problems of "the period in which he writes" then "the worse historian he is likely to be." The job of the historian, he declared (this was in the era of the Memorial Day Massacre, Guernica, and the Nuremberg Laws) is "to know whether . . . certain events, or sequences of events, happened at certain past times, and what . . . the characters of those events were." When philosophers suggest this is not the first business of a historian, Lovejoy said, "they merely tend to undermine his morals as a historian."

At the bottom of the fear of engagement, it seems to me, is a confusion between ultimate values and instrumental ones. To start historical enquiry with frank adherence to a small set of ultimate values—that war, poverty, race hatred, prisons, should be abolished; that mankind constitutes a single species; that affection and cooperation should replace violence and hostility—such a set of commitments places no pressure on its advocates to tamper with the truth. The claim of Hume and his successors among the logical positivists, that no *should* can be proved by what *is,* has its useful side, for neither can the moral absolute be disproved by any factual discovery.*

Confusion on this point is shown by Irwin Unger, in his article "The 'New Left' and American History," [5] where he says:

> If there has been no true dissent in America; if a general consensus over capitalism, race relations, and expansionism has prevailed in the United States; if such dissent as has existed has been crankish and sour, the product not of a maladjusted society but of maladjusted men—then American history may well be monumentally irrelevant for contemporary radicalism.

* If our ultimate aim is human happiness and particular arrangements of the races in residential patterns are *means,* then the fact that integration of the races in a particular situation did not prove a happy solution need not be hidden for fear it might hurt our ultimate values. That fact would show us that integration in itself is not sufficient to produce happiness—it may set us to look for other factors—and we would even keep our minds open to the possibility that integration could produce unhappiness, either in certain situations or conceivably in all situations. I present this illustration not for its factual accuracy, but as an example of how honesty is not foreclosed by "subjectivity" if one keeps the ultimate values distinct from the instrumental ones.

Unger seems to believe that a radical historian who is opposed to capitalism *must* find such opposition to capitalism in the American past in order to make the study of history worthwhile for him; the implication is that if he does not find such opposition he may invent it, or exaggerate what he finds. But the factual data need not contain any premonition of the future for the historian to advocate such a future. The world has been continually at war for as long as we can remember; yet the historian who seeks peace, and indeed who would like his research to have an effect on society in behalf of peace, need not distort the martial realities of the past. Indeed, his recording of that past and its effects may itself be a very effective way of reminding the reader that the future needs kinds of human relationships which have *not* been very evident in the past.

(Unger continues to make the same mistake in this essay when, discussing William A. Williams' *The Contours of American History,* he notes that it shows general American acceptance of private property and says *"The Contours* proves a constant embarrassment to the younger radical scholars.")

For an American historian with an ultimate commitment to racial equality there is no compulsion to ignore the facts that many slaveholders did not use whips on their slaves, that most slaves did not revolt, that some Negro officeholders in the Reconstruction period were corrupt, or that the homicide rate has been higher among Negroes than whites. But with such a commitment, and more concerned to shape the future than to recount the past for its own sake, the historian would be driven to point out what slavery meant for the "well-treated" slave; to explain how corruption was biracial in the 1870's as in all periods; to discuss Uncle Tomism along with the passivity of Jews in the concentration camps and the inertia of thirty million poor in an affluent America; to discuss the relationship between poverty and certain sorts of crime.*

---

* The problem of *lying* is not the most serious one. If a historian lies, someone will soon find him out. If he is irrelevant, this is harder to deal with. We have accepted truth as criterion, and we will rush to invoke it, but we have not yet accepted relevance.

Unyielding dedication to certain *instrumental* values, on the other hand—to specific nations, organizations, leaders, social systems, religions, or techniques, all of which claim their own efficacy in advancing the ultimate values—creates powerful pressures for hiding or distorting historical events. A relentless commitment to his own country may cause an American to glide over the elements of brutality in American "diplomatic history" (the term itself manufactures a certain aura of gentility). Compare, for instance, James Reston's pious column for Easter Sunday, 1965, on the loftiness of American behavior toward other countries, with Edmund Wilson's harsh, accurate summary of American expansionism in his introduction to *Patriotic Gore.*

It was rigid devotion to Stalin, rather than to the ultimate concerns of a humane Marxism, that led to fabrication of history in the Soviet Union about the purges and other things. After 1956, a shift in instrumental gods led to counter-fabrication. With the advent of the cold war, the United States began to outdo the Soviet Union in the large-scale development of government-supported social science research which assumed that an instrumental value—the nation's foreign policy—was identical with peace and freedom.

Thus, teams of social scientists under contract to the armed forces took without question the United States government's premise that the Soviet Union planned to invade Western Europe, and from this worked out all sorts of deductions for policy. Now it turns out (and we are told this by the same analysts) that premise was incorrect. This is replaced not by the overthrow of dogma itself, but by substituting a new assumption—that Communist China intends to take over all of Asia and eventually the world—and so the computers have begun to click out policy again. The absolutization of an instrumental value—in this case, current U. S. foreign policy (in other cases, Soviet policy or Ghanaian policy or whatever) distorts the results of research from the beginning.*

* One of the contributions the historians can make is to disprove the absolute value of certain social instruments by revealing their weaknesses and failures—thus helping us guard against total approval of any particular nation, race, ideology, party. Pieter Geyl, for instance, in *Encounters in History,* Meridian, 1961, makes the point that history can prevent us

Knowing that commitments to instrumental values distort the facts often leads scholars to avoid commitment of any kind. Boyd Schafer, reporting for the American Historical Association on the international congress of historians held in Vienna in the summer of 1965, notes an attempt at one session to introduce the question of Vietnam. The executive body of the Congress "firmly opposed the introduction of any current political question," saying the organization "had been and could only be devoted to scientific historical studies." Here were twenty-four hundred historians from forty nations, presumably an enormous assembly of data and insights from all branches of history; if this body could not throw any light on the problem of Vietnam, what claim can anyone make that history is studied to help us understand the present?

It testifies to the professionalization, and therefore the dehumanization of the scholar, that while tens of thousands of them gather annually in the United States alone, to hear hundreds of papers on scattered topics of varying significance, there has been no move to select a problem—poverty, race prejudice, the war in Vietnam, alternative methods of social change—for concentrated attention by some one conference.

But if a set of "ultimate values"—peace, racial equality, economic security, freedom of expression—is to guide our questioning, without distorting our answers, what is the source of these values? Can we prove their validity?

It is only when "proof" is identified with academic research that we are at a loss to justify our values. The experiences of millions of lives over centuries of time, relived by each of us in those aspects common to all men, *prove* to us that love is preferable to hate, peace to war, brotherhood to enmity, joy to sorrow, health to sickness, nourishment to hunger, life to death. And enough people recognize these values (in all countries, and inside all social systems) so that further academic disputation is only a stumbling block to action. What we see and feel (should we not view human emotion as crystallized, ineffable rationality?) is more formally stated as a fact of social psychology in Freud's broadest definition

---

from hating a whole people, a whole civilization, by the understanding it gives.

of Eros and in Erik Erikson's idea of "the more inclusive identity." *

How should all this affect the actual work of the historian? For one thing, it calls for an emphasis on those historical facts which have hitherto been obscured, and whose recall would serve to enhance justice and brotherhood. It is by now a truism that all historical writing involves a selection of facts out of those which are available. But what standards should govern this selection?

Harvard philosopher Morton White, anxious to defend "historical objectivity" against "the hurried flight to relativism," says that the "ideal purpose of history" is "to tell the whole truth." [6] But since it is impossible to have historical accounts list all that has taken place, White says the historian's job is to give a shorter, "representative" list. White values "impersonal standards" and "a neutral standpoint." The crux of this argument is based on the notion that the fundamental aim of the historian is to tell as much of the story of the past as he can.

Even if it were possible to list *all* the events of a given historical period, would this really capture the human reality of this period? Can starvation, war, suffering, joy, be given their due, even in the most complete historical recounting? Is not the *quality* of events more important than their quantity? Is there not something inherent in setting the past on paper which robs human encounter of its meaning? Does not the attention to either completeness or representativeness of "the facts" only guarantee that the cool jelly of neutrality will spread over it all, and that the reader will be left in the mood of the writer—that is, the mood of detached scholarship? And if this is so, does not the historian, concerned with the quality of his own time, need to work on the list in such a way as to try to restore its human content?

In a world where justice is maldistributed, historically and now, there is no such thing as a "neutral" or "representative" recapitulation of the facts, any more than one is dealing "equally" with a starving beggar and a millionaire by giving each a piece of bread.

---

* For an extended discussion on this point—that beyond intuitive and existential "proof" of these values there is a wealth of biological, psychological, cultural, and historical evidence to support them—see Abraham Edel, *Ethical Judgement: The Use of Science in Ethics,* Free Press, 1955.

The condition of the recipient is crucial in determining whether the distribution is just.

Our best historians, whether or not they acknowledge it, take this into account. Beard's study of the making of the Constitution was hardly a representative list of the events connected with the Philadelphia Convention. He singled out the economic and political backgrounds of the Founding Fathers to illustrate the force of economic interest in political affairs, and he did it because (as he put it later) "this realistic view of the Constitution had been largely submerged in abstract discussion of states' rights and national sovereignty and in formal, logical, and discriminative analyses of judicial opinions." *

When C. Vann Woodward wrote *The Strange Career of Jim Crow* he chose instances of equal treatment for Southern Negroes in public facilities, voting, transportation, in the 1880's. These were certainly not "representative." But he chose to emphasize them because he was writing in a time (1954) when much of the American nation, North and South, seemed to believe that segregation was so long and deeply entrenched in the South that it could not be changed. Woodward's intent was to indicate that things have not always been the same in the South.**

Similarly, the "Freedom Primer," used in the deep South by the Student Nonviolent Coordinating Committee, carefully selects from the mass of facts about the Negro in America those stories of heroism and rebellion which would give a Mississippi black child a sense of pride and worth, precisely because those are the feelings which everything around him tries to crush. (Yet one should not hesitate to point out, to a black child who developed

* This larger point is often forgotten in the meticulous critiques of Beard's specific data by scholars. For instance, see Robert E. Brown, *Charles Beard and the Constitution: A Critical Analysis of an Economic Interpretation of the Constitution,* Princeton, 1956, where Brown's main correction is that the Constitution favored "middle-class property owners" whose holdings were in land as opposed to Beard's emphasis on holdings in more disposable wealth.

** As with Robert Brown and Beard, the scholarly critics often miss Woodward's main point, which is *not* invalidated by the evidence of segregation alongside slavery, as in "Racial Segregation in Ante Bellum New Orleans," by Roger A. Fisher, *American Historical Review,* February 1969.

the notion that blacks could do no wrong, that history also showed some unheroic Negroes.)

The examples I have given are not "neutral" or "representative," but they are *true* to the ideal of man's oneness and to the reality of his separateness. Truth only in relation to what is or was is one-dimensional. Historical writing is most *true* when it is appropriate simultaneously to what was in the past, to the condition of the present, and to what should be done in the future. Let me give a few examples.

How can a historian portray the twenties? It was a time of glittering "prosperity," with several million unemployed. There were floods of new consumer goods in the stores, with poverty on the farm. There was a new class of millionaires, while people in city slums struggled to pay the rent and gas bills. The two hundred largest corporations were doubling their assets, but Congressman Fiorello LaGuardia, representing a working-class district in East Harlem, wrote in 1928: [7]

> "It is true that Mr. Mellon, Mr. Ford, Mr. Rosenwald, Mr. Schwab, Mr. Morgan and a great many others not only manage to keep their enormous fortunes intact, but increase their fortunes every year. . . . But can any one of them improve on the financial genius of Mrs. Maria Esposito or Mrs. Rebecca Epstein or Mrs. Maggie Flynn who is keeping house in a New York tenement raising five or six children on a weekly envelope of thirty dollars . . . ?"

A "comprehensive" picture of the twenties, the kind most often found in American history textbooks, emphasizes the prosperity, along with amusing instances of governmental corruption, a summary of foreign policy, a dash of literature, and a bit on the K.K.K. and the Scopes Trial. This would seem to be "representative"; it leaves the reader with an unfocused mishmash, fogged over by a general aura of well-being. But wouldn't a history of the twenties be most true to both past facts and future values if it stressed the plight of many millions of poor behind the facade of prosperity? Might not such an emphasis on the twenties, if widespread, have hastened the nation's discovery (not made until the 1960's) of poverty amidst plenty?

There is still another flaw in the exhortation to the historian to give a "representative" account of his subject: he is not writing in an empty field; thousands have preceded him and have weighted the story in certain directions. When the Marxist historian Herbert Aptheker wrote *American Negro Slave Revolts,* he was giving heavy emphasis to a phenomenon in which only a small minority of slaves had participated. But he was writing in an atmosphere dominated by the writings on slavery of men like Ulrich Phillips, when textbooks spoke of the happy slave. Both southern and northern publics needed a sharp reminder of the inhumanity of the slave system. And perhaps the knowledge that such reminders are still necessary induced Kenneth Stampp to write *The Peculiar Institution.*

The earth has for so long been so sharply tilted on behalf of the rich, the white-skinned, the male, the powerful, that it will take enormous effort to set it right. A biography of Eugene Debs (Ray Ginger's *The Bending Cross*) is a deliberate focusing on the heroic qualities of a man who devoted his life to the idea that "while there is a lower class, I am in it; while there is a criminal element, I am of it; while there is a soul in prison, I am not free." But how many biographies of the radical Debs are there, compared to biographies of John D. Rockefeller or Theodore Roosevelt? The selection of the topic for study is the first step in the weighting of the social scales for one value or another.

Let me give one more illustration of my point that there is no such thing as any one true "representative" account of a complex phenomenon, and that the situation toward which the assessment is directed should determine the emphasis (without ignoring the counter-evidence, it is important to add). In the debate between Arnold Toynbee (*A Study of History*) and Pieter Geyl (*Encounters in History*), Geyl objects to Toynbee's emphasis on the failures of Western civilization and suggests that the West's successes should be more heavily stressed. Behind the debate, one can see the Cold War, with Geyl reacting sharply and sensitively to any account of the world which implies more condemnation of the Western countries than of the Communist nations. But what is crucial in assessing the Geyl-Toynbee debate is not one's view of the past. All of us, Toynbee as well as Geyl, could readily agree on a list of the sins committed by the Communist nations and probably also agree on a list of the sins of the West. Where would that leave us, in view of the difficulty of quantifying this situation and declaring a "winner" as if in a baseball game? The crucial element is the present and the question of what we, the receivers of any assessment, will do in the present. And since Toynbee is addressing himself to the readers of the West primarily, he is implying that for Westerners to take a more critical view of their own culture will lead to more beneficial results (for those values esteemed by critics of both East and West) than to engage in self-congratulation. Since the argument about the past is insoluble, one does better directing his judgment toward the present and future.*

The usual distinction between "narrative" and "interpretive" history is not really pertinent to the criterion I have suggested for writing history in the public sector. It has often been assumed that narrative history, the simple description of an event or period, is "low level" history, while the interpretation of events, periods, individuals is "high level" and thus closer to the heart of a socially concerned historian. But the narration of the Haymarket Affair, or the Sacco-Vanzetti Case, to someone with a rosy picture of the American court system, has far more powerful effect on the present than an interpretation of the reasons for the War of 1812. A factual recounting of the addresses of Wendell Phillips constitutes (in a time when young people have begun to be captivated by the idea of joining social movements) a far more positive action on

---

* Confusion on this point is shown by William Bark, reviewing Pieter Geyl's *Encounters in History* (Meridian, 1961), *History and Theory,* Vol. IV, 1964. Bark connects the desire for free enquiry into history with the defense of the West against criticism. He says: "Those who believe in unrestricted historical study believe in the civilization of which their free historical interpretations are one of the cultural products and without which there could be no such study of history. When that civilization and that history are attacked, no matter how persuasively, as being meaningless and on the verge of collapse, such historians can be expected to engage in controversial discussions. . . ." Bark makes clear the past-oriented approach which leads to Geyl's defense of the West when he says: "Geyl's great service has been his insistence on standards in the writing of history and on the proper role of history as preserver of faith in the past, therefore of health and balance" (p. 107).

behalf of social reform than a sophisticated "interpretation" of the abolitionists which concludes that they were motivated by psychological feelings of insecurity. So much of the newer work on "concepts" in history gives up both the forest and the trees for the stratosphere.

If the historian is to approach the data of the past with a deliberate intent to further certain fundamental values in the present, then he can adopt several approaches. He may search at random in documents and publications to find material relevant to those values (this would rule out material of purely antiquarian or trivial interest). He can pursue the traditional lines of research (certain periods, people, topics: the Progressive Period, Lincoln, the Bank War, the Labor Movement) with an avowed "presentist" objective. Or, as the least wasteful method, he can use a problem-centered approach to the American past. This approach, used only occasionally in American historiography, deserves some discussion.

The starting point, it should be emphasized, is a *present* problem. Many so-called "problem approaches" in American history have been based on problems of the past. Some of these may be extended by analogy to a present problem (like Beard's concern with economic motive behind political events of the eighteenth century), but many of them are quite dead (the tariff debates of the 1820's; the character of the Southern Whigs; Turner's frontier thesis, which has occupied an incredible amount of attention). Not that bits of relevant wisdom cannot be extracted from these old problems, but the reward is small for the attention paid.*

---

* Benedetto Croce writes: "For dead history revives, and past history again becomes present, as the development of life demands them." He says that as soon as you become *interested* in a thing of the past, it becomes contemporary. His distinction between *history* and *chronicle* is based on this present-mindedness, for history is contemporary, chronicle is the dead past, and Croce says: "First comes history, then chronicle. First comes the living being, then the corpse; and to make history the child of chronicle is the same thing as to make the living be born from the corpse." (Quoted in Hans Meyerhoff, *Philosophy of History in Our Time,* Doubleday [Anchor edition], 1959, p. 52.) His metaphor recalls the Orozco mural in the Dartmouth College library, where skeletons in academic robes bring forth baby skeletons.

Teachers and writers of history almost always speak warmly
(and vaguely) of how "studying history will help you understand
our own time." This usually means the teacher will make the point
quickly in his opening lecture, or the textbook will dispose of this
in an opening sentence, after which the student is treated to an
encyclopedic, chronological recapitulation of the past. In effect,
he is told: "The past is useful to the present. Now you figure out
how."

Barrington Moore, discussing the reluctance of the historian to
draw upon his knowledge for suggestive explanations of the present, says: "Most frequently of all he will retreat from such pressures into literary snobbishness and pseudo cultivation. This takes
the form of airy generalizations about the way history provides
'wisdom' or 'real understanding.' . . . Anyone who wants to
know how this wisdom can be effectively used, amplified and cor-
rected, will find that his questions usually elicit no more than irri-
tation." [8]

To start historical enquiry with a present concern requires ignoring the customary chronological fracture of the American past:
the Colonial Period; the Revolutionary Period; the Jacksonian Period; and so on, down to the New Deal, the War, and the Atomic
Age.* Instead, a problem must be followed where it leads, back
and forth across the centuries if necessary.

David Potter has pointed to the unconfessed theoretical assumptions of historians who claim they are not theorizing.[9] I
would carry his point further: all historians, by their writing, have
some effect on the present social situation, whether they choose to
be presentists or not. Therefore the real choice is not between

* John Higham, *Reconstruction in American History,* Harper (Torchbook edition), 1962, declared concern "with the rethinking that American
history has undergone in recent years," and said each of the essays "tells
how a standard topic in American history was understood a generation
ago and how its interpretation has altered since that time." But the fresh-
ness of new interpretation was trapped by that book inside stale and pur-
poseless categories—the "standard" topics: Puritanism, the Revolution, the
West, the Jacksonian Period, the Civil War, the Progressive Tradition,
Emergence to World Power. Two of the essays it must be said, were fresh
topics ("The Working Class" and "The Quest for National Character").

shaping the world or not, but between doing it deliberately or un-consciously.*

Psychology has contributed several vital ideas to our under-standing of the role of the historian. In the first place, the psy-chologist is not recording the events of the patient's life simply to add to his files, or because they are "interesting," or because they will enable the building of complex theories. He is a therapist, de-voted to the aim of curing people's problems, so that all the data he discovers are evaluated in accord with the single objective of therapy. This is the kind of commitment historians, as a group, have not yet made to society.

Second, there is Harry Stack Sullivan's notion of the psycholo-gist as "participant." Whether the psychologist likes it or not, he is more than a listener. He has an effect on his patient. Similarly, the historian is a participant in history by his writing. Even when he claims neutrality he has an effect—if only, with his voluminous production of irrelevant data, to clog the social passages. So it is now a matter of consciously recognizing his participation, and deciding in which direction his energies will be expended.

An especially potent way of leading the historian toward a presentist, value-directed history is the binding power of social ac-tion itself. When a group of American historians in the Spring of 1965 joined the Negroes marching from Selma to Montgomery they were performing an unusual act. Social scientists sometimes speak and write on public policy; rarely do they bodily join in ac-tion to make contact with those whose motivation comes not from thought and empathy but from the direct pain of deprivation. Such contact, such engagement in action, generates an emotional at-tachment to the agents of social change which even long hours in the stacks can hardly injure.

---

* Irwin Unger's complaint that: "The young radicals' efforts are gener-ally governed not by the natural dialogue of the discipline but by the con-cerns of the outside cultural and political world" ignores the point that there is no "natural dialogue" of the discipline, but only a dialogue im-posed by the concerns of the outside world, whether the historian chooses to recognize this fact or not. "The 'New Left' and American History," *American Historical Review,* July 1967.

Surely there is some relationship between the relative well-being of professors, their isolation in middle-class communities, their predictable patterns of sociality, and the tendency to remain distant, both personally and in scholarship, from the political battles of the day. The scholar does vaguely aim to serve some social purpose, but there is an undiscussed conflict between problem-solving and safety for a man earning fifteen thousand dollars a year. There is no deliberate avoidance of social issues, but some quiet gyroscopic mechanism of survival operates to steer the scholar toward research within the academic consensus.

When Arthur Mann writes that: "Neither dress, style, nor accent unifies the large and heterogeneous membership of the American Historical Association," he adds immediately: "Yet most writers of American history belong to the liberal intelligentsia that voted for John F. Kennedy and, before him, for Adlai Stevenson, Harry S. Truman, Franklin D. Roosevelt, Alfred E. Smith, Woodrow Wilson, Theodore Roosevelt, and William Jennings Bryan." [10] In other words, historians have almost all fitted neatly into that American consensus which Richard Hofstadter called "The American Political Tradition." So when it is said (again, by Mann) that Richard Hofstadter is a "spectator" while Arthur Schlesinger (who wrote loving books about Jackson, FDR, Kennedy) "writes history as he votes" it is because this country only hands ballots to Republicans and Democrats, to conservatives and liberals, while yearning radicals like Richard Hofstadter are given no one to vote for in this political system. Hofstadter might well write a sequel, *The American Historical Tradition* describing among historians the same kind of liberal consensus he found in American politics—a consensus which veers toward mild liberalism in politics, and which therefore ensures that where the historian does go beyond irrelevancy to engagement, it is a limited engagement, for objectives limited by the liberal Democratic frame. Mann shows his own entrapment inside this frame by his comment that the progressives, lauded by almost all American historians, "transformed the social Darwinian jungle of some eighty years ago into the humane capitalistic society it is today." Five years after this statement was published the urban ghettos in America were exploding in rebellion against this "humane capitalistic society."

Engagement in social action is not indispensable for a scholar to direct his scholarship toward humane concerns; it is part of the wonder of people that they can transcend their immediate circumstances by leaps of emotion and imagination. But contact with the underground of society, in addition to spurring the historian to act out his value-system, might also open him to new data: the experiences, thoughts, feelings of the invisible folk all around us. This is the kind of data so often missed in official histories, manuscript collections of famous personalities, diaries of the literate, newspaper accounts, government documents.*

I don't want to exaggerate the potency of the scholar as activist. But it may be that his role is especially important in a liberal society, where the force available for social change is small, and the paralysis of the middle class is an important factor in delaying change. Fact can only buttress passion, not create it, but where passion is strained through the Madisonian constitutional sieve, it badly needs support.

The black revolution has taught us that indignation stays alive in the secret crannies of even the most complacent society. Niebuhr was right in chiding Dewey that intellectual persuasion was not enough of a force to create a just America. He spoke (in *Moral Man and Immoral Society*) of his hope that reason would not destroy that "sublime madness" of social passion before its work was done. Perhaps reason may even help focus this passion.

Except for a scattered, eloquent, conscience-torn few, historians in America have enjoyed a long period of luxury, corresponding to that of a nation spared war, famine, and (beyond recent memory) imperial rule. But now, those peoples who were not so spared are rising, stirring, on all sides—and even, of late, in our midst. The rioting Negro poor, the student-teacher critics on Vietnam, the silent walls around state prisons and city jails—all are remind-

---

* Rowland Berthoff, in his essay "The Working Class" in John Higham, *The Reconstruction of American History,* says: "The egalitarianism of this country of the common man . . . is a peculiarly middle-class doctrine. . . . The historians of the poor and the disadvantaged have, therefore, ordinarily approached them as special cases. . . . Accordingly the main stream of American historiography has flowed past these social backwaters, except in so far as they have presented special problems to the middle-class commonality."

ers in this, the most luxurious of nations, that here, as well as abroad, is an exclusiveness based on race, or class, or nationality, or ideology, or monopolies of power.

In this way, we are forced apart from one another, from other people in the world, and from our freedom. To study this exclusiveness critically, and with unashamed feeling, is to act in some small way against it. And to act against it helps us to study it, with more than sharpness of eye and brain, with all that we are as total human beings.

3

What is radical history?

Historical writing always has some effect on us. It may reinforce our passivity; it may activate us. In any case, the historian cannot choose to be neutral; he writes on a moving train.

Sometimes, what he tells may change a person's life. In May 1968 I heard a Catholic priest, on trial in Milwaukee for burning the records of a draft board, tell (I am paraphrasing) how he came to that act:

> I was trained in Rome. I was quite conservative, never broke a rule in seminary. Then I read a book by Gordon Zahn, called *German Catholics and Hitler's Wars*. It told how the Catholic Church carried on its normal activities while Hitler carried on his. It told how SS men went to mass, then went out to round up Jews. That book changed my life. I decided the church must never behave again as it did in the past; and that I must not.

This is unusually clear. In most cases, where people turn in new directions, the causes are so complex, so subtle, that they are impossible to trace. Nevertheless, we all are aware of how, in one degree or another, things we read or heard changed our view of the world, or how we must behave. We know there have been many people who themselves did not experience evil, but who became persuaded that it existed, and that they must oppose it. What makes us human is our capacity to reach with our mind beyond our immediate sensory capacities, to feel in some degree what others feel totally, and then perhaps to act on such feelings.

I start, therefore, from the idea of writing history in such a way as to extend human sensibilities, not out of this book into other

35

books, but into the going conflict over how people shall live, and whether they shall live.

I am urging value-laden historiography. For those who still rebel at this—despite my argument that this does not determine answers, only questions; despite my plea that aesthetic work, done for pleasure, should always have its place; despite my insistence that our work is value-laden whether we choose or not—let me point to one area of American education where my idea has been accepted. I am speaking of "Black Studies," which, starting about 1969, began to be adopted with great speed in the nation's universities.

These multiplying Black Studies programs do not pretend to just introduce another subject for academic inquiry. They have the specific intention of so affecting the consciousness of black and white people in this country as to diminish for both groups the pervasive American belief in black inferiority.

This deliberate attempt to foster racial equality should be joined, I am suggesting, by similar efforts for national and class equality. This will probably come, as the Black Studies programs, not by a gradual acceptance of the appropriate arguments, but by a crisis so dangerous as to *demand* quick changes in attitude. Scholarly exhortation is, therefore, not likely to initiate a new emphasis in historical writing, but perhaps it can support and ease it.

What kind of awareness moves people in humanistic directions, and how can historical writing create such awareness, such movement? I can think of five ways in which history can be useful. That is only a rough beginning. I don't want to lay down formulas. There will be useful histories written that do not fit into preconceived categories. I want only to sharpen the focus for myself and others who would rather have their writing guided by human aspiration than by professional habit.

1. *We can intensify, expand, sharpen our perception of how bad things are, for the victims of the world.* This becomes less and less a philanthropic act as all of us, regardless of race, geography, or class, become potential victims of a burned, irradiated planet. But even our own victimization is separated from us by time and the fragility of our imagination, as that of others is separated from us because most of us are white, prosperous, and within the walls

of a country so over-armed it is much more likely to be an aggressor than a victim.

History can try to overcome both kinds of separation. The fascinating progression of a past historical event can have greater effect on us than some cool, logical discourse on the dangerous possibilities of present trends—if only for one reason, because we learn the end of that story. True, there is a chill in the contemplation of nuclear war, but it is still a contemplation whose most horrible possibilities we cannot bring ourselves to accept. It is a portent that for full effect needs buttressing by another story whose conclusion is known. Surely, in this nuclear age our concern over the proliferation of H-bombs is powerfully magnified as we read Barbara Tuchman's account of the coming of the First World War: [1]

> War pressed against every frontier. Suddenly dismayed, governments struggled and twisted to fend it off. It was no use. Agents at frontiers were reporting every cavalry patrol as a deployment to beat the mobilization gun. General staffs, goaded by their relentless time-tables, were pounding the table for the signal to move lest their opponents gain an hour's head start. Appalled upon the brink, the chiefs of state who would be ultimately responsible for their country's fate attempted to back away but the pull of military schedules dragged them forward.

There it is, *us*. In another time, of course. But unmistakably us.

Other kinds of separation, from the deprived and harried people of the world—the black, the poor, the prisoners—are sometimes easier to overcome across time than across space: hence the value of historical recollection. Both the *Autobiography of Malcolm X* and the *Autobiography of Frederick Douglass* are history, one more recent than the other. Both assault our complacency. So do the photos on television of blacks burning buildings in the ghetto today, but the autobiographies do something special: they let us look closely, carefully, personally behind the impersonality of those blacks on the screen. They invade our homes, as the blacks in the ghetto have not yet done; and our minds, which we tend to harden against the demands of *now*. They tell us, in some small

degree, what it is like to be black, in a way that all the liberal cli-
chés about the downtrodden Negro could never match. And thus
they insist that we act; they explain why blacks are acting. They
prepare us, if not to initiate, to respond.

Slavery is over, but its degradation now takes other forms, at
the bottom of which is the unspoken belief that the black person
is not quite a human being. The recollection of what slavery is
like, what slaves are like, helps to attack that belief. Take the letter Frederick Douglass wrote his former master in 1848, on the
tenth anniversary of his flight to freedom: [2]

> I have selected this day to address you because it is the anni-
> versary of my emancipation . . . Just ten years ago this beautiful
> September morning yon bright sun beheld me a slave—a poor, de-
> graded chattel—trembling at the sound of your voice, lamenting that
> I was a man . . .
>
> When yet but a child about six years old I imbibed the determina-
> tion to run away. The very first mental effort that I now remember on
> my part, was an attempt to solve the mystery, Why am I a slave . . .
> When I saw a slave driver whip a slave woman . . . and heard her
> piteous cries, I went away into the corner of the fence, wept and pon-
> dered over the mystery . . . I resolved that I would someday run
> away.
>
> The morality of the act, I dispose as follows: I am myself; you are
> yourself; we are two distinct persons. What you are, I am. I am not by
> nature bound to you nor you to me. . . . In leaving you I took noth-
> ing but what belonged to me . . .

Why do we need to reach into the past, into the days of slavery?
Isn't the experience of Malcolm X, in our own time enough? I see
two values in going back. One is that dealing with the past, our
guard is down, because we start off thinking it is over and we
have nothing to fear by taking it all in. We turn out to be wrong,
because its immediacy strikes us, affects us before we know it;
when we have recognized this, it is too late—we have been moved.
Another reason is that time adds depth and intensity to a problem
which otherwise might seem a passing one, susceptible to being
brushed away. To know that long continuity, across the centuries,

of the degradation that stalked both Frederick Douglass and Malcolm X (between whose lives stretched that of W. E. B. Du-Bois, recorded in *The Souls of Black Folk* and *Dusk of Dawn*) is to reveal how infuriatingly long has been this black ordeal in white America. If nothing else, it would make us understand in that black mood of today what we might otherwise see as impatience, and what history tells us is overlong endurance.

Can history also sharpen our perception of that poverty hidden from sight by the foliage of the suburbs? The poor, like the black, become invisible in a society blinded by the glitter of its own luxury. True, we can be forcefully reminded that they exist, as we were in the United States in the 1960's when our sensibilities had been sharpened by the civil rights revolt, and our tolerance of government frayed by the Vietnamese war. At such a time, books like Michael Harrington's *The Other America* jabbed at us, without going back into the past, just supplying a periscope so that we could see around the corner, and demanding that we look.

Where history can help is by showing us how other people similarly situated, in other times, were blind to how their neighbors were living, in the same city. Suppose that, amidst the "prosperity" of the 1950's, we had read about the 1920's, another era of affluence. Looking hard, we might find the report of Senator Burton Wheeler of Montana, investigating conditions in Pennsylvania during the coal strike of 1928: [3]

> All day long I have listened to heartrending stories of women evicted from their homes by the coal companies. I heard pitiful pleas of little children crying for bread. I stood aghast as I heard most amazing stories from men brutally beaten by private policemen. It has been a shocking and nerve-racking experience.

Would this not suggest to us that perhaps in our time too a veil is drawn over the lives of many Americans, that the sounds of prosperity drown out all else, and the voices of the well-off dominate history?

In our time, as in the past, we construct "history" on the basis of accounts left by the most articulate, the most privileged members of society. The result is a distorted picture of how people live, an underestimation of poverty, a failure to portray vividly the situations of those in distress. If, in the past, we can manage to find the voice of the underdog, this may lead us to look for the lost pleas of our own era. True, we could accomplish this directly for the present without going back. But sometimes the disclosure of what is hidden in the past prompts us, particularly when there is no immediate prod, to look more penetratingly into contemporary society. (In my own experience, reading in the papers of Fiorello LaGuardia the letters from the East Harlem poor in the twenties, made me take a second look at the presumed good times of the fifties.)

Is the picture of society given by its victims a true one? There is no one true picture of any historical situation, no one objective description. This search for a nonexistent objectivity has led us, ironically, into a particularly retrogressive subjectivity, that of the bystander. Society has varying and conflicting interests; what is called objectivity is the disguise of one of these interests—that of neutrality. But neutrality is a fiction in an unneutral world. There are victims, there are executioners, and there are bystanders. In the dynamism of our time, when heads roll into the basket every hour, what is "true" varies according to what happens to your own head—and the "objectivity" of the bystander calls for inaction while other heads fall. In Camus' *The Plague,* Dr. Rieux says: "All I maintain is that on this earth there are pestilences, and there are victims, and it's up to us, so far as possible, not to join forces with the pestilences." Not to act is to join forces with the spreading plague.

What is the "truth" about the situation of the black man in the United States in 1968? Statistics can be put together which show that his position has improved. Statistics can be put together which show that his situation is as bad as it always was. Both sets of statistics are "true." * But the first leads to a satisfac-

---

* See Vivian Henderson, *The Economic Status of Negroes,* Southern Regional Council, 1963. One sentence in the *Report of the National Advisory Commission on Civil Disorders,* Bantam, 1968, p. 13, reveals the complexity: "Although there have been gains in Negro income nationally, and a decline in the number of Negroes below the 'poverty level,' the condition of Negroes in the central city remains in a state of crisis."

tion with the present rate of change; the second leads to a desire for quickening the rate of change. The closest we can come to that elusive "objectivity" is to report accurately *all* of the subjectivities in a situation. But we emphasize one or another of those subjective views in any case. I suggest we depart from our customary position as privileged observers. Unless we wrench free from being what we like to call "objective," we are closer psychologically, whether we like to admit it or not, to the executioner than to the victim.

There is no need to hide the data which show that some Negroes are climbing the traditional American ladder faster than before, that the ladder is more crowded than before. But there is a need—coming from the determination to represent those still wanting the necessities of existence (food, shelter, dignity, freedom)—to emphasize the lives of those who cannot even get near the ladder. The latest report of the Census Bureau is as "true," in some abstract sense, as the reports of Malcolm X and Eldridge Cleaver on their lives. But the radical historian will, without hiding the former (there are already many interests at work to tell us that, anyway) emphasize those facts we are most likely to ignore —and these are the facts as seen by the victims.

Thus, a history of slavery drawn from the narratives of fugitive slaves is especially important. It cannot monopolize the historiography in any case, because the histories we already have are those from the standpoint of the slaveholder (Ulrich Phillip's account, based on plantation diaries, for instance), or from the standpoint of the cool observer (the liberal historian, chastising slavery but without the passion appropriate to a call for action). A slave-oriented history simply fills out the picture in such a way as to pull us out of lethargy.

The same is true in telling the story of the American Revolution from the standpoint of the sailor rather than the merchant,[4] and for telling the story of the Mexican War from the standpoint of the Mexicans. The point is not to omit the viewpoint of the privileged (that dominates the field anyway), but to remind us forcibly that there is always a tendency, now as then, to see history from the top. Perhaps a history of the Opium War seen through Chinese eyes would suggest to Americans that the

Vietnamese war might also be seen through Vietnamese eyes.*

2. *We can expose the pretensions of governments to either neutrality or beneficence.* If the first requisite for activating people is to sharpen their awareness of what is wrong, the second is to disabuse them of the confidence that they can depend on governments to rectify what is wrong.

Again, I start from the premise that there are terrible wrongs all about us, too many for us to rest content even if not everyone is being wronged. Governments of the world have not been disposed to change things very much. Indeed, they have often been the perpetrators of these wrongs. To drive this point at us strongly pushes us to act ourselves.

Does this mean I am not being "objective" about the role of governments? Let us take a look at the historical role of the United States on the race question. For instance, what did the various American governments do for the black person in America right after the Civil War? Let's be "objective," in the sense of telling .*all* the facts that answer this question. Therefore we should take proper note of the Thirteenth, Fourteenth, Fifteenth Amendments, the Freedman's Bureau, the stationing of armed forces in the South, the passage of civil rights laws in 1866, 1870, 1871, and 1875. But we should also record the court decisions emasculating the Fourteenth Amendment, the betrayal of the Negro in the 1877 Hayes-Tilden agreement, the nonenforcement of the civil rights acts. Ultimately, even if we told all, our emphasis in the end would be subjective—it would depend on who we are and what we want. A present concern, that citizens need to act themselves, suggests we emphasize the unreliability of government in securing equal rights for black people.

Another question: to what extent can we rely on our government to equitably distribute the wealth of the country? We could take proper account of the laws passed in this century which seemed directed at economic justice: the railroad regulation acts of the Progressive era, the creation of the graduated income tax in

---

* See the letter of Commissioner Lin to Queen Victoria in Teng, Ssu-yü, and Fairbank, John K., *China's Response to the West,* Harvard University, 1954, p. 24.

the Wilson administration, the suits against trusts initiated in the Theodore Roosevelt and Taft administrations. But a *present* recognition of the fact that the allocation of wealth to the upper and lower fifths of the population has not fundamentally changed in this century would suggest that all that legislation has only managed to maintain the status quo. To change this, we would need to emphasize what has not so far been emphasized, the persistent failure of government to alter the continuing inequities of the American economic system.

Historians' assessments of the New Deal illustrate this problem. We can all be "objective" by including in any description of the New Deal both its wealth of reform legislation and its inadequacies in eradicating poverty and unemployment in America. But there is always an emphasis, subtle or gross, which we bring to bear on this picture. One kind of emphasis adds to a feeling of satisfaction in how America has been able to deal with economic crisis. Another stimulates us to do more ourselves, in the light of the past failure at dealing with the fundamental irrationality by which our nation's resources are distributed. The needs of the present suggest that the second kind of historical presentation is preferable.*

Thus, it is worth putting in their proper little place the vaunted liberal reforms of the Wilson administration. For instance, in a situation like the Ludlow Massacre of 1914, Wilson called out the federal troops not when the striking miners of Colorado were being machine-gunned by the Baldwin-Felts detectives or their homes burned by the National Guard, but when they began to arm and retaliate on a large scale. To take another case, it is useful to

---

* This should not be confused with "the search for culpability," as Jerald S. Auerbach puts it, criticizing the New Left critics of the New Deal. The point is not to denounce the New Deal of FDR, nor to praise it; that kind of historical evaluation is useless, as I suggest in my discussion of responsibility in Chapter 17 of this book. Auerbach, in "New Deal, Old Deal, or Raw Deal: Some Thoughts on New Left Historiography," *Journal of Southern History,* February 1969, mistakes the intention of those who (like myself in *New Deal Thought,* Bobbs-Merrill, 1966, or like Paul Conkin, in *The New Deal,* Thomas Crowell, 1967) stress the inadequacies of the Roosevelt reforms. Our aim is not castigation of past politics, but stimulation of present citizens.

know that social security measures were proposed in 1935 beyond those supported by FDR, but that he pushed more moderate proposals. In the light of our belated recognition that social security payments are now and have always been pitifully inadequate, how we view FDR's social security program may or may not reinforce our determination to change things.

A radical history, then, would expose the limitations of governmental reform, the connections of government to wealth and privilege, the tendencies of governments toward war and xenophobia, the play of money and power behind the presumed neutrality of law. It would illustrate the role of government in maintaining things as they are, whether by force, or deception, or by a skillful combination of both—whether by deliberate plan or by the concatenation of thousands of individuals playing roles according to the expectations around them.

Such motivating facts are available in the wealth of data about present governments. What historical material can do is to add the depth that time imparts to an idea. What one sees in the present may be attributable to a passing phenomenon; if the same situation appears at various points in history, it becomes not a transitory event, but a long-range condition, not an aberration, but a structural deformity requiring serious attention.

For instance, we would see more clearly the limitations of government investigating committees set up to deal with deep-rooted social problems if we knew the history of such committees. Take Kenneth Clark's blunt testimony to the National Advisory Commission on Civil Disorders, which was set up after the urban outbreaks of 1967. Pointing to a similar investigation set up after the 1919 riot in Chicago, he said: [5]

> I read that report . . . of the 1919 riot in Chicago, and it is as if I were reading the report of the investigating committee on the Harlem riot of '35, the report of the investigating committee on the Harlem riot of '43, the report of the McCone Commission on the Watts riot. I must again in candor say to you members of this Commission—it is a kind of Alice in Wonderland—with the same moving picture, reshown over and over again, the same analysis, the same recommendations, and the same inaction.

3. *We can expose the ideology that pervades our culture—using "ideology" in Mannheim's sense: rationale for the going order.* There is the open sanctification of racism, of war, of economic inequality. There is also the more subtle supportive tissue of half-truths ("We are not like the imperialist powers of the nineteenth century"); noble myths ("We were born free"); pretenses ("Education is the disinterested pursuit of knowledge"); the mystification of rhetoric ("freedom and justice for all"); the confusion of ideals and reality (The Declaration of Independence and its call for revolution, in our verbal tradition; the Smith Act and its prohibition of calls for revolution, on our lawbooks); the use of symbols to obscure reality ("Remember the *Maine,*" vis-à-vis rotten beef for the troops); the innocence of the double standard (deploring the violence of John Brown; hailing the violence of Ulysses Grant); the concealment of ironies (using the Fourteenth Amendment to help corporations instead of Negroes).

The more widespread is education in a society, the more mystification is required to conceal what is wrong; church, school, and the written word work together for that concealment. This is not the work of a conspiracy; the privileged of society are as much victims of the going mythology as the teachers, priests, and journalists who spread it. All simply do what comes naturally, and what comes naturally is to say what has always been said, to believe what has always been believed.

History has a special ability to reveal the ludicrousness of those beliefs which glue us all to the social frame of our fathers. It also can reinforce that frame with great power, and has done so most of the time. Our problem is to turn the power of history—which can work both ways—to the job of demystification. I recall the words of the iconoclast sociologist E. Franklin Frazier to Negro college students one evening in Atlanta, Georgia: "All your life, white folks have bamboozled you, preachers have bamboozled you, teachers have bamboozled you; I am here to debamboozle you."

Recalling the rhetoric of the past, and measuring it against the actual past, may enable us to see through our current bamboozlement, where the reality is still unfolding, and the discrepancies still not apparent. To read Albert Beveridge's noble plea in the

Senate January 9, 1900, urging acquisition of the Philippines with "thanksgiving to Almighty God that He has marked us as His chosen people, henceforth to lead in the regeneration of the world," and then to read of our butchery of the Filipino rebels who wanted independence, is to prepare us better for speeches about our "world responsibility" today. That recollection might make us properly suspicious of Arthur Schlesinger's attempt to set a "historical framework" for Vietnam comprised of "two traditional and entirely honorable strands in American thinking," one of which "is the concept that the United States has a saving mission in the world." [6] In the light of the history of idea and fact in American expansionism, that strand is not quite honorable. The Vietnam disaster was not, as Schlesinger says, "a final and tragic misapplication" of those strands, a wandering from a rather benign historical tradition, but another twining of the deadly strands around a protesting foreign people.

To take another example where the history of ideas is suggestive for today: we might clarify for ourselves the puzzling question of how to account for American expansion into the Pacific in the post-World War II period when the actual material interests there do not seem to warrant such concern. Marilyn B. Young, in her study of the Open Door period, indicates how the mystique of being "a world power" carried the United States into strong action despite "the lack of commercial and financial interest." Thus, "The Open Door passed into the small body of sacred American doctrine and an assumption of America's 'vital stake' in China was made and never relinquished." [7] Her book documents the buildup of this notion of the "vital stake," in a way that might make us more loath to accept unquestioningly the claims of American leaders defending incursions into Asian countries today.

For Americans caught up in the contemporary glorification of efficiency and success, without thought of ends, it might be liberating to read simultaneously *All Quiet on the Western Front* (for the fetid reality of World War I) and Randolph Bourne's comment on the American intellectuals of 1917: [8]

They have, in short, no clear philosophy of life except that of intelligent service, the admirable adaptation of means to ends. They are vague as to what kind of a society they want or what kind of society America needs, but they are equipped with all the administrative attitudes and talents necessary to attain it . . . It is now becoming plain that unless you start with the vividest kind of poetic vision, your instrumentalism is likely to land you just where it has landed this younger intelligentsia which is so happily and busily engaged in the national enterprise of war.

4. *We can recapture those few moments in the past which show the possibility of a better way of life than that which has dominated the earth thus far.* To move men to act it is not enough to enhance their sense of what is wrong, to show that the men in power are untrustworthy, to reveal that our very way of thinking is limited, distorted, corrupted. One must also show that something else is possible, that changes can take place. Otherwise, people retreat into privacy, cynicism, despair, or even collaboration with the mighty.

History cannot provide confirmation that something better is inevitable; but it can uncover evidence that it is conceivable. It can point to moments when human beings cooperated with one another (the organization of the underground railroad by black and white, the French Resistance to Hitler, the anarchist achievements in Catalonia during the Spanish Civil War). It can find times when governments were capable of a bit of genuine concern (the creation of the Tennessee Valley Authority, the free medical care in socialist countries, the equal-wages principle of the Paris Commune). It can disclose men and women acting as heroes rather than culprits or fools (the story of Thoreau or Wendell Phillips or Eugene Debs, or Martin Luther King or Rosa Luxemburg). It can remind us that apparently powerless groups have won against overwhelming odds (the abolitionists and the Thirteenth Amendment, the CIO and the sit-down strikes, the Vietminh and the Algerians against the French).

Historical evidence has special functions. It lends weight and depth to evidence which, if culled only from contemporary life, might seem frail. And, by portraying the movements of men over time, it shows the possibility of change. Even if the actual change has been so small as to leave us still desperate today, we need, to spur us on, the faith that change is possible. Thus, while taking proper note of how much remains to be done, it is important to compare the consciousness of white Americans about black people in the 1930's and in the 1960's to see how a period of creative conflict can change people's minds and behavior. Also, while noting how much remains to be done in China, it is important to see with what incredible speed the Chinese Communists have been able to mobilize seven hundred million people against famine and disease. We need to know, in the face of terrifying power behind the accusing shouts against us who rebel, that we are not mad; that men in the past, whom we know, in the perspective of time, to have been great, felt as we do. At moments when we are tempted to go along with the general condemnation of revolution, we need to refresh ourselves with Thomas Jefferson and Tom Paine. At times when we are about to surrender to the glorification of law, Thoreau and Tolstoi can revive our conviction that justice supersedes law.

That is why, for instance, Staughton Lynd's book, *Intellectual Origins of American Radicalism,* is useful history. It recalls an eighteenth-century Anglo-American tradition declaring: [9]

> . . . that the proper foundation for government is a universal law of right and wrong self-evident to the intuitive common sense of every man; that freedom is a power of personal self-direction which no man can delegate to another; that the purpose of society is not the protection of property but fulfillment of the needs of living human beings; that good citizens have the right and duty, not only to overthrow incurable oppressive governments, but before that point is reached to break particular oppressive laws; and that we owe our ultimate allegiance, not to this or that nation, but to the whole family of man.

In a time when that tradition has been befogged by cries on all sides for "law and order" and "patriotism" (a word playing on the ambiguity between concern for one's government and concern for one's fellows) we need to remind ourselves of the *depth* of the humanistic, revolutionary impulse. The reach across the centuries conveys that depth.

By the criteria I have been discussing, a recollection of that tradition is radical history. It is therefore worth looking briefly at why Lynd's book has been criticized harshly by another radical, Eugene Genovese, who is a historian interested in American slavery.[10]

Genovese is troubled that *Intellectual Origins of American Radicalism* is "plainly meant to serve political ends." If he only were criticizing "the assumption that myth-making and falsifying in historical writing can be of political use" (for instance, the history written by so-called Marxists in the Stalinist mode) then he would be right. But Genovese seems to mean something else, for Lynd is certainly telling us the straight truth about the ideas of those early Anglo-American thinkers. He says a historical work should not deal with the past in terms of "moral standards abstracted from any time and place."

Specifically, Genovese does not like the way Lynd uses the ideas of the Declaration of Independence as a kind of "moral absolutism" transcending time, connecting radicals of the eighteenth century with those of the twentieth, while failing to discuss "the role of class or the historical setting of the debates among radicals." He is critical of the fact that "Lynd never discusses the relation of these ideas to the social groups that hold them" and claims Lynd "denies the importance of the social context in which ideas occur," rather seeing the great moral truths as "self-evident and absolute." This means to Genovese that Lynd "thereby denies the usefulness of history except for purposes of moral exhortation." He says Lynd leaves out "the working class, the socialist movements" and the "counter-tendencies and opposing views of the Left," thus making the book "a travesty of history."

It is a powerful and important criticism. But I believe Genovese is wrong—not in his description of what Lynd does, but in his estimate of its worth. His plea not to discuss the past by moral standards "abstracted from time and place" is inviting because we (especially we professional historians) are attached to the anchor of historical particularity, and do not want some ethereal, utopian standard of judgment. But to abstract from time and place is not to remove completely from time and place; it is rather to remove enough of the historical detail so that common ground can be found between two or more historical periods—or more specifically, between another period and our own. (It is, indeed, only carrying further what we must of necessity do even when we are discussing *the* moral standard of any one time and place, or *the* view of any one social movement—because all are unique on the most concrete level.) To study the past in the light of what Genovese calls "moral absolutism" is really to study the past *relative* to ideals which move us in the present but which are broad enough to have moved other people in other times in history.

The lure of "time and place" is the lure of the professional historian interested in "my period" or "my topic." These particularities of time and place can be enormously useful, depending on the question that is asked. But if the question being asked is (as for Lynd): What support can we find in the past for values that seem worthwhile today?—a good deal of circumstantial evidence is not especially relevant. Only if *no* present question is asked, does all the particular detail, the rich, complex, endless detail of a period become important, without discrimination. And that, I would argue, is a much more abstract kind of history, because it is abstracted from a specific present concern. That, I would claim, is a surrender to the absolute of professional historiography: Tell as much as you can.

Similarly, the demand for "the role of class" in treating the natural-right ideas of Locke, Paine, and others, would be very important if the question being asked was: how do class backgrounds and ideas interact on one another (to better understand the weaknesses of both ideological and utopian thinking today). But for Staughton Lynd's special purpose, another emphasis was required. When one focuses on history with certain questions, much is left out. But this is true even when there is a lack of focus.

Similar to the professional dogma requiring "time and place" is a dogma among Marxist intellectuals requiring "the role of class" as if this were the touchstone for radical history. Even if one replaced (as Genovese is anxious to do) the economic determinism of a crude Marxism with "a sophisticated class analysis of historical change," discussing class "as a complex mixture of material interests, ideologies, and psychological attitudes," this may or may not move people forward toward change today. That—the total effect of history on the social setting today—is the criterion for a truly radical history, and not some abstract, absolute standard of methodology to which Marxists as well as others can get obsessively attached.

For instance, Genovese agrees that one of the great moral truths Lynd discusses—the use of conscience against authority as the ultimate test for political morality—was a revolutionary force in the past. But for Genovese this is a historical fact about a particular period, whereas: "Lynd seeks to graft them on to a social-ist revolution, the content of which he never discusses. He merely asserts that they form the kernel of revolutionary socialist thought, although no socialist movement has ever won power with such an ideology. . . ." This is precisely the reason for asserting a moral value shared by certain eighteenth-century thinkers (and, on a certain level, by Marx and Engels): that socialist movements thus far have *not* paid sufficient attention to the right of conscience against *all* states. To be truly radical is to maintain a set of tran-scendental beliefs (yes, absolutes) by which to judge and thus to transform any particular social system.

In sum, while there is a value to specific analysis of particular historical situations, there is another kind of value to the unearth-ing of ideals which cross historical periods and give strength to beliefs needing reinforcement today. The trouble is, even Marx-ist historians have not paid sufficient attention to the Marxian ad-monition in his *Theses on Feuerbach:* "The dispute over the real-ity or nonreality of thinking which is isolated from practice is a purely scholastic question." Any dispute over a "true" history cannot be resolved in theory; the real question is, which of the several possible "true" histories (on that elementary level of fac-tual truth) is *true,* not to some dogmatic notion about what a radical interpretation should contain, but to the practical needs for social change in our day? If the "political ends" Genovese warns against and Lynd espouses are not the narrow interests of a nation or party or ideology, but those humanistic values we have not yet attained, it is desirable that history should serve political ends.

5. *We can show how good social movements can go wrong, how leaders can betray their followers, how rebels can become bureaucrats, how ideals can become frozen and reified.* This is needed as a corrective to the blind faith that revolutionaries often

develop in their movements, leaders, theories, so that future actors for social change can avoid the traps of the past. To use Karl Mannheim's distinction, while *ideology* is the tendency of those in power to falsify, *utopianism* is the tendency of those out of power to distort. History can show us the manifestations of the latter as well as the former.

History should put us on guard against the tendency of revolutionaries to devour their followers along with their professed principles. We need to remind ourselves of the failure of the American revolutionaries to eliminate slavery, despite the pretensions of the Declaration of Independence, and the failure of the new republic to deal justly with the Whiskey Rebels in Pennsylvania despite the fact a revolution had been fought against unjust taxes. Similarly, we need to recall the cry of protest against the French Revolution, in its moment of triumph, by Jacques Roux and the poor of Gravillers, protesting against profiteering, or by Jean Varlet, declaring: "Despotism has passed from the palace of the kings to the circle of a committee." * Revolutionaries, without dimming their enthusiasm for change, should read Khrushchev's speech to the Twentieth Party Congress in 1956, with its account of the paranoid cruelties of Stalin.

The point is not to turn us away from social movements but into *critical* participants in them, by showing us how easy it is for rebels to depart from their own claims. For instance, it might make us aware of our own tendencies—enlightened though we are—to be paternal to the aggrieved to read the speech of the black abolitionist Theodore S. Wright, at the 1837 Utica convention of the New York Anti-Slavery Society. Wright criticized "the spirit of the slaver" among white Abolitionists. Or we might read the reply of Henry Highland Garnet in 1843 to the white Abolitionist lady who rebuked him for his militancy: [11]

You say I have received "bad counsel." You are not the only person who has told your humble servant that his humble productions have been produced by the "counsel" of some Anglo-Saxon. I have

---

* For a marvelous historical document of this aspect of the French Revolution, see Scott, ed., *The Defense of Gracchus Babeuf Before the High Court of Vendôme,* University of Massachusetts Press, 1967.

expected no more from ignorant slaveholders and their apologists, but I really looked for better things from Mrs. Maria W. Chapman, anti-slavery poetess and editor pro tem of the Boston *Liberator* . . .

The history of radical movements can make us watchful for narcissistic arrogance, the blind idolization of leaders, the substitution of dogma for a careful look at the environment, the lure of compromise when leaders of a movement hobnob too frequently with those in power. For anyone joyful over the election of socialists to office in a capitalist state, the recounting by Robert Michels of the history of the German Social Democratic Party is enlightening. Michels shows how parliamentary power can be corrupting, because radicals elected to office become separated from the rank and file of their own movement, and are invested with a prestige which makes it more difficult to criticize their actions.[12]

During the discussions in the Reichstag concerning the miners' strike in the basin of the Ruhr (1905), the deputy Hue spoke of the maximum program of the party as "utopian," and in the socialist press there was manifested no single symptom of revolt. On the first occasion on which the party departed from its principle of unconditional opposition to all military expenditure, contenting itself with simple abstention when the first credit of 1,500,000 marks was voted for the war against the Hereros, this remarkable innovation, which in every other socialist party would have unquestionably evoked a storm from one section of the members . . . aroused among the German socialists no more than a few dispersed and timid protests.

Such searching histories of radical movements can deter the tendency to make absolutes of those instruments—party, leaders, platforms—which should be constantly subject to examination.

That revolutionaries themselves are burdened by tradition, and cannot completely break from thinking in old ways, was seen by Marx in the remarkable passage opening *The Eighteenth Brumaire of Louis Bonaparte:*

Men make their own history, but they do not make it just as they please; they do not make it under circumstances chosen by themselves, but under circumstances directly found, given and transmitted from the past. The tradition of all the dead generations weighs like a nightmare on the brain of the living. And just when they seem engaged in revolutionizing themselves and things, in creating something entirely new, precisely in such epochs of revolutionary crisis they anxiously conjure up the spirits of the past to their service and borrow from them names, battle slogans and costumes in order to present the new scene of world history in this time-honored disguise and this borrowed language . . .

How to use the past to change the world, and yet not be encumbered by it—both skills can be sharpened by a judicious culling of past experience. But the delicate balance between them cannot come from historical data alone—only from a clearly focused vision of the human ends which history should serve.

History is not inevitably useful. It can bind us or free us. It can destroy compassion by showing us the world through the eyes of the comfortable ("the slaves are happy, just listen to them"—leading to "the poor are content, just look at them"). It can oppress any resolve to act by mountains of trivia, by diverting us into intellectual games, by pretentious "interpretations" which spur contemplation rather than action, by limiting our vision to an endless story of disaster and thus promoting cynical withdrawal, by befogging us with the encyclopedic eclecticism of the standard textbook.

But history can untie our minds, our bodies, our disposition to move—to engage life rather than contemplating it as an outsider. It can do this by widening our view to include the silent voices of the past, so that we look behind the silence of the present. It can illustrate the foolishness of depending on others to solve the problems of the world—whether the state, the church, or other self-proclaimed benefactors. It can reveal how ideas are stuffed into us by the powers of our time, and so lead us to stretch our minds beyond what is given. It can inspire us by recalling those few moments in the past when men did behave like human beings, to prove it is *possible*. And it can sharpen our critical faculties so that even while we act, we think about the dangers created by our own desperation.

These criteria I have discussed are not conclusive. They are a rough guide. I assume that history is not a well-ordered city (despite the neat stacks of the library) but a jungle. I would be foolish to claim my guidance is infallible. The only thing I am really sure of is that we who plunge into the jungle need to think about what we are doing, because there *is* somewhere we want to go.

4

Inequality

Somehow, the notion of American uniqueness persists. It is "God's Country and Mine," Jacques Barzun has said.[1] There is a common belief that our country has from birth been favored, by Providence or by Circumstance, in being unencumbered with harsh class lines, with solidified privilege, with a stubborn aristocracy, with a mass of illiterate peasantry, with all those things that plagued Europe until the dawn of modern times. A naked continent, rare idealism and courage among settlers weeded out by hardship and three thousand miles of ocean, the equalitarian demands of the frontier—these combined, we are often told, for a physically crude but socially immaculate conception.

Our birth, therefore, was of a new civilization, truly new, not a copy of the Old World. In Tocqueville's words, we were "born free."

A Whig preacher named Calvin Colton in 1844 summed up a belief about America that still represents the dominant self-image:[2]

> Ours is a country where men start from an humble origin . . . and where they can attain to the most elevated positions, or acquire a large amount of wealth, according to the pursuits they elect for themselves. No exclusive privileges of birth, no entailment of estates, no civil or political disqualifications stand in their path, but one

has as good a chance as another, according to his talents, prudence or personal exertions. This is a country of self-made men, than which nothing better could be said of any state of society.

The self-deception of Colton (there was slavery in the South, and in the North the factory system had a brutal grip on many Americans) applies to every period of this country's history, from our colonial origins to our imperial present. The fact is, we were born far from free, and far from equal, and through centuries of enormous growth in territory, resources, population, that initial inequality continued.

Why, then, does the myth persist?

Judgments depend on the criteria we use. Americans, evaluating their own country, generally use as their base other places in the world. In all the harping on the special equalitarianism of America, what is really implied, and only occasionally stated, is not that we were really free or really equal but that we were *more* free and equal than Europe. A new society, physically open and structurally loose, does have—for a time, in some of its parts, to a certain degree—more opportunities for changing one's status than an old, encrusted society.

Even this comparative statement about American equality depends for its truth on one enormous premise: that we not count the black slaves in America (20 percent of the population on the eve of the American revolution). It started early—the bland assessment of this country *after* putting the slaves aside. This is one of the unchanging aspects of our self-evaluation—that we mention the Negro with proper lamentation, and then put him in brackets while we make our total judgment of American civilization. Both slavery and segregation have always been treated as special phenomena, to be mentioned then forgotten, because they spoil all estimates about democracy, freedom, and equality in this country.

But even aside from this dishonesty, there is something wrong with the use of other countries—Europe, or Asia to make the contrast even more dramatic—as a basis for evaluation. Why not use as our norm the ideal society, that which has never existed on earth, that mythic society which has eliminated (to use Jacques

Barzun's phrase) "irrational privilege." I would call irrational that privilege which comes from the distorted distribution of abundant resources.

The distinction between these two criteria (Europe's rigid class system on the one hand; an ideal society on the other) is not that the first is realistic (comparing us with existing reality elsewhere), while the other is idealistic (measuring us against a goal unattained anywhere). Both are realistic, in the sense that they have effects on reality. But the first suits a historical scholarship which uses the past not only as its starting point but as its end; the second suits a view of history which is designed to change the present toward a desired future. Both kinds of historiography are able to use, with accuracy and competence, the data of the past. But the choice of criteria makes one kind of history contemplative, academic, and the other kind existential, active.

What follows then is a discussion of class inequality in America, drawing briefly on data from two periods—the colonial and the contemporary. The point is not to conclusively *prove* something about America, but rather to suggestively question the happy myth of equalitarianism, as a way of prodding us to bolder changes than so far called forth by the "welfare state."

THE LESS THAN IMMACULATE CONCEPTION

A hundred years before the Declaration of Independence, the first revolt broke out in the American colonies, not against England, but against the entrenched power of the Virginia aristocracy. A Royal Commission's confidential report to the crown, after the rebellion had been suppressed and its leaders hanged, described the leader of the 1676 uprising, Nathaniel Bacon: [3]

    . . . a person whose lost and desperate fortunes had thrown him into that remote part of the world about fourteen months before and fram'd him fitt for such a purpose. . . . He was said to be about four or five and thirty yeares of age, indifferent tall but slender, black-hair'd and of an ominous, pensive, melancholly Aspect, of a pestilent and prevalent Logical discourse tending to atheisme. . . . he seduced the Vulgar and most ignorant people to believe (two thirds of each county being of that Sort) Soe that theire whole hearts and hopes were set now upon Bacon. Next he charges the Governour as negligent and wicked, treacherous and incapable, the Lawes and Taxes as unjust and oppressive and cryes up absolute necessity of redress. Thus Bacon encouraged the Tumult and as the unquiet crowd follow and adhere to him, he listeth them as they come in upon a large paper, writing their name circular wise, that their Ring-Leaders might not be found out. Having connur'd them into this circle, given them Brandy to wind up the charme, and enjoyn'd them by an oath to stick fast together and to him . . . and the oath being administered he went and infected New Kent County ripe for Rebellion.

The rebellion was a complex phenomenon, immediately stirred by the feeling of frontier farmers that the Virginia government was ignoring their needs, but its essence was a rising of a lower class against the privileges, political and economic, of a higher class. A contemporary of Bacon's, Thomas Mathews, wrote of the debate in the Virginia Assembly over motions to inspect the tax structure, which the governor asked to be delayed, "tho' such of that Indigent People as had no benefits from the Taxes groand under our being thus Overborn." [4]

Our first settlers brought with them across the ocean the class distinctions of the Old World. The American wilderness modified and complicated these distinctions, but it did not eliminate them. And the more the population grew—the greater the wealth, the more complex the society—the sharper became the differences between upper and lower classes. The white indentured servant supplied the basic lower-class labor force in the seventeenth century, the Negro slave in the eighteenth century, both supplemented by town laborers of various types. At the upper levels of society there grew a colonial aristocracy, whose way of life separated it more and more from the lower classes. The fact that in between these extremes was a fairly large middle class of independent small farmers mitigated the total amount of deprivation, and also served to block out—as this middle class has done throughout American history—the vision of a significant part of the population (about one-third of the total) in physical or economic bondage.

But even that landowning yeoman class, except for a small

number who managed to push up through the social apertures, was shut off from real economic or political power. Bacon's Rebellion, like a number of other colonial uprisings, was a spontaneous foaming of indignation on the part of this class. Nathaniel Bacon complained, a year before his revolt, in 1675: "The poverty of the country is such that all the power and sway is got into the hands of the rich, who by extortious advantages, having the common people in their debt, have always curbed and oppressed them in all manner of ways."

By 1700, there were fifty families in Virginia with wealth equivalent to $50,000, a huge sum for those days, especially for a new frontier society. These fifty families sat at the pinnacle of a pyramid whose broad base was the labor of indentured servants and slaves. The rich families owned the plantations, sat on the governor's council, served as local magistrates. In Maryland, where the settlers were under the rule of a semi-feudal proprietor whose right to control the whole colony had been granted by the English King, there were five revolts between 1650 and 1689 against the proprietor.

The claim that America was "born free" is sometimes traced to the fact that the new nation borrowed the ideas of John Locke. But it was Locke himself who wrote the "Fundamental Constitutions" of the Carolinas, which set up a feudal-type aristocracy, headed by eight seigniors, and eight barons, who would own 40 percent of the colony's land. Only the head of a barony could be governor, the Fundamental Constitutions provided; and only owners of five hundred acres could be deputies in the assembly. The attempt of the proprietors to enforce these arrangements under frontier conditions led to conflict and martial law. The Fundamental Constitutions never were able to work as planned, but a small group of wealthy proprietors did run the colony as absentee landlords. A conflict over control of the land led to a revolt in 1719. While the immediate cause of the revolt was the land-hunger of five hundred poor immigrants, the uprising was taken over by the large rice planters and English merchants, who succeeded in getting rid of the proprietors in order to obtain a royal government which would favor their interests. In North Carolina, which became a separate crown colony, half a million acres were monopo-

lized by large speculators by 1750, including all of the good farming country near the coast. Poor squatters on these lands fought
all through that period over rent payments.

Similar battles with proprietors over land were fought by small
farmers in Pennsylvania, New Jersey, and New York. It was these
same yeomen, constantly in debt, who battled against the colonial
governments for the issuance of paper money. In Boston, debtors
succeeded in issuing land bank notes worth fifty thousand pounds,
and when the merchants refused to accept the paper money, farmers marched on the city. Leaders of the march were jailed, and
the bank was outlawed. (Among the ruined men was the father of
Sam Adams.) In Rhode Island, Newport merchants succeeded in
prohibiting the wide distribution of paper money demanded by
debtor-farmers.

New York was the closest thing to a feudal state in the American colonies. Under the patroonship system created by the Dutch
along the Hudson River, gigantic landed baronies were created,
where the barons held not only economic, but political and judicial control over the lives of their tenants. One Hudson Valley estate alone—Rensselaerswyck—included 700,000 acres. And when
the British took over in 1664, the huge estates continued, with
the Duke of York, as proprietor, holding the powers of a despot.

Governor Fletcher of New York gave one of his favorites, Captain John Evans, an area of close to a half-million acres, for a
token annual payment of twenty shillings. Under Fletcher, three-
fourths of the land in New York was granted to about thirty people. The only difference with Lord Cornbury as governor, in the
early 1700's, was that he favored groups of speculators, rather
than individuals. One grant was for two million acres.

The desperate revolt in New York of Jacob Leisler and his followers, in 1689, was at bottom a class uprising against a combination of wealthy landowners and merchants, with the religious and
political issues of England's Glorious Revolution supplying a con-
venient starting point. Leisler was hanged, and despite the gradual introduction of some political reforms, the handing out of
huge estates to a privileged few continued, sharpening the lines
between very rich and very poor. The period before the American
Revolution in New York was full of tenant outbreaks, whose class

character was sometimes concealed by the fact that they were frequently led and used by rival groups of land speculators.

Harassed and ignored small farmers were helpless against the power of colonial land speculators, merchants, and government officials. A petition came from the town of Deerfield in 1678 to the Massachusetts General Court: "You may be pleased to know that the very principle and best of the land; the best for soile; the best for situation; as lying in ye center and midle of the town: and as to quantity, nere half, belongs unto eight or nine proprietors. . . ." Also within the colonial working class should be counted tens of thousands of sailors and dockworkers of various kinds—about thirty-five hundred counted in Salem and Boston alone in the early eighteenth century.

There is not much to be said here about the slaves in colonial society, except to reiterate that no account of class relationships and distribution of wealth and power in America can, in justice, leave the slaves out of the reckoning; to do so is to accept the pre-Civil War judgment of them as less than human beings. It needs to be emphasized that slaves constituted one-fifth of the entire colonial population by the time of the Revolution and were in *all* of the colonies, North and South, though their heaviest concentration was in Virginia and South Carolina (where they were a majority of the population). That their treatment as the bottom class was universal is shown clearly by the law passed in 1693 by the Quaker legislature of Pennsylvania, authorizing any persons "to take up Negroes, male or female, whom they shall find gadding abroad . . . to take them to jail, there to remain that night, and that without meat or drink, and to cause them to be publicly whipped next morning with 39 lashes, well laid on their bare backs, at which their said master or mistress shall pay 15 pence to the whipper."

On March 28, 1771, the *Virginia Gazette* ran an announcement: "Just arrived at Leedstown, the Ship *Justitia,* with about one Hundred Healthy Servants, Men Women & Boys. . . . The Sale will commence on Tuesday the 2nd of April. . . ." Ranking just above the slave in the colonial class structure, and yet so often close to the slave in misery and deprivation that he has often been termed "a semi-slave" was the indentured servant. Indentured servants, the chief source of labor in the seventeenth century, continued to pour into the colonies in the eighteenth century; two-thirds of Pennsylvania's immigrants, for instance, were white servants. The institution of indenture did not die out until the early part of the nineteenth century, and it is probable that more than a quarter of a million persons served as indentured servants during the colonial period. These were indigent Europeans who, in return for passage to America, signed contracts (either voluntarily or by force, for many were convicts and vagrants in England) guaranteeing five or seven years of servile labor to an American master.

To this day, the way people travel is a key to their social and economic class; in colonial times this was true to the point of death. The indentured servants were at times packed into ships much like the screaming, dying African slaves, with as many as six hundred forced into a boat meant to carry three hundred. On one trip thirty-two children were thrown into the ocean as a result of starvation and disease.*

Indentured servants had some rights that slaves did not have, like the right to sue in court, but the court was generally friendlier to the owner than to the servant. They could not marry without permission, could be separated from their families at will, could be whipped for various offenses. Pennsylvania law in the seventeenth century said that marriage of servants "without the consent of the Masters . . . shall be proceeded against as for Adultery, or fornication, and Children to be reputed as Bastards." [5] The great numbers of ads for runaway servants tell something about the conditions under which they lived and worked, conditions adjudicated by judges who took the word of the master, one contemporary observer noted, "ten to one." [6]

Returning to Germany from America in the mid-eighteenth century, Gottlieb Mittelburg wrote of the privations of his fellow

* See Abbot Smith, *Colonists in Bondage,* University of North Carolina, 1947, especially pp. 147–51 on the forced transportation of poor children. On the horrendous conditions of the voyage (on one ship making a trip in 1732, 100 of the 150 passengers died of starvation), see Karl Geiser, *Redemptioners and Indentured Servants in the Colony and Commonwealth of Pennsylvania,* Tuttle, Morehouse, & Taylor, 1901, especially Chapter 5, "The Voyage."

Germans in servitude in Pennsylvania. He said many asked him to let others in Germany know what they were suffering so they would not be enticed into slavery. Contemporary accounts of the good living conditions of indentured servants need to be taken cautiously in view of the fact that most of these were written for the purpose of inducing immigration. They should be placed against letters like the following, written at the time: "Whoever is well off in Europe better remain there. Here is misery and distress, same as everywhere, and for certain persons and conditions incomparably more than in Europe." And:

> O Dear Father, belive what I am going to relate the words of truth and sincerity, and Ballance my former bad conduct to my sufferings here, and then I am sure you'll pitty your Distressed Daughter, What we unfortunat English people suffer here is beyond the probability of you in England to conceive, let it suffice that I one of the unhappy Number, am toiling almost Day and Night, and very often in the Horses druggery . . . and then tied up and whipp'd to that Degree that you'd not serve an Annimal, scarce any thing but Indian Corn and Salt to eat and that even begrudged nay many Negroes are better used, almost naked, no shoes nor stockings to wear, and the comfort after slaving dureing Masters pleasure, what rest we get is to rap ourselve up in a Blanket and ly upon the Ground, this is the deplorable condition your poor Betty endures. . . .[7]

John Adams wrote about Massachusetts, as late as the Revolutionary period: "Perhaps it may be said that in America we have no distinctions of ranks . . . ; but have we not laborers, yeomen, gentlemen, esquires, honorable gentlemen, and excellent gentlemen?" There were rich and poor in the colonies, and the distinction was clear not only in economic and political power, but in every aspect of daily living. Poor and rich lived in different kinds of houses, ate different foods, entertained themselves in different ways, were addressed with different degrees of respect, and were buried differently. An early eighteenth-century traveler stopped off at "a dirty poor house, with hardly anything in it but children, that wallowed about like so many pigs" and in another home was "forced to pig together" with ten people in a room.

By the latter part of that century, prosperous merchants and planters lived in lavish mansions with ornate Chippendale furniture and elaborate china, drank claret, port, and Madeira (while the poor drank "kill-devil" rum). Even frontier societies can support an idle aristocracy, if the differences in wealth are sharp enough. Josiah Quincy wrote about a sojourn in Maryland: "I spent yesterday chiefly with young men of fortune; they were gamblers and cockfighters, hound-breeders and horse-jockies."

In Massachusetts, the law forbade a woman from wearing silk hoods and scarves unless her husband was worth two hundred pounds. The upper class were called Master and Mistress, the ordinary people Goodman and Goodwife. The upper class did not get whippings if they broke the law. The poor did. One-fifth to one-sixth of the population were servants in seventeenth-century Massachusetts.

In a study of five important colonial towns—Boston, New York, Philadelphia, Newport, Charles Town—Carl Bridenbaugh concludes: "The colonists who came to settle in the villages brought with them the social order then existing in England or Holland, and sought with considerable success to set up a similar system in America." They "were thoroughly indoctrinated with prevailing ideas of social inequality. . . . and they certainly had never heard of a classless society." [8] His work enables us to give quick sketches of the class society in these five towns.

BOSTON: "The leaders of early Boston were gentlemen of considerable wealth who, in association with the clergy, eagerly sought to preserve in America the social arrangements of the Mother Country. By means of their control of trade and commerce, by their political domination of the inhabitants through church and Town Meeting, and by careful marriage alliances among themselves, members of this little oligarchy laid the foundations for an aristocratic class in seventeenth century Boston." [9] Rich merchants erected mansions, persons "of Qualitie" traveled in coaches or sedan chairs, had their portraits painted, wore periwigs, and filled themselves with rich food and Madeira. At times of crisis, the maldistribution of wealth brought food shortages, and one night in 1713, a Bostonian recorded "the Riot Committed that night . . . by 200 people in the Comon, thinking to find Corn there."

It was in that year that Cotton Mather wrote: ". . . the distressed Families of the Poor to which I dispense, or procure needful Relief, are now so many, and of such daily Occurrence, that it is needless for me here to mention them." The Bostonian rich lived in "elaborate town houses, beautifully appointed, and filled with elegant furniture . . . a corps of servants, black and white. . . . Boston gentlewomen dressed in the latest and most expensive London clothese and bedecked themselves with lavish jewelry." The rich began to spend so much money on elaborate funerals that the General Court had to pass laws against extraordinary funeral expenses.

NEWPORT: As in Boston, Bridenbaugh finds "the town meetings, while ostensibly democratic, were in reality controlled year after year by the same group of merchant aristocrats, who secured most of the important offices. . . ." A contemporary described the Newport merchant aristocracy: ". . . the men in flaming scarlet coats and waistcoats, laced and fringed with brightest glaring yellow. The Sly Quakers, not venturing on these charming coats and waistcoats, yet loving finery, figured away with plate on their sideboards." Common sailors, warehousemen, dockworkers formed the lower strata of town society (with slaves and servants below them). In the summer of 1730 a quarrel between the "gentleman's party" and one representing town workers led to a mob rising in the town.

NEW YORK: Negro slaves made up a much larger part of the working class in Northern towns than is generally recognized. In 1720, of New York's population of 7000, 1600 were Negroes, and Wall Street was designated as the market place where slaveowners could hire them out by the day or the week. In the bloody Negro insurrection of 1712 in New York City, twenty-one slaves were executed.

When, in 1735, John Van Zandt horsewhipped his slave to death for having been found on the streets by the night watch, the New York City coroner's jury said: "The Correction given by the

Master was not the Cause of his Death . . . but it was by the visitation of God." In 1741, another Negro insurrection in New York led to the burning to death of fifteen Negroes, the hanging of eight more.

The New York aristocracy was the most ostentatious of all. Bridenbaugh tells of: "Window hangings of camlet, japanned tables, gold-framed looking glasses, spinets and massive eight-day clocks. . . . richly carved furniture, jewels and silverplate. . . . Black house servants." The middle classes lived fairly comfortably, but far below the style of the rich; poor laborers and free Negroes, just above the servant-slave rank, lived at the edge of poverty.

A letter to Peter Zenger's New York *Journal* in 1737 spoke of the poor children in New York: "I believe it would be a very shocking Appearance to a moralized Heathen, were he to meet with an Object in Human Shape, half starv'd with Cold, with Cloathes out at the Elbows, Knees through the Breeches, Hair standing on end. . . . From the age about four to fourteen they spend their Days in the Streets. . . . then they are put out as Apprentices, perhaps four, five, or six years. . . ."

With variations in detail, the sharpness of class distinctions were similar in Charles Town and Philadelphia.

THE PROBLEM OF HISTORICAL SELECTION

If the colonial period of our history constitutes our birth and infancy we were not "born free." We were born amidst slavery, semi-slavery, poverty, land monopoly, class privilege, and class conflict. And this is not putting it as starkly as we might, for history has always been written by the upper and middle classes, and has only rarely been able to capture even a glimpse of the actual misery of lower-class life. The very nature of intellectual discourse on inequalities in wealth guarantees an overall tone of moderation and detachment, just as American history written by whites tends to complacency on the race issue. It takes the rare artistic talent of a Zola, Dickens, or Melville to even approach the terrible reality masked by historical description.

Three points have been omitted from this discussion so far, all of which support the temper lying behind the concept that we were "born free." One is that whatever conditions were in America for the lower classes, they were worse in Europe. This is true, *if* we follow the American historian's custom of leaving out Negro slavery from assessments of the social condition which are not primarily concerned with race. An amended statement would read: the lower-class white Anglo-Saxon farmer, worker, and servant was better off in America than in England.

The second point is: the mobility from lower to upper classes was much greater in the American colonies. The evidence so far indicates a flat yes to this statement. Much has been made of the social mobility in America but we are beginning now to see, in the emerging countries of Asia and Africa, the same kind of dynamic, shooting mobility that we had in our early years; it seems to come with any fresh, vigorous society and is not unique to our nation. This mobility, even at its best, in America as elsewhere, has always been a prize for the few, and has not affected the position of the vast majority. It gives to society both the zest and the deception that Irish Sweepstakes winners gave not long ago to the Lower East Side of New York City.

The third point in favor of the "born free" idea is that we in America had, almost from the very beginning, a large middle class, something not existent in the feudal-aristocratic societies of the Old World or the despotisms of the Orient, and so, if not luxury, a degree of comfort was spread to larger proportions of the population than had ever been done before. This should also be recorded flatly as a truth, with this reminder: that it was made possible, from the beginning, by slavery and servitude, and that, throughout our history, the laudable fact of a large, well-fed middle class has obscured the existence of an equally large, ill-fed lower class.*

Thus, we have a problem in historical objectivity. We can, as I have just done, make out a case for a class society in colonial

---

* In his study, *The Social Structure of Revolutionary America,* Princeton University Press, 1965, Jackson Turner Main estimates a "permanent proletariat" black and white, of 30 percent at the time of the Revolution. That seems remarkably close to the twentieth-century estimate of the permanently poor.

America, and for glaring inequalities of wealth and status. We can also, as has been done many times, make out a case for a fluid class structure and a rather prosperous society. Both descriptions focus on different aspects of the same complex reality. It is also possible to do as most historians, and refuse to make out a "case" at all, but to present enough facts to supply the needs of polemicists on both sides. This, while useful, represents a social detachment which ignores human need.

If one wants to avoid neutrality, and if both a case for equality and a case for inequality can be extracted from the same body of historical material, which shall the social analyst emphasize? That depends on his criterion: If his standard of judgment for characterizing American society is the comparable state of equality in most other countries of the world, then the emphasis is on American class fluidity, the comfort of the large middle class, the relatively good position even of many members of the lower class. If his standard is an ideal society where "irrational privilege" is nonexistent, then his emphasis is on the still-deplorable condition of the lower classes and on the maldistribution of wealth. But which standard should be applied? I would argue that the choice is neither arbitrary nor capricious nor instinctive, but can be rationally determined by the relationship of social needs to social possibilities at any given time.

It is a problem that is not confined to the issue we are here discussing, but to all situations where an analyst understands that his analysis enters into history and must have *some* effect (even so-called neutrality, or "objectivity," has its effect) and needs to decide whether to emphasize progress already made, or distance from the goal still to be achieved. There are two situations which warrant, I think, a stress on progress already achieved: when it is necessary to encourage those dubious of the possibility of progress; or when there is no chance of substantially improving conditions, and focusing on the ideal would only result in false expectations and terrible frustration. Human happiness seems to depend on the balance of expectations and fulfillment. If there is no possibility of fulfillment, it is socially desirable to reduce expectations (Buddhism, with its exhortation to eliminate *desire,* has this function).

The first of the above reasons—combating pessimism—is sufficiently operative today to warrant maintaining, as a minor theme in social analysis of the national condition, the fact of achieved progress in relation to other countries, and in relation to the past. But the second reason does not exist for us; in our incredibly wealthy America, with its capacity to eliminate poverty completely and forever, to distribute health facilities, education, and housing to all sections of the population in needed quantities, there should be a shouting stress on our unfulfilled capacity and on the shamefulness of existing inequality.

To emphasize inequality in the colonial period is not to make any judgment on what was done or was not done to change the situation in that time; it is rather useless—because it is too late— to "judge" the past. The only socially useful judgments are of the present, and the helpful thing about reading the past is that it may have the effect on the observer that Aristotle saw in the tragic drama—a heightened perception of one's own life as a result of viewing and feeling, through the magnifier of space and time, the failures of another's experience. This, I suggest, is the most useful function of historical analysis. It is our *present* needs which require a focus on the class inequalities of the American past.

But what of the present?

CLASS TODAY

Three news items from contemporary America.

In the summer of 1961, a young father in Council Bluffs, Iowa, named William Maguire, used a rope to strangle three of his children to death, then, with his remaining child, a six-year-old boy, drove his auto head-on into a parked truck, killing them both. Maguire left a note addressed to his wife, who had been ill for some time and in a hospital: "Sorry, but this is best way out. Pains in back after accident Feb. 9, 1961, and bills since then. I can't take it any longer. All three kids in trouble all the time makes it worse. Love. Mac."

Around the same time in New York City: "With the eyes of thousands of theatre-goers and other persons fastened on him, an unemployed father of five children balanced precariously for an hour atop the flashing sign above the Manhattan Hotel last night before being pulled to safety. From his perch more than 400 feet above Eighth Avenue, the man shouted incoherently of lies he had been told and sobbed that he could not support his children."

In the fall of 1962, in Atlanta: "Neighbors stopped Mrs. Mary H. Harden, a 35-year-old mother of three, from burying her sons alive on a construction site adjacent to the new expressway. . . . At a hearing on Monday Mrs. Harden said that she had tried to 'put them out of their misery.' She also said that neither she nor the children had eaten from Thursday until Saturday, and that she had been evicted from her Forrest Road residence."

One needs to put aside on occasion first-rate newspapers, quality magazines, and other respectable sources of news about American civilization, and pick up the big-city tabloids, to read about the family knifings, the suicides, the drownings of babies by their mothers, and the thousands of other horrors that dramatize the huge (and to middle-class America, invisible) underworld of poverty in the United States. These outbursts of frantic violence induced by economic distress might be dismissed as only isolated and rare incidents, if we were not confronted with the statistics of American poverty, which indicate that for every sensational item in the newspapers there are hundreds of thousands of stories of personal tragedy, grief, misery, being played out behind closed doors all over the country, unnoticed by that two-thirds of the nation which shares somewhat in the shallow prosperity of our "affluent society."

The 20,000 Americans who commit suicide every year * represent only the sharpest point of a pyramid of anguish which at its base probably includes forty million Americans—that 20 percent of the families who earn between $1000 and $4000 a year (of the twelve million single people, 20 percent earn under $1000 a year) [10]—a pyramid whose construction materials are varied in outward appearance, but whose essential ingredient is the same: poverty. We have always deluded ourselves about American prosperity; this is a sacred bubble which few are anxious to puncture publicly. We quote happily the "average" American sal-

* There were 21,281 suicides in 1966. *Statistical Abstract of the U.S., 1969,* p. 58.

ary (in the last few years, over $7000), and receive the feeling of satisfaction that comes with knowing all Americans are doing well these days. There is no better way to conceal the sharp edges of individual suffering than to wrap them all in the smooth round packages of national "averages."

Our country looks different, however, when you break it into economic classes, and see how well each class does. In 1966, about 30 percent of the population (about seventy million people) were in families earning under $5000 a year, with about half that number earning under $3000 a year. ($3000 was just about the cost of maintaining one son or daughter in a private college or university for a year.) About 40 percent of the population were in families earning between $5000 and $10,000 a year—enough money not to be considered poor, but not enough to avoid a desperate struggle to pay basic bills. And 30 percent of the population earned over $10,000 a year.[11]

Measured by European or Asian standards, this is affluence. Measured against the enormous wealth produced in the United States, this is a horrendously inefficient distribution of that wealth. Granted that there is a relatively large, comfortable middle class, there is something grossly unfair in the wealthiest fifth of the population getting 40 percent of the nation's income, and the poorest fifth getting 5 percent (a ratio virtually unchanged from 1947 to 1966).

Statistics cannot accurately depict the condition of that thirty million people below the $3000-a-year level. Farm workers in Massachusetts were described as follows in the *Boston Sunday Globe,* October 2, 1966:

> A farm north of Boston is an example of conditions at their worst. The men work for 95 cents an hour. They work up to fourteen hours a day, seven days a week. They live in a shack with cardboard on the floor. The farmer does not allow the men off the farm to shop. He does not allow them to have visitors. There are twenty men on the farm. Their one toilet is an outhouse. A priest saw how the men live and work, and described their conditions as "slavery."

When Robert Lampman testified before Congress in 1960 for the National Bureau of Economic Research, he reported that the top one percent of the nation (about 400,000 families) own over one-fourth of all tangible wealth (money, stocks, bonds, mortgages, real estate) in the United States, as well as 75 percent of the value of all corporate stock in the United States. Even if there were a gradual improvement in the distribution of income it would take a very, very long time to cut significantly into this disproportionate allocation of wealth.

In fact, the changes in the relative position of very rich and very poor are insignificant, while incomes in the middle ranges have gone up markedly. The bottom tenth of the population got one percent of the total money income in 1947, and still one percent in 1960; the top tenth's share decreased from 33 percent to 27 percent.[12] Between 1950 and 1960 both the lowest one-fifth and the highest one-fifth of American families increased their take-home pay by the same percentage. But this meant that in dollars, the lowest one-fifth earned $500 more, while the upper one-fifth earned $5000 more. Percentages deceive.

Again, statistics dull the sensibilities about wealth and poverty. Whether you are poor or rich determines the most fundamental facts about your life: whether or not you are cold in the winter while trying to sleep; whether or not you suffocate in the summer; whether or not you live among vermin or rats; whether the smells around you all day are sweet or foul; whether or not you have adequate medical care; whether or not you have good teeth; whether or not you can send your children to college; whether or not you can go on vacation, or have to take an extra job at night; whether you can afford a divorce, or an abortion, or a wife, or another child.

No statistics can tell us in personal terms about those thirty or forty or fifty or sixty million human beings in this country who are up against it: the porters, the waiters, the unskilled factory workers, the delivery "boys," the maids and office cleaners, the migrant workers, the filling station attendants, the hangers-on, the tenant farmers, the petty clerks—the people who have to drink or take drugs, the physically disabled, the mentally disturbed, the foreigner in a strange land, the Negro in his own land, the aged staring through the window.

These people are all invisible, until you begin to look for them.

Then, they suddenly appear everywhere. There are places where they can be seen in bunches: the emergency ward of a city hospital, the bus terminal in any town in America, the employment offices in the rundown section of the city, street corners at seven in the morning, the little-traveled roads and byways of the American countryside, the subways of New York City, the low-income housing projects, and the slums alongside. The man named "Wash" in Faulkner's story, the "Assistant" of Bernard Malamud, the discarded athletic coach in John Updike's *Rabbit, Run*—these are not fictional characters. There are millions of them in America, impoverished spiritually as well as economically.

Government spokesmen have tended to perpetuate the myth of classlessness. In August, 1961, testifying before the Joint Economic Committee of Congress, Marriner Eccles, of the Federal Reserve Board made light of the rise in interest rates, which some people had charged would benefit banks and rich bondholders. Government bonds, he said "are very widely distributed." But the *Federal Reserve Bulletin* of July 1959 indicated that 73 percent of all family spending units in the nation owned no savings bonds whatsoever, and of the total of 42.5 billions in savings bonds, 36 billion dollars was owned by 5 percent of the spending units.

The class nature of the American economy is reflected in the tax structure, but this is hidden from those without the time or training to study taxes. For instance, in President John F. Kennedy's first administration he proposed a "tax cut." Newspapers then talked endlessly of a "tax cut." Everybody passed very quickly over the really crucial questions: how much of a cut for the rich, how much for the poor, how much for corporations, how much for families earning under $4000 a year. The president talked of an "across-the-board" tax cut, but an expert on tax law pointed to "a hidden tilt." In Kennedy's proposal, a married person with two dependents who earned $4580 a year would increase his take-home pay after taxes by $124. A married person with two dependents who earned $143,454 a year would increase his take-home pay after taxes by thousands of dollars.[13]

Taxation is loaded intrinsically with tensions of class, but these are concealed in newspaper reports and public statements, behind vague, general phrases which make no class differentiation. More than anyone, it is the low-income groups which are kept in the dark about the tax structure. The middle class has gone to college and can figure things fairly well. The upper class hires blue-chip accountants to do its figuring.

The great tax revolution of the past few decades consists of the shifting of the national tax burden onto the low and lower-middle groups. Glib percentage-quoters, talking of 90 percent from the rich, and only 20 percent from the poor, are evading the facts almost as much as the rich are evading taxes. In 1929, persons earning under $10,000 paid less than one-twentieth of the income tax revenue. By 1956, they paid two-thirds of the total revenue. On the other hand, taxpayers earning over $100,000 paid two-thirds of the total income tax revenue in 1929, but by 1956 paid only one-twentieth of total revenue. Today, five-sixths of the income tax comes from the lowest income-tax bracket, the 20 percent bracket.

Low-income people simply didn't pay federal income taxes in 1929. Today, they do. A man with a wife and two children who earns $4000 needs every cent he can keep; but the federal government can take $240 of this in taxes. Even if the $100,000-earner were left with only $25,000 (which doesn't happen), on whom is the burden greater? Chambers of commerce complain about "confiscatory" taxes, pointing to the 91 percent tax for incomes over $200,000, but nobody making that much pays 91 percent. In 1956, the Treasury took only about 37 percent of the over-$200,000 incomes. *Fortune Magazine,* not unfriendly to the rich, compared the high-bracket taxation situation to "dipping deeply into great incomes with a sieve."

A survey made by the Brookings Institution in 1966 of the tax laws found that people with annual incomes over $1,000,000 paid out only 26.7 percent of their total income in Federal income taxes.[14] In 1961, seventeen Americans with incomes over $1,000,-000 and thirty-five with incomes over $500,000 paid no taxes.[15] In that same year a Negro maintenance man I knew in Atlanta, with no savings, earning a dollar an hour, was called to the Internal Revenue Office to pay up several hundred dollars in back taxes. Not sophisticated in the ways of income-tax forms, he had done as so many in his class; he had gone to an "accountant" who charged five dollars for a hasty job of filling out his return.

The rich, instead of calling it salary, take much of their money in expense accounts, a popular way of increasing income without paying taxes. Perhaps five billion dollars a year are involved in expense accounts, which means that the Treasury, not taxing these, loses over a billion dollars. One dairy company executive and his wife deducted from taxable income $16,000 for a safari to Africa, on the ground that it publicized his business. Another manufacturer deducted $269,000 for a tropical island, fishing cruisers, and air transport, to entertain guests. Another deducted $10,000 to take customers to the Kentucky Derby. All these were allowed by the courts.

One researcher on the tax system, pointing to the hundred or so special provisions in the tax code, commented: "One thing virtually all the special provisions have in common is that however reasonable or meritorious they may seem, they help the upper-bracket taxpayer most and do little or nothing for the low-income group." [16] He noted that the joint-return provision saved $40 for a man earning $4000 a year and $22,180 for someone earning $200,000 a year.

Congress' most notorious tampering with the effect of taxation on income distribution in the postwar period was to grant a special depletion allowance of 27.5 percent of gross income for the oil industry, which went ahead in 1953 to take two billion dollars out of its taxable revenue. A Dartmouth professor showed the House Ways and Means Committee (which listened but did not act) that one company, over a twenty-year period, on an investment of $200,000, could write off $600,000 against taxes. Individual wage-earners have no comparable right to write off 50 percent of their net income each year for "depletion" as this oil company could do.[17]

Is America a class society—that is, a country of very rich and very poor? A clear-cut affirmative answer was always beclouded by the fact that in between the very rich and very poor was always that great middle class. In recent years, as the middle class has moved out to the suburbs, the picture became more stark; left in the city are the very rich and the very poor. All one needs to do is take a long walk through any large city in the United States, to affirm the fact that we are indeed a class society.

True, this is not unique to America. Everywhere you go in the world you see class societies. But there is one fact peculiar to the United States; we are the one country in the world that has no excuse for such contrasts of affluence and misery, because we are so enormously wealthy. One economist has noted how puny are the gestures we make, in our most generous moments, toward change: "A society whose gross income rises by $40 billion a year may even find the heart to give an annual increment of $1 billion for the most unfortunate of its poor. In the general structure of society and politics, this charity changes nothing." [18]

I have thrust quickly into the colonial picture and into the contemporary one to find a fact common to this country at its birth and in its maturity—the unjust distribution of its resources. I use the word "unjust" based on two criteria. One is the unheard-of wealth of this nation. The other is that modern ideal of equality, whether expressed in the Jeffersonian phrase that "all men are created equal" in the right to pursue happiness—or the Marxian idea that men should receive from an affluent society "according to their need." The perception that all the lauded progress toward the welfare state has done little to alter that basic historic inequality might spur us to more radical solutions.

5

The Ludlow Massacre

In their scholarly history of the labor movement, we find this terse statement by Selig Perlman and Philip Taft: "On April 20, 1914, the Colorado coal strike was brought to the attention of the entire country by the gruesome burning of eleven children and two women in the Ludlow tent colony." [1]

The event they describe became known as the Ludlow Massacre. It was the culminating act of perhaps the most violent struggle between corporate power and laboring men in American history. Despite five thousand pages of testimony, taken at the time by Congressional investigating bodies,* it remains an obscure event, rarely mentioned in textbooks on American history.**

I recall it now, but not for its dramatic particulars, which might, in their uniqueness, be seen as a set of events happily submerged in the new welfare state. Rather, I find in it a set of suggestions

* That testimony is the basic source of this essay. It consists of Senate document No. 415, which is the last three volumes of the nine-volume report issued by the Industrial Relations Commission, pp. 6347–8903. (U.S. Commission on Industrial Relations, *Report and Testimony,* Government Printing Office, Washington, 1916); and a two-volume report by the House Mines and Mining Committee, *Conditions in the Coal Mines of Colorado,* (Government Printing Office, Washington, 1914). The House testimony (except for the Appendix) was taken just before the Ludlow Massacre, the Industrial Relations Commission testimony shortly afterward.

** For instance, in the otherwise very detailed *Encyclopedia of American History,* edited by Richard Morris, Harper & Row, 1965, there is no mention of the Colorado strike. Nor is it mentioned in Samuel Eliot Morison's *Oxford History of the American People,* Oxford University Press, 1965. (Of course, I do not mean it is deliberately omitted. The process of "forgetting" in history is more complex than that.) There is an excellent chapter on the Colorado strike in Samuel Yellen, *American Labor Struggles,* Harcourt, Brace, 1936.

about the relations between people and government which, stripped of their particularity, are still alive (so that, in place of miners, we might see blacks; in place of unions we might see student movements or welfare rights organizations). I find, from 1914 to 1969, a continuity of governmental behavior which is easily forgotten if one is distracted by the intricately embroidered veil of words and gestures, or by the specificities of the Colorado countryside: the mining canyons, the strange and unrepeatable sounds, colors, tones, of that time, that place.

I would point to several elements in that continuity, and let the reader judge, from the facts of the Colorado events, from what we know of contemporary America, whether I am concluding too much from too little:

1. The firm connection between entrenched wealth and political power, manifested in the decisions of government, and in the machinery of law and justice.

2. The team play of the federal system, in which crass action by local police on behalf of the rich and powerful is modified—especially after resistance develops—with a more masked but still biased intervention by the national government.

3. The selective control of violence, in which government power is fumbling and incompetent in dealing with corporate and local police violence, sure and efficient in dealing with the violence of protest movements.

4. The somewhat different style of the national government (without difference in substance) in dealing with those outside its bounds who are helpless to resist and impotent as an internal political force—that is, with foreigners (Mexico, 1914; Dominican Republic, 1965). The style there is more like a local police force dealing with the locally powerless.

5. The opiate effect of commissions and investigations.

But let us turn to Colorado, 1913–1914.

Formed under the enormous weight of the Rockies, soft coal was found in Southern Colorado not long after the Civil War. Railroads moved south from Denver, north from New Mexico. Settlers, coming down the old Santa Fe trail, converged on the banks of the Purgatory River, just east of the Rockies and about fifteen miles north of the New Mexican border, and built the town of Trinidad.* The great Colorado Fuel and Iron Corporation, along with smaller companies, sank shafts into the hillsides, advertised for immigrant labor, and lowered workers into the earth to remove the coal.

In 1902, Colorado Fuel and Iron was purchased by John D. Rockefeller. Then, in 1911, he turned his interests (about 40 percent of the stock, more than enough to control) over to his son, John D. Rockefeller, Jr., who made major policy decisions from his office at 26 Broadway in New York City.

Two hundred and fifty feet, three hundred, four hundred feet below the surface—in blackness so complete it seemed alive, grotesque—men hacked away at the face of the coal seam with hand picks. Their helpers shoveled the coal into waiting railroad cars, which were drawn through tunnels by mules to the main shaft, and lifted to the surface to the top of the tipple, the coal then showering down through the sorting screens onto flat cars. The average coal seam was about three feet high, so the miner worked on his knees or on his side. The ventilation system depended on the manipulation of tunnel doors by "trapper boys"—often thirteen- or fourteen-year-old children being initiated into mining.

At the edge of the mountains, in steep-walled canyons, were the camps where the miners lived, in sagging, wooden huts, with old newspapers nailed to the walls to keep out the cold. Nearby were the mine buildings and the coke ovens, with clouds of soot clogging the air. Behind the huts was a sluggish creek, dirty-yellow, laden with mine slag and camp refuse, alongside which the children played.

The mining camps were feudal kingdoms run by the coal corporation, which made the "laws"; curfews were imposed, suspicious strangers were not allowed to visit the homes, the company store must be patronized, the company doctor used. The laws were enforced by company-appointed marshals. The teachers and preachers were picked by the company. By 1914, Colorado Fuel and Iron owned twenty-seven mining camps, and all the land, the

* Michael Beshoar, *All About Trinidad and Las Animas County,* Stearn Printing House, Denver 1882. See also House Mines and Mining Committee, *Conditions in the Coal Mines of Colorado,* p. 7.

houses, the saloons, the schools, the churches, the stores.[2] Company superintendents, in charge of the camps, were described once by a corporation employee as "uncouth, ignorant, immoral, and in many instances the most brutal set of men. . . . Blasphemous bullies." *

At first the miners were Welshmen and Englishmen, who had gained experience in their home countries. But in the 1880's and 1890's, the new immigration brought Italians, Greeks, Poles, Hungarians. There were also many Mexicans and Negroes.**

Colorado Fuel and Iron became unmistakably the major political force in Colorado. A letter from C.F.&I. Superintendent Bowers to the secretary of John D. Rockefeller, Jr., written in May 1913, summed up the situation: ***

> The Colorado Fuel & Iron Company for many years were accused of being the political dictator of southern Colorado, and in fact were a mighty power in the whole state. When I came here it was said that the C.F.&I. Co. voted every man and women in their employ without regard to their being naturalized or not; and even their mules, it used to be remarked, were registered, if they were fortunate enough to possess names.

Bowers told Rockefeller that the company, in the 1904 election campaign, had contributed $80,605, and that it "became notorious in many sections for their support of the liquor interests. They established saloons everywhere they possibly could." A sheriff elected with company support became a partner in sixteen liquor stores in the mining camps.

---

* Statement by Rev. Eugene S. Gaddis, Superintendent of the Sociological Department of the Colorado Fuel and Iron Corporation during the strike, to the U.S. Commission on Industrial Relations, May 19, 1915. For descriptions of life in the mining camps see George Korson, *Coal Dust on the Fiddle,* Folklore, 1965, also McAlister Coleman, *Men and Coal,* Farrar & Rinehart, 1943.

** In 1901, out of 7500 employees of C.F.&I., 500 were Negroes. Sterling Spero and Abram Harris, *The Black Worker,* Atheneum, 1968.

*** George P. West, *Report on the Colorado Strike,* Government Printing Office, 1915, p. 46. This is the official summary of the report of the Commission on Industrial Relations.

Apparently, Bowers' entrance onto this scene did not change the situation. Company officials continued to be appointed as election judges. Company-dominated coroners and judges prevented injured employees from collecting damages. Polling places were often on company property. In Las Animas County, John C. Baldwin, a gambler, bartender, and friend of Colorado Fuel and Iron, was jury foreman in 80 percent of the county cases. During the strike, Governor Ammons was questioned about civil liberties in the state of which he was chief executive, and his interviewer, Rev. Atkinson, reported this exchange: [3]

Rev. Atkinson: Have you no constitutional law and government in Colorado?

Gov. Ammons: Not a bit in those counties where the coal mines are located.

Rev. Atkinson: Do you mean to say that in large sections of your state there is no constitutional liberty?

Gov. Ammons: Absolutely none.

One Colorado official told the House Committee investigating the strike: "It's very seldom you can convict anyone in Huerfano County if he's got any friends. Jeff Farr, the sheriff, selects the jury and they're picked to convict or acquit as the case may be." [4]

In early 1913, the United Mine Workers, which had unsuccessfully led a strike in the southern Colorado coal fields ten years before, began another organizing drive. It asked the mine operators to negotiate. The operators refused and hired the Baldwin-Felts Detective Agency. The governor sent his deputy labor commissioner to Trinidad to investigate what seemed a growing tension. Hundreds of deputies were sworn in by the sheriffs of Las Animas and Huerfano Counties.

On the evening of August 16, 1913, a young United Mine Workers organizer named Gerald Lippiatt arrived in Trinidad by train, walked down the main street through a Saturday night crowd, exchanged angry words with two Baldwin-Felts detectives who had recently been deputized, and was shot to death.

The two detectives, George Belcher and Walter Belk, were released on $10,000 bond, while a coroner's jury was formed. On it were six Trinidad men: the manager of the Wells Fargo Express

Company, the cashier of the Trinidad National Bank, the president of the Sherman-Cosmer Mercantile Company, the manager of the Columbia Hotel, the proprietor of a chain of mercantile stores, and John C. Baldwin, gambler and saloonkeeper, who acted as foreman.[5]

There were conflicting reports to the jury on who fired first, how many shots were fired, and what was said between Lippiatt and the detectives. The only details on which all witnesses agreed was that Lippiatt walked down the street, encountered Belcher and Belk, exchanged gunfire with Belcher, and was killed. The first man to reach Lippiatt, a miner named William Daselli, said Belk reached for his gun, Belcher pulled his gun and fired, and Lippiatt fell, fired from the ground, wounding Belcher in the thigh, then fell for the last time. When Daselli raised Lippiatt's head, he said, Belk's gun was still trained on him.*

The jury's verdict was: justifiable homicide.

The pace of union organizing in the mining canyons now quickened. Secret meetings were held, in churches, at picnics, in abandoned mine workings hidden in the mountains. A convention was called for mid-September in Trinidad, and delegates were elected at hundreds of meetings.

Meanwhile, the Baldwin-Felts Agency was importing hundreds of men, from the saloons and barrelhouses of Denver, and from points outside the state, to help break the impending strike. In Huerfano County, by September 1, 326 men were deputized by Sheriff Jeff Farr, all armed and paid by the coal companies.[6]

The miners' convention, with 280 delegates, opened in the Great Opera House of Trinidad. For two days, rank-and-file miners registered their complaints: that they were robbed of from 400–800 pounds on each ton of coal, that they were paid in scrip worth ninety cents on the dollar (a violation of Colorado law), that the eight-hour law was not observed, that the law allowing miners to elect checkweighmen of their own choice was completely ignored, that their wages could only be spent in company stores

---

* Accounts of the shooting are found in the *United Mine Workers Journal* for August 21 and August 28, 1913. Also in Michael Beshoar, *Out of the Depths,* Golden Bell, Denver, 1957 (a biography of strike leader John Lawson).

and saloons (where prices were 25–40 percent higher), that they were forced to vote according to the wishes of the mine superintendent, that they were beaten and discharged for voicing complaints, that the armed mine guards conducted a reign of terror which kept the miners in subjection to the company. Their average daily wage was $1.68 for eight hours, $2.10 for ten hours.[7] Casualty rates were twice as high in Colorado as in other mining states.

The high point of the Trinidad convention was the appearance of Mary Jones (the fabled Mother Jones), eighty-year-old organizer for the United Mine Workers, just back from a bitterly fought strike in the coal fields of West Virginia. Mother Jones represented a radical view (she had been one of the founders of the IWW) inside the rather conservative United Mine Workers (which had, for instance, supported Governor Ammons and the Democratic Party in 1912 against Progressive and Socialist candidates).* Mother Jones' speech deserves to be quoted at length: [8]

> The question that arises today in the nation is an industrial oligarchy. . . . What would the coal in these mines and in these hills be worth unless you put your strength and muscle in to bring them? . . .
>
> I went into the state of West Virginia. . . . There I saw women that had been beaten to death and a babe of the coming generation was beaten to death and murdered by the Baldwin-Felts thugs in the womb of her mother. That is in America, my friends, and I said "I will never leave the state until the Baldwin thugs leave too" and I didn't. . . .
>
> Three thousand men assembled in Charlestown and we marched up with banners, with demands upon those banners, and we walked into the state house grounds, for they are ours, and we have a right to

---

* Michael Beshoar wrote: "John Lawson and his miners were naive on the subject of politics. They invariably regarded the Democratic Party as the champion of the downtrodden, a position that could not have been sustained had they had the experience to draw obvious conclusions from the party's record in the state." (*Out of the Depths.*) Beshoar was a grandson of Dr. Michael Beshoar, a physician friendly to the miners in early Colorado history.

take possession of them if we want to. . . . I called a committee and I said, "Here, take this document into the governor's office and present it to him. Now don't get on your knees. We have got no kings in America. Stand on both your feet with your head erect" said I, and present that document to the governor, and they said "Will we wait?" and I said, "No, don't wait, and don't say your honor," said I, because very few of those fellows have any honor. . . .

And there was that meeting. I would give the United States Treasury if I had it, boys, if there had been someone there with a pen who grasped the sociology of that meeting—he would have paralyzed the world with it. . . . Men came from the mountains with toes out of their shoes, with stomachs empty. . . . Fifteen hundred men came there, the militia was there, the Baldwin thugs came there. . . . When I was about to close the meeting I said, "Boys, let Mother tell you one thing." And they said, "What, Mother?" And I said, "Liberty is not dead, she is only quietly resting, waiting only for you to call" and that voice of fifteen hundred men rang the air, reached to Heaven, and they said, "Oh God, Mother, call her, call her now!". . .

Sure we'll get in the bullpen. There is nothing about that. I was in jail. God Almighty, what if you do, you built the jail! I was jailed . . . and tried in Federal court and the old judge said "Did you read my injunction?" I said I did. "Did you notice that that injunction told you not to look at the mines and did you look at them?" "Certainly," I said. "Why did you do it?" the judge said. "Because there was a judge bigger than you, and he gave me my eyesight, and I am going to look at whatever I want to."

A lickspittle of the court comes up, and he says, "You must say your Honor, this is the court, His Honor on the bench." Yes, that was His Honor on the bench, the fellow behind the counter with the mustache. . . .

You have collected more wealth, created more wealth, than they in a thousand years of the Roman Republic, and yet you have not any. . . .

When I get Colorado, Kansas, and Alabama organized, I will tell God Almighty to take me to my rest. But not before then!

The convention, rebuffed by the company again on requests to negotiate, voted to call a strike for September 23, 1913.

On that day, an epic scene took place in the coal districts of Southern Colorado. Eleven thousand miners, about 90 percent of the workers in the mines, gathered their families and their belongings on carts and mules and on their backs, and marched out of the mining camps to tent colonies set up in the countryside by the union.* One observer wrote: [9]

> All the tents had not yet arrived and the elements seemed to be in league with the operators. For two days it rained and snowed. There was never a more pitiful sight than the exodus of those miners fortunate enough to get wagons for their household goods. It rained all day Tuesday, and there streamed into Trinidad from every road miners with their wives and kids, crowded up on top of pitifully few household things.

Mother Jones testified later that twenty-eight wagonloads of personal belongings came into the Ludlow tent colony that day, on roads deep in mud, with the horses weary, and mothers carrying tiny babies in their arms. Tents and mattresses were wet, and the children had to sleep on those mattresses that night.[10]

The largest of the tent colonies was at Ludlow, a railroad depot eighteen miles north of Trinidad, on a direct line to Walsenburg, at the edge of Colorado Fuel and Iron property. There were four hundred tents here, for a thousand people, including 271 children. In the course of the strike, twenty-one babies were born in this colony. Later a National Guard officer, reporting to the governor, said of the Ludlow colony: "The colony numbered hundreds of people of whom only a few families were Americans. The rest were for the most part Greeks, Montenegrins, Bulgars, Servians, Italians, Mexicans, Tyroleans, Croatians, Austrians, Savoyards, and other aliens from the Southern countries of Europe." **

Violence began immediately. The Baldwin-Felts Agency constructed a special auto, steel-armored, with a Gatling gun mounted

---

* President Welborn of C. F. & I. estimated 70 percent of C. F. & I. struck. West, *Report on the Colorado Strike.*

** Edward Boughton, *Report to the Governor* (Denver, 1914). Boughton headed a military commission asked to report to the governor on the events of April 20, 1914.

on top, which became known as the Death Special. It roamed the countryside, and on October 17, attacked the tent colony at Forbes, killing one man, leaving a ten-year-old boy with nine bullets in his leg.[11] Around the same time, two rows of armed guards marched forty-nine miners to Trinidad, with the Death Special crawling along to the rear, its guns trained on the strikers' backs. When G. E. Jones, a member of the Western Federation of Miners (the militant miners' union which helped form the IWW) tried to photograph the armored car, Albert Felts, manager of the Baldwin-Felts Agency, beat him unconscious with the butt of his pistol. Jones was then arrested for disturbing the peace.[12]

That same month, a steel-clad train manned by 190 guards with machine guns and rifles, headed for the Ludlow colony. It was intercepted by a detachment of armed miners, and a battle took place in which one mine guard was killed. *The New York Times* commented, after this first small victory for the union: "The situation is extremely critical tonight. More than 700 armed strikers are reported to be in the field against the mine guards.[13]

By this time there had been at least four battles between strikers and guards, and at least nine men had been killed—mostly strikers. The tent colonies were in a state of siege, with machine guns and high-powered searchlights perched on inaccessible ridges, constantly aimed at the tents.

On October 28, 1913, Governor Ammons declared martial law, issued an order forbidding the import of strikebreakers from outside the state, and ordered General Chase of the Colorado National Guard, to move his troops into the strike district. It was one of those "balanced" political moves, in which the concession to one side (the ban on imported strikebreakers) is unenforced, and that to the other side (the reinforcement of the mine guards by government troops) effectively carried out. Some of the pressures behind Ammons' calling of the Guard are explained in a letter written by Vice-President Bowers of C.F.&I. to John D. Rockefeller, Jr., in New York: [14]

> You will be interested to know that we have been able to secure the cooperation of all the bankers of the city, who have had three or four interviews with our little cowboy governor, agreeing to back

the State and lend it all funds necessary to maintain the militia and afford ample protection so our miners could return to work. . . . Besides the bankers, the chambers of commerce, the real estate exchange, together with a great many of the best business men, have been urging the governor to take steps to drive these vicious agitators out of the state. Another mighty power has been rounded up on behalf of the operators by the getting together of fourteen of the editors of the most important newspapers in the state.

After five weeks of terror organized by the mine operators' private army, the striking miners were ready to believe that the National Guard, representing the government of the United States, had come to restore order. At the Ludlow tent colony, pennies and nickels were collected to buy a large American flag, to greet the Guard. A thousand men, women, children, gaunt from lack of food, lined up on the road from the railroad station to the Ludlow colony, dressed in their Sunday best, the children in white, waving little American flags, a hastily assembled band, dressed in faded Greek and Serbian army uniforms, playing "The Union Forever." From the station marched the first troop of cavalry, with General Chase himself on a prancing white stallion, then a small detachment of field artillery, then two regiments of infantrymen, in wide-brimmed hats and yellow leggings. The miners and their wives and children shouted greetings and sang until the last troops had disappeared past the colony, down Berwind Canyon.[15]

But the National Guard turned out to be no different than the Baldwin-Felts men, during that cold, hungry winter of 1913–14. In December, a teen-ager was accosted on the road near the Ludlow colony by Lieutenant Linderfeldt, a stocky, beribboned veteran of the Spanish-American War, and knocked unconscious by the lieutenant's fists. A women's parade in Trinidad in January was attacked by cavalry, and a frightened sixteen-year-old girl, trying to get away, was kicked in the chest by a man on a rearing white horse—General Chase. The leader of the Ludlow colony, a college-educated Greek man named Lou Tikas, was beaten by Linderfeldt and dragged off to jail.*

* These and the other instances of National Guard brutality cited in this essay are part of a 600-page compilation of eyewitness reports by the

The National Guard made 172 arrests that winter. A Welsh woman named Mary M. Thomas, mother of two, was held for three weeks in a vermin-ridden cell. One striker, forced to sleep on an icy cement floor, died after twenty-five days. A nineteen-year-old girl, pregnant, was dragged through an alley by National Guardsmen one night until she lost consciousness. One miner's wife, Mrs. Yankinski, was home with four children when militiamen broke into her home, robbed her money, and broke her little girl's nose with a kick. In the town of Segundo, a group of drunken Guardsmen forced some children to march about the city for two hours, prodding them with bayonets to keep them moving. Marro Zeni, a miner, was forced to stay awake in his cell for five days by soldiers, who threw water in his face, and jabbed him continually with bayonets.[16]

There was violence by the strikers. Strikebreaker Pedro Armijo was murdered near the Aguilar tent colony. A mine clerk named Herbert Smith, scabbing in a Colorado Fuel and Iron mine, was brutally beaten near Trinidad. Strikers fired on the Forbes mining camp, where strikebreakers were living, and were dispersed by an infantry company. Four mine guards were killed at LaVeta while escorting a scab. And on November 20, 1913, George Belcher, the killer of Lippiatt, was leaving a Trinidad drug store, stopped on the corner to light a cigar, and was killed by a single rifle shot by an unseen gunman.*

Governor Ammons rescinded his order against out-of-state strikebreakers, and the National Guard began escorting strikebreakers to the mines. A trainload of such men from St. Louis, disembarking in the mine area, were protected by militiamen with unsheathed bayonets. A House committee heard testimony on the violation of federal peonage laws. "Salvatore Valentin, a Sicilian, told the committee that he had been brought from Pittsburgh

---

Colorado State Federation of Labor, which were the basis for a short report, *Militarism in Colorado* (published in Denver, 1914), by William Brewster of the Yale Law School.

* The instances of miners' violence are reported in *The Military Occupation of the Coal Strike Zone of Colorado,* a report to the Governor by the Adjutant-General's office, 1914. The killing of Belcher was reported in the *International Socialist Review,* February 1914.

through deception, and forced to work in the Delagua mine. One of his fellow strikebreakers, he said, was shot and killed in the mines by an unknown person." *

Early in January 1914, Mother Jones came back to Trinidad, "to help my boys," and was immediately deported by the National Guard. Eluding three detectives, she returned, but over a hundred militiamen stormed the Toltec Hotel in Walsenburg, and took her prisoner. She was held in prison for twenty days, with two armed sentinels outside her door. When women paraded in Trinidad to protest her arrest, eighteen were jailed.[17] When General Chase reported later to the governor on the conduct of the National Guard, he wrote: "It is hoped that a just and discriminating public will in the end come to realize the disinterested service of these champions of the state's integrity and honor."

As Spring approached in 1914, funds for the Guard began to run out. The payroll alone was $30,000 a month, and critics pointed to the disproportionate number of officers: 397 officers to 695 privates. The state was heavily in debt to the bankers. As it became unable to pay salaries, the regular enlisted militia dropped out, and their places were taken by mine guards of Colorado Fuel and Iron, now in Guard uniforms, drawing their pay from the company.

In early April, 1914, Governor Ammons recalled all but two companies of the National Guard, consisting now mostly of mine guards in the pay of C.F.&I. and under the command of Major Pat Hamrock, a local saloonkeeper, and Lieutenant Linderfeldt. They were stationed on a rocky ridge overlooking the thousand men, women, and children who lived in the tent colony at Ludlow.[18]

On Monday morning, April 20, two dynamite bombs were exploded in the hills above Ludlow by Major Hamrock's men—a signal for operations to begin. At 9 A.M. a machine gun began firing into the tents, and then others joined. Women, holding children, ran from tent to tent, seeking shelter, crying out wildly.

* * *

* *New York Times,* February 11, 1914. Dozens of accusations of peonage appear in House Mines and Mining Committee, *Conditions in the Coal Mines of Colorado,* pp. 48, 749, 1239, 1363, 1374, 1407, and other places in the hearings.

Some managed to escape into the hills. Others crawled into the dark pits and caves which had been dug under a few of the tents. Miners left the tents to draw off the fire, flung themselves into deep arroyos (gashes left by old creek beds) and fired back. One eyewitness reported later: [19]

> The firing of the machine guns was awful. They fired thousands and thousands of shots. There were very few guns in the tent colony. Not over fifty, including shotguns. Women and children were afraid to crawl out of the shallow pits under the tents. Several men were killed trying to get to them. The soldiers and mine guards tried to kill everybody; anything they saw move, even a dog, they shot at.

The old feud between strike leader Tikas and Lieutenant Linderfeldt came to its end that afternoon. Tikas was in the big tent, finding shelter for women and children, helping the wounded, when a telephone, its wires amazingly intact, started ringing. It was Linderfeldt, up on the ridge. He wanted to see Tikas—it was urgent, he said. Tikas refused. The phone rang again and again. Tikas answered, said he would come.

Carrying a white flag, Tikas met Linderfeldt on the hill. The Lieutenant was surrounded by militiamen. The only eyewitness report is from a young engineer visiting Colorado with a friend, who saw the scene from a nearby cliff. They saw the two men talking, then Linderfeldt raised his rifle and brought the stock down with all his strength on Tikas' skull. The rifle broke in two as Tikas fell, face downward. "As he lay there, we saw the militiamen fall back. Then they aimed their rifles and fired into the unconscious man's body. It was the first murder I had ever seen. . . ." [20]

Two other strikers, unarmed and under guard, met their deaths on the hill in a similar manner. The machine guns continued firing into the tents, and five people died in their fire. One of them was Frank Snyder, ten years old. His father told about it: [21]

> Frank was sitting on the floor . . . and he was in the act of stooping to kiss or caress his sister. . . . I was standing near the front door of my tent and I heard the impact of the bullet striking the boy's head and the crack . . . as it exploded inside of his brain.

As the sun fell behind the Black Hills, the firing lessened. Now soldiers moved down the slopes into the shadows alongside the tents, drenched the canvas with coal oil, and set the tents afire. The visiting engineer later described the scene: [22]

> We watched from our rock shelter while the militia dragged up their machine guns and poured a murderous fire into the arroyos from a height by Water Tank Hill above the Ludlow depot. Then came the firing of the tents. I am positive that by no possible chance could they have been set ablaze accidentally. The militiamen were thick about the northern corner of the colony where the fire started, and we could see distinctly from our lofty observation place what looked like a blazing torch waved in the midst of the militia a few seconds before the general conflagration swept through the place.

While bullets whistled through the flaming canvas, people fled in panic from their tents and from the caves beneath. A dispatch to *The New York Times* reported some of the results: [23]

> A seven-year-old girl dashed from under a blazing tent and heard the scream of bullets about her ears. Insane from fright, she ran into a tent again and fell into the hole with the remainder of her family to die with them. The child is said to have been a daughter of Charles Costa, a union leader at Aguilar, who perished with his wife and another child. . . . James Fyler, financial secretary of the Trinidad local, died with a bullet in his forehead as he was attempting to rescue his wife from the flames. . . . Mrs. Marcelina Pedragon, her skirt ablaze, carried her youngest child from the flames, leaving two others behind. . . . An unidentified man, driving a horse attached to a light buggy, dashed from the tents waving a white flag, just after the fire started. When ordered to halt he opened fire with a revolver and was killed by a return volley from the militia.

The tents became crackling torches, and for hours the countryside shone in a ghastly light, while men, women, and children roamed through the hills, looking for others in their families. At 8:30 P.M. the militia "captured" the Ludlow tent colony, now a smoldering pile of ashes.

It was on the following day, April 21, that a telephone linesman, going through the ruins, lifted a twisted iron cot that covered one of the pits dug beneath the tents for shelter. There he found the mangled, charred bodies of two women and eleven children, heaped together in what had been a desperate struggle to escape.

Funerals for the dead were held in Trinidad; according to the Trinidad Red Cross, twenty-six bodies of strikers had been found at Ludlow.[24] Then the miners turned from the coffins of the dead and took up arms, joined by union miners from a dozen neighboring camps, who left wives and children behind, and swarmed over the hills, carrying arms and ammunition. From Denver, the day after the discovery of the Ludlow death pit, United Mine Workers' officials issued a "Call to Arms": *

> Organize the men in your community in companies of volunteers to protect the workers of Colorado against the murder and cremation of men, women, and children by armed assassins in the employ of coal corporations, serving under the guise of state militiamen.
>
> Gather together for defensive purposes all arms and ammunition legally available. . . .
>
> The state is furnishing no protection to us and we must protect ourselves. . . . We intend to exercise our lawful right as citizens to defend our homes and our constitutional rights.

Three hundred armed strikers marched from tent colonies in neighboring Fremont County to help. Others came overland in the dark, carrying guns and ammunition. The press reported a series of encounters between soldiers and strikers in an area of three square miles south of Ludlow, the battlefield isolated by the cutting of telephone and telegraph wires. Four train crews of the Colorado and Southern Railroad refused to take soldiers and ammunition from Trinidad to Ludlow. There was talk of a general strike in Colorado.

* House Mines and Mining Committee, *Conditions in the Coal Mines of Colorado,* Vol. II, Appendix. The call was signed by John Lawson and other U.M.W. officials, and by Ernest Mills, secretary-treasurer of the Western Federation of Miners.

Near Aguilar, the Empire mine was besieged, the tipple burned, the mouth of the slope caved in by dynamite explosions. Three mine guards were reported dead there, two mine shafts were in ashes, and the press reported that "the hills in every direction seem suddenly to be alive with men." Two hundred militia and company guards along the tracks at Ludlow were cut off from the rest of the district by "armed bands of strikers whose ranks are swelled constantly by men who swarm over the hills from all directions." At Colorado Springs, three hundred union miners quit work to go to the Trinidad district, carrying revolvers, rifles, and shotguns.[25]

The first legal move came from Pueblo, where a federal grand jury returned indictments against eight striking miners on charges of attacking the company post office at Higgins, Colorado.

Governor Ammons reported an attack on Delagua and Hastings by the miners. An attack on Berwind mine was expected momentarily. Now the Trinidad mayor and Chamber of Commerce appealed to President Woodrow Wilson to intervene.[26]

President Wilson was busy at this time with Mexico. Several American sailors from a vessel which was blockading Mexico as an act of pressure against the Huerta regime on April 9, 1914, went ashore at Tampico and were arrested. The American admiral demanded that Mexico apologize, hoist the American flag, and give it a 21-gun salute. Wilson gave Mexico until April 19 to act. Meanwhile, twenty-two thousand men and fifty-two ships were ready.* The Mexican foreign minister responded that Mexico would exchange salutes with the United States, would even salute first, but would not salute unconditionally. The officer who had arrested the American sailors was under arrest, he said, and the Americans had been freed even before investigation. "Mexico had yielded," he said, "as much as her dignity will permit. Mexico trusts to the fairmindedness and spirit of justice of the American people." [27]

On April 20th, Wilson asked Congress for the right to use armed force: "There can in what we do be no thought of aggression or selfish aggrandizement. We seek to maintain the dignity and

* *New York Times,* April 20, 1914. The headline read: "Campaign Worked Out by Naval Experts in Recent Months Now Being Carried Out in Detail."

authority of the United States only because we wish always to keep our great influence unimpaired for the uses of liberty, both in the United States, and wherever else it may be employed for the benefit of mankind." [28]

The New York Times carried an editorial on the Mexican affair: [29]

> Just as when we went to war with Spain there were those who insisted that we should ignore the destruction of the *Maine* . . . so there are now those who hold that Huerta is in the right and that he has given us no cause of offense. As to that, we may trust the just mind, the sound judgment, and the peaceful temper of President Wilson. There is not the slightest occasion for popular excitement over the Mexican affair; there is no reason why anybody should get nervous either about the stock market or about his business.

Without waiting for Congress, Wilson ordered American naval forces to act. On April 21, the day of the discovery of the death pit at Ludlow, American ships bombarded Vera Cruz, landed ten boatloads of marines, and occupied the city. Over a hundred Mexicans were killed.

Business men had been asking for intervention in Mexico ever since the Mexican Revolution of 1910 created a threat to American investments in Mexican oil, mines, land, and railroad—which totaled a billion dollars by 1913. Now there was enthusiasm for Wilson's move. The *Times* reported: *

> The five hundred or more business men who attended the luncheon of the Members Council of the Merchants Association of New York jumped to their feet yesterday when William C. Breed, the toastmaster, called upon those present to express their loyalty to President Wilson "to whatever course he shall determine necessary to restore peace, order and a stable government in the Republic of Mexico."

It took President Wilson several days to turn his attention to Colorado. Meanwhile, the armed revolt of the miners was growing

* *New York Times,* April 23, 1914. By July, Huerta was forced out of office. In November, the U.S. occupation forces withdrew from Vera Cruz.

there. A troop train leaving Denver to carry soldiers to the strike zone ran into trouble. Eighty-two men in Company C mutinied and refused to go to the district. "The men declared they would not engage in the shooting of women and children. They hissed the 350 men who did start and shouted imprecations at them." [30]

Five thousand people demonstrated in Denver, standing in a pouring rain on the lawn in front of the capitol. A resolution was read, asking that Hamrock, Linderfeldt, and other National Guard officers be tried for murder, that the state seize the mines and operate them. Governor Ammons was denounced as a traitor and accessory to the murder, and Colorado citizens were asked to arm themselves for self-protection. The Denver Cigar Makers Union voted to send five hundred armed men to Ludlow and Trinidad in the morning, and women of the United Garment Workers Union in Denver announced that four hundred of their members had volunteered as nurses to aid the Colorado strikers. [31]

All over the country meetings and demonstrations took place in support of the Colorado miners. Upton Sinclair and others picketed Rockefeller's office at 26 Broadway, in funeral garb. In front of the church where Rockefeller sometimes preached Sunday sermons, a minister was clubbed by police while protesting the Massacre. The usually mild Eugene Debs, angered by the Colorado events, wrote: [32]

> The time has come for the United Mine Workers and the Western Federation of Miners to levy a special monthly assessment to create a Gunmen Defense Fund. This Fund should be sufficient to provide each member with the latest high power rifles, the same ones used by the corporation gunmen, and 500 rounds of cartridges. In addition to this, every district should purchase and equip and man enough Gatling and machine guns to match the equipment of Rockefeller's private army of assassins. This suggestion is made advisedly, and I hold myself responsible for every word of it.

With the National Guard in Colorado unable to control the marauding miners, with damages amounting to millions of dollars, and over twenty killed since the Massacre, pressure grew for President Wilson to restore order with federal troops. The formal request was made by Governor Ammons, but a powerful informal signal was flashed by *The New York Times,* whose reaction, representing important elements in business and political circles, deserves a moment's attention.

The *Times'* first account of the Ludlow Massacre was an inaccurate one. Its headline read: "Women and Children Roasted in Pits of Tent Colony as Flames Destroy It. Miners Store of Ammunition and Dynamite Exploded, Scattering Death and Ruin." [33] The *Times* had been unsympathetic to the miners throughout the strike; now it expressed horror at the killing of women and children. However, it seemed to be most angry that the militia and the authorities had been stupid enough to create a situation on which the strikers might capitalize to their advantage. Here is the *Times* editorial following the Massacre: [34]

> Somebody blundered. Worse than the order that sent the Light Brigade into the jaws of death, worse in its effect than the Black Hole of Calcutta, was the order that trained the machine guns of the state militia of Colorado upon the strikers' camp at Ludlow, burned its tents, and suffocated to death the scores of women and children who had taken refuge in the rifle pits and trenches. . . . Strike organizers cannot escape full measure of blame for the labor war. . . . But no situation can justify the acts of a militia that compels women and babes to lie in ditches and cellars twenty-four hours without food or water, exposes them to cannon and rifle fire, and lets them die like trapped animals in the flames of their camp. . . . when a sovereign State employs such horrible means, what may not be expected from the anarchy that ensues?

Two days later, when the miners had taken up arms against the militia, the *Times* ran another editorial: [35]

> With the deadliest weapons of civilization in the hands of savage-minded men, there can be no telling to what lengths the war in Colorado will go unless it is quelled by force. The President should turn his attention from Mexico long enough to take stern measures in Colorado.

The indignation at the militia, such as it was, had lasted about a day. The *Times* had never, in the course of the long violent series of attacks on the miners, called for federal intervention to stop that. Once the miners took up arms, it became concerned for order. A week after the Massacre, another *Times* editorial criticized two clergymen, Rev. Percy Stickney Grant of Manhattan, and Rev. John Howard Melish of Brooklyn, who had denounced from their pulpits the actions of the National Guard against the strikers.

The *Times* said about the sermons: [36]

> These are sympathetic utterances and differ from cold impartiality. . . . There are those who think that infamy in Colorado consists in the fact that the militia are shooting workers. It may be contended that there is something like infamy in the opposition of workers to society and order. The militia are as impersonal and impartial as the law.

On April 29, Woodrow Wilson sent federal troops into Colorado to bring order.[37] Secretary of War Garrison asked everyone to surrender their arms to federal troops. The commander of the federal forces prohibited the import of strikebreakers from other states, banned picketing, and protected scabs.[38]

For the next seven months, the air was filled with talk of negotiations, peace offers, mediation plans. The governor appointed an investigating commission. The Mines and Mining Committee of the House and the Industrial Relations Commission of the Senate held hearings, while federal troops patrolled the strike area. Testimony for House and Senate added up to over five thousand pages. The strike petered out, was officially called off in December 1914. The Union had not won recognition. Sixty-six men, women, and children had been killed. Not one militiaman or mine guard had been indicted for crime.* Under the weight of volumes of words,

---

* On the contrary, John Lawson, the strike leader, was, a year later, tried and convicted of murder. He was accused of murdering John Nimmo, one of the army of deputies paid by the companies. No effort was made to prove Lawson fired the fatal shot; he was held responsible because he led the strike, was at the Ludlow tent colony the day of the battle. The judge, Granby Hillyer, was a former attorney for Colorado Fuel and Iron and had helped prepare cases against the strikers. The jury was chosen by a panel selected by the sheriff of Las Animas County. Lawson's conviction was later overturned. West, *Report on the Colorado Strike,* p. 22.

suspended from the tips of bayonets, the miners' resistance was crushed.

How shall we read the story of the Ludlow Massacre? As another "interesting" event of the past? Or as supporting evidence for an analysis of that long *present* which spans 1914 and 1970. If it is read narrowly, as an incident in the history of the trade union movement and the coal industry, then it is an angry splotch in the past, fading rapidly amidst new events. If it is read as a commentary on a larger question—the relationship of government to corporate power and of both to movements of social protest—then we are dealing with the present. Then we see a set of characteristics which have persisted, not only in American history, but in the history of all nations, although the forms vary. Then we see the complex alternating techniques of brute force and innocent solicitude, and the rain of investigations, words, negotiations, commissions, denunciations—all adding up to inches of progress and the basic retention of power and wealth where it now resides. Of course things have changed; there are now larger portions of material benefits meted out to the underdog; there are now more subtle methods used by both government and business in dealing with resistance * and more modern weapons (gas, planes) ** when other methods fail. And one set of victims exchanged for others of different color, nationality, geography as their tolerance runs dry.

The story can be read as a problem in personal responsibility, which leads to a continuing, inane argument about blame. Shall we blame John D. Rockefeller, Jr., who testified after the Massacre that he and his company had been fighting to defend the workers' right to work? (A Congressman had asked him: "You'll do that, even if you lose all your money, and have all your em-

---

* Note the bewildering variety of government agencies and commissions to represent welfare and beneficence; note that Rockefeller, after the Colorado strike, hired Ivy Lee, the nation's leading public relations man, and how public relations has become a vital part of government and business operations; note that the Rockefeller Foundation, new at the time of the strike, stepped up its activities, and that foundations in general multiplied.

** I write this shortly after police in Berkeley, California, carried out the first aerial gas attack on a domestic demonstration (May 1969).

ployees killed?" And Rockefeller answered: "It's a great principle. It's a national issue." [39]) Or should we blame his managers, or the Governor, or the President? Or Lieutenant Linderfeldt?

Or—shall we look beyond blame? In that case, we might see a similarity in behavior among the privileged (and their followers) in all times, all countries: the willingness to kill for a great principle—the word "principle" a euphemism for keeping the fruits of the earth divided according to present rules. Then, we might see that the killing is not the result of an elitist conspiracy, but of a social structure larger than the consciousness of any of its parts. With such a vision, we might conclude that the responsibility belongs to no one in the past, but to us today, to figure out—by acts as much as by thought—how to dismantle that structure, while constructing one which does not require as its indispensable work force a team comprised of executioners and victims.

6

LaGuardia in the Jazz Age

There is an underside to every Age about which history does not often speak, because history is written from records left by the privileged. We learn about politics from the political leaders, about economics from the entrepreneurs, about slavery from the plantation owners, about the thinking of an age from its intellectual elite.

It is the victors who give names to the wars, and the satisfied who give labels to the ages. But what did the Crusades mean to the peasants who died in them, or the Renaissance to the vast majority who suffered while the Medicis financed art, or the Enlightenment to the unenlightened, or the Era of Good Feeling to the slaves in Virginia, or the Progressive Period to girls in the Lawrence textile mills, or the New Deal to blacks in Harlem?

Sometimes we search hard, and find the narratives of those in chains, or other bits and scraps of evidence showing all was not as we thought. And sometimes there are men or women on the border of their time or their class, who manage to save for us, by a great effort, the traces of what history tends to bury. Even then, we get only the faintest glimpse of what a war was to the wounded, or an epoch to the vast, silent numbers who populated it—like artifacts from a buried civilization, only hinting at what was endured.

In the United States, the twenties were the years of Prosperity, and Fiorello LaGuardia is one of its few public figures who suspected to what extent that label was a lie. The twenties were also, to later generations, a time of quiet isolation from foreign affairs. LaGuardia did not believe this. The twenties also became known as a time of national political consensus, when a general mood of well-being softened political combat. LaGuardia tried to speak for those left out of the consensus, those whose votes were tallied but whose condition was ignored.

Fiorello LaGuardia was elected to Congress in 1916, went off to fly on the Italian front for the American army, ran again successfully for Congress in 1922. From then until 1933 he viewed the national scene from his seat in the House, and through the eyes of his constituents, looking out of their tenement windows in East Harlem.

From this vantage point, the "prosperity" of the twenties seemed a bitter joke; under the raucous cries of the Jazz Age, LaGuardia, listening closely, could hear the distinct sound of the blues. For many Americans, the high living of the twenties was only a spectacle seen from the cheap seats, and when they left the theater they went home, not to Babylon, but to what Robert and Helen Lynd have called "the long arm of the job." LaGuardia was one of a handful of men in Washington who recognized this fact, and acted upon it.

He set his stocky body and rasping voice against all the dominant political currents of his day. While the Klan membership soared into the millions, and nativists wrote their prejudices into the statute books, LaGuardia demanded the end of immigration restriction. When the marines were dispatched to make the Caribbean an American lake, LaGuardia demanded their recall. Above the jubilant message of the ticker tapes, LaGuardia tried to tell the nation about striking miners in Pennsylvania. As Democrats and Republicans lumbered like rehearsed wrestlers in the center of the political ring, LaGuardia stalked the front rows and bellowed for real action. He did not get it, but we need to listen for those echoes, to see what was then and still is undone, to look beneath the fogged membrane that hides the shame of our own age.

LaGuardia was born in a modest flat in Greenwich Village, of a Jewish mother from Trieste, and an Italian father who was a gifted musician, having come to America as arranger for the famous soprano Adelina Patti. His father joined the American army as bandmaster, and during the Spanish-American War died of food poisoning, one of the thousands of victims of the "embalmed beef" sold to the Quartermaster Corps by the big packinghouses. All his life, Fiorello LaGuardia would blame "profiteers" for his father's death.

He worked in the American consulates in Budapest and Fiume,

then as an interpreter for immigrants on Ellis Island. He went to law school at night, walked the picket lines with striking garment workers in Manhattan, and became attracted to the Progressive wing of the Republican party, surprising the machine men by his victory in 1916. In Congress, he introduced a bill (pigeonholed, as were virtually all his bills during his career) asking the death penalty for anyone selling inferior supplies to the armed forces in wartime. He denounced the Espionage Act of 1917 which forbade "scurrilous, abusive" criticism of the government. He fought to ease the tax burden on the poor, and urged that the national government regulate the food industry in peace as well as war. He supported World War I as meaning liberation for the millions of subjects of the Hapsburg Empire, and left Congress to fly bombing raids behind Austrian lines. But when the war ended and Wilson's "self-determination" was lost in the power struggles of the peace conferences, LaGuardia became bitter about the "war to make the world safe for democracy."

The Republican party kept trying to get LaGuardia out of the way, while using him to pick up immigrant votes. They eased him in as President of the New York City Board of Aldermen in 1920–21 (there were 100,000 Italian voters in New York City) but he became a political nuisance. He denounced the Republican legislature for ejecting five duly elected Socialist members, raged at the Republican governor for not restoring the five-cent fare, and went up to Albany to tell a cheering crowd of tenants demanding rent relief that he had come to the capitol "not to praise the landlord, but to bury him."

To get LaGuardia out of the way of a possible gubernatorial campaign in 1922, the Republican machine offered him the Congressional candidacy in East Harlem—a Jewish-Italian tenement district on the upper East Side of New York. He accepted and outlined his political philosophy for the New York *World:* "I stand for the Republicanism of Abraham Lincoln; and let me tell you that the average Republican leader east of the Mississippi doesn't know anything more about Abraham Lincoln than Henry Ford knows about the Talmud. I am a Progressive."

LaGuardia's Democratic opponent in the 1922 race was Herman Frank, whose backers grew desperate as polling time drew near, and sent out Rosh Hashonoh cards to every Jewish voter in the district, referring to "the Italian LaGuardia, who is a pronounced anti-Semite and Jew-hater," and appealing for support of Herman Frank, "a Jew with a Jewish heart."

LaGuardia was furious. He proceeded to dictate, in Yiddish, a letter which was distributed throughout the district, challenging Frank to debate the issues of the campaign, but in the Yiddish language. When Frank ignored this (he could not speak Yiddish) LaGuardia set out on a tour of the Jewish district, making three speeches in Yiddish. His opponent was seeking votes, LaGuardia asserted, on the ground that he was a Jew: "After all, is he looking for a job as a *schamas*, or does he want to be elected Congressman?" (A *schamas* is the caretaker of a synagogue.) LaGuardia won the election by 245 votes.

‒ In Congress once again, LaGuardia continued to confound the Democrats, exasperate the Republicans, and confuse the Socialists. A New York Republican leader said of him: "He is no Republican at all. He is no more a Republican than the representatives of Soviet Russia are Republicans."

Aided by a small group of Congressmen from New York and Chicago, LaGuardia fought the mounting tide of nativism in the twenties. He denounced the drastic restriction of immigration, and particularly the "national origins" method of determining quotas which was designed to limit the number of immigrants from Southern and Eastern Europe. The floor of the House was the scene of bitter exchanges between the proponents of restriction and LaGuardia. "We have too many aliens in this country . . . we want more of the American stock," declared Elton Watkins of Oregon. "Education and environment do not fundamentally alter racial values," Michigan's Grant Hudson said. Tincher of Kansas drew loud applause by urging his colleagues to "think, act and do real Americanism" and warning that one day, if immigration continued as in the past, Congressmen would have to address the Speaker of the House "in Italian or some other language."

The restriction bills were "unscientific," LaGuardia retorted, the "result of narrow-mindedness and bigotry" and "inspired by influences who have a fixed obsession on Anglo-Saxon superiority." Angered by a reference to the "Italian bloc" from New

York made by Kentucky's Fred Vinson, LaGuardia referred to the illiteracy of the Blue Ridge mountain folk. This drew a stirring response from another Kentuckian, who rose to his full height and declared that his constituents "suckle their Americanism and their patriotism from their mother's breast . . . and I resent the gentleman's insolent, infamous, contemptible slander against a great, honest, industrious, law-abiding, liberty-loving, God-fearing, patriotic people."

Restriction became law, but the debate continued through the twenties. LaGuardia exchanged arguments in a national magazine with a writer who insisted: "The time to gird our loins for battle is here and now," and cried for resistance against "the inroads of the degeneracy which arises from the mixture of unassimilable and disharmonic races." LaGuardia called the national origins plan "the creation of a narrow mind, nurtured by a hating heart." But the time was not right for his views. The Klan was never more powerful. (Vice-President Charles Dawes himself, as LaGuardia put it, had "praised them with faint damn.") The American Legion, the Harding, Coolidge, and Hoover administrations, and even "Progressives" from the midwest like Norris and Borah and Johnson were on the other side. LaGuardia swam powerfully, but with increasing futility, against the nativist tidal wave of the twenties.

LaGuardia's mightiest verbal barrages were to be aimed, however, at the myth of universal prosperity in the twenties. The riotous New Year celebrations that ushered in 1922 could barely be heard above the general din, for it was an era identified in terms of sound—the "Roaring Twenties," the "Jazz Age." The noise was, all agreed, simply the joyful gurgle of prosperity.*

* Part of it, however, was the sound of violence, which seems to scar every age of high living. F. Scott Fitzgerald wrote: "A classmate killed his wife and himself on Long Island, another tumbled 'accidentally' from a skyscraper in New York. One was killed in a speakeasy in Chicago; another was beaten to death in a speakeasy in New York and crawled home to the Princeton Club to die; still another had his skull crushed by a maniac's axe in an insane asylum where he was confined. These are not catastrophes that I went out of my way to look for—these were my friends; moreover, these things happened not during the depression but during the boom." From his article "Echoes of the Jazz Age," *Scribner's,* November 1931.

Prosperity was real for substantial numbers of Americans.* Those who made more than two thousand dollars a year, 40 percent of all families, could buy a fair share, either in cash or on the installment plan, of the exciting new gadgets and machines crowding the show windows in every city and town. For the 305,000 people who received 15 percent of the total national income, there were more expensive autos, as well as jewels, furs, and endless amusements. Because spending is by its very nature a conspicuous activity, and because frolic is more newsworthy than a ten-hour day in a textile mill, the general aura of the twenties— prosperity and well-being—was that given to it by its most economically active members.

Amid the general self-congratulation, however, amid the smug speeches of the business leaders, and the triumphant clatter of ticker-tape machines, millions of Americans worked all day in mines, factories, and on patches of rented or mortgaged land. In the evening they read the newspaper or listened to the not-yet-paid-for radio and looked forward to Saturday night, when they might hold their mouths under the national faucet for a few drops of the wild revelry that everyone spoke about. For the fact was that a large section of the American population was living sparely and precariously and, though not jobless and impoverished (as many would be a decade later), were shut out of the high, wild, and prosperous living that marked the upper half of the population.

After a detailed study of economic conditions in the twenties, George Soule concluded that while production and profits rocketed in bursts of happy speculation, "the American people did not all enjoy the ride." [1] From 1919–28, productivity grew 40 percent, compared to a 26 percent rise in real earnings,[2] so that "business did not fully share its productive gains with earners and consumers by a combination of wage increases and price reduction." This led to a "tremendous growth of profits for the more fortu-

---

* Unemployment declined, 1921–27, from 4,270,000 to 2,055,000. Real wages rose. The number of prosperous farmers grew, so that by 1929, 25,000 farms had gross incomes over $20,000 a year. *Recent Social Trends: Report of the President's Research Committee on Social Trends,* McGraw-Hill, 1933, Vol. II, p. 820.

nately situated sectors of business and for the big corporations that dominated them." [3] From 1922–29, while real wages per capita in manufacturing advanced at a rate of 1.4 percent a year, common stockholders gained 16.4 percent a year.[4]

The classic sociological study of the twenties, that of Muncie, Indiana, in the Lynds' *Middletown*, shows graphically that ordinary working people did not share the prosperity of that time and went about their mundane lives day to day never free from "the long arm of the job." In Middletown, whose thirty thousand people lived much like people in the hundreds of other industrial towns scattered across the nation, there were two clearly defined groups: "the Working Class and the Business Class."

The Lynds reported: "As one prowls Middletown streets about six o'clock of a winter morning one notes two kinds of home: the dark ones where the people still sleep, and the ones with a light in the kitchen where the adults of the household may be seen moving about, starting the business of the day." A speaker urging parents to help children by making of breakfast a "leisurely family reunion" did not realize that for two-thirds of the city's families "the father gets up in the dark in winter, eats hastily in the kitchen in the gray dawn, and is at work from an hour to two and a quarter hours before his children have to be at school." [5]

When some people looked behind the facade to catch a glimpse of suffering, their voices were either shouted down or ignored.* Merle Curti wrote: [6]

> It was, in fact, only the upper ten percent of the population that enjoyed a marked increase in real income. But the protests which such facts normally have evoked could not make themselves widely or effectively felt. This was in part the result of the grand strategy of the major political parties. In part it was the result of the fact that almost all the chief avenues to mass opinion were now controlled by large-scale publishing industries.

Not all voices were stilled. There were some too eloquent, too powerful, or simply too insistent to be ignored: Sinclair Lewis,

---

* F. Scott Fitzgerald wrote about this period: "It was borrowed time . . . the whole upper tenth of a nation living with the insouciance of grand ducs and the casualness of chorus girls." *Op. cit.*

Theodore Dreiser, John Dos Passos, H. L. Mencken, Oswald Garrison Villard, Lewis Mumford. They spoke to their generation with kindliness or with cynicism, with anger or with irony. They probed into the vitals of the social structure, sometimes crudely, sometimes delicately, but in any case deriding the cult of material wealth and the deification of orthodoxy.

And in Congress, a small group of Progressives and Socialists tried to jab at the conscience of their age. Among them the most vociferous, the most colorful, the most radical was Fiorello La-Guardia, the Congressman from East Harlem.

When the issue of extending the wartime rent controls rose, La-Guardia argued in Congress for the rights of tenants. Landlords had used college professors and legal experts to support their arguments, LaGuardia said: [7]

> . . . but gentlemen, with all of their experts, with all of their professors, with all of their legal talent, there is no argument that can prevail when a man with a weekly income and a family to support is compelled to pay out of his income such a large proportion that there is not sufficient left to properly care for and nourish his children. That is the condition in New York City; that is the condition in Washington, D.C. . . .

LaGuardia was aware that the farmer was getting little for his work, and the consumer was paying too much for his food. He told Congress: [8]

> Some of my friends sometimes refer to me as a radical. If by that they mean that I am seeking radical changes in the very conditions which brought about the disparity between the exorbitant retail prices of food and the starvation prices paid to the farmer, I am not at all shocked by being called a radical. . . . Something is radically wrong when a condition exists that permits the manipulation of prices, the creation of monopolies on food to the extent of driving the farmer off his farm by foreclosures and having thousands of underfed and ill-nourished children in the public schools of our cities.

What LaGuardia asked was comprehensive legislation establishing national regulation of transportation, marketing, and money. "You have protected the dollar and disregarded the producers. You have protected property and forgotten the human being, with the result that we have legalized a cruel system of exploitation. Now we are approaching the time when a real change is necessary." [9]

In early 1926, LaGuardia told the House about the rise in meat prices in New York City, and of his request for aid from the Department of Agriculture. *"This* is the help I got," he said, holding up a pamphlet on the economical use of meat. The Department had also sent him a pamphlet on "Lamb and Mutton and Their Uses in the Diet," despite the fact, he said, that 90 percent of the people in New York could not afford lamb chops.

"Why, I have right here with me . . ." LaGuardia said, and pulled out of his vest pocket a rather scrawny lamb chop. This had cost thirty cents in New York, he said. Then he reached into another pocket and pulled out a steak, saying: "Here is $1.75 worth of steak." Then out of another pocket, a roast, commenting: "Now here is a roast—three dollars worth of roast. What working man's family can afford to pay three dollars for a roast this size?" [10]

The cattle grazer, he noted, was getting two and one half to five cents a pound, while the consumer paid seventy-five to eighty cents a pound. This meant, he concluded, that the packinghouse monopolies were making unjustifiably large profits and could afford to cut prices substantially.

LaGuardia appeared on a dozen different sectors of the labor front throughout the twenties, wherever he thought his voice could have some effect. He walked the picket line and then spoke at a Madison Square Garden meeting supporting the 1926 garment strike in New York,[11] and several months later aided striking paper-box makers. He denounced the use of "kidnapped" Chinese strikebreakers to replace striking American sailors and attacked the Pullman Company for preventing the organization of twelve thousand Pullman porters.[12] He fought for pay raises for government workers and even made the sports pages by denouncing "baseball slavery" and calling for the unionization of baseball players.[13]

Testifying before the House Civil Service Committee, LaGuar-

dia declared that women earning $1200 a year in government serv-
ice could not attend church on Sunday because they had to stay
home to do their own washing. "They talk of Andrew Mellon being a great financier," he said. "Gentlemen, it is easy to play with
hundreds of millions of dollars, but a woman who can keep her
family clean and decent on $1200 a year is a real financier." [14]

When anthracite miners in eastern Pennsylvania went on strike
in August 1925, LaGuardia called for government ownership of
the mines: [15]

> There seems to be one solution only. This country is blessed
> with a rich supply of coal. It is not the invention of any one man, it is
> God's gift to the people of America. It requires human labor to dig
> the coal, bring it back from the bowels of the earth so it may be used
> for the benefit of mankind. The American people all have an interest
> in this coal. The government should . . . take such actions as even-
> tually will put the government in possession of the gift of God that
> surely was intended to be used for the benefit of all American people.

Two years later, when another strike, this time against a series
of wage cuts, tied up the Pennsylvania coal fields, LaGuardia visited the strike area. He interviewed strikers, their wives, and children, and his anger reached the boiling point. Once again he saw
the labor injunction in action when a group of men and women
were arrested by state police for mass picketing in violation of a
federal court injunction. He watched children hide under their
beds in miners' shacks because the day before strikebreakers had
poured volley after volley of bullets through the windows of the
school at Broughton just before 350 children were to be dismissed.
He told newspapermen: [16]

> I have never seen such thought-out, deliberate cruelty in my
> life as that displayed against the unfortunate strikers by the coal oper-
> ators and their army of coal and iron police. Imagine, gentlemen, a
> private army, with its private jail, where the miners are unlawfully de-
> tained and viciously assaulted! . . . I have been preaching American-
> ism as I understand it, where justice and freedom and law and order
> prevail, but these miners and their families don't even get a shadow of

it. . . . Asbestos will not hold the statements I shall make on the floor of the House.

Throughout the decade, LaGuardia clashed with the seventy-year-old Secretary of the Treasury, Andrew W. Mellon, the man described by William Allen White as the "guardian angel of all that the Chamber of Commerce held sacred in its white marble palace." [17] The vast Mellon empire included coal, coke, gas, oil, and aluminum. "No other Croesus," a biographer of Mellon wrote, "had levied toll on so many articles and services." [18] War contracts boosted the already considerable Mellon fortune, which one day would reach two billion dollars. One hundred Mellon companies were connected through a two hundred and fifty million-dollar banking institution, Union Trust.

Mellon's various tax proposals in the twenties had one basic theme: to lower taxes on high incomes. For instance, his first report to Congress, in 1921, recommended tax cuts, but only on incomes over $66,000 a year. Attacked by Bob LaFollette of Wisconsin, Mellon replied: [19]

> Any man of energy and initiative in this country can get what he wants out of life. But when that initiative is crippled by a tax system which denied him the right to receive a reasonable share of his earnings, then he will no longer exert himself, and the country will be deprived of the energy on which its continued greatness depends.

LaGuardia fought the Mellon Plan in Congress. When a stenographer wrote to him in complaint, he replied: "I readily understand your anxiety and that of your co-workers on the taxes over $200,000 a year. I was a stenographer once and I remember how much I had to worry about my income over $200,000 a year." [20]

Despite LaGuardia and a few others, the Mellon principles won out in the tax bills passed by Congress, and the business community celebrated. The president of Columbia University, Nicholas Murray Butler wrote happily to a Republican leader: "I am just back from Pittsburgh where on Saturday night there took place at the Chamber of Commerce dinner the most magnificent demonstration in favor of Secretary Mellon that is possible to imagine. . . . It was really a great occasion." [21]

Profiteering enraged LaGuardia. When a railroad official who had been convicted of a million dollar fraud was fined $12,500 with no jail sentence, on the ground that the man had a weak heart, LaGuardia told the press: "If Joyce with a weak heart stole a million dollars, what would he have done if he had a strong heart?" [22]

Through correspondence with people in his district, and through Vito Marcantonio, who was on constant duty at Harlem House on 116th Street, LaGuardia kept in touch with the problems of people in his district. He attacked the I.R.T. and a court decision allowing it to raise its fare to seven cents.[23] He denounced the establishment of "an exclusive club for exclusive people in Central Park," noting that "out of season fruit from distant tropics, rare species of fish specially imported and choice morsels to tickle the tongue of the fastidious gourmand were menued and their high prices featured. Not since Nero banqueted and fiddled while Rome was burning has such contempt for the rights, comfort and feelings of the people been shown." [24]

As 1928 drew to a close, LaGuardia accompanied a reporter on a tour of homes in the poorer districts of the city in connection with the newspaper's annual relief fund, and reported: "I confess I was not prepared for what I actually saw. It seemed almost incredible that such conditions of poverty could really exist." [25] The article was lost amid reports of a city dancing, singing, and shouting with joy to usher in the year 1929.

If there was an underside to the "Age of Prosperity" in the twenties, there was also an underside to the "isolationism" that many have attributed to that period. The label is due, partly, to the fact that students of that period have concentrated on American rejection of the League of Nations and the World Court. However, as William Appleman Williams has pointed out, the United States emerged from the war as the industrial and financial leader of the world, and would, therefore, regardless of its participation or nonparticipation in political agreements, play the key role in the world economy.[26] It was the leading producer of coal, pig iron, and petroleum, creditor of most of Europe, and investor in enterprises which ringed the globe.

The nation's economic nationalism—its insistence on war debt payments and towering tariff barriers—was a reflection, not of isolationism, but of an intervention in world affairs based on cash returns rather than democratic ideals. The State Department, throughout the twenties, exercised strong influence on private loans to other nations, partly in order to ensure political "stability" in certain areas like the Caribbean. Herbert Feis writes that in this period: "We acted as banker to the whole needy world. Private capital provided the funds. But the American Government concerned itself with the lending operations." [27]

Despite the Wilsonian cry for self-determination in the peace treaties, the United States was established as a dominant power in the Caribbean, having purchased the Virgin Islands during the war, possessing a naval base in Cuba, and exercising such control over the Republic of Panama, Nicaragua, Haiti, and the Dominican Republic as to make them "virtual protectorates." [28] Furthermore, American influence in the Far East extended from the Aleutian Islands to Hawaii and across the western Pacific to the Philippines.

The United States was cautious about the League of Nations, but at the same time the Coolidge Administration was acting with force and determination to protect American investments and political power in the Caribbean area. By 1924 the finances of half of the twenty Latin American states were being directed to some extent by the United States.[29] When other tactics did not work, marines were dispatched—to Haiti, the Dominican Republic, and Nicaragua. The realities did not match Coolidge's promise in his inaugural address: "America seeks no earthly empire built on blood and force. . . . The legions which she sends forth are armed, not with the sword, but with the cross."

Nicaragua was a vivid example of marine diplomacy at work. Her proximity to Panama, and the ever-present possibility of a trans-Nicaraguan canal, gave Nicaragua a special place in the plans of the State Department, while fruit and lumber investments gave American private business groups a sphere of interest there. Ever since 1909, when a United States-aided revolution had overthrown the Liberal Zelaya government, a pattern of Yankee intervention was established, with bank credits and marines standing guard alternately over shaky conservative governments.*

After the withdrawal of the American marines in 1925, a Liberal revolution got under way, and when rebel forces pushed on toward Managua in spite of pro-government actions by United States naval forces, "American fruit and lumber companies sent daily protests to the State Department." [30]

On January 8, 1927, American marines were ordered to station themselves in Fort Loma, commanding the Nicaraguan capital, and two days later Coolidge sent a special message to Congress, saying: **

I am sure it is not the desire of the United States to intervene in the internal affairs of Nicaragua or of any other Central American republic. Nevertheless, it must be said, that we have a very definite and special interest in the maintenance of order and good government in Nicaragua at the present time.

In the next six weeks, five thousand United States troops landed, and the United States gave the Nicaraguan government three thousand rifles, two hundred machine guns, and three million rounds of ammunition. Later, the State Department said: [31]

In entering into the transaction the United States government followed its customary policy of lending encouragement and moral support to constitutional governments beset by revolutionary movements intended to overthrow the established order.

* Elihu Root said in 1915 that "the present government with which we are making this treaty is really maintained in office by the presence of the United States marines in Nicaragua." Council on Foreign Relations, *Survey of American Foreign Relations,* 1929, pp. 167–197.

** Ruhl J. Bartlett, *The Record of American Diplomacy,* p. 546. Graham H. Stuart, *Latin America and the United States,* Appleton-Century-Crofts, 1955, says: "The first landing of troops was declared to be solely for the protection of American lives and property, but there was little evidence that American lives and property were in jeopardy." p. 332.

Secretary of State Frank Kellogg explained to the Senate Foreign Relations Committee that the threat of Communist influences in Nicaragua had brought on American intervention.

LaGuardia, asked to comment on Kellogg's statement, called it "aldermanic stuff." There was no proof of Communist activity in Nicaragua, he said, adding: "The protection of American life and property in Nicaragua does not require the formidable naval and marine forces operating there now. Give me fifty New York cops and I can guarantee full protection." [32]

LaGuardia wrote a constituent that Kellogg, back in November, had planted the story of Communist activities in the press by asking various wire services to print such a story. The Associated Press had complied. When LaGuardia made this accusation publicly, the State Department denied it, and when LaGuardia said that he had conferred with Kellogg and had gotten the impression that no forces would be sent to Nicaragua, Kellogg denied the conference had taken place.[33]

In April 1927 Coolidge, harassed by a nationwide barrage of criticism, ordered Colonel Henry L. Stimson to negotiate peace between the rival factions in Nicaragua. Stimson reported later how he met rebel leader Moncada under "a large black thorn tree" and in thirty minutes reached an agreement on peace terms.[34] This included American supervision of elections to be held in 1929, the appointment of Liberal governors in six of the country's thirteen departments, and the maintenance of marines in Nicaragua.*

LaGuardia kept up a constant stream of criticism. He wrote to Kellogg: "Permit me to state, Mr. Secretary, that universal suffrage and the secret ballot are absolutely inconsistent with uniformed marines and fixed bayonets. The two cannot be harmonized." [35]

---

* Moncada's concession was born of a sense of futility in the face of overwhelming power. He said at the time of his acceptance: "I am not inhuman. . . . I cannot advise the nation to shed all its patriotic blood for our liberty, because in spite of this new sacrifice, this liberty would succumb before infinitely greater forces and the country would sink more deeply within the claws of the North American eagle." Council on Foreign Relations, *op. cit.,* p. 195.

Stimson, on the other hand, felt that the United States had "no cause to be ashamed" of its effort "to do an unselfish service to a weak and sorely beset Central American State." His argument that the United States had not transgressed upon Nicaraguan sovereignty was based on his belief that every step taken was upon the request of the Nicaraguan government.[36]

The arguments of the twenties in connection with Nicaragua could be transplanted easily to the sixties in connection with Vietnam. So could the arguments on poverty, prices, taxation made in that era be transferred to our own. If there is a persistence of policy and rhetoric in American history from that decade to this one (and beyond) we are helped to find it by those few who, like LaGuardia, dug beneath the surface and held up to public view that which had been hidden. This suggests, perhaps, what people with energy, with voices, sensing the suffering beneath the smugness of their age, might do in any time.

7

The Limits of the New Deal

When we compel the past to speak, we want neither the gibberish of total recall nor the nostalgia of fond memories; we would like the past to speak wisely to our present needs. And so we have a good reason for trying to recapture some of the lost dialogue of the New Deal years—that which was carried on, with varying degrees of tension, inside and outside the Roosevelt circle.

The New Dealers themselves were articulate, humane, and on occasion profound. Among them were the "brain trust" (Adolf A. Berle, Raymond Moley, Rexford Guy Tugwell), the cabinet members (Henry Wallace, Frances Perkins, Harold Ickes, and others), the administrators of the alphabetic agencies (Harry Hopkins, David Lilienthal, and others), the Congressional spokesmen (Robert F. Wagner, Hugo Black, and others). And above them all was Franklin D. Roosevelt himself. They had no clearly defined set of goals, beyond that of extricating the nation from the depression of 1929–32. In the course of easing the crisis, however, they found themselves—pushed partly by the cries of alarm on all sides, partly by inner humanitarian impulses—creating new laws and institutions like the Tennessee Valley Authority, the social security system, farm subsidies, minimum wage standards, the National Labor Relations Board, and public housing.

These accomplishments were considerable enough to give many Americans the feeling they were going through a revolution, and yet they successfully evaded any one of a number of totalitarian abysses into which they might have fallen. So it is not surprising that the New Deal left a glow of enthusiasm, even adoration, in the nation at large.

Yet, when it was over, the fundamental problem remained—and still remains—unsolved: how to bring the blessings of immense natural wealth and staggering productive potential to every person in the land. Also unsolved was the political corollary of that problem; how to organize ordinary people to convey to national leadership something more subtle than the wail of crisis (which speaks for itself); how to communicate the day-to-day pains felt, between emergencies, in garbage-strewn slums, crowded schools, grimy bus stations, inadequate hospital wards, Negro ghettos, and rural shacks—the environment of millions of Americans clawing for subsistence in the richest country in the world.

When the reform energies of the New Deal began to wane around 1939 and the depression was over, the nation was back to its normal state: a permanent army of unemployed; twenty or thirty million poverty-ridden people effectively blocked from public view by a huge, prosperous, and fervently consuming middle class; a tremendously efficient yet wasteful productive apparatus that was efficient because it could produce limitless supplies of what it decided to produce, and wasteful because what it decided to produce was not based on what was most needed by society but on what was most profitable to business.*

What the New Deal did was to refurbish middle-class America, which had taken a dizzying fall in the depression, to restore jobs to half the jobless, and to give just enough to the lowest classes (a layer of public housing, a minimum of social security) to create an aura of good will. Through it all, the New Dealers moved in an atmosphere thick with suggestions, but they accepted only enough of these to get the traditional social mechanism moving again, plus just enough more to give a taste of what a truly far-reaching reconstruction might be.

This harsh estimate of New Deal achievements derives from the belief that the historian discussing the past is always commenting—whether he realizes it or not—on the present; and that because he is part of a morally responsible public, his commen-

---

* In *The Affluent Society* (Houghton Mifflin, 1958), John Kenneth Galbraith has pointed eloquently to the American economy's emphasis on private rather than public needs. Michael Harrington's *The Other America* (Macmillan, 1963), and Leon Keyserling's *Poverty and Deprivation in the United States* (Conference on Economic Progress, 1962) testify to continuing large blocs of poverty thirty years after the New Deal.

tary should consider present needs at the expense, if necessary, of old attachments. It is fruitless today to debate "interpretations" of the New Deal. We can no longer vote for or against Roosevelt. We can only affect the world around us. And although this is the 1960's, not the 1930's, some among us live very high, and some live very low, and a chronic malaise of lost opportunities and wasted wealth pervades the economic air.*

It is for today, then, that we turn to the thinking of the New Deal period. Although the New Deal gave us only fragments of solutions, it did leave us—perhaps because those were desperate years, and desperation stimulates innovation—with a public discussion more intense and more sweeping than any we have had before or since. People outside the New Deal entourage, invited or not, joined that discussion and extended the boundaries of political and economic imagination beyond those of the New Dealers—sometimes to the left, sometimes to the right, sometimes in directions hard to plot.

Among these were philosophers, writers, critics, lawyers, poets, college professors, journalists, dissident politicians, or commentators without special portfolio. Their names are still known today: John Dewey, Charles Beard, Reinhold Niebuhr, Paul Douglas, Stuart Chase, John Maynard Keynes, Norman Thomas, Oswald Garrison Villard, Heywood Broun, Max Lerner, Morris Cohen, Walter White, Edmund Wilson, Felix Frankfurter, John Steinbeck, John L. Lewis, Upton Sinclair.

Their thinking does not give us facile solutions, but if history has uses beyond that of reminiscence, one of them is to nourish lean ideological times with the nectars of other years. And although the present shape of the world was hardly discernible in 1939, certain crucial social issues persist in both eras. Somehow, in the interaction between the ideas of the New Dealers themselves and those of social critics who gathered in various stances and at various distances around the Roosevelt fire, we may find suggestions or approaches that are relevant today.

* David Bazelon, in *The Paper Economy* (Random House, 1963), and Robert Theobald, in *Free Men and Free Markets* (C. N. Potter, 1963), give trenchant critiques of the American economy in the 1960's.

I

The word "pragmatic" has been used, more often perhaps than any other, to describe the thinking of the New Dealers.* It refers to the experimental method of the Roosevelt administration, the improvisation from one step to the next, the lack of system or long-range program or theoretical commitment. Richard Hofstadter, in fact, says that the only important contribution to political theory to come out of the Roosevelt administration was made by Thurman Arnold, particularly in his two books, *The Symbols of Government* and *The Folklore of Capitalism*. Hofstadter describes Arnold's writing as "the theoretical equivalent of FDR's opportunistic virtuosity in practical politics—a theory that attacks theories." [1] As the chief expression of Roosevelt's "ideology," Arnold's work deserves some attention.

All through both his books, in a style of cool irony, Arnold cuts away at "preconceived faiths," "preconceived principles," "theories and symbols of government," "high-sounding prejudices," "traditional ideals," "moral ideals," "permanent cures." In the last paragraphs of *The Symbols of Government,* he writes:

> So long as the public hold preconceived faiths about the fundamental principles of government, they will persecute and denounce new ideas in that science, and orators will prevail over technicians. So long as preconceived principles are considered more important than practical results, the practical alleviation of human distress and the distribution of available comforts will be paralyzed. . . . The writer has faith that a new public attitude toward the ideals of law and economics is slowly appearing to create an atmosphere where the fanatical alignments between opposing political principles may disappear and a competent, practical, opportunistic governing class may rise to power. . . . [2]

Because the Roosevelt administration did, in fact, experiment and improvise without a total plan, FDR's "pragmatism" has

---

* A representative statement is Arthur M. Schlesinger, Jr.'s, in *The Politics of Upheaval* (Houghton Mifflin, 1960), "For Roosevelt, the technique of liberal government was pragmatic. . . . Nothing attracted Roosevelt less than rigid intellectual systems." p. 649.

come, for many, to be the most important statement about the thinking of the New Dealers. This emphasis on the method rather than on the substance of that thinking tends to obscure what may be its greatest significance.*

Most statesmen experiment: Tsar Nicholas instituted a Duma, Lenin encouraged private enterprise for several years, Bismarck sponsored social welfare measures, Mao Tse-tung introduced back-yard steel furnaces, and George Washington supported a national bank. These examples show that experimentation can be linked to a variety of social ideals. Some statesmen engage in more experiments than others, and in a time of crisis one who is willing to undertake a vast number of them deserves commendation, as Roosevelt does. The truly important question that can be asked about the thinking of any government is: in what direction, and how far, is it willing to experiment? What goals, what ideals, what expectations direct that experimentation?

Thurman Arnold himself contributed to this misplaced emphasis on method rather than substance. He was so anxious to demolish old myths that stood in the way of the welfare measures of the New Deal that mythology itself became his chief concern. He was so intent on sweeping away old debris, that he became obsessed, ironically, with a folklore of his own, in which the idea of debris-clearing crowded out the concept of what he wanted to plant in the cleared area.

Examining Arnold's *The Symbols of Government,* one sees that what started him on a crusade against myths was that he sought to expose the symbolism that stood in the way of bringing cheap electric power to people and of instituting relief, public works, social security.** His strongest expression on social justice was his statement that: "Those who rule our great industrial feudalism still believe inalterably the old axioms that man works efficiently only for

---

* A notable exception is William E. Leuchtenburg, *Franklin D. Roosevelt and the New Deal* (Harper & Row, 1963), pp. 344–346.

** *The Symbols of Government,* Yale University Press, 1935, pp. 16, 110–111, 120. Hofstadter, in *The Age of Reform,* Knopf, 1955, p. 318, analyzes the words that recur frequently in Arnold's books to show his movement away from the Progressivist moralism. Yet even to make this point he finds he must include the word "humanitarian" because it appears so frequently.

personal profit; that humanitarian ideals are unworkable as the principal aim of government or business organization; that control of national resources, elimination of waste, and a planned distribution of goods would destroy both freedom and efficiency." *

As was true of his associate, Thurman Arnold, FDR's experimentalism and iconoclasm were not devoid of standards and ideals. They had a certain direction, which was toward governmental intervention in the economy to prevent depression, to help the poor, and to curb ruthless practices in big business. Roosevelt's speeches had the flavor of a moral crusade. Accepting the nomination at the Democratic Convention of 1932, he said that "the Federal Government has always had and still has a continuing responsibility for the broader public welfare," and pledged "a new deal for the American people." In a campaign speech that year at the Commonwealth Club in San Francisco, he said: "Our government . . . owes to every one an avenue to possess himself of a portion of that plenty sufficient for his needs, through his own work." In his 1936 speech accepting the nomination, he spoke of the power of the "economic royalists" and said: "Our allegiance to American institutions requires the overthrow of this kind of power."

But FDR's ideas did not have enough clarity to avoid stumbling from one approach to another: from constant promises to balance the budget, to large-scale spending in emergencies; from an attempt to reconcile big business interests and labor interests (as in the National Recovery Act), to belated support for a pro-labor National Labor Relations Act; from special concern for the tenant farmer (in the Resettlement Administration), to a stress on generous price supports for the large commercial farmer (in the Agricultural Adjustment Act of 1938).

His ideas on political leadership showed the same indecision, the same constriction of boundaries, as did his ideas about eco-

---

* *The Symbols of Government*, pp. 259–260. Arnold was so reluctant to admit he possessed a set of values that Sidney Hook, reviewing *The Folklore of Capitalism*, took him at his word (or rather at his emphasized words), and described him as one who believed "all standards and ideals are nonsense." *University of Chicago Law Review*, V, April 1938, pp. 341–357.

nomic reform. Roosevelt was cautious about supporting the kind of candidates in 1934 (Socialist Upton Sinclair in California, Progressive Gifford Pinchot in Pennsylvania) who represented bold approaches to economic and social change; and when he did decide to take vigorous action against conservative Congressional candidates in 1938, he did so too late and too timorously. He often attempted to lead Congress in a forceful way to support his economic program; yet his leadership was confined to working with the existing Congressional leadership, including many Southern conservatives who ruled important committees. Roosevelt's political daring did not extend to building new political forces among the poor, the unemployed, the tenant farmers, and other disadvantaged groups, with whose support he might have given the country a bolder economic program.

The circle of men around Roosevelt, the cabinet members and administrators, were an odd mixture of liberals and conservatives who often worked at cross-purposes. Rexford Guy Tugwell, a bold advocate of national planning to help the lower-income groups, was close to Roosevelt for several years; but so was Raymond Moley, who believed in a kind of planning more beneficial to business interests. Even the liberal New Dealers, with rare exceptions, hesitated to carry their general concern for the underprivileged too far. Frances Perkins, the Secretary of Labor, had the humanitarian instincts of a first-rate social worker, but she seemed often to be trailing behind the labor movement, rather than helping to give it direction. (The most advanced piece of New Deal labor legislation was the Wagner Act, but Secretary Perkins wrote later: "I myself, had very little sympathy with the bill.") Progressive Secretary of the Interior Harold Ickes was offset by conservative Secretary of Commerce Daniel Roper. And although Roper was succeeded in 1939 by Harry Hopkins, there remained in the cabinet a powerful force for fiscal conservatism and budget-balancing—Secretary of the Treasury Henry Morgenthau.

The experimentalism of the New Deal, in short, had its limits: up to these limits, Roosevelt's social concern was genuinely warm, his political courage huge, his humanitarian spirit unfailing; beyond them, his driving force weakened. Thus, by 1938, with the nation out of the worst of the depression, with a skeletal structure of social reform in the statute books, and with that year's Congressional elections showing a sudden waning of political approbation, the Roosevelt program began to bog down. As it slid to its close, it left behind a mountain of accomplishment, and ahead, mountains still unclimbed. Many millions—businessmen, professionals, unionized workingmen, commercial farmers—had been given substantial help. Many millions more—sharecroppers, slum-dwellers, Negroes of North and South, the unemployed—still awaited a genuine "new deal."

II

Why did the New Deal sputter out around 1938–39? One important factor seems to be that the urgency of 1933–35 was gone. By 1939, although there were still nine million unemployed, the sense of panic was over. After all, unemployment was normal in America. Harry Hopkins had said in 1937 that even in prosperity it was "reasonable to expect a probable minimum of 4,000,000 to 5,000,000 unemployed." [3] The American nation had developed over the years a set of expectations as to what constituted "normal" times; and by 1938 it was approaching these.

Hopkins' statement and the administration's inaction indicate that the ideals of the New Dealers did not extend very far beyond the traditional structure of the American economy. They had wanted to get out of the terrible economic despair of 1932 and 1933 and to establish certain moderate reforms. These aims had been accomplished. True, some of the New Dealers, including FDR himself, did speak of what still remained to be done. But once the nation was restored to close to the old balance—even if income was still distributed with gross inequality, even if rural and urban slums crisscrossed the land, even if most workingmen were still unorganized and underpaid, and a third of the nation still, in FDR's words, "ill-nourished, ill-clad, ill-housed"—the driving force of the New Deal was gone.

Why were the expectations and ideals of the New Deal (its folklore, its symbols, according to Thurman Arnold) so limited? Why did the New Dealers not declare that the government would continue spending, experimenting, and expanding governmental enterprises—until no one was unemployed, and all slums were gone from the cities, until no family received below-subsistence incomes and adequate medical care was available to everyone, until anyone who wanted a college education could get one? True, there were political obstacles to realizing such objectives, but to state them as *goals* would itself have constituted the first step toward overcoming those obstacles. For this might have enabled FDR to do what political scientist James MacGregor Burns asserts was not done: to build "a solid, organized mass base" among labor and other underprivileged groups.[4]

Humanitarianism pure and simple can go only so far, and self-interest must carry it further. Beyond the solicitude felt by the New Dealers for the distressed, beyond the occasionally bold rhetoric, there was not enough motive power to create a radically new economic equilibrium; this would have to be supplied by the groups concerned themselves; by the tenant farmers, the aged, the unemployed, the lowest-paid workers in the economy. Those who *did* organize—the larger farm operators, the several million industrial workers who joined the CIO—improved their position significantly. But as Paul Douglas, then an economics professor at the University of Chicago and later a United States Senator, wrote in 1933:

> Along with the Rooseveltian program must go . . . the organization of those who are at present weak and who need to acquire that which the world respects, namely, power. . . . Unless these things are done, we are likely to find the permanent benefits of Rooseveltian liberalism to be as illusory as were those of the Wilsonian era.[5]

Many organized movements sprang up in the 1930's, spurred by need and encouraged by the new atmosphere of innovation. The Townsend Movement sought $200 a month pensions for the aged. Father Charles Coughlin's panacea of "Social Justice" was heard by millions of radio listeners. Huey Long, the Louisiana Senator, excited many others with his "Share the Wealth" plan. The National Negro Congress, the Farmers Union, and the American Youth Congress all represented special needs and all hurled their energies into the boiling political pot in Washington.

But there was no political program around which these disparate groups could effectively unite. And many of them began to lose their thrust when their demands were partially met. Even the Congress of Industrial Organizations, the largest and most successful of those mass movements born in the depression and stimulated by New Deal legislation, came eventually to represent a special interest of its own.

The Madisonian argument that political stability would be assured in a federal republic of many states, because an uprising in one would die for lack of support, applied also in the economic sphere, where no single economic interest, fierce as it might be in its own domain, ever developed a concern wide enough to embrace society at large. Perhaps one reason is that in the United States every little rebellion, every crisis, has been met with enough concessions to keep general resentment below the combustible level, while isolated aggrieved groups fought their way up to the point of complacency.*

But if—as Paul Douglas forecast—the underprivileged are the only ones who can supply the driving force for a sharp change in their condition, then it is probably the intellectuals of society who will furnish the theories, state the ideals, define the expectations. And so it is from those thinkers who clustered, half-friendly, half-reproachful, around the New Deal, their ideological reach less restrained, perhaps, by the holding of power, that our generation may find suggestions.

III

Almost immediately, with John Dewey, we are brought face to face with the proof that it is not the fact of experimentalism, but the definition of its boundaries, that is of supreme significance. He was one of the fathers of American pragmatism, the theoretician par excellence of the experimental method. In an article of 1918,

---

* Gabriel Kolko, in *The Triumph of Conservatism* (Free Press, 1963), pp. 302–304, advances his theory of "political capitalism," and distinguishes between "the rhetoric of reform" and its "structural results," and argues that what we call "reform" is really the use by capitalists of "a centralized state power to meet problems they could not solve themselves."

he expressed the view of pragmatic experimentation that he held to the end of his life in 1952.

> The question is whether society . . . will learn to utilize the intelligence, the insight and foresight which are available, in order to take hold of the problem and to go at it, step by step, on the basis of an intelligent program—a program which is not too rigid, which is not a program in the sense of having every item definitely scheduled in advance, but which represents an outlook on the future of the things which most immediately require doing, trusting to the experience which is got in doing them to reveal the next things needed and the next steps to be taken.[6]

Roosevelt and Dewey were both experimentalists and they both operated within a range of ideals; but that range, for John Dewey, involved goals that went well beyond Roosevelt's farthest bounds. Roosevelt wrote to newspaper publisher Roy Howard on September 2, 1935, that his legislation was "remedial," described the New Deal program as involving "modifications in the conditions and rules of economic enterprise" and said that: "This basic program, however, has now reached substantial completion." Undoubtedly he was bending over backward to satisfy an anxious and influential citizen. And his program did go on to embrace a minimum wage law, public housing, and other measures. But that was largely because of the momentum already created for reform and because of pressures among the public. The Roosevelt vision had been stretched almost to its limits.

In Dewey's 1935 lectures at the University of Virginia, he said:

> The only form of enduring social organization that is now possible is one in which the new forces of productivity are cooperatively controlled and used in the interest of the effective liberty and the cultural development of the individuals that constitute society. Such a social order cannot be established by an unplanned and external convergence of the actions of separate individuals, each of whom is bent on personal private advantage. . . . Organized social planning, put into effect for the creation of an order in which industry and finance are socially directed . . . is now the sole method of social action by which liberalism can realize its professed aims.[7]

Both Roosevelt and Dewey believed in moving step by step. But FDR wanted to preserve the profit system; Dewey was willing to reshape it drastically. Because Dewey's aim was larger, his steps were longer ones, taken two or three at a time, and were less haphazard. "In short," he said, "liberalism must now become radical. . . . For the gulf between what the actual situation makes possible and the actual state itself is so great that it cannot be bridged by piecemeal policies undertaken *ad hoc*." [8] Dewey was very conscious of the dangers of totalitarianism, but he believed that the spirit of free expression could remain alive, even while liberalism went on to "socialize the forces of production." [9] Among pragmatists, apparently, crucial distinctions exist.

Part of Roosevelt's "pragmatism" was his rejection of doctrinaire ideas of the left.[10] Marxism was in the air all around him. Many intellectuals were enthusiastic about the Five Year Plans of Soviet Russia. British Marxists were influential: Harold J. Laski lectured and wrote extensively in the United States; John Strachey popularized the concepts of socialism in *The Nature of Capitalist Crisis* (1935) and other works. Some in depression-ridden America were attracted to Marxism's claims that society could be analyzed "scientifically": that economic crisis was inevitable where production was complex and gigantic, yet unplanned; that exploitation of working people was built into a system where private profit was the chief motive; that the state was not neutral but an instrument of those who held economic power; that only the working class could be depended on to take over society and move it toward a classless, strifeless commonwealth. A true pragmatist might at least have explored some of the suggestions of Marxist thought. Roosevelt's thinking, however, remained in a kind of airtight chamber that allowed him to regulate what currents he would permit inside—and Marxism was not one of them.

Nevertheless, to steer clear of the theories of the Marxists, as of the Hooverian folklore of "free enterprise," "thrift," and "laissez-faire," left a vast middle ground of which Roosevelt explored only one sector. Edmund Wilson, for instance, a social critic and essayist, also rejected Marxian dialectics; yet he tried to extract from it some truths. He wrote with apparent warmth of the idea that (as he put it, in an imaginary restatement of a more acceptable Marxism): ". . . if society is to survive at all, it must be reorganized on new principles of equality." [11] Others, not Marxists, but more demanding in their notion of reform than was the New Deal, reconnoitered beyond its ideological fences.

Reinhold Niebuhr, a theologian and social philosopher who carried the Social Gospel to new borders in the 1930's, urged that "private ownership of the productive processes" be abandoned,[12] yet he hoped that through an alliance among farmers, industrial workers, and the lower income classes, the transition to a new order could be accomplished without violence. Stuart Chase, an economist who wrote a series of widely selling books in the 1930's, suggested that old alternatives had been swept aside by the onrush of technology, that the choice was no longer between capitalism and socialism; there was a need, he said, for some uncategorizable collectivist society whose "general objective will be the distribution of the surplus, rather than a wrangling over the ownership of a productive plant which has lost its scarcity position.[13]

William Ernest Hocking, a Harvard philosopher, asked for "collectivism of a sort," but neither the collectivism of a "headless Liberalism" or of a "heady" Communism or Fascism. He wrote: "What the State has to do with production is to drive into economic practice the truth that there is little or no capital whose use is not 'affected by a public interest.' " Hocking said: "Economic processes constitute a single and healthy organism only when the totality of persons in a community who have a right to consume *determine what is produced. . . .*" [14] Hocking was setting goals quite beyond the Rooseveltian ones.

Upton Sinclair, a muckraker since the early part of the century, preached a non-Marxist, home-grown socialism that attracted enough adherents to bring him very close to winning the gubernatorial election in California in 1934.* Sinclair prophesied that "in a cooperative society every man, woman, and child would have the equivalent of $5000 a year income from labor of the able-bodied young men for three or four hours per day." [15] This prophecy was certainly utopian in 1933, but such vision, even if it were

* He won easily in the primary over liberal George Creel, but then, lacking FDR's support, lost to an anti-New Dealer.

going to be bent and modified in practice, might carry a program of social reform much further—and perhaps win more powerful blocs of electoral support—than did the more moderate goals of the New Deal.

A program may be pragmatic in its willingness to explore various means, yet be certain of its goals; it may be limited in how far it is willing to go, and yet be clear about the direction of its thrust. There is a difference between experimentation and vacillation. Robert MacIver, a distinguished social scientist, was impressed in 1934 by the variety of new institutions created under Roosevelt, but wondered if they meant "the inauguration of a period of social and cultural reformation." He asked: "The new institutions are here, but the essential point is—Who shall control them?" [16] There was uncertainty about the New Deal, particularly in its first two years, when the National Recovery Act set out to create large planning organizations for industry in which big business seemed to be making the important decisions. It led some liberals and radicals to see in it possible Fascist aims,* led some important businessmen to support it,** and kept political loyalties crisscrossed in a happy chaos.

After 1935 (although ambiguity remained in specific areas like trust-busting), the overall direction of the New Deal became clear: it was sympathetic to the underprivileged, and to organized labor, and it was pervaded by a general spirit of liberal, humanitarian reform. But also the scope of the New Deal became clear. This limitation is shown in a number of issues that the New Deal faced, or sometimes tried to avoid facing, between 1933 and 1939: the problem of planning; the question of how to deal with monopolistic business; the controversy over deficit financing and the extension of public enterprise; the creation of an adequate system of social security.

---

* For example, William Z. Foster, for the Communists; Norman Thomas, for the Socialists; and I. F. Stone, as an independent radical.

** Russell Leffingwell, of J. P. Morgan and Company; Edward Filene, of the Boston mercantile family; Richard Whitney, president of the New York Stock Exchange; and many others.

IV

When Roosevelt told students at Oglethorpe University during his 1932 campaign that he was in favor of "a larger measure of social planning," it was not clear how large this measure was. Was he willing to go as far as his own advisor, Columbia professor Rexford Guy Tugwell? Tugwell attacked the profit motive, said that "planning for production means planning for consumption too," declared that "profits must be limited and their uses controlled," and said he meant by planning "something not unlike an integrated group of enterprises run for its consumers rather than for its owners." The statement, he said, that "business will logically be required to disappear" is "literally meant" because: "Planning implies guidance of capital uses. . . . Planning also implies adjustment of production to consumption; and there is no way of accomplishing this except through a control of prices and of profit margins." To limit business in all these ways, he said, meant in effect "to destroy it as business and to make of it something else." [17]

Raymond Moley, who had a direct role in shaping Roosevelt's early legislation, also deplored the lack of planning in the New Deal. But Moley was interested in planning for quite different groups. Tugwell was concerned with the lower classes' lack of purchasing power. Moley, although he too was moved by a measure of genuine concern for deprived people, was most worried about "the narrow margin of profit" and "business confidence." [18] In the end, Roosevelt rejected both ideas. Whatever planning he would do would try to help the lower classes, for example, the Tennessee Valley Authority. On the other hand, the planning would not be national; nor would it interfere with the fundamental character of the American economy, based as it was on corporate profit; nor would it attempt any fundamental redistribution of wealth in the nation. And the TVA embodied these limitations too because it represented *piecemeal* planning.

David Lilienthal's defense of this method, in his book on the TVA, comes closest to the New Deal approach. "We move step by step—from where we are," wrote Lilienthal.[19] Not only was any notion of national economic planning never seriously considered, but after the TVA, the moving "step by step" did not carry very far. Housing developments and several planned communities were inspiring, but came nowhere near matching the enormity of the national need.

Ambiguity persisted longest in the policy toward monopoly and oligopoly. The NRA was a frank recognition of the usefulness—or at least, the inevitability—of large enterprise, when ordered by codes. The Securities Exchange Commission and the Public Utilities Holding Company Act moved back (but weakly, as William O. Douglas recognized at the time) [20] to the Brandeis idea of trying to curb the size and strength of large enterprises. Roosevelt's basic policy toward giantism in business, although he vigorously attacked "economic royalists" in 1936, remained undetermined until 1938, when he asked Congress for a sweeping investigation of monopoly. And although he was clearly returning to the idea of restraining the power of big business, one sentence in his message to Congress reveals his continuing uncertainty: "The power of the few to manage the economic life of the Nation must be diffused among the many or be transferred to the public and its democratically responsible government."

The first alternative was an obviously romantic notion; the second was really much farther than either Congress or FDR was prepared to go. Hence, the Temporary National Economic Committee, after hearing enough testimony to fill thirty-one volumes and forty-three monographs, was unwilling, as William Leuchtenburg writes, "to tackle the more difficult problems or to make recommendations which might disturb vested interests." [21] Roosevelt had come close to expressing, but he still did not possess, nor did he communicate to the nation, a clear, resolute goal of transferring giant and irresponsible economic power "to the public and its democratically responsible government." The restraints on the New Dealers' thinking is shown best perhaps by Adolf A. Berle, who said that prosperity depended on either a gigantic expansion of private activity or nationalization of key industries. Yet, knowing private industry was not going to fill the need, he did not advocate nationalization—nor did any other New Dealer.

Roosevelt was experimental, shifting, and opportunistic in his espousal of public enterprise and the spending that had to accompany such governmental activity. As James MacGregor Burns says: "Roosevelt had tried rigid economy, then heavy spending, then restriction of spending again. He had shifted back and forth from spending on direct relief to spending on public works." [22] The significant measure, however, was not the swings of the pendulum, but the width of the arcs. When FDR went all-out for spending, it was still only a fraction of what the British economist John Maynard Keynes was urging as a way of bringing recovery. An American Keynesian, Professor Alvin Hansen, was arguing that the economy was "mature" and therefore required much more continuous and powerful injections of governmental spending than was being given.*

Roosevelt himself had introduced into public discussion the idea of a "yardstick," which the Tennessee Valley Authority represented—a public enterprise that would, by competing with private producers, force them to bend more toward the needs of the consumer. (Later FDR tried, unsuccessfully, to get Congress to introduce "seven little TVA's" in other river valleys.) But the vast implications of the concept were left unexplored. When political scientist Max Lerner called for government-owned radio stations and government-subsidized newspapers to break into the growing monopolization of public opinion by giant chains, there was no response.[23] TVA, a brief golden period of federal theater, a thin spread of public housing, and a public works program called into play only at times of desperation, represented the New Deal's ideological and emotional limits in the creation of public enterprise.

It is one thing to experiment to discover the best means of achieving a certain objective; it is quite another thing to fail to recognize that objective. The Social Security System, as set up, was not an experiment to find the best type of system. Roosevelt knew from the beginning that it was not the most effective way to handle the problems of poverty for the aged, the unemployed, and the helpless. Behind the basic political problem of getting the bill passed lay fundamental narrowness of vision. Social security expert Abraham Epstein pointed this out at the time,[24] and it was

---

* In late 1937, Secretary of the Treasury Henry Morgenthau, Jr., speaking to the American Academy of Political Science, said the 1933 emergency was over; now the budget could be balanced. He suggested cuts in public works, unemployment relief, and farm benefits.

noted on the floor of Congress.[25] Henry E. Sigerist, a physician and student of welfare medicine in other countries, wrote patiently and clearly about the need for socialized medicine, answered the arguments against it, and explained how it might operate.[26]

Thus, if the concept of New Deal thought is widened to include a large circle of thinkers—some close to the administration itself, others at varying distances from it—we get not panaceas or infallible schemes but larger commitments, bolder goals, and greater expectations of what "equality" and "justice" and "security" meant.

V

For our view of the New Deal as a particularly energetic gyroscopic motion putting the traditional structure aright again, we have what the natural scientists might call a set of "controls"—a way of checking up on the hypothesis—one in the area of race relations, another in the experience of war.

In the field of racial equality, where there was no crisis as in economics, where the gyroscope did not confront a sharply tilted mechanism, there was no "new deal." The special encumbrances of the depression were lifted for Negroes as for many other Americans, but the *permanent* caste structure remained unaltered by the kind of innovations that at least threatened the traditional edifice in economics. The white South was left, as it had been since the Compromise of 1877, to deal with blacks as it chose—by murder, by beatings, by ruthless exclusion from political and economic life; the Fourteenth Amendment waited as fruitlessly for executive enforcement as it had in all earlier administrations since Grant. Washington, D.C., itself remained a tightly segregated city. And the Harlems of the North continued as great symbols of national failure.

The warm belief in equal rights held by Eleanor Roosevelt, as well as by FDR himself, the appointments of Mary McLeod Bethune, Robert Weaver, and others to important secondary posts in the government, even the wide distribution of relief and WPA jobs, were not enough to alter the fundamental injustice attached to being a Negro in the United States. The disposition of the New Deal to experiment could have led to important accomplishments, but the clear goal of ending segregation, as with comparable objectives in economics, was never established.

With the coming of World War II, economic and social experimentation blossomed under Roosevelt's leadership and involved a good measure of national planning, jobs for everyone, and a vast system of postwar educational benefits to eighteen million veterans. There was little inhibition; new, radically different national goals were not required for the traditional objective of winning at war. With such a goal, policy could be fearless and far-reaching.

Some coming generation perhaps, while paying proper respects to the spirit of the New Deal, may find (in William James' phrase) "the moral equivalent of war"—in new social goals, new expectations, with imaginative, undoctrinaire experimentation to attain them. If, in such an adventure, the thought of the past can help, it should be put to work.

8

Abolitionists and the tactics of agitation

Few groups in American history have taken so much abuse as that mixed crew of editors, orators, runaway slaves, free Negro militants, and gun-toting preachers known as the Abolitionists. Many laymen sympathetic to the Negro have been inspired by Garrison, Phillips, Douglass, and the rest. Scholars, on the other hand (with a few exceptions), have either scolded the Abolitionists for immoderation, or psychoanalyzed them as emotional deviates in need of recognition.

It is tempting to reverse the psychological game and speculate about what it is in the lives of academic scholars that keeps them at arm's length from the moral fervor of one of history's most magnificent crusades. But it may be more useful to examine the actions of the Abolitionists, to connect them with later agitators against racial exclusiveness, and thus to assess the value of "extremists," "radicals," and "agitators" in bringing desired social change.

At issue are a number of notions held by liberal-minded people who profess aims similar to the radical reformers, but urge more moderate methods. To argue a case too heatedly, they point out, provokes the opponent to retaliation. To urge measures too extreme alienates possible allies. To ask for too much too soon results in getting nothing. To use vituperative language arouses emotions to a pitch that precludes rational consideration. To set up a clash of extremes precipitates sharp conflict and violence.

All of these tactical sins have been charged, at different times, by different people, to the American Abolitionists. Today the same charges are being made about the more militant elements in the black movement. These charges—both then and now—have not been closely scrutinized as part of a discussion of preferable approaches to change. Twentieth-century man, marking the transition from chaotic renovation of the social fabric to purposeful social action, needs to give much more careful consideration than before to the tactics of such action.

There is no denying the anger, the bitterness, the irascibility of the Abolitionists. William Lloyd Garrison, dean of them all, wrote in blood in the columns of the *Liberator* and breathed fire from the speakers' platforms all over New England. He spoke abroad in brutal criticism of America: "I accuse the land of my nativity of insulting the majesty of Heaven with the greatest mockery that was ever exhibited to man." He burned the Constitution before several thousand witnesses on the lawn at Framingham, calling it "source and parent of all other atrocities—a covenant with death and an agreement with hell" and spurred the crowd to echo, "Amen!" He provoked his opponents outrageously, and the South became apoplectic at the mention of his name. South Carolina offered $1500 for conviction of any white person circulating the *Liberator,* and the Georgia legislature offered $500 for Garrison's arrest and conviction.

Wendell Phillips, richer, and from a distinguished Boston family, was no softer. "Don't shilly-shally, Wendell," his wife whispered to him as he mounted the speaker's platform, and he never did. The anger that rose in him one day in 1835 as he watched Boston bluebloods drag Garrison through the streets never left him, and it remained directed at what he considered America's unbearable evil—slavery. "The South is one great brothel," he proclaimed. Neither gradualism nor Garrison's language of nonresistance was for Phillips. "No sir, we may not trifle or dally. . . . Revolution is the only thing, the only power, that ever worked out freedom for any people." The piety of New England did not intimidate him: "The American church—what is it? A synagogue of Satan." On that same green where Garrison burned the Constitution, Phillips said: "We are very small in numbers; we have got no wealth; we have got no public opinion behind us; the only thing that we can do is, like the eagle, simply to fly at our enemy, and pick out his eyes."

Even Garrison and Phillips seem moderate against the figure of John Brown, lean and lusty, with two wives and twenty children, filled with enough anger for a regiment of agitators, declaring personal war on the institution of slavery. Speeches and articles were for others. The old man studied military strategy, pored over maps of Southern terrain, raised money for arms, and planned the forcible liberation of slaves through rebellion and guerrilla warfare. On Pottawatamie Creek in the Bleeding Kansas of 1856, on the Sabbath, he struck one night at an encampment of pro-slavery men, killing five with cold ferocity. On his way to the gallows, after the raid on Harpers Ferry arsenal in Virginia in the fall of 1859, he wrote: "I John Brown am now quite certain that the crimes of this guilty land will never be purged away; but with Blood."

The black Abolitionist Frederick Douglass, newly freed from slavery himself and long a believer in "moral suasion" to free the others, talked with John Brown at his home in 1847 and came away impressed by his arguments. Two years later, Douglass told a Boston audience: "I should welcome the intelligence tomorrow, should it come, that the slaves had risen in the South, and that the sable arms which had been engaged in beautifying and adorning the South were engaged in spreading death and devastation." He thought the Harpers Ferry plan wild, and would not go along; yet, to the end, he maintained that John Brown at Harpers Ferry began the war that ended slavery. "Until this blow was struck, the prospect for freedom was dim, shadowy, and uncertain. . . . When John Brown stretched forth his arm the sky was cleared."

These were the extremists. Did they hurt or help the cause of freedom? Did their activities bring a solution at too great a cost? If we can answer these questions, and others, we may illuminate the tactics of present agitators and immoderates, whose cries, if not so shrill as Garrison's, are as unpleasant to some ears, and whose actions, if not so violent as John Brown's, are just as distasteful to those who urge caution and moderation.

In the first four pages of a well-known book on Civil War politics, *Lincoln and the Radicals,* T. Harry Williams describes Abolitionists, individually and collectively, with the following epithets: "radical . . . zealous . . . fiery . . . scornful . . . revolutionary . . . spirit of fanaticism . . . hasty . . . Jacobins . . . aggressive . . . vindictive . . . narrowly sectional . . . bitter . . . sputtering . . . fanatical . . . impractical . . . extreme." Like other words of judgment frequently used to enliven historical accounts, such terms have not been carefully analyzed; while they serve as useful approximations of a general attitude held by the writer (to be transferred without question to the reader) they fail to make the kinds of distinction necessary to precise understanding. For example, the word "extremist," used perhaps more often than any other to characterize the Abolitionists, deserves inspection.

Now, if we are told that a woman is extremely beautiful, a man extremely kind, a mechanic extremely skillful, or a child extremely healthy, we find it admirable. In politics, however, the label "extremist" carries unfavorable implications. It may mean that the person desires social change more sweeping than that requested by most people; in a period when most people are willing to free the slaves, but not to enfranchise them, an advocate of equal rights is considered an extremist. Or it may mean someone who urges more drastic action than most to attain a commonly desired goal; a person, that is, who advocates slave revolts (as did John Brown) rather than compensated emancipation followed by colonization abroad (as did Lincoln). Yet, in any real political situation, the alternative plans of action advocated are usually much fewer than the total range of possibilities. The most extreme suggestion put forward at a given time will be labeled "extremist" even though it may be far less sweeping than other possible courses of action.

For instance, William Lloyd Garrison, regarded as an extremist by his antagonists and by modern historians alike, did not seek goals as far-reaching as he might have. Around 1830 he explained "immediate abolition" as follows: "Immediate abolition does not mean that the slave shall immediately exercise the right of suffrage, or be eligible to any office, or be emancipated from law, or be free from the benevolent restraints of guardianship." (Yet suffrage was not objectionable to Thaddeus Stevens, Charles Sumner, and Garrison in 1865.) Wendell Phillips, another "extremist," opposed the use of violence to free the slaves. He said, in 1852: "The cause of three millions of slaves, the destruction of a great national institution, must proceed slowly, and like every other change in public sentiment, we must wait patiently for it." (John Brown was not so patient.) Charles Sumner, the "radical"

Republican in the Senate, did not urge going beyond the Constitution, which gave Southern states the right to maintain slavery if they chose. (Garrison, burning the Constitution, was less restrained.)

The point is plain: we are not precise in our measure of "extremism." Writers may call "extreme" any proposal more drastic than that favored by the majority of articulate people (or by the writer). In a society in which the word "extreme" has a noxious political odor and in which the literate community is enamored of an Aristotelian golden mean, we often hurl that word unjustifiably at a proposal extreme only in a context of limited alternatives. Consider: The NAACP, denounced all over the South as radical and virtually Communistic, began to look respectable and law-abiding when the sit-ins and Freedom Riders moved into mass extralegal action in 1960 and 1961. And the White Citizens Councils could lay claim to espousing "moderate" racial views as long as the K.K.K. was around.

With the criterion for extremism so flexible, with the limits constantly shifting, how can we judge the value of a position by whether it is "extreme" or "moderate"? (We accept such labels in the first place because they afford us a test simple enough to avoid mental strain and also because it is comfortable—especially for intellectuals who do not share the piercing problems of the deprived and thus face no *extreme* problems—to presume that the "moderate" solution is the best.) One gauge of value might be the nature and severity of the problem. Modest evils may be dislodged by a few sharp words, but the elimination of slavery clearly required drastic action, and the Abolitionists did not pretend that they were gentle and temperate; they quite consciously measured their words to the enormity of the evil. In his famous declaration in the first issue of the *Liberator,* January 1, 1831, Garrison said: "On this subject I do not wish to think or speak or write with moderation. No! No! Tell a man whose house is on fire to give a moderate alarm; tell him to moderately rescue his wife from the hands of the ravisher; tell the mother to gradually extricate her baby from the fire into which it has fallen—but urge me not to use moderation in a cause like the present."

How evil was slavery? A complex phenomenon, different in every individual instance, its whole range of variation was set in a framework of unspeakable inhumanity. At its "best," slavery was a ferocious attack on man's dignity. And at its worst, slavery was, as Allan Nevins has said, "the greatest misery, the greatest wrong, the greatest curse to white and black alike that America has ever known." Ads for fugitive slaves in the Southern press (as many as 5400 advertisements in a year) contained descriptions like the following to aid apprehension: "Stamped N.E. on the breast and having both small toes cut off." "Has on a large neck iron, with a huge pair of horns and a large bar or band of iron on his left leg." "Branded on the left cheek, thus 'R,' and a piece is taken off her left ear on the same side; the same letter is branded on the inside of both legs." One plantation diary reads: "Whipped every fieldhand this evening." A Natchez slave who attacked a white man was chained to a tree and burned alive.

Against this, how mild Garrison's words seem.

G. F. Milton, in *The Eve of Conflict,* writes of the Abolitionists' "deep-seated passions" and "the emotional flood . . . psychic forces clamoring for expression . . . a drive for reform, change, agitation, which boded ill for any arbitrament of intelligence." Thoreau, Parker, and other reformers, he says, "showed a remarkably keen insight into latent mass emotions and did not hesitate to employ appropriate devices to mobilize the mob mind." Fanaticism, irrationality, emotionalism—these are the qualities attributed again and again, in a mood of sharp criticism, to the Abolitionists; and indeed, to radical reformers today. How valid is the criticism?

If being "emotional" means creating a state of excitement, both for oneself and for others, then we need not argue. What *is* arguable is the notion that "emotionalism" is to be deplored.

Intellectuals and scholars are generally taken aback by emotional display. It often appears an attack on reason. "Dispassionate" is a favorite term of praise; the words "calm . . . judicious . . . reasonable" seem to belong together. We recall the Hitlers, the Southern demagogues of racism, the religious charlatans and faith healers. And yet, if we sit in a Negro Baptist Church in the deep South in the summer of 1964, listen to the crowd sing, "We shall overcome . . ." and hear it cry "Freedom! Freedom!" even the most intellectual among us may well feel a surge of joy and love, only slightly damped by a twinge of uneasiness at our spontaneous display of emotion. We are uneasy, I would suggest, because of a failure to recognize that emotionalism is a *morally neutral* instrument; that it serves a positive purpose when linked to laudable goals; that it is not "irrational" but "nonrational" because, being merely an instrument, its rationality is derived only from the value of the goal toward which it is directed.

When, at a moment of high tension in the battle over slavery, William Lloyd Garrison first heard the freed Negro Frederick Douglass speak, at a crowded meeting in Nantucket, he cried out: "Have we been listening to a man—or a thing?" The audience stirred. In this flash of words and transferred emotion, a group of New England men and women, far removed from the plantation and its daily reminders of human debasement, were confronted with an experience that made them more ready to act against an evil whose meaning flooded in on them for perhaps the first time. The "Horst Vessel" song drove the Nazi myrmidons, but the "Battle Hymn of the Republic" inspired anti-slavery fighters. The agitation of emotions by words or actions is an art; as such, it is an instrument of whatever moral camp employs it. And what needs to be said finally, if only to assuage the embarrassment of the emotionally aroused intellectual, is that there is no necessary connection between emotionalism and irrationality. Indeed, emotion can be used to make decisions more rational, if we mean decisions based on greater knowledge and if we concede that knowledge involves not only information but intensity. Who "knows" more about slavery—the man who has in his head the available statistics and calmly goes about his business, or the man who has less data, but is moved by a book or by an orator to feel the reality of slavery with such depth that he will establish a station on the underground railroad?

Closely linked to the theme of emotionalism, and in part because of it, is the charge of distortion and exaggeration, which is often made against reformist agitators today as in the past. The Abolitionists, historian Avery Craven wrote in *The Coming of the Civil War,* spread thousands of distortions about the South. "For more than two decades, these molders of public opinion steadily created the fiction of two distinct peoples contending for the right to preserve and expand their sacred cultures. . . . In time, a people came to believe . . . that the issues were between right and wrong; good and evil." Thus persons with an abiding concern for the truth are often led to keep a safe distance from the concerns of agitators.

It is important, however, to make a distinction between outright misstatements of fact or personal slander and the exaggeration or selection of aspects of a complex truth that support the viewpoint of the reformer. False statements have indeed been made by radical reformers; and this is especially unpardonable, for if the reformer speaks the truth, then he needs no falsification of the evidence to back his case. But charges of distortion are apt to be more subtle: once one passes simple factual statements ("On March 3, 1851, field hand —— was whipped by his master") and begins to deal with the general characterization of social institutions (such as Mr. Nevins' statement that slavery was "the greatest misery . . . the greatest curse . . .") words like "true" and "false" cannot be applied simply. (This is that philosophical realm dealing with the theory of knowledge, a field in which historians frequently cavort without paying much attention to the rules; philosophers, meanwhile, discuss the rules in their studies and rarely look out the window to see how the game is being played.) Slavery was a complex institution, and no one statement describes it fully.

Now, there is an answer to the problem of how to state simply a complex truth—but it requires an engaged outlook rare among scholars. If in teaching a child to be careful crossing the street I say, "You can be killed by an automobile," I single out of the total complex of reality that small percentage of automobile incidents in which people are killed. I am fully aware I am not telling the whole truth about the "traffic problem," but emphasizing that portion of the truth which supports a desirable action.

In *Lincoln and the Radicals,* T. Harry Williams complains that as a result of Abolitionist agitation, it "was widely believed that slavery had brutalized the Southern character." This Abolitionist emphasis, on first thought, does not depict total reality; not every white Southerner was brutalized by slavery. Yet, it awakens the idea that just to *live* in such a system without protest is a sign of brutalization. What seemed an oversimplification turns out to grasp a subtle truth applicable to both past and present.

It is paradoxical that historians, presumably blessed with perspective, should judge the radical from within the narrow moral base of the radical's own period, while the radical assesses his immediate society from the vantage point of a future, better era. If progress is desirable, and if escape from the bonds of the immediate is healthy, whose perspective is more appealing—that of the agitator, or that of the scolding historian? Wendell Phillips, speaking affectionately of the Abolitionist leader, Angelina Grimké, said: "Were I to single out the moral and intellectual trait which won me, it was her serene indifference to the judgement of those about her." That kind of indifference (David Riesman calls it inner-directedness) is hard to find in contemporary scholarship.

The two sides of the argument over the wisdom of agitation in the tactics of social reform were aptly summed up in Boston in pre-Civil War years. Samuel May, speaking of Garrison, said: "He will shake our nation to its center, but he will shake slavery out of it." Reverend Lyman Beecher said: "True wisdom consists in advocating a cause only so far as the community will sustain the reformer." The agitator, declare moderate reformers, shakes so hard that he makes compromise impossible, alienates friends, and delays rather than speeds the coming of reform.

Compromise was not disdained by the Abolitionists; they were fully conscious that the outcome of any social struggle is almost always some form of compromise. But they were also aware that to compromise in advance is to vitiate at the outset that power for progress which only the radical propels into the debate. Phillips said: "If we would get half a loaf, we must demand the whole of it." The Emancipation Proclamation itself was a compromise, the tortured product of a long battle between radicals and moderates in and out of the Lincoln administration, and only the compelling force of the Abolitionist intransigents made it come as soon as it did.

The real question is: Can moderation ever be an effective tactic for sweeping reform? It is often thought that the agitator alienates potential allies by his extremism. Lewis Tappan, the wealthy New

Yorker who financed many Abolitionist activities, wrote anxiously to George Thompson, the British Abolitionist: "The fact need not be concealed from you that several emancipationists so disapprove of the harsh, and, as they think, the un-Christian language of the *Liberator,* that they do not feel justified in upholding it." This, in general, was the feeling of the Executive Committee of the American Anti-Slavery Society in the early years of the movement. Undoubtedly, the Society itself was not diverted from its aim by Garrison's immoderation; they were concerned lest others be alienated.

But who? The slaveholder? The slave? The moderate reformer? The open-minded conservative? Different sections of the population respond differently to the same appeal. Why should the radical soften his language or his program to please that element of the population which cannot possibly be pleased by anything short of total surrender of principle? The slaveholders themselves pointed out the impossibility of their being won over by moderate overtures. In 1854, the editor of the Richmond *Enquirer* wrote: "That man must be a veritable verdigreen who dreams of pleasing slaveholders, either in church or state, by any method but that of letting slavery alone." For the groups most inimical to reform, it is doubtful that moderation is effective. It was Nat Turner's violent slave revolt in Virginia in 1831 that led the Virginia legislature into its famous series of discussions about the abolition of slavery. "For a while indeed," Ralph Korngold writes, "it seemed that what years of propaganda by the Quakers had failed to accomplish would come as a result of Turner's bloodletting."

When friends of reformers rail against harsh words or strong action, it is clear that they themselves will not be put off because of it. Thus if neither extreme can be moved by tactics or moderation, the decisive group becomes that which shifts back and forth depending on circumstances. Garrison was quite aware that most of the American population to which he was appealing was not sympathetic with his views. But he was persuaded, as were Phillips and other leading Abolitionists (John Brown felt it, and acted it, if he did not express it intellectually), that only powerful surges of words and feelings could move white people from their complacency about the slave question. To his friend Samuel May, who urged him to keep more cool, saying: "Why, you are all on fire," Garrison replied: "Brother May, I have need to be all on fire, for I have mountains of ice about me to melt."

We can check historical record to see whether the vituperative language of Garrison, the intemperate appeals of Wendell Phillips, retarded or advanced popular sentiment against slavery. In the 1830's a handful of men cried out against slavery and were beaten, stoned, and shot to death by their Northern compatriots. By 1849, antislavery sentiment was clearly increasing, and some of the greatest voices in America were speaking out for abolition. James Russell Lowell asked curtly of those who charged the Abolitionists with retarding the movement: "Has there really been a change of public opinion for the worse, either at the North or the South, since the *Liberator* came into existence eighteen years ago?" By 1860, when millions of Americans were convinced that slavery was an evil, open insurrection by John Brown brought more public support than Garrison had achieved with words thirty years before.

It is when we enter the realm of politics that the tactics of the agitator raise the greatest alarm. The moderate observer often thinks the radical injudicious in making extreme demands of the man in office, but he fails to distinguish between the social role of the politician and that of the agitator. In general, this distinction has been perceived more clearly by reformers than by politicians. Wendell Phillips put it neatly: "The reformer is careless of numbers, disregards popularity, and deals only with ideas, conscience, and common sense. . . . He neither expects nor is overanxious for immediate success. The politician dwells in an everlasting now. . . . His office is not to instruct public opinion but to represent it." The observer who is critical of the radical may be unconsciously visualizing a world peopled only with radicals, a world of incessant shouting, lamenting, and denunciation. But it would be good for him also to imagine a world without any radicals—and to remember that, in all ages, it has been first the radical, and only later the moderate, who has extended his hand to men knocked to the ground by the social order. When Horace Greeley charged Garrison with fanaticism, James Russell Lowell retorted: "Why God sent him into the world with that special mission and none other. . . . We would not have all men fanatics, but let us be devoutly thankful for as many of that kind as we can get. They are by no means too common as yet."

Abraham Lincoln provides the very archetype of the politician so moderate as to require the pressure of radicals to stimulate action. It is hard to find a set of statements more clearly expressive of the politician's ambivalence than those Lincoln made during his race for the Senate against Stephen Douglas in 1858. He told a Chicago audience in July:

> Let us discard this quibbling about this man and the other man, this race and the other race being inferior, and therefore they must be placed in an inferior position.

And in September, he told an audience in southern Illinois:

> I am not, nor ever have been, in favor of bringing about in any way the social or political equality of the white and black races. . . . I will say in addition that there is a physical difference between the white and black races which, I suppose, will forever forbid the two races living together upon terms of social and political equality; and inasmuch as they cannot so live, that while they do remain together, there must be the position of the superiors and the inferiors; and that I, as much as any other man, am in favor of the superior being assigned to the white man.

The most shocking statement about Lincoln—all the more shocking when we realize its essential truth—was made by Frederick Douglass in 1876 at the unveiling of the Freedman's monument in Washington:

> To protect, defend, and perpetuate slavery in the United States where it existed Abraham Lincoln was not less ready than any other President to draw the sword of the nation. He was ready to execute all the supposed Constitutional guarantees of the United States Constitution in favor of the slave system anywhere inside the slave states. He was willing to pursue, recapture, and send back the fugitive slave to his master, and to suppress a slave rising for liberty, though his guilty master were already in arms against the Government. The

race to which we belong were not the special objects of his consideration. Knowing thus, I concede to you, my white fellow citizens, a preeminence in his worship at once full and supreme. First, midst, and
last, you and yours were the objects of his deepest affection and his
most earnest solicitude. You are the children of Abraham Lincoln.
We are at best only his stepchildren, children by adoption, children by
force of circumstances and necessity.

In the absorbing dialogue—sometimes articulated, sometimes
unspoken—between Abraham Lincoln and the Abolitionists, we
see the classic posture of the politician vis-à-vis the radical reformer. It would be wrong to say that Lincoln was completely a
politician—his fundamental humanitarianism did not allow that—
and wrong to say that the Abolitionists did not occasionally play
politics, but on both sides the aberrations were slight, and both
played their respective roles to perfection.

Albert Beveridge, in his biography of Lincoln, saw him as a man
who "almost perfectly reflected public opinion." Lincoln opposed
repeal of the Fugitive Slave Law, was silent on the violence in
Kansas and the beating of Sumner, and followed the tactic of saying nothing except on issues most people agreed on—like stopping
the extension of slavery. During the secession crisis, and through
most of the war, Lincoln's stand on slavery was so ambiguous and
cautious as to make the British Abolitionist George Thompson tell
Garrison: "In no one of his utterances is there an assertion of a
great principle—no appeal to right or justice. In everything he
does and says affecting the slave, there is the alloy of expediency."
Lincoln's first desire was to save the Union; Abolition was secondary and he would sacrifice it, if necessary, to maintain the republican rule over the entire nation.

While Lincoln kept reading the meter of public opinion, the
Abolitionists, in massive ideological waves, assaulted both the
public and the meter-reader. In the winter of 1861–62, 50,000
persons heard Wendell Phillips speak. Millions read his speeches.
Petitions and delegations besieged Lincoln at the White House.
Garrison went easy on Lincoln, but his own writings had created
an army of impatients. The evidence is that Lincoln, who had reflected public opinion well enough in 1860 to win the election,

was not abreast of it in 1861 and 1862 on the issue of slavery. And this is a point of huge significance: although both the politician and the agitator have their own special roles to play in man's fitful march toward Utopia, the agitator, who takes his own actions into account, is dynamic, while the political meter-reader is static. Thus political decisions tend to be conservative, for the politician is so preoccupied with the evaluation of existing forces that his own power is expended in *reading* public opinion rather than in *changing* it.

When Presidents *have* been more than reflectors of a consensus, their energies have usually been exerted for nationalistic rather than reformist goals. Lincoln, Wilson, Roosevelt, and Truman worked hard to create popular support for the wars they administered; but the reforms of Teddy Roosevelt and Wilson were largely diluted toasts to Populist and Progressive protest. Franklin D. Roosevelt's New Deal comes closest to a dynamic effort to push through a reform program while creating the sentiment to support it. But on the racial question, from Lincoln to Kennedy and Johnson, the man at the pinnacle of national political power has chosen to play the cautious game of responding to the powerful push of "extremists," "troublemakers," and "radicals." For Lincoln it was the Abolitionists; for Kennedy the Freedom Riders and Birmingham demonstrators, for Johnson the Mississippi summer workers. The man sitting in the White House has a power to change public opinion a thousand times greater than agitators can achieve by protest and outcry. So far, however, no one with Presidential power had played so dynamic a role for racial equality.

There is no point—except for the abstract delight that accompanies historical study—in analyzing the tactics of the agitator in history unless we can learn something from it that is of use today. We have, after a hundred years, successors to the Abolitionists: the sit-in agitator, the Freedom Rider, the voter-registration worker in Mississippi. Every objection—and every defense—applicable to the Abolitionist applies also to his modern-day counterpart.

When the sit-in movement erupted in the South in the Spring of 1960, it seemed a radical, extreme departure from the slow, law-court tactics of the N.A.A.C.P., which had produced favorable court decisions but few real changes in the deep South; it upset

Southern white liberals sympathetic to the 1954 Supreme Court school decision. But the advent of the Freedom Rides in 1961— busloads of integrated Northerners riding through the most backward areas of the deep South in direct and shocking violation of local law and custom—made the sit-ins seem a rather moderate affair. And the emergence of the militantly anti-white Black Muslims made the integrationist advocates of nonviolence seem even more moderate. "Extremism" is still a relative term.

Garrison's old argument that his radicalism was pitched to the level of the evil he was opposing is directly applicable to the new young radicals of the American South. Is sitting at a lunch counter in a white restaurant and refusing to leave really a very extreme measure in relation to the evil of segregation? The element of emotionalism, too, has a special place in the current movement for racial equality. Every important demonstration and action has been accompanied by church meetings, singing, fiery oratory. But this is an instrument consciously adapted to a most rational objective: securing in fact as well as in theory the basic principles of the Declaration of Independence and the Fourteenth Amendment. Martin Luther King played on the emotions of his people, but contained them within a controlled rationality directed toward carefully defined goals.

Does the race agitator today exaggerate the truth about the conditions of the black? To be a Negro in America, for most Negroes, most of the time, does not mean beatings or lynchings. But for all Negroes in America, all of the time, it does mean a fundamental hurt that exceeds statistics. America is not one mad orgy of lynching and brutality, as Communist propaganda might have it. But there is a kind of permanent brutality in the atmosphere that *nobody's* propaganda has quite accurately described. And thus no accusation directed against the white is much of an exaggeration. As for the moderate exhortation to compromise, the angry but cool black students in the South did learn the lesson well: apply full pressure; then the final compromise will be at the highest possible level.

The role of the politician vis-à-vis the agitator was revealed as clearly in the Kennedy Administration as it was under Lincoln. Like Lincoln, Kennedy read the meter of public concern and reacted to it, but never exerted the full force of his office to change the reading drastically. He too had a measure of humanitarianism, but it took the shock of Birmingham to bring from him his first clear moral appeal against segregation and his first move for civil rights legislation (the Civil Rights Act of 1964). Lyndon Johnson also neglected—even while modern-day Abolitionists were murdered in Mississippi—to revoke the Compromise of 1877 and decisively enforce federal law in that state.

Behind every one of the national Government's moves toward racial equality lies the sweat and pain of boycotts, picketing, beatings, sit-ins, and mass demonstration. All of our recent administrations have been funnels into which gargantuan human effort—organized by radical agitators like Martin Luther King and the young militants of the Student Nonviolent Coordinating Committee—has been poured—to emerge at the other end in slow dribbles of social progress. No American President from Lincoln on has seen the immense possibilities for social change that lie in a *dynamic* reading of public opinion. Progress toward racial equality in the United States may come, but this is because agitators, radicals, and extremists—black and white together—are giving the United States its only living reminder that it was once a revolutionary nation.

9

Psychoanalyzing the dissenter: two cases

(*DAVID DONALD AND THE ABOLITIONISTS; LEWIS FEUER AND THE STUDENT REBELS*)

I

David Donald does not fit neatly into the traditional camps of historians arguing about (mostly against) the Abolitionists.* He is sympathetic with the aims of the Abolitionists (I recall that at Columbia University in the early 1950's, Donald was very much moved—as we all were—during his lecture on Garrison and Phillips). Still, he feels much more at home with Lincoln's cautious pragmatism than with the "rigid ideologists" who pressured the President to act against slavery. Donald's interpretation of the Abolitionists is psychological; he turns their crusade into a sour playing-out of personal frustrations on the social stage.**

In *Lincoln Reconsidered,* Donald aims to use social psychology and sociology to explore the minds and actions of the Abolitionists. He wants to find out why they were what they were. "According to their voluminous memoirs and autobiographies, they were simply convinced by religion, by reading, by reflection, that slavery was evil, and they pledged their lives and their sacred honor to destroy it."

* See Louis Ruchames, "Charles Sumner and American Historiography," *Journal of Negro History,* April 1953. Also Fawn Brodie, "Who Defends the Abolitionists?" in *The Anti-Slavery Vanguard,* edited by Martin Duberman, Princeton University Press, 1965.

** I will be referring in this essay to two of Donald's books: his Pulitzer Prize-winning study, *Charles Sumner and the Coming of the Civil War,* Knopf, 1960, and his book of essays, *Lincoln Reconsidered,* Knopf, 1956.

Donald is not satisfied with this. It turns out, however, to be much more convincing as an explanation than the causal factors he ultimately finds to be crucial. His use of the word "simply" indicates that he feels the answer is much more complex. But if those factors named above (religion, reading, reflection) are too simple, can it not be that the complexity we seek is in a more detailed, analytical examination of just those factors, or related factors, rather than a leap into a completely different realm of explanation? In other words, the mere simplicity of these cited factors is not sufficient argument to warrant deserting them completely.

Yes, Donald says, he knows the Abolitionists were sincere, but why should such sincerity be concentrated in the 1830's of all times? The answer, it seems to me, is perhaps "simple." Abolitionism, while it surged upward dramatically in the 1830's, was a continuing phenomenon in American history in every decade from the American Revolution until the Civil War. The greatest growth of Abolitionism did not take place in the 1830's, but in the 1840's and 1850's. So why give to the 1830's some mysterious preeminence, one so strong as to demand a special causal complex specifically tied to that decade?

The best way to answer the question he poses, Donald says, is "to analyze the leadership of the Abolitionist movement." He draws up a list of 250 Abolitionist leaders, but eliminates a number who joined after 1840, on the rather unwarranted assumption that since the Abolitionist movement entered politics in the 1840's those who joined in this period were "political" Abolitionists, and therefore outside the concern of his analysis.

After his eliminations, he has 106 people who constituted "the hard core of active antislavery leadership in the 1830's." Now Donald goes into that series of statistical maneuvers which have become popular among social scientists enamored of IBM machines: the tabulation of characteristics. He finds for instance, that in 1831 the median age of his group is twenty-nine, and concludes, "Abolitionism was thus a revolt of the young." While the significance of this conclusion for social inquiry is itself elusive (how many reform movements are led by the old except for the Townsend movement?), wouldn't it be as justifiable to take the median age in 1839 rather than in 1831, the last year rather than the first year of that decade which Donald is studying? In that case the median age becomes thirty-eight. But really, how important is all this?

The tabulating machine goes to work again and finds that 60 percent of the Abolitionist leaders come from New England. This discovery only throws another weight into the rather fruitless battle between those historians emphasizing the Middle West as the center of Abolitionism (like Benjamin Thomas in his study of Theodore Weld) and those preoccupied with Garrison and Phillips.

Now we come to the crux of Donald's argument. "The parents of the leaders generally belonged to a clearly defined stratum of society. Many were preachers, doctors, or teachers; some were farmers and a few were merchants; but only three were manufacturers . . . none was a banker, and only one was an ordinary day laborer. . . . These families were neither rich nor poor." In other words, they were of middle-class background in general. And this, as we shall see, is vital information.

"Virtually all the parents were staunch Federalists." Since they lived in that part of the country which was the stronghold of Federalism, and in exactly that era when the Federalist Party held undisputed positions of leadership, it is hard to find this surprising.

Donald's thesis begins to emerge here, and it would be well to keep it in mind as we pursue further his methodology and findings. It is that the Abolitionists grew up in a world swiftly urbanizing, industrializing, with no niche for them; and rather than be by-passed by this "bustling democracy of the 1830's" they took to agitation as a means of becoming leaders. Donald works throughout his essay to support this thesis. "In New York, antislavery was strongest in those counties which had once been economically dominant but which by the 1830's, though still prosperous, had relatively fallen behind their more advantageously situated neighbors." Even if there is a clear causal connection between those two phenomena does the fact that the "county" has fallen behind economically mean that Donald's subjects in that county have also fallen behind, and that therefore we can automatically assume they match his conception of the Abolitionist as a bypassed person?

"As young men, the fathers of Abolitionists had been leaders of their communities and states; in their old age they were elbowed aside by the merchant prince, the manufacturing tycoon, the corporation lawyer." Are not most people elbowed aside in their old age in any dynamic economy? In view of Donald's emphasis on the family background, it would be interesting to inquire into the siblings of his Abolitionist leaders, since they certainly shared the same parents and background. Why is it that the brothers and sisters of these Abolitionist leaders were not also in the movement? There are the Tappan brothers, of course (neither bypassed in the economic race, but rather doing very well) and the Grimké sisters. But what of all the other siblings?

The tabulating machine, once set to work, does not know where to stop. Donald finds it "difficult to tabulate the religious affiliations of antislavery leaders. Most were troubled by spiritual discontent and they wandered from one sect to another seeking salvation. It is quite clear, however, that there was a heavy Congregational-Presbyterian and Quaker preponderance." And recent studies "confirm the conclusion that, except in Pennsylvania, it is correct to consider humanitarian reform and Congregational-Presbyterianism as causally interrelated." It would help to know how those studies were carried out, and it would be interesting to know exactly *why* there should be a special causal connection between "Congregational-Presbyterianism" and humanitarian reform. And how important is this, if "most" of the Abolitionists "wandered from one sect to another." And why would the existence of Quakerism in Pennsylvania break this causal connection linking reform and Congregational-Presbyterianism?

Donald finds it significant that "only thirteen of the entire group were born in any of the principal cities of the United States." Since they were born at the end of the eighteenth and beginning of the nineteenth century, were they not part of that great mass of the American people who were *not* born in "principal cities." Donald finds Abolition "distinctly a rural movement" and quotes not his New England majority but Weld, a member of the Midwest minority, to prove this. But most Abolitionist activity—newspaper editing, lecturing, etc.—went on in the cities, and was directed at city people.

He cites, correctly, Garrison's and others' unsympathetic feelings toward labor, but pays little attention to Wendell Phillips' strong pro-labor sympathies. However, he ends up saying: "Actually, it is clear that the Abolitionists were not so much hostile to labor as indifferent to it." This is not hard to understand in the world of the 1830's, when manufacturing was still only a thin segment of American economic life, and trade unions were in their infancy. He explains away the attacks by Emerson, Parker, Sumner on the "Lords of the Loom" as mainly an attack on "the morality of old New England" rather than on exploitation.

"Here then," he finds, "is a composite portrait of Abolitionist leadership. Descended from old and socially dominant [are ministers, teachers, farmers "socially dominant"] Northeastern families, reared in a faith of aggressive piety [but most "wandered from one sect to another"] and moral endeavor, educated for conservative leadership, these young men and women who reached maturity in the 1830's faced a strange and hostile world." But weren't there thousands of other young Americans who fit this description—and why didn't they ·become Abolitionist leaders? "Social and economic leadership was being transferred from the country to the city, from the farmer to the manufacturer, from the preacher to the corporation attorney." Isn't this the story not only of the 1830's, but of the 1840's, 1850's, 1870's, 1890's, etc.—in fact the story of American development? The Abolitionists wanted to lead, Donald says, but could find no followers. "They were an elite without function, a displaced class in American society." But Wendell Phillips could easily have had almost any function he wanted in society, and the same for Charles Sumner. As for Garrison, his background does not clearly fit the above portrait.

Thus, Donald concludes ". . . agitation allowed the only chance for personal and social self-fulfillment." These leaders were "aliens in the new industrial society." Their "appeal for reform was a strident call for their own class to reexert its former social dominance." But what former "social dominance" had there been for a group which Donald himself says was not upper class but middle class, not rich manufacturers or leading politicians but teachers, ministers, doctors, farmers?

Illogic feeds on itself. "An attack on slavery was their best, if

quite unconscious attack upon the new industrial system." Here
we have a simplistic, and quite unsupported case of Freudian
"transference." The Abolitionists really hated the new industrial
system, but took it out on the slaveholders. Why not take it out
on the slaves? Why not take it out on the politicians? Why not take
it out on foreigners? Why not take it out on the industrial system
itself, directly? If they were opposed to the new industrial system,
why try to destroy the great obstacle to the full development of
this industrial system—the slave plantation system of the South?
Psychoanalysis is so much more enticing as a theory to explain
a social movement than the older, cruder, and so much more be-
lievable notion: that these people were moved by what they saw,
heard about, read about; that while their personal lives may very
well have been unfulfilled for any one of a number of reasons—
the exact *direction* in which they sought fulfillment was decided
by the specific impact that the horror of slavery made on their
consciousness.

"Reform gave meaning to the lives of this displaced social
elite." But wouldn't anti-reform also give meaning? In other
words, if we grant that those conditions Donald describes as surrounding the Abolitionists created a vacuum this still does not determine exactly what is required to fill that vacuum. The facts of
anxiety, of search, of displacement, of being pushed aside, may
motivate people to become leaders of a movement, but it doesn't
explain why they should become leaders of a particular *kind* of
movement. When we read in Donald's essay: "Basically, Abolitionism should be considered the anguished protest of an aggrieved
class against a world they never made" we can as easily substitute
the name of any protest movement for that of Abolitionists. Donald's specific aim, of telling us why this specific group, the Abolitionists, spurted forward at this specific time, the 1830's, becomes
dissipated into this general conclusion: unfulfilled people become
leaders of movements against the existing order.

I do not claim to know why the Abolitionists became Abolitionists. In a number of years of intimate contact with, and constant
questioning of white Southerners who have become modern-day
Abolitionists—that is, leaders of the desegregation movement—I
have had a hard time finding out exactly why these particular peo-

ple developed the kind of social consciousness that they did. My own attitude toward causation is based on the belief that it is such a complex affair that only when you start off with a particular social aim in mind can you disentangle a definable thread from the causative skein. General searches for causation are doomed from the start, I think.

If it would help us increase the rank of reform leaders by finding some specific x factor whose presence makes persons socially conscious, we might try to isolate it. If we see experience and ideology as causative factors, we can try to bring people into direct contact with social problems, and with books about them, in the hope that this may produce, out of every hundred such persons, one leader. I see no particular social aim in Donald's causative investigation, except that it demeans the lofty idealism of the Abolitionists by presenting them as social malcontents whose real concern is not the misery of the slave but their own place in society.

The psycho-social thesis serves another purpose for Donald. He finds it hard, apparently, to believe that the Abolitionists criticized and attacked Lincoln because he was slow to abolish slavery. This is too simple an explanation—and too easily supported by the evidence. There must be some psychological malaise at the bottom of their hostility; the Abolitionists didn't like Lincoln because of his "plebeian origins, his lack of Calvinistic zeal, his success in corporate law practice, and his skill in practical politics." There is no evidence for this, except that once we accept the unsupported theory about why the Abolitionists became Abolitionists, this seems a logical corollary.

Against Donald's thesis we have the historical facts that the Abolitionists were most angry against Lincoln when he was most hesitant about slavery, that they came to his support when they felt he was moving toward Abolition, that Garrison and Phillips became dramatically more pro-Lincoln once he seemed committed to a course that would end the slave system. We are involved in a peculiar kind of social science, where we must not believe what people say. If the Abolitionists say they don't like Lincoln because he is not militant enough against slavery, it must really be because he is a successful politician in the new society which granted them no such success.

Donald would have us believe that the Abolitionists were opposed to Lincoln because "by his effective actions against slavery
he left the Abolitionists without a cause. . . . For them, Abraham Lincoln was not the Great Emancipator; he was the killer of
the dream." First, Lincoln's actions against slavery were hardly effective. His chief actions were directed toward winning the war,
and his effectiveness was largely in this sphere; the Emancipation
Proclamation itself was seen by him as useful in winning the war;
it certainly was not directly effective in freeing the slaves. That
took the Thirteenth Amendment, and more. Second, what proof,
beyond Donald's own dubious psychological explanation of Abolitionist frustration, is there that the Abolitionists were *sorry* when
slavery ended? We may, with as much justification, accuse every
reform movement in history of regretting its own success because
it is then deprived of a cause.

Shortly after his statement about Lincoln's "effective actions"
against slavery, Donald attacks the Abolitionists for criticizing
Lincoln's hesitation to move on slavery. "Unburdened with the
responsibilities of power, unaware of the larger implications of
actions, they criticized the President's slowness, doubted his good
faith, and hoped for his replacement by a more vigorous emanci-
pationist. Such murmurings and discontents are normal in American political life; in every village over the land there is always at
least one man who can tell the President how the government
ought to be run." Here Donald is missing what the Abolitionists
themselves saw clearly, that the President had his role—and they
had theirs. Donald doesn't see that their prodding of the President
is based on an acute perception of exactly what Donald recognizes as inherent in the Presidency—the tendency of the office to
read public opinion and to act in careful consonance with the
reading.

If Donald understood the role of the agitator as a deliberate
pressure upon the nerve centers of the politician, he would not
look, as he does, for mysterious psychological maladjustments to
explain the agitator's actions. "When a patient reacts with excessive vehemence to a mild stimulus, a doctor at once becomes suspicious of some deep-seated malaise." Is slavery a mild stimulus,
and is a historian a doctor of sorts, with a specialty in psycho-

therapy? "Similarly, the historian should be alert to see in extraordinary and unprovoked violence of expression the symptom of some profound social or psychological dislocation." Was the Abolitionists' violence of expression unprovoked? Here may be the causal explanation for Donald's search for psychological disorder. Is it possible that academic historians are too far removed from the seat of social injustice to understand that deep, burning feeling of hostility which some people develop in the face of evil? If the historian really feels the depths of the social blight which leads an agitator to agitate, then he has no need to look for psychological disturbance.

Donald's biography of Sumner reveals the same search for psychological factors to explain Sumner's powerful hatred of slavery. "Through the influence of Channing, his views on international peace, on prison discipline, and on slavery came to be more carefully thought out and more articulately expressed, but not until personal unhappiness increased Sumner's sensitivity to social injustice did he take an active part in agitating these issues." How many people in public life are unhappy personally without increasing their sensitivity to social injustice? Perhaps personal unhappiness does intensify whatever feelings have already developed in a person. But if so, its role is a supporting and enhancing one, not a causative one, and does not deserve the major attention Donald gives it as a factor in Sumner's intransigent Abolitionism. It so happened that in those very years when Sumner's personal unhappiness increased, the slavery question became more intense, and many other individuals, whose personal lives were different from Sumner's, developed the same kind of increased militancy on the slave issue.

Here is a passage from Donald's biography:

> For as long as Sumner could remember, he had detested slavery. His father taught him that Negroes deserved not merely freedom, but equality and happiness as well. . . . Reading Lydia Maria Child's *An Appeal in Favor of that Class of Americans called Africans,* a tract published in 1833, further helped convince Sumner of the injustice of both slavery and racial discrimination. He found his first actual sight of slaves, on his trip to Washington in 1834, shock-

ing, and he was outraged by the bullying proslavery tone Calhoun's disciples adopted during the 1830's. In 1836 he wrote to Lieber: "We are becoming abolitionists at the North fast."

Sumner's European travels had further strengthened his belief that the United States must abolish slavery. Everywhere abroad he was told that slavery was his country's disgrace.

Is this not enough to constitute the major complex of causes for Sumner's strong Abolitionist feelings? Why do we need to stress his personal difficulties when, as Donald says: "His views were anything but unique, for virtually everyone in Massachusetts shared them."

Can we not reasonably assume that when an evil is severe enough it will stimulate thinking, feeling people—who have been placed in its path by some odd and complex combination of personal and social circumstances—to act against it? This kind of commonsense explanation for the emergence of radical agitators emphasizes that something is wrong with society. The psychological explanations currently popular among some historians emphasize that something is wrong with the agitator. One explanation says: men become radicals because there is evil in the world. The other says: men become radicals because they are psychologically disturbed. Both explanations can be supported by "evidence." Ultimately, which explanation we choose probably depends on whether or not we think the condition of our society today demands more radicals.

II

Lewis Feuer's book, *The Conflict of Generations,* appeared in 1969, a year in which campus demonstrations against the war in Vietnam, for Black Studies programs, for university reform, took place all over the country. Students occupied administration buildings, blocked the passage of army recruiting officers, interfered with representatives of the Dow Chemical Company, protested against R.O.T.C., disrupted commencement exercises.

The Conflict of Generations reveals Feuer's anger at the student movements of today, and in it he invents a theory to legitimize his anger. His theory asserts that student movements, through the last century and a half, driven by some parricidal urge against their elders, have invariably turned to nihilism and terrorism (to irrationality, at the least) and have thus, time after time, set back the march of progress in the world. The bulk of the book is a historical "proof" of his theory—with chapters on the German, Bosnian, Russian, Chinese, Japanese, and other student movements, giving special attention to the current movement in the United States.

At the beginning and end of his large book, Feuer throws in enough statements about the "eternal duality" of selflessness and violence, of idealism and irrationality in student movements, to give the look of that "balanced judgment" which academicians can no more discard than their pants. But in between those few sympathetic murmurs we get nothing but a long cacophony of complaint about the young.

In Feuer's demonology, student movements (and therefore, ultimately, "generational conflict") have been responsible in varying degrees for the following disasters:

1. World War I: because Gavrilo Princip, the Archduke's assassin, was a member of a student movement (Feuer's chapter heading is: The Bosnian Student Movement Blindly Provokes the First World War).

2. Hitlerism: because the 1819 assassination of the dramatist Kotzebue by a member of a German student group led to the repressive Karlsbad decrees, and thus the student movement "was largely responsible for the defeat of German constitutionalism" whereupon "the heritage of the German student movement of 1817 was transmitted to the Nazis."

3. The Bolshevik Revolution: because Alexander II "was about to give a constitution" when a student threw the bomb that killed him, and because Moscow University students preferred revolutionary groups to the Constitutional Democrats, who stood for "the virtues of liberal judgment." (Support of World War I, we might note, was one of these virtues.)

4. Stalinism (he was a "rebellious theological student"): because students assassinated Kirov in 1934 and Komsomol members plotted to assassinate Stalin the following year, which infuriated him.

5. World War II: because student pacifism in the thirties caused "a weakening of the resistance which should have been made to Hitler." (Chamberlain, Daladier, and the American Neutrality Acts are absent; did the students or did the governments have the guns and the power to intercede in Spain and Czechoslovakia? The young radicals can't win with Feuer. He damns them for the Oxford Pledge against war. But when they go off to fight and die in Spain he sees this grouchily as "death in obedience to a drive that was so ill-understood that it set a young man on its quest in a back-to-the-people heroism.")

6. The Chinese Communist Revolution: because "Mao's conflict with his father and its primacy as a motivation for his political ideas were typical of the Chinese students who emerged with him." And by 1926 and 1927 "responsible authorities were flouted." (To call Chinese authority, whether in government or education, "responsible" in that time is to show profound ignorance of Chinese history.)

7. Castroism: because for the student Castro "the United States became a surrogate father to be blamed." (What other reason could there possibly be for a Cuban to resent the United States?)

8. Espionage and treason in America: because "the reason-blinding passion of generational hatred begot a corrupted idealism which led to treason." (Feuer is speaking of the Rosenbergs.)

9. The silence of the fifties: because "the sons rejected the fathers' political gods as broken idols."

10. McCarthyism: because the legacy of the American Student Union was "moral entrapment . . . guilt and consequent depoliticization." But Feuer, like so many righteous critics of the fallen McCarthy, is a fan at heart. He says William Remington was "involved in tawdry espionage." I find obnoxious Feuer's bland acceptance of a court decision in the McCarthy era (challenged by Learned Hand, never reviewed by the Supreme Court, based on the testimony of a paid informer and Remington's divorced wife) of a man convicted of perjury and then murdered in prison.

The value of Feuer's book is that, by carrying to absurdity what other social scientists do with more sophistication, it may awaken us to their methodological inanity and to their deadly aimlessness. How often are we bedazzled by some pretentious concept (often in the form of a catchphrase) which "fits" all elements of the subject under discussion, not noticing that it fits all subjects under all discussions?

Bio-psychological "causes" of human catastrophe are especially appealing because they can be discovered anywhere you look at human behavior. (It is a little like attributing suicide leaps to the law of gravity.) They are also marvelous reinforcers of the going order because they have no operable corrective (unless it is geno-surgery). Explanations of social events by castration complexes insure impotency.

Psychological explanations are comforting to those of us who don't want our little worlds upset, because they emphasize the irrationality of the protester rather than the irrationality of that which produces protest. It seems much easier for us to believe that Abolitionists were vehement because they were upward-striving than that they grasped in some small way the horror of slavery. It is easier to believe that students have "intense, unresolved Oedipal feelings, a tremendous attachment to their mothers, and a violent hostility to their fathers" rather than that they are outraged at a society which (speaking precisely) will not let them live.

Of course, rebels and protesters engage in irrational behavior; of course their tactics are a compound of ingeniousness and desperation, compassion and masochism. Any fool can find the sex drives in black slaves, the indiscriminate resentment of old by young. But the beginning of wisdom is a sense of proportion. Pope Pius XII in his inner mind may have justified his inaction on the gassing of the Jews by thinking about their shrewd ways. We are all tempted to be Deputies for similar, more intellectualized reasons, in a time when there are no more observers in the world, and we are all Jews.

The three-page *Theses on Feuerbach* will guide us better than the five hundred pages of Feuer's book. That can be found in *Marx and Engels: Basic Writings on Politics and Philosophy* (edited by Lewis Feuer, some years ago). The ideas there are not infallible, but they are wise and humane (and, incidentally, more understanding of capitalists than Feuer is of the young). We learn there that the world has real problems which are historically rooted in the particular ways we order our lives. We also learn that these problems are operable, if we will only stop interpreting, and start acting.

10

Liberalism and racism

In the twenties, liberal anthropologists repudiated the theories of Houston Chamberlain and Madison Grant, which attributed the Negro's special and tragic history in America to a set of genetic characteristics marking him as not only physically different but intellectually and morally inferior.* In the forties, liberal historians began to turn from the racist assumptions of scholars like Ulrich Phillips and John Burgess.

Thus, in the past fifty years American liberals began to search for the roots of "the Negro problem" not in innate characteristics, but in acquired attitudes, not in genetics, but in history. This approach, substituting history for biology as a determinant of race relations, took about three hundred years (thinking back to the first shipload of blacks to Jamestown in 1619) to become dominant in politics and the academy. The liberal view of history, however, was a limited one, for it asserted that the plight of the Negro in America had been determined by slavery and segregation—by John Calhoun, George Fitzhugh, Ben Tillman, and John Rankin.

What was left out of the historical accounting was the role of American liberalism, as a collaborator by acquiescence or default, with American racism. The result of this omission was to leave two things unexplained: Why a *minority* of slaveholders had exerted such a powerful effect on the leading liberal revolutionary

* The evidence of belief in biological inferiority goes back to sixteenth and seventeenth century England. See Winthrop D. Jordan, *White Over Black,* U. of North Carolina Press, 1968, Ch. 1. In Virginia, almost as soon as court records began to be kept (1624), racial prejudice appears (1630) in the case of a white man Hugh Davis, who is ordered "to be soundly whipt . . . for abusing himself . . . by defiling his body by lying with a Negro." Helen Catterall, *Judicial Cases Concerning American Slavery and the Negro,* Vol. I, Da Capo, 1968.

nation of the eighteenth and nineteenth centuries; and why the apogee of racial liberalism in the Kennedy and Johnson administrations of the 1960's also brought disillusionment, alienation, and a surge of black radicalism.

This essay is intended only to sketch the history of American liberalism's relationship to the Negro. It suggests—and if the sketch were filled out I believe the suggestion would be strengthened—that current black radicalism is a reasonable response to the hypocrisy which has always tainted that relationship.

Note first, that the forced passage of millions of black slaves to the New World in the sixteenth, seventeenth, eighteenth, and nineteenth centuries was concomitant with the basic features of what we proudly call Western Civilization. Large-scale slavery was a product not of the Dark Ages, but of the Renaissance and the Scientific and Commercial Revolutions; it was expanded not by feudal baronies but by the new national states; its most powerful impetus was not manorialism but capitalism; it was justified not by pagan ritual but by Christian doctrine (by the spokesmen for the Protestant Reformation as well as the Church of Rome).

One of the great sources of American liberal philosophy is John Locke, who also wrote the Fundamental Constitutions for Carolina when it was colonized in 1669, which included the passage: "every freeman of Carolina shall have absolute power and authority over his negro slaves, of what opinion or religion soever." And in Massachusetts, presumably important in creating the American liberal heritage even in the colonial period, the Body of Liberties of 1641 included the provision:

There shall never be any bond slavery, villeinage, or captivity among us, unless it be lawful captives taken in just wars and such strangers as willingly sell themselves or are sold to us.

That word "unless" represents eloquently the deception of self and others that marked liberal America.

American liberalism came to power in the Revolution, and reached its most romantic theoretical expression in the Declaration of Independence. The famous paragraph of Jefferson's which was stricken from the Declaration is often represented as libertarian. But it was directed more at the British slave trade than at

American slavery, and reserved its strongest anger not for the institution of slavery, but for those who would encourage slave revolts. The King was castigated not just for "this execrable commerce" but for "exciting those very people to rise in arms among us."

It was not Jefferson or other liberals who made the first gesture toward emancipation, but Lord Dunmore, Governor General of Virginia, who, six months before the Declaration of Independence was written, declared free all slaves who would bear arms to put down the colonial rebellion. Neither the royalist Lord Dunmore, nor the conservative General Washington, nor the liberal Thomas Jefferson, were moved, except by the exigencies of war and self-interest, to act against Negro slavery. Washington at first opposed the enlistment of Negroes, both free and slave, in the Continental Army, but Dunmore's successful plea stimulated a reversal of policy, and about five thousand free Negroes were eventually permitted to enlist in the Revolutionary army.

Thus, from the very beginning of our national history, it was established that the attitude of government toward the Negro would be determined by expediency, and by the conflict of contending interests, with whatever compromises emerged from such contention. The Revolution was disruptive enough of society to break the loose moorings of slavery in the North, but not elsewhere.

The Constitution put national union first and Negro freedom last, a priority arrangement to which Lincoln later would explicitly subscribe; it was no wonder that Garrison saw fit to burn it publicly.[1] There was fiery debate on the three-fifths compromise, and on the slave trade, neither issue touching the *existence* of slavery. But there was virtually no debate on the fugitive slave provision in Article IV, Section 2: "No person held to service or labor in one state, under the laws thereof, escaping into another shall, in consequence of any law or regulation therein, be discharged from such service or labor, but shall be delivered up on claim of the party to which such service or labor may be due." Roger Sherman pointed out that the return of runaway horses was not demanded with such specific concern, but he got no support from the other members of the Convention.

Southern slavery may have been a "peculiar institution" between the Revolution and the Civil War, but it was sustained and protected by the official policy of the Government of the United States, in all three branches: Congress, the Presidency, the Supreme Court. (The nation managed nonetheless, in the age of Metternich, to remain the symbol of freedom to many in Europe and Latin America.) In 1793, two years after it enacted the Bill of Rights, Congress enacted its first fugitive slave law. And although it proceeded to outlaw the slave trade in 1807 (the slave uprisings in Haiti and in the South had made control of slavery a matter of life and death), the law went unenforced from the beginning, as John Hope Franklin has pointed out.[2] The illicit slave trade, which brought perhaps 250,000 blacks to this country between 1808 and 1860, was really, in Franklin's words "the first underground railroad."

The folk vision of Andrew Jackson has always seen him as one of the great democratic presidents. Arthur Schlesinger, Jr., in his biography, reinforced this picture. He portrayed Jackson, along with Jefferson, as an early prototype of New Deal pluralistic liberalism, "a society in which no single group is able to sacrifice democracy and liberty to its own interests." [3] Schlesinger did not, however, see the white man as such a group, or pay much attention to the anti-Negro aspect of Jackson's liberalism. It was not just that Jackson was himself a slaveholder; he urged Congress, in his message of December 1835, to pass a law to prohibit the circulation of Abolitionist literature in the Southern states. The law was not passed, largely because Southerners themselves did not think it necessary, but Jackson's Postmaster General, and succeeding ones, simply closed their eyes to the fact that local postmasters in the South were removing antislavery literature from the mails.

Roger Taney was Jackson's Attorney General, and appointed by him as Chief Justice of the Supreme Court. His opinion in the Dred Scott case was not an aberration; its conclusion that the Negro was property followed logically the dominant attitude in the federal government. Even Justice Joseph Story, who was considered antislavery, accepted this principle in his 1842 opinion on *Prigg v. Pennsylvania,* when he denied Pennsylvania's right to interfere with the forcible seizure of a runaway slave by his owner.

The quotation used by Leon Litwack as a headnote to his book *North of Slavery* deserves to be repeated, as epitomizing the attitude of the "liberal" half of the country toward the Negro in the period before the civil war; it is from Charles Mackay's account of his tour of North America in 1857–58:

> "We shall not make the black man a slave; we shall not buy him or sell him; but we shall not associate with him. He shall be free to live, and to thrive, if he can, and to pay taxes and perform duties; but he shall not be free to dine and drink at our board—to share with us the deliberation of the jury box—to sit upon the seat of judgment, however capable he may be—to plead in our courts—to represent us in the Legislature—to attend us at the bed of sickness and pain—to mingle with us in the concert-room, the lecture-room, the theatre, or the church, or to marry with our daughters. We are of another race, and he is inferior. Let him know his place—and keep it." This is the prevalent feeling, if not the language of the free North.

The cautious, legalistic, and politically opportunistic approach of Abraham Lincoln has often been noted.* Slavery itself was ended not because of an upsurge of moral resentment in the North, or an insistence on the principle of freedom by the federal government. It was ended because the political and economic interests of the slaveholders clashed with those of the Northern politicians and business interests to the point of war. Expediency, flavored with morality, brought emancipation, and only after prolonged, unrelenting pressure on Lincoln by Abolitionists.[4]

The betrayal of the Negro by liberal Republicans (mistakenly called "radical Republicans"), after emancipation and a brief fling of Negro participation in Southern politics, was to be expected. "Radical Reconstruction" was not based on genuine Negro power, but on the Negro's usefulness—for a while—to Northern politicians. By the second Grant administration it was becoming clear to the dominant forces in the North that the road to their own prosperity and power did not lie in Negro suffrage. Businessmen and politicians needed domestic tranquillity more than any-

---

* See especially the chapter on Lincoln in Richard Hofstadter, *The American Political Tradition,* Alfred Knopf, 1948.

thing else, and this could only be secured with the cooperation of the white elite of the South. C. Vann Woodward has documented how this realization became firm in Washington years before the Wormley Compromise of 1877.[5]

Willie Lee Rose, in her study of the sea islands during and after the Civil War, *Rehearsal for Reconstruction,* notes that with the granting of the franchise, the government thought it had done all it had to do for the Negro. Education and economic freedom, however, were overlooked, and without these as a base, the vote turned out to be meaningless.[6] The fact is that the national government's priorities were different from the Negro's, so that without independent power of his own, the Negro was dependent on the winds of chance blowing the national vessel his way. The winds were right for a few years, but no more.

The Compromise of 1877, based as it was on the reality of the Negro's impotence, was to remain operative for a long time. As Woodward said: "There were no serious infringements of the basic agreements of 1877—those regarding intervention by force, respect for state rights, and the renunciation of Federal responsibility for the protection of the Negro." The Civil Rights Act of 1875 represented a last gasp by the equalitarians in Congress, and when it was voided by the Supreme Court in 1883, this represented, Woodward says, "a sort of validation of the Compromise of 1877." *

The North had signed a nonaggression pact with the South, which meant that the South was now free to commit aggression against the Negro. After 1877, the situation of the Negro descended to what Rayford Logan has called "the nadir." In the eighteen years from 1882 to 1900, 1645 Negroes were lynched. It was the national government that stood by and watched, much as it had watched the institution of slavery before 1860, once again pointing to its legal impotence.**

* *Reunion and Reaction,* p. 266. An unpublished paper by John Hope Franklin also documents the failure of the Justice Department to enforce the 1875 Act.

** For a richly documented account of the period between the Civil War and World War I see Rayford W. Logan, *The Betrayal of the Negro: From Rutherford B. Hayes to Woodrow Wilson,* Collier Books, 1965.

This legal argument was more difficult to sustain with the Fourteenth Amendment, but Justice John Harlan was the only member of the Supreme Court who insisted that the Civil War had emancipated the Negro, not just in name, but in every way. His argument in the Civil Rights Cases of 1883 could have been used as a legal base for protecting the Negro, but no one cared. The rest of the court turned the Fourteenth Amendment to the uses of the corporations, and the fact that the due process clause was now used to protect the property of big business rather than the lives of Negroes represented perfectly the priorities of that age.

The coming of Woodrow Wilson and Theodore Roosevelt, in the "progressive" era, did not change this situation at all. Wilson, in an article in the *Atlantic Monthly* in 1901, said the last thirty years had been a time of unprecedented progress and noted, with apparent approval, that the nation had lost the "passion" of the sixties. There were bloody anti-Negro race riots in 1898 (Greenwood, South Carolina, and Wilmington, North Carolina), in 1904 (Statesboro, Georgia, and Springfield, Ohio), in 1906 (Atlanta, Georgia; Brownsville, Texas; Greensburg, Indiana), and finally in 1908, in Springfield, Illinois, where a mob killed and wounded scores of Negroes. In the Statesboro riot, Theodore Roosevelt was urged to use military power to arrest mob leaders. His Attorney General replied that the Justice Department could not take action. When an Assistant Attorney General prepared evidence for a grand jury, the Attorney General said the federal government had no jurisdiction, and the grand jury was discharged.

Woodrow Wilson was the epitome of American liberalism. He was willing to fight for equal rights for all Princeton boys, but Negroes were another matter. He introduced segregation in the Post Office and Treasury Departments, on the ground that this would result in the least friction. When violence broke out in 1917 in East St. Louis and forty Negroes were stabbed, clubbed, hanged, shot to death, Wilson spoke out against it, but took no action. He offered the same narrow legal ground which his predecessors and successors took: that the murder of Negroes was a local matter, not within the jurisdiction of the Fourteenth Amendment, although that Amendment had been passed precisely to interfere with the right of the states to treat Negroes differently than whites.[7]

The reality of *Negro* powerlessness in the Progressive Period is best illustrated by the fact that although race riots had stimulated the formation of the NAACP in 1910, it was whites who dominated the organization; W. E. B. Dubois was the only Negro officer. (At this time Booker T. Washington was touring Europe saying the United States was making rapid progress in the field of race relations.) American definitions of "Progressive" and "Liberal" have always been based on issues outside of racial equality; hence Thomas Jefferson, Andrew Jackson, Woodrow Wilson, and Theodore Roosevelt are all part of the American liberal tradition, despite their coldness to the Negro.

Certainly the crowning achievements of the Age of Reform came in the New Deal, and nowhere can we find a better test of the thesis that American liberalism has never considered the Negro question one of top priority. FDR, in relieving the distress of the nation's poor, thereby gave relief to the Negro, who was among the poorest. But this only restored the Negro to his pre-depression status: to the miserable ghettos of the North; to subservience, poverty, and violence in the South. Roosevelt's biographer, Frank Freidel, has written: "President Roosevelt seemed ready to leave well enough alone in questions that involved white supremacy." [8]

Roosevelt learned a lesson which was passed on to subsequent presidents (perhaps the idea came from Theodore Roosevelt's dinner invitation to Booker T. Washington): the placement of a few important Negroes in high government posts could substitute for genuine social change. Secretary of the Interior Ickes, himself a member of the NAACP, had several Negroes in important positions in his department (the "Black Cabinet"). Mrs. Roosevelt made some kindly speeches on behalf of Negro rights. FDR himself spoke out against lynching. But he gave no real support to anti-lynching bills, and the federal government remained as inactive against Southern violence as ever. Walter White wrote bitterly in 1935 about the "U.S. Department of (White) Justice," which he said "may lay claim to one hundred percent performance in at least one branch of its activities—the evasion of cases involving burning questions of Negro rights." [9]

The Negro, without power himself, and low on the priority list of even the most liberal of national administrations, had to wait once again for a confluence of expediency and morality in national affairs. This came with the Second World War, where national survival was at stake, and now, as with the Revolutionary and Civil Wars before, an impetus was created toward Negro emancipation. The desegregation of the armed forces, begun in the Truman administration, was intended to meet the raised expectations of Negroes who had fought in large numbers in the war; because it did not constitute direct interference with Southern politics it was not politically dangerous.*

In 1954 came the Supreme Court's decision in the Brown Case. Like the Emancipation Proclamation, the decision had its greatest effect where vested interests were weakest (in the border states)—and least effect in the hard-core States of the deep South (South Carolina, Georgia, Mississippi, Alabama, Louisiana, Arkansas). There were a few dramatic instances of immediate and massive school desegregation (Washington, Baltimore, Louisville), but the life of the Negro in the South—and indeed in the nation—remained basically as before. President Eisenhower's use of troops in Little Rock in 1957 was a sharp break with the reluctance of past presidents to display federal power in the South; but it was a token gesture. The Deep South, with but marginal changes, successfully kept the Negro segregated despite the Supreme Court decision.**

Another liberal President (Andrew Jackson) had once said of a Supreme Court Justice, "John Marshall made his decision; now let him enforce it." The Supreme Court could not enforce its own decisions; and no President of the United States, in the context of American liberal tradition, would act decisively to enforce the succession of court decisions outlawing racial discrimination in schools and other public facilities. It was Negro impatience with the slow workings of American liberalism that brought the demonstrative phase of the Negro revolt. Liberals saw the rise of Negro

* The historian William C. Berman, who has worked extensively with the *Truman Papers,* suggests that the rival candidacy of Henry Wallace in 1948 was an important factor pushing Truman toward his decision.

** See the report of the *Southern Regional Council* in 1967, "Lawlessness and Disorder: Fourteen Years of Failure in Southern School Desegregation."

militancy as a reaction to Southern segregationist intransigence, but it was just as much a reaction to the timorousness of the national government.

The revolt began with the Montgomery bus boycott of 1955, continued with the sit-ins of 1960, the Freedom Rides of 1961, the mass marches in Albany, Georgia in 1961 and 1962, the demonstrations in Birmingham in 1963, the Mississippi Summer of 1964. These were the first mass expressions of Negro power exploding within the political structure. They unsettled Washington sufficiently to bring a series of concessions: the Civil Rights Acts of 1957, 1960, 1964, 1965. Almost everything in the new legislation could have been accomplished by executive action, based on the Fourteenth and Fifteenth Amendments. But the passage of laws was useful to the national government; it shifted attention from demonstrations in the streets to debates in Congress, and created the appearance of enormous achievement. The new laws, however, like those passed a century earlier, were not vigorously enforced.

The fate of voting legislation was an example. Voting discrimination against Negroes was explicitly made illegal by the Fifteenth Amendment; all it needed was Presidential enforcement. However, it became the subject of Congressional action in 1957, and again in 1960, each time with meager results. More legislation was passed in 1964, once more with little change. Finally, came the Voting Rights Act of 1965. When all this had been done, the Department of Justice was still acting feebly, utilizing the federal registrar provision of the 1965 act in only a small portion of the areas where such registrars were needed. Now, finally, a significant increase in Negro registration began to appear in the deep South; but with economic power still absent, the Southern Negro was bound to repeat the history of the First Reconstruction, when the franchise, without an economic base, turned out to be an illusory promise.

The limits of American liberalism's accomplishments for the Negro were clear by 1969. A few Negroes had the money and the courage to take advantage of the laws outlawing discrimination in hotels, restaurants, parks, transportation facilities. *Some* Negroes had the incentive and the courage to register to vote. But two overwhelming realities persisted. One was the physical helplessness of the Negro in the face of violence committed by private persons and by the police, while the federal government, through the Department of Justice, insisted that it could not legally protect Negroes against such violence.* And second, was the continuing, desperate poverty of the Negro, in the rural areas of the South, and in the festering ghettos North and South.** Nothing in the whole spate of liberal legislation touched these two facts.

This failure of American liberalism at a time of heightened expectations explains the black uprisings in the big cities outside the South: in Harlem in 1964, in Los Angeles in 1965, in Chicago in 1966, and in 150 cities in 1967. These were, for the most part, unorganized, spontaneous bursts of rage at the life of the Negro in the ghetto. They recalled the prophecy in Langston Hughes' poem about "a dream deferred" when he finally asks: "Or does it explode?"

The long, consistent story (only outlined in these pages) *** of the failure of the United States, even in its most liberal hours, to allow justice to the black man, does not add up to a deliberate plot against him. But neither does it suggest a set of accidents. It does bespeak a set of factors, built deep into American society, which perpetuate racial injustice whether the national leaders are liberal or conservative, Republican or Democrat, Southern or Northern.

What are these factors? I would propose, without extended argument, the following:

1. The historical fact of slavery, which casts the spell of infe-

---

* For a casuistic defense of federal inaction, see Burke Marshall's *Federalism and Civil Rights,* Columbia University Press, 1964; and for a devastating critique of Marshall, see the review of his book by a former Justice Department attorney, Richard Wasserstrom, in the *University of Chicago Law Review,* Winter, 1966.

** See the Report of the *National Advisory Commission on Civil Disorders,* Ch. 7.

*** For a more detailed account of the coldness of the Kennedy and Johnson administrations to the black person in America, see my book, *SNCC: The New Abolitionists,* Beacon Press, 1964. Also see *Law Enforcement in Mississippi,* Southern Regional Council, 1964. And the Civil Rights Commission Report, *Law Enforcement,* 1965.

riority over the black person. It is a spell which could be lifted, and in the absence of other factors would dissipate, but added to everything else is a reinforcement of institutionalized degradation.

2. The economic fact of capitalism, which puts profit and property before human rights, whether for slaveholders or real estate dealers; which distributes wealth inequitably, creating a class of poor. And if there must be a class of poor in the country, other factors will see to it that the blacks will dominate that class.

3. The political fact of power and privilege, exerted by an elite for an elite (despite Lincoln's noble words, which represented hope, not reality) and which, in any choice between betrayal of ideals and loss of privilege, will choose betrayal.

4. The psychological fact of racism, which insures that when physical difference is accompanied by other motives (such as those named above) subordination will take on a special cruelty.

None of these factors is peculiar to American liberalism. Racism exists in other countries, whether autocratic or democratic, capitalist or socialist. All that is asserted here is the falseness of the claim that American liberalism escapes the brutalities of other systems. What is implied is that no government, not even the most praised, can be entrusted with the liberties of its citizens, who will always have to fight for their own safety, security, and dignity.

11

Albany, Georgia, and the New Frontier

Traditionally, historians avoid writing the history of contemporary events. But why? Yesterday is the past, as is the nineteenth century. A perspective one year after an event is no less valuable than a perspective a hundred years later, only different. And if historians must rely for data of the past on the reporting of others, which they then cherish as "primary sources," why should they not create their own primary sources for both present and future use?

It is from this viewpoint that I offer in the following pages a history of the Albany, Georgia, racial crisis of 1961–62.[1] Six years after the Montgomery bus boycott, and shortly after the freedom rides of 1961, Albany became the scene of the first of those mass revolts against local police power which have shaken the South and the nation in the past decade. It is a study in detail of the general historical pattern traced in the preceding chapter.

Many Georgians call it All-benny. Before the Civil War, this was cotton and slave country, and Albany was a trading center, the seat of Dougherty County. W. E. B. DuBois, in *The Souls of Black Folk,* described the area:

> For a radius of a hundred miles about Albany stretched a great fertile land, luxuriant with forests of pine, oak, ash, hickory, and poplar, hot with the sun and damp with the rich black swampland; and here the cornerstone of the Cotton Kingdom was laid.

By the turn of the century, Albany was a placid little town. Blacks outnumbered whites, slavery was gone, and segregation was firmly in place.

Today, the city is a four-hour drive by automobile straight south from Atlanta, past scraggly cotton, clusters of Black Angus cattle, and beautiful brown fields of pecan trees. Wide-avenued and clean, it lies south of Kinchafoonee Creek, on the banks of the Flint River. It is a commercial center for Southwest Georgia, where corn, cattle, and pecans are traded. "Tenth fastest booming city in the U.S.A.," the man at the Chamber of Commerce told me. "There's the rating—in black and white."

But Albany always rated higher for whites than for blacks, and this was at the root of the mass demonstrations and mass arrests that shook the city in December 1961 and then again the following summer.

Negroes made up 40 percent of Albany's population (23,000 out of 56,000) and zero percent of its political officials. Whites and blacks had different perceptions of their city. Again and again, I was told by whites—in the office of a political leader, in the anteroom of a businessman, in the living room of a middle-class family: "Albany has always had good race relations. . . . Our colored folks are satisfied. . . . We have made considerable progress." To blacks, the "peace" that had been true of Albany was paid for by them—in a grossly unequal distribution of social goods. To them the "progress" (the paving of some streets in Negro neighborhoods, the lighting of the Negro football field, the building of an air-conditioned Negro school) was a set of mild reforms inside a huge prison.

In the year 1961, a Negro arrived in Albany on the colored part of the bus, entered a colored waiting room, drank from a colored fountain, used a colored restroom, walked eight blocks to find a restaurant which would feed him, and traveled six miles to find a colored motel. Once inside the city, he had better avoid trouble: the courtrooms were segregated, the jails were segregated, the judges, juries, sheriffs, deputies, and city police were all white. Tax forms for Negroes had a special color. He might get a job, but only after color had narrowed the field to a slit. "If I can do a job as good as a white man, why shouldn't I have it?" a Negro porter asked me as we stood on the steps of the white church where he was employed.

Early in 1961, the century-long quiescence of Albany Negroes began to break. Perhaps it was shaken by the sit-ins, freedom rides, and boycotts which had been successful elsewhere in the South, perhaps vaguely stirred by the rise of colored peoples in Africa and Asia, or, more likely, by a combination of factors too complex for easy categorization.

In February, a group of Negro leaders in Albany presented the city commissioners with a request to initiate the desegregation of certain municipal facilities. The Albany *Herald,* the city's only daily (owned by James Gray, the most powerful political figure in Albany), answered for the City Commission and flatly rejected the request. About the same time, sporadic incidents occurred on the campus of the Negro college in town, Albany State, where marauding whites in automobiles threw eggs, fired shots, and tried to run down a Negro student.

It was against this background of local unrest, frustration, and developing action that the Atlanta-based Student Nonviolent Coordinating Committee (SNCC) sent a team into Albany in September 1961 to register Negro voters. SNCC was born out of the sit-in struggles of 1960 and was staffed by a small group of former college students who had experienced jailings and beatings in the sit-ins and freedom rides. They set up an office in a run-down little building two blocks from the Shiloh Baptist Church, began to register Negro voters in the city, and through their enthusiasm and energy acted as a catalyst to a community which had already begun to stir.

On November 1, 1961, in direct response to the freedom rides of that summer, the Interstate Commerce Commission handed down its ruling that all train and bus facilities used for interstate commerce were to be desegregated and were to show signs announcing this. SNCC was ready to test the ruling in the segregated terminals of Albany on the very first day of its existence. A white college girl from Memphis named Salynn McCollum served as witness when a group of Negro students walked into the white waiting room of the Trailways Bus Terminal in Albany and were ordered out by police. SNCC notified the Department of Justice.

That was the first test of whether the national government would enforce the ICC ruling. It failed the test. Nothing came of the complaint.

A few weeks later, the Albany Movement was formed—of SNCC, the local NAACP, the colored ministerial alliance, and other Negro groups. They expressed their determination to attack discrimination in all areas. One of the leaders said: "The kids were going to do it anyway . . . they were holding their own mass meetings and making plans . . . we didn't want them to have to do it alone."

On the morning of November 22, three members of the Youth Council of the NAACP in Albany were arrested by Chief of Police Pritchett for returning to the Trailways Terminal lunchroom after he had ordered them out. And in the afternoon, two Albany State students were arrested for going into the white waiting room. (They became the first of forty students expelled by Albany State College for participating in the Movement.) With these two incidents, the Department of Justice failed its second and third tests. It did nothing.

The fourth test, on December 10, was the most dramatic. With several hundred Albany Negroes at the railroad station to greet them, an integrated SNCC group of eight rode from Atlanta to Albany, sat together in the white car, entered the white waiting room at the Albany terminal, were ordered out by Chief Pritchett, and were arrested as they were leaving the terminal and getting into automobiles. They were charged with obstructing traffic, disorderly conduct, and failure to obey an officer. A. C. Searles, editor of the Negro weekly *Southwest Georgian,* watched the scene and reported: "There was no traffic, no disturbance, no one moving. The students had made the trip to Albany desegregated without incident. Things had gone so smoothly I think it infuriated the chief."

Again, the Department of Justice failed, and by that failure ignited the conflict that exploded in Albany the week before Christmas 1961.

Now the Albany Movement went into action. The next seven days saw a series of mass meetings by the Negro community and marches downtown by over a thousand Albany Negroes, singing and praying, asking freedom for the arrested students and, as one woman said after her release from prison, "to get our rights." The long silence in Albany was ending.

When the trial of the freedom riders was to take place at the city courthouse two days after the arrest, over four hundred Negro high school and college students marched downtown to protest, singing as they went by the courthouse. Police cars with loudspeakers ordered them to disperse, but they continued to walk. Then they were herded into a fifteen-foot-wide alley running alongside City Hall, where they waited in a driving rain for two hours as police booked them one by one on the same charges levied against the freedom riders. Three different demonstrations took place the next day: a prayer meeting in front of City Hall, and two marches; hundreds more were arrested. Chief of Police Pritchett told newsmen: "We can't tolerate the NAACP or the SNCC or any other nigger organization to take over this town with mass demonstrations."

On Friday night, Martin Luther King, Jr., invited by the Albany Movement Executive Committee, arrived from Atlanta with Rev. Ralph Abernathy and spoke to a packed prayer meeting at the Shiloh Baptist Church. King told the audience of over a thousand: "Don't stop now. Keep moving. Don't get weary. We will wear them down with our capacity to suffer." The next day he led two hundred and fifty hymn-singing men, women, and youngsters down Jackson Street toward the county courthouse. Police Chief Pritchett stopped them two blocks from the City Hall and asked King if he had a parade permit. King said, "We are simply going to pray at City Hall." Pritchett ordered the entire group arrested for parading without a permit.

The total arrested now stood at 737, with many people farmed out to prisons in nearby counties. Late Saturday night, sound trucks moved through the city calling military personnel back to the Air Force and Marine Corps bases. Police closed bars and liquor stores.

Negotiations between the Albany Movement and city officials ended a few days later with a verbal agreement on the calling off of demonstrations, the release of those in jail, and a promise by the city to hear Negro demands. People streamed out of the jails to the Shiloh Baptist Church and I listened to their stories. Charles Sherrod, just out of Terrell County jail, told of Sheriff Zeke Mathews who announced to his prisoners: "There'll be no damn singin' and no damn prayin' in my jail." Sherrod told him: "We may be in jail, but we're still human beings and still Christians." The Sheriff hit him in the face. They took him into another room, and another officer hit him.

Fifty-one women had been sent to the Lee County stockade. There was no place to sleep, just wet and dirty mattresses in the cell.

Eula Jackson spent four days in "Bad Baker" county jail: "Peas and grits are what they gave us. They would put it on the floor and kick it into the cell. I didn't eat for four days."

Another woman: "We were eighty-eight in one room from Saturday night to Monday night, with twenty steel bunks and no mattresses. . . . Sheriff took us to Camilla. On the bus he told us: 'We don't have no singin', no prayin', and no handclappin' here.' "

A man arrested Saturday night: "No one put a hand on me, but I feel like I been beaten. When you sleep on steel and concrete you are automatically sore. I'm a trailer driver, on the job a year, came back to work this morning, found I got no job. They told me: 'You a Freedom Marcher.' "

Another man: "Forty-two of us in a cell for twelve in the city jail. Then we were put in a bullpen, sixty men, sixteen beds, all standin' up on one another. The food? Oh bad, man!"

A young married woman, senior at Albany State College, left two children with her mother and demonstrated Wednesday evening. She slept on an iron cot in the city jail and got sick. For two days she ate nothing. Slater King, in the same prison, tried to slip his food to her through a hole in the door, but a guard came along and hit him in the back.

One of the women had worked a year at a cleaning establishment. Thirty dollars a week, $28.10 net. Six days a week, twelve hours a day. When she was forced to work until 10 P.M. one night and got no extra pay, she left her job, got another. Now, with her arrest, that job was gone too.

It wasn't the prison conditions that hurt these people deep inside, but the reason for it all. The young woman from Albany State said: "I didn't expect to go to jail for kneeling and praying at City Hall."

That truce of December 1961 did not take much time to fall

apart. On Friday, January 12, 1962, an eighteen-year-old Negro girl named Ola Mae Quarterman, a former student at Albany State College, sat down in a front seat of an Albany city bus. The driver left his seat, poked his finger near her face, and the conversation went something like this: "Don't you know where you're supposed to sit?" Her reply: "I paid my damn twenty cents and I can sit where I want." He called a policeman and she was arrested and jailed. The reason for the arrest, Police Chief Pritchett said, was that she had used vulgar language ("damn").

"I used the word 'damn' in regard to my twenty cents, not to the driver," Miss Quarterman later stated at a federal court hearing, but the distinction seemed lost on the court. At that hearing, the city attorney tried to establish that she was arrested for using vulgar language, rather than for sitting in the front of the bus. It was all part of an elaborate judicial game played in Southern courtrooms in which everyone pretends that the race of the arrested person was the farthest thing from the policeman's mind, and tries to invent interesting new charges for the arrest.

But Ola Mae Quarterman did not want to play. When the city attorney asked, "You weren't tried for sitting where you were sitting, were you?" she replied quietly, "That's what they said," and then repeated more loudly for the benefit of the court, *"That's what they said."*

She was found guilty of using "obscene" language, and a boycott by Negroes of the city bus system, already under way, was intensified. In less than three weeks the company, dependent for much of its revenue on Negro customers, halted operations.

Later in January, the Albany Movement presented its requests for desegregation of various city facilities to the City Commission, as provided in the December agreement. The Commission denied all the requests, saying: "The demand for privileges will scarcely be heard, wherever and whenever voiced, unless . . . arrogance, lawlessness, and irresponsibility subside." Negro leaders could "earn acceptance for their people," the Commission said, "by encouraging the improvement of their moral and ethical standards."

In March, the trial of the original Freedom Riders jailed by Chief Pritchett on December 10 began in the county court. When Charles Sherrod entered the courtroom that morning, he walked down front to the "white" section and was immediately knocked to the floor by Chief Deputy Lamar Stewart, who pulled him back to the rear of the courtroom. Bob Zellner and two other white defendants, Tom Hayden and Per Laursen, as well as Tom's wife, Sandra Hayden, sat down next to Sherrod in the rear. Deputies pounced on them and dragged them out of the courtroom. One deputy pulled Mrs. Hayden over a row of seats and pushed her through a revolving door. Judge Carl E. Crow watched all of this and then told newsmen: "The officers were enforcing a rule of the court."

About the same time, a Negro cafe-operator in Albany named Walter Harris was shot to death by a policeman who claimed Harris had attacked him with a knife while resisting arrest. Perhaps there was a need now to make up for the silence that had followed previous slayings of Negroes by police officers for "resisting arrest." Perhaps there was a recollection of Charles Ware, in prison since 1960, who had been shot repeatedly through the neck by officers of Baker County for "resisting arrest." At any rate, twenty-nine adults and teen-agers appeared in front of City Hall after the Harris shooting, to protest. Refusing to disperse, they were arrested, and when some youngsters lay down on the sidewalk in a show of passive resistance they were picked up and carried into police headquarters.

Meanwhile, Martin Luther King, Jr., and Ralph Abernathy had been called back to Albany from Atlanta to stand trial for leading that parade in December. The defense attorneys argued that the arrests were based on the desire to maintain segregation, that they violated the First Amendment rights of free speech and assembly, as well as the Fourteenth Amendment right to equal protection of the laws. But the city said race was not an issue in the arrests at all; the Chief of Police was merely enforcing a statute that required a permit for parades. When Chief Pritchett was asked how a "parade" was defined, he said there was no definition. "Then it's anything you want to make it?" The reply: "In my opinion, yes."

King and Abernathy were found guilty, sentenced to forty-five days in jail. Defense attorney asked the judge for the legal citations on which his decision was based. The judge said he didn't have any, but that it was based on "general research of the law."

The defendants chose jail rather than the fine, and excitement rose in Albany and throughout the nation. With a mass prayer meeting scheduled by the Albany Movement for City Hall, Mayor Kelley flew to Columbus to see Federal District Judge J. Robert Elliott. Elliott, an old associate of the Talmadges in Georgia politics and a public supporter of segregation, had just been appointed to his post by President Kennedy. At midnight on Friday, July 20, on the eve of the scheduled prayer meeting, Elliott issued an omnibus injunction that barred "unlawful picketing, congregating or marching in the streets . . . participating in any boycott in restraint of trade" and, in fact, "any act designed to provoke breaches of the peace."

With the temporary restraining order in effect, the planned Saturday afternoon demonstration did not take place, but in the evening a group of one hundred and sixty persons, young and old, began to walk from Shiloh Baptist Church toward City Hall, and were arrested under orders of Chief Pritchett. Many of the marchers were thirteen and fourteen years old, and they were sent to Camilla in nearby Mitchell County. "They call it a juvenile detention place," one youngster said. "But it's just an old jailhouse." Sixty-four were put in a cell designed for twelve children, fifty-two others in a cell designed for eight.

Two days later, Mrs. Slater King, wife of the Albany Movement's vice-president, and in her sixth month of pregnancy, drove to Camilla with a group of other Negro women to take food to the daughter of a friend. She had her three children along and was carrying one of them. Two deputies ordered the group away from the outer fence around the jail. "All you niggers get away from the fence," one of them demanded. The women began to move away, Mrs. King walking slowly to her car. One of the deputies pointed her out, cursed her, and said if she did not hurry, she would be arrested. She turned and said, "If you want to arrest, go ahead." The next thing she knew she was kicked and knocked to the ground. An officer hit her twice on the side of her head and she lost consciousness. She revived in about ten minutes and since no one else in her car could drive, managed to drive back to Albany. Months later, Mrs. Slater King lost her baby.

One of the young people arrested that week was a white SNCC field worker from Cincinnati named William Hansen; he was promptly put into the white section of Dougherty County jail. Depositing him in the cell, a deputy said to a trusty: "This is one of those guys who came down here to straighten us out." The trusty replied: "Well, I'll straighten him out." As Hansen sat on the cell floor reading a newspaper, he was attacked and beaten into unconsciousness. His jaw was broken, his lip was split, and a number of ribs were broken. He was then transferred to the city jail.

Late that afternoon, Attorney C. B. King, brother of Slater King, and the only Negro lawyer in Albany, visited Sheriff Cull Campbell to check on the condition of Hansen. Seeing King in his office, the Sheriff said: "Nigger, haven't I told you to wait outside?" King turned to say something. The Sheriff pulled a walking stick out of a basket (a sign on the basket says they are made by the blind and sell for fifty cents to courthouse visitors) and brought it down with all his force on King's head. The attorney staggered from the office, blood streaming down his face and onto his clothes, and made his way across the street to Chief Pritchett, who called for medical aid.

New York *Times* reporter Claude Sitton quoted Sheriff Campbell as saying, "He didn't get out so Goddammit, I put him out." Sitton also noted in his story that "Chief Pritchett had more than 160 city, county and state law enforcement officers standing by to prevent violence." Pritchett had just arrested twenty-eight Negroes for praying and singing for fifteen minutes in front of City Hall. He called the beating of King "very regrettable."

A month later, arriving in Albany on my second visit, I went to see Sheriff Campbell. The basket of walking sticks was in the hall. The Sheriff invited me into his office and said: "You're not with the goddam niggers, are you?" I thought it better not to reply. Instead, I asked him about the affair of Attorney King. He stared at me. "Yeh, I knocked hell out of the son-of-a-bitch, and I'll do it again. I wanted to let him know . . . I'm a white man and he's a damn nigger."

In early August, a white couple and six Negroes were arrested in Albany for attempting to use a bowling alley. Among them was sixteeen-year-old Shirley Gaines, who had spent time in jail in Camilla back in April when she protested the killing of Walter Harris by police. Arrested at the bowling alley, she sat on the steps waiting for the paddy wagon to park nearby. As she waited, she later told me, two policemen threw her dress over her head, held her by her legs, dragged her down the stone steps to the bottom, and left her lying there. A man came along and kicked her in the side, and when she cried out, a policeman standing nearby said, "Nigger, you can holler louder than that," then dragged her into the paddy wagon. With her back hurt, she lay on the floor inside City Hall. A man kept opening a swinging door near her, hitting her head each time. As she kept crying out, a policeman dashed water in her face to quiet her, and another called, "Holler, nigger."

A policeman then carried her, meanwhile kicking her with his knee, into the paddy wagon again, pushed her on the floor, and took her to Putney Hospital. But when the examiner found she couldn't rise since her back still hurt, she was taken to a city doctor. The doctor shone a light on her back, announced he found no injury, and said: "There ain't nothing wrong with that nigger. She got a good kickin'." She spent a day in city jail, then was examined by a Negro osteopath who found her back bruised and scarred.

Police Chief Pritchett was hailed in newspapers all over the country that summer for preventing violence in Albany. An Atlanta *Constitution* reporter did a piece on Pritchett in which he did not conceal his admiration. A reporter for the New York *Herald Tribune* said Pritchett "brought to Albany a standard of professional achievement that would be difficult to emulate in a situation so made to order for violence. . . ."

It was a classic example of what Americans have usually meant by the prevention of violence, the maintenance of law and order: the perpetuation of the usual distribution of goods and liberties favoring the rich and the white, ignoring the poor and the black; the subjugation, by police power, of anyone daring to challenge the going order. Chief Pritchett earned praise, North and South, among conservatives and liberals, by simply putting into prison every man, woman, and child who dared protest in any way the infringement of rights guaranteed to them by the Constitution. He had arrested more than a thousand people for praying, singing, marching, or picketing. He did not make a single move toward arrest when Sheriff Campbell, just across the street, bludgeoned C. B. King and the attorney staggered, still bleeding, into Pritchett's office.

In an incident reported by journalist Murray Kempton, a tiny boy showed up in the line of Negroes being booked at Albany's City Hall after a protest parade. "How old are you?" Chief Pritchett asked.

"Nine," the boy replied.

"What is your name?" the Chief asked.

"Freedom, freedom," was the response.

The Chief said: "Go home, freedom."

What was the national government doing all this time?

Constitutionally, the federal government has the power, via the First Amendment, the Fourteenth Amendment, and a set of laws passed after the Civil War, to enforce with any means it chooses the rights of its citizens—to speech and assembly, to freedom from racial discrimination—in every corner of the Union, local officials notwithstanding. It can secure a network of injunctions to bar in advance interference with constitutional rights. It can use federal agents to prevent local officials or private persons from depriving citizens of their rights. It can prosecute police officers or anyone else who violates someone's constitutional rights.*

Never in its history has the government of the United States used these powers to protect effectively black people against police action depriving them of their liberties. And in the case of Albany, Georgia, the administration of John F. Kennedy, who had promised a "New Frontier," was no exception.

Throughout the events of December 1961, the FBI dutifully sat

---

* For extended legal argument on this, see my chapter, "Which Side Is the Federal Government On?" in *SNCC: The New Abolitionists,* Beacon, 1964. Also, see Jack Greenberg, *Race Relations and American Law,* Columbia University Press, 1959. Also, Leon Friedman, ed., *Southern Justice,* Pantheon, 1965.

in its office in Albany and took dozens upon dozens of affidavits from Negro citizens complaining that their constitutional rights had been violated by city and county officials. But they got no action. In the spring and summer of 1962, hundreds of Negroes were once again deprived of their constitutional rights by city and county officials. Again, no action. Speaking of the FBI, a young Negro told me bitterly, "They're a bunch of racists."

In the midst of the December arrests, *The New York Times* reported from Albany: "The Justice Department was watching developments here closely." Nine months later, after shotgun blasts ripped into a home in Terrell County where Negro and white registration workers were staying, a Department of Justice spokesman said in Washington: "We are watching the situation very, very closely."

In June 1962 six months after several flagrant violations of the ICC ruling, the Atlanta *Journal*'s Washington correspondent reported: "The U.S. Justice Department has launched an investigation of alleged bus station segregation in Albany." In July several Department of Justice lawyers were sent to Albany. On the 26th of that month, according to the Atlanta *Constitution,* Mayor Kelley conferred in Washington with Attorney General Robert Kennedy. The newspaper report said: "Kelley said he told Kennedy that Albany's racial problems are dealt with by local people. Kelley said Kennedy agreed with him."

Whether or not Kelley was telling the truth, the Attorney General of the United States *acted* as if he were.

The Atlanta *Journal*'s Washington correspondent reported in July: "Justice Department officials described the Albany trouble Monday as 'a tense situation' but added that Mayor Asa Kelley and Chief of Police Laurie Pritchett 'have certainly indicated a strong desire to maintain order.' They said they had received no evidence that Albany police are not furnishing adequate law protection." This was immediately after Attorney C. B. King, with more than one hundred city and county police nearby, had received his bloody beating at the hands of the Dougherty County Sheriff.

Near the end of the summer, after receiving angry telegrams, after the picketing of the White House by citizens from both North and South, and after face-to-face pleas from Roy Wilkins of the

NAACP and William Kunstler of the American Civil Liberties Union, the Department of Justice made two weak legal moves: First, it entered a friend-of-the-court brief to support the Albany Movement's request that an injunction against further demonstrations be denied; and second, it asked for an injunction (after a violation of voting rights in Terrell County so outrageous that usually calm reporters on the scene were upset) to prevent certain officials in Southwest Georgia from interfering with voter-registration activities.

Only once in the Albany troubles did the national administration show a real burst of energy; that was when Martin Luther King, Jr., was jailed on July 10. The President asked for a report, the Attorney General got busy, the Assistant Attorney General in charge of civil rights made telephone calls, and the next day King was out of jail. But there was no such deep concern for the hundreds of ordinary citizens in Albany who went to jail about the same time for basically the same reason.

In the summer of 1963, the United States government, so passive in the Albany events of the previous year, moved into action: the Department of Justice initiated its first large-scale criminal prosecution—against eight Negro leaders and a white student in the Albany Movement.

It all arose out of an incident in "Bad Baker" County in 1961. A Negro named Charlie Ware had been shot four times, while in handcuffs, as he was taken into custody by the Sheriff. Charging a violation of his civil rights under federal law, Ware sued the Sheriff for $125,000. At the trial, held in Macon in April 1963, an all-white jury dismissed the claim.

One of the jurors was Carl Smith, who owned a supermarket in Albany. Businessmen in Albany had been picketed for over a year as part of a general boycott by the Albany Movement, but when Carl Smith's store was picketed, shortly after the Ware trial ended, FBI agents seemed to be swarming all over the place. And shortly afterward, the Albany Movement leaders were indicted, tried, and convicted for conspiring to obstruct justice by picketing and boycotting Smith's supermarket, or for perjury in connection with the charges of picketing.

The picket signs around Smith's store had asked that Smith hire

Negroes in his store; no signs mentioned the Ware trial. After one day of picketing, Smith—who had been grossing over $200,000 a year, closed up the store, "driven out of business," thus establishing a perfect federal case.

During the trials, it was disclosed that at least thirty-eight FBI agents had worked on the prosecutions. Never, during all the beatings and jailings of the past two years, had there been that many FBI agents in evidence in Albany. The prosecutions could not have been undertaken without the approval (or, to put it more cautiously, over the opposition) of Attorney General Robert Kennedy. A representative of the Department of Justice came down from Washington to sit with the U.S. Attorney during the trials. Negroes drawn for possible jury service were removed by the peremptory challenge of the government of the United States.

It was an irony of shattering proportions. My own reaction was to think immediately of Slater King, whom I had interviewed in Albany right after the beating of his wife by deputy sheriffs, and who had spoken of the indifference of the FBI men who were investigating her complaint. He had been jailed and physically abused. His brother had received a bloody caning at the hands of the sheriff. None of this led to federal action. Then his wife had lost the baby she was carrying at the time she was beaten. Now he was convicted and sentenced to a year in jail, in an action initiated by the United States Government.*

All the events of those years in Albany, Georgia—the rhetoric of the "New Frontier" notwithstanding—gave powerful evidence, once more, that the American Government, in its action and in its passivity, was on the side of power and privilege and the white race.

I recall particularly driving from dirt road onto dirt road deep in the cotton and peanut land of Lee County to talk to James Mays, a teacher and farmer. He showed me the damage done by thirty bullets which hours before, in the middle of the night, had been fired through the doors and windows of his house, and had crashed into the walls around the heads of nineteen sleeping persons, most of them children. At dawn, he had quickly lettered a

---

* Ultimately, the convictions were thrown out on appeal. In 1969, Slater King was killed in an auto accident.

sign of protest and stood, holding it up, on the main road to Leesburg. It was clear that, although he was a member of a nation whose power stretched around the globe and into space, James Mays was on his own.

After Albany, the betrayal by the national government continued, despite oratory from the White House and more laws passed by Congress. The pattern of brutality against the Negro and inaction by the United States Government was repeated dozens of times in Alabama, Mississippi, and elsewhere in the Deep South. Starting in 1965, it would also become dramatically clear in cities of the North. That pattern, so obvious in the Albany crisis, so pervasive in America as to suggest much more than an aberration susceptible to liberal reform, helps explain the rise of angry militancy, Black Power, and the new revolutionary spirit among young black people in this country.

12

Aggressive liberalism

The concept of paradox is useful to our innocence. We keep it as a last defense, first erecting two other barriers. The first is not to look for, or not to see, those facts that challenge our deepest beliefs. The second is (when the world will not tolerate our ignorance) to keep separate in our consciousness those elements which, brought together, would explode the myths of our culture. When both those restraining walls collapse, we fall back, as an emergency measure, on the explanation: It's one of those paradoxes—an incredible but true combination.

With this triple defense, the liberal democracy of the Western world, bedecked with universal suffrage, parliamentary representation, technological progress, mass education, Bills of Rights, social welfare, has managed to maintain its reputation for beneficence—despite its record of imperialism, war, racism, and exploitation. The unpleasant facts are first ignored (or made pallid by judicious juxtaposition with the more blatant sins of others). Then they are kept in a different compartment of the brain. Then, when the brain is so jostled that separation becomes impossible, the essential goodness of what we call Western Civilization is kept intact by the concept of paradox. Thus, liberalism can remain unscratched by the most prurient of juxtapositions, and the entire social system for which it is the shorthand symbol—the bad as well as the good—can remain unquestioned.

It is the first line of defense that this essay will deal with—the forgetting of discomfiting facts. The myth that refuses to be discomfited is that the United States, as might be expected from its behavior at home, is a peculiarly decent nation abroad.

Perhaps we took the myth, along with mother's milk, from British liberalism. A British historian, Geoffrey Barraclough, writing of German expansionism at the time of the First World War, says: "Easy though it is to criticize the imperialism of the French and British in Africa or China, their worst enormities simply do not compare. For all its faults British imperialism had a genuine idealistic component, a sense of service and mission expressed in India by Curzon and in Egypt by Cromer." [1]

"Idealistic components" have always been handy in aggressive international behavior. The chastity of Helen in the Trojan Wars, the sanctity of Christ's birthplace in the Crusades—and one can multiply the components indefinitely—no more altered the basic fact of conquest, murder, exploitation than did the more sophisticated rationale of the British liberals in the Boer War. As D. A. N. Jones has written about Winston Churchill's role at that time: [2]

> Churchill lent an air of nobility to ugly realities. He had come to Parliament, in 1901, as the war correspondent from South Africa, able to present the Boer War as a grand duel between blood-brothers. Some, he said, in his maiden speech, were prepared to "stigmatize this as a war of greed. . . . This war from beginning to end has only been a war of duty."

Churchill praised the white enemy for not arming the black population: "The Black Peril . . . is the one bond of union between the European races." In a letter to his wife in 1907, Churchill, a junior Minister in the Liberal Government, talks of ". . . 150,000 more natives under our direct control. . . . There will not, I think, be any bloodshed. . . . Thus the Empire grows under Radical Administration!" *

Was this a "paradox" of British liberalism? Only if one ignores parallel features of liberalism at home which cast doubt on the total appraisal traditionally made of liberal democracy in the West. For instance, Churchill is "all for government intervention to assist the poor, to take the railways and canals into public ownership, to establish a national minimum wage. It was all talk." He was also saying: "As for tramps and wastrels, there ought to be

---

* From *Winston S. Churchill: Young Statesman 1901–1914*, edited by Randolph Churchill, quoted by D. A. N. Jones, *New York Review of Books*, May 23, 1968.

proper Labour Colonies where they could be . . . made to realise their duty to the State. . . ." And in 1911, as Home Secretary, he accompanied the police who were after some foreign-born burglars alleged to be anarchists. The suspects' house was burned down; two corpses were found, and Churchill wrote to the Prime Minister: [3]

> I thought it better to let the house burn down rather than spend good British lives in rescuing those ferocious rascals. I think I shall have to stiffen the administration of the Aliens Act a little. . . .

To reply to the claim of "paradox" in American liberalism, we would have to place its external conduct alongside the facts of its domestic policies. But first, the external conduct itself requires a more scrupulous examination than is usually given: whether in the elementary school textbooks which glorify America's wars, or in the more sophisticated academic circles where benign motives and other "idealistic components" are thought to make American foreign policy notably more admirable than that of other nations.*

A quick survey of American foreign policy shows that aggressiveness, violence, and deception accompanied, from our first years as a nation, the development of those domestic attributes which (seen in isolation from *other* domestic traits) made us the prototype of Western liberal democracy. This survey is of course a selective one, but for purposes of taking a hard look at our nation in a time of social crisis, it is a useful corrective to more orthodox selection. I suspect there is an important difference between individuals and nations which supports the idea of a critical selection. For a person, the overlooking of past miscreancy may have a positive effect on future conduct, as a psychological spur

---

* This insistence on our purity reaches absurd lengths. In 1968, *Life* magazine carried a picture of a Vietnamese girl whose leg was amputated after she was shot down by a United States helicopter. Dr. Howard Rusk, President of the World Rehabilitation Fund, wrote: "I think the readers of *Life* should know that young Tran would not have had an artificial limb had it not been for the American people working through the U.S. Agency for International Development."

to change. For nations, there is not that sensitivity. A hardened, mindless mechanism requires not psychological encouragement but a taking apart and reassembling by its citizens—a task so arduous as to be spurred only by a sense of great peril, reinforced by a concentrated recollection of the number of times the mechanism has failed.

It was in our first diplomatic efforts as a new nation—the making of the peace treaty with England—that, despite the nobility of sentiment that accompanied a war for independence and the goals of the Declaration of Independence, we began to show the cupidity of our elders. Bradford Perkins, in his review of Richard B. Morris' *The Peacemakers,* makes the point as precisely as one could make it: [4]

> . . . like most American historians, Richard Morris seems to assume that, because the envoys served a noble people, their cynical and even dishonest efforts are to be excused, whereas their European counterparts are to be condemned because they served less enlightened states. In fact Jay, Franklin, and Adams triumphed precisely because they adopted the brutal morality of their contemporaries. They betrayed their instructions and the spirit of the alliance with France to obtain great benefits for their country. They cannot, as Morris seems to imply, be defended on moral grounds. They initiated, their contemporaries echoed, and their countrymen since have reaffirmed the false claim that Americans normally act with a morality superior to that of statesmen of other nations.

The peace that followed the Revolutionary War was a nervous one, accompanied by the first waves of post-independence nationalist passion. The British were holding on to their military and trading posts on the northern frontier, the Spanish were in the Floridas to the south, the French soon in possession of New Orleans and the vast Louisiana territory to the north, and the Indians everywhere. War fever rose and fell in those years, against the British under Washington, against the French under Adams (intensified by the French Revolution), against also (ironically—but irony is normal in international affairs) those Irish revolutionaries who came to this country with the same fierce anti-British feeling that we held in our Revolution.

From the first, aggressive expansion was a constant of national ideology and policy, whether the administration was "liberal" or "conservative"—that is, Federalist or Republican, Whig or Democrat, Democrat or Republican. The first and greatest act of territorial expansion was taken by Jefferson, in a legally dubious purchase, the President conveniently overlooking the fact that he was receiving, in effect, stolen goods (for Napoleon was violating a treaty with Spain by selling Louisiana).

Expansionism was given a moral justification; the nation had a "natural right" to security in the West, it was said. This was the customary jump in modern history, from an idealistic nationalism invoked to justify independence from colonial rule, to the stretching out over others' territory by a new nation. "The very peoples who had drunk most deeply of the new humanitarian nationalism succumbed most readily to the expansionist intoxication which led into the age of imperialism," writes Arthur K. Weinberg, in his classic study, *Manifest Destiny*.

France had leaped from Rousseau to Napoleon, and the United States from the Declaration of Independence to (as Weinberg puts it) "the extension of its rule over an alien people—Indians—without their consent." And it was the author of the phrase "consent of the governed," Jefferson himself, who sent troops into the Louisiana Territory to guard against Indian outbreaks at the time of purchase. He had written in 1787 that "it may be taken for a certainty that not a foot of land will ever be taken from the Indians without their own consent." The argument now used to justify taking this land from the Indians was that they were not cultivating it. But a score of years later, when the Indians began to settle down in the South and to cultivate the land, they were driven out (by Andrew Jackson, Jefferson's descendant in the "liberal" tradition).*

Expansionism, with its accompanying excuses, seems to be a constant characteristic of the nation-state, whether liberal or con-

* For an account of the long, murderous battle against the Indians see John Tebbel and Keith Jennison, *The American Indian Wars*, Harper & Row, 1960.

servative, socialist or capitalist. I am not trying to argue that the liberal-democratic state is especially culpable, only that it is not less so than other nations. Russian expansionism into Eastern Europe, the Chinese moving into Tibet and battling with India over border territories—seem as belligerent as the pushings of that earlier revolutionary upstart, the United States. And in these cases, the initial revolution followed by others, led to a paranoid fear of revolution beyond the real potential.

Thus, six years after the American Revolution, France was convulsed in hers. After the turn of the century, Latin America caught fire: Haiti the first, suspiciously close to the American shore, then Venezuela, Argentina, Chile, and the rest. Europe's despots pointed accusingly at the United States, much as we now point to Soviet Russia (or more lately to China or Cuba) whenever there are rumblings of change anywhere in the world. The philosophy of Manifest Destiny in America was not far from the Soviet rationale today, that (in Weinberg's words) "one nation has a preeminent social worth, a distinctively lofty mission, and consequently unique rights in the application of moral principles." Socialism and liberalism both have advantages over feudal monarchies in their ability to throw a benign light over vicious actions.

On the eve of the war of 1812, the Madison administration, by a combination of subversive agitation and deception, took from under the nose of Spain the territory of West Florida, a strip of land along the Gulf of Mexico reaching as far west as Baton Rouge. Expansionist elements in the Southern states, encouraged and perhaps helped materially by the Madison administration, revolted against Spanish authority, set up a Lone Star Republic, and asked to join the United States. It was a preview in certain respects of the later annexation of Texas. According to Thomas A. Bailey, Secretary of State James Monroe "went so far as to falsify the dates of certain important documents" to show that the territory belonged to the United States as part of the Louisiana Purchase.[5] Spain was too heavily involved in war with Napoleon to do much about it, but several years later, the London *Times* said: "Mr. Madison's dirty, swindling manoeuvres in respect to Louisiana and the Floridas remain to be punished."

A century and a half of historical research have not solved the question of exactly why the United States went to war with England in 1812. The grievance concerning British impressment of American seamen seems hopelessly knotted with expansionist aims. But whatever the complex of actual reasons, there is no doubt about the powerful generation of expansionist sentiment at this point in American history. Congressman John Randolph of Virginia, suspicious of the imperial designs of John Calhoun and Henry Clay, told the House of Representatives that the impressment issue was false. "Agrarian cupidity, not maritime right, urges the war," he said. "Ever since the report of the Committee . . . we have heard but one word—like the whip-poor-will, but one eternal monotonous tone—Canada! Canada! Canada!"

As if to corroborate this accusation, the Nashville *Clarion* asked: "Where is it written in the book of fate that the American Republic shall not stretch her limits from the Capes of the Chesapeake to Nootka Sound, from the isthmus of Panama to Hudson Bay?" The entire North American continent lay waiting.

The war of 1812 ended too indecisively for the United States to extend her territorial possessions at the expense of Britain. But there was Spain, controlling Florida. In 1817, Andrew Jackson, now a military hero, went into action. Given the right by the American Government to cross the Florida border in pursuit of pillagers—Seminole Indians, runaway slaves, white renegades— he did just that, and then more. He seized most of the important Florida posts, confiscated the royal Spanish archives, replaced the Spanish governor with an American, executed two Englishmen, and declared that United States tax laws would operate in Florida. For this, he became a national hero.

This led to what appears benignly in our textbook charts as "The Florida Purchase." Secretary of State John Quincy Adams insisted that Spain cede Florida, and promised to take care of American citizens' claims against Spain, amounting to five million dollars, but not a cent went to Spain for the Florida territory. As Bailey sums up: [6]

However much we may applaud the masterly diplomacy of Adams, there are features of the negotiation that are not altogether savory. Spain, to be sure, was shuffling, dilatory, and irresponsible; the United States was rough, highhanded and arrogant. Some writers have called the acquisition of Florida a case of international bullying. Others have called it Manifest Destiny—the falling of ripe fruit.

The Monroe Doctrine has been invested with a good deal of patriotic sentiment, accompanied by only a vague sense of what it was all about. In the 1920's, Christian Science leader Mary Baker Eddy took a full-page ad in *The New York Times,* heading it: "I believe strictly in the Monroe Doctrine, in our Constitution, and in the laws of God."

As we look into it, the Monroe Doctrine begins to look like the common tendency of all new nations to build a *cordon sanitaire* around themselves, and indeed to stretch that far beyond the needs of self-defense. Russia in Eastern Europe, China in South Asia, Egypt in the Middle East, have all showed the same behavior. And in August of 1960, the Prime Minister of Ghana, Kwame Nkrumah, told his National Assembly that he "would not be so presumptuous as to put forward a Monroe Doctrine for Africa" but that he thought African problems should be settled by African states. His statement had just the tone of righteousness and just the tone of paternal supervision that marked the United States in 1823, when James Monroe's presidential message to Congress promised that the United States would not interfere in the internal concerns of European countries, but also warned that "we should consider any attempt on their part to extend their system to any portion of this hemisphere as dangerous to our peace and safety."

There is considerable doubt that the Monroe Doctrine saved either independence or democracy in Latin America, but there is little doubt that it served as a justification, by President Polk and later by Theodore Roosevelt, for the expansion of American influence in Latin America. Interestingly, Metternich in central Europe saw this commonplace action of modern nationalism with the same ideological phobia that the United States sees the Soviet Union and other Communist nations. He responded to the Monroe Doctrine as follows: "These United States of America . . . lend new strength to the apostles of sedition and reanimate the courage of every conspirator. If this flood of evil doctrines and pernicious examples should extend over the whole of America, what would become of our religious and political institutions. . . ."

The spirit of Manifest Destiny was strong in those very decades of the early nineteenth century when the nation was creating institutions marking it as liberal and democratic: the extension of suffrage, the popular election of the President, the spread of public education, the flowering of literature. One of the nation's leading orators, Edward Everett, in an oration commemorating the battle of Bunker Hill in 1836, told his audience:

> . . . wherever there are men living, laboring, suffering, enjoying—there are our brothers. Look then still further abroad, honored friends and patriots! Behold in distant countries, in other quarters of the globe, the influence of your example and achievements in stimulating the progress of social improvement. Behold the mighty spirit of Reform striding like a giant through the civilized world and trampling down established abuses at every step! . . . Behold him working out his miracles in France, knocking off the shackles of neighboring nations in Spanish America, pursuing his course, sometimes triumphant, sometimes temporarily trodden under foot, betrayed by false friends, overwhelmed by superior force, but still in the main, forward and onward over Spain, Portugal, Italy, Germany, Greece!

The liberal West, now fat, rich, and spread-eagled over the world, points with alarm at the upstart righteousness of the Communist states, the messianic fervor of the new nationalism in Asia and Africa. But liberalism, at a similar stage in its development, showed the same character. Tocqueville wrote in the 1830's: "Nothing is more embarrassing in the ordinary intercourse of life, than this irritable patriotism of the Americans."

In this same period the most popular American historian was George Bancroft, who saw American democracy as God's special gift to the universe. His historical study of the United States, Bancroft said, aimed "to follow the steps by which a favoring Providence, calling our institutions into being, has conducted the nation to its present happiness and glory." Shall we rest on the explanation of "paradox" when we recall that at this same time, the nation was putting people in prison for debt, herding free men into labor gangs under the most brutal conditions, and enslaving that one-sixth of its population which was black?

The administration of Andrew Jackson, who is seen sometimes as an early New Dealer, a conveyer of the liberal Jeffersonian tradition, was a particularly truculent one. The Cherokees were established in the south as a separate nation, by treaty after treaty which they signed with the United States. They were industrious, progressive, and peaceful. Their government was more democratic and their educational system more advanced than those of Georgia, North Carolina, and Tennessee, in whose mountain fastnesses the Cherokees maintained their society. When Georgia in 1832 defied a Supreme Court ruling that only the national government had jurisdiction over Cherokee territory, Andrew Jackson supported Georgia with his famous statement: "John Marshall has made his decision, now let him enforce it."

Jackson, after all, was an old Indian fighter, and he pushed through Congress an Indian Removal Act to force the Cherokees out. A few years later, General Winfield Scott invaded with 7000 troops. The Cherokees were put in concentration camps, their homes burned, and 14,000 of them herded onto the long trek westward, the "Trail of Tears," during which 4000 men, women, and children died.

Any confidence in the special benignity of a "democratic" nation's foreign policy is shaken, at the least, by this episode. Four years after the crushing of the Hungarian revolt, Premier Khrushchev of the Soviet Union declared that the Hungarian situation was now settled to everyone's satisfaction. Andrew Jackson's handpicked successor, President Martin Van Buren, said about the Cherokee removal operation: "The measures authorized by Congress at its last session have had the happiest effects. . . . The Cherokees have emigrated without any apparent reluctance."

It was an aggressive war against Mexico that extended the nation's boundaries to the Pacific. In the 1819 treaty with Spain the United States had given up any claim to Texas. But this did not stop it from trying to bribe Mexican officials to sell Texas, as by United States Minister Anthony Butler in Jackson's administration. This failing, it gave active support to the revolution which separated Texas from Mexico and made it, for ten years, the Lone Star State. The United States had its eye not only on Texas, but on California and all the land between—about half of what was then Mexico. After Texas was annexed in 1845, President Polk sent secret instructions to his confidential agent in California, Thomas O. Larkin, to work for annexation.

Polk first tried to buy California and New Mexico, but Mexico refused, whereupon he sent troops into the disputed territory between the Nueces River and the Rio Grande, which both Texas and Mexico claimed. When Polk took the question of war to his cabinet, the suggestion was made that it would be better for Mexico to start the war. By some remarkable coincidence, a dispatch that same night reported Mexicans coming into the disputed area, and a battle ensued, with sixteen American casualties. Polk asked Congress to declare war, saying that Mexico "has invaded our territory and shed American blood upon the American soil." Polk's claim to be protecting Texas was rather weak, in view of the fact that in nine years Mexico had made no effort to retake Texas.

The war was won without difficulty, and the 1848 Treaty of Guadalupe Hidalgo gave the United States what it wanted: New Mexico, California, and the disputed territory in Texas—altogether, half of Mexico. The United States could even point to its restraint in not taking all of Mexico. During the war, that thought had been widespread. At a Jackson Day dinner, Senator Dickinson of New York had offered a toast to "A more perfect Union, embracing the whole of the North American continent." The liberal New York *Evening Post* urged America not to withdraw from Mexico, saying:

Now we ask, whether any man can coolly contemplate the idea of recalling our troops from the territory we at present occupy and . . . resign this beautiful country to the custody of the ignorant cowards and profligate ruffians who have ruled it for the last 25 years? Why, humanity cries out against it. Civilization and Christianity protest.

Expansionism was neither liberal nor conservative, Southern or Northern. It was a trait of the American nation, as of other nations, as of any unit bursting with power and privilege in a competitive, lawless world. The sentiment of the New York *Post* was not much different from that of Jefferson Davis, the Senator from Mississippi, who wrote just before the Civil War:

> We may expand so as to include the whole world. Mexico, Central America, South America, Cuba, the West India Islands, and even England and France we might annex without inconvenience . . . allowing them with their local legislatures to regulate their local affairs in their own way. And this sir, is the mission of this Republic and its ultimate destiny.

It was, indeed, in the direction of worldwide power, that the United States Government moved. It expanded, in the years between the Revolution and the Civil War, from a thin strip along the Atlantic to a huge continental power fronting the oceans. It did this by purchase and by pressure, by aggression, by deceit, and by war. It used these varied weapons against Spaniards, Frenchmen, Indians, Mexicans—and all with an air of arrogant righteousness, with the idea that to spread the American flag far and wide was to confer on other peoples the greatest gift in the world.

After 1890, we moved out into the Caribbean and the Pacific, as far as the coastal waters of China. That story is too well known to recount in detail: the "splendid little war" with Spain; the annexation of Hawaii, and the Philippines and the ugly war of extermination against the Filipino rebels; the taking of Puerto Rico and the establishment of a protectorate over Cuba; the shrewd creation of a Republic of Panama, pulling the site for a canal from under Colombia; the waves of marines into the Caribbean—Haiti, the Dominican Republic, Nicaragua; the bombardment and occupation of Vera Cruz; in the meantime the concern with profit and influence in China and Japan by the judicious use of gunboats, dollars, and diplomacy. With World War I we became the banker of the world; with World War II we spread military bases onto every land mass, every ocean in the world, intervened openly or stealthily in Greece, Lebanon, Guatemala, Cuba, the Dominican Republic, Korea, Vietnam. By 1969, the Japanese had to protest the use of their former island, Okinawa, to store deadly nerve gas for American military use.

These, in terse summary, are the facts we tend either to ignore or to so mix into the rich potpourri of American history as to obscure them. Extricated, they force us to deal with them alongside the kindly view of our society as a summit of liberal, democratic achievement in world history. Refusing to simply separate "liberalism" at home from aggression abroad, refusing also to end the discussion by speaking of "paradox," we can attempt a reconciliation from one or another direction.

That is, we can find that our behavior abroad is not as bad as it seems on first look, that it is indeed invested with some of the saving characteristics we find in domestic liberalism. For instance, Frederick Merk, in *Manifest Destiny and Mission in American History, a Reinterpretation,* is unhappy with the idea that manifest destiny and imperialism represent the actual American spirit. He finds they are exceptions, and that the true American mood was that of "mission," of liberating other peoples, that the United States has been, in the main, "idealistic, self-denying, hopeful of divine favor for national aspirations, though not sure of it."

I would suggest another way of looking at the facts: that there is a similar principle operating in domestic affairs and foreign affairs—for presumably liberal states as for other kinds of states: that in a world which has not yet developed either the mind or the mechanism for humane cooperation, power and privilege tend to be as rapacious as the degree of resistance by the victims will permit. That aggression at home is more disguised, more sporadic, more controlled than that abroad comes from the development of countervailing forces at home, while those abroad have usually been helpless before the marauding foreign power. Where internal groups have been similarly helpless they have been treated as ruthlessly as enemies in wartime: the blacks, the Indians, the workingmen before they organized, the students when they dared to challenge authority.

All this suggests that we need to stop looking with special fondness on that group of Western states which represent, in those millions of textbooks distributed in high schools and colleges, "Western civilization." Their external behavior is not an unfortunate departure from character. It is what their internal behavior would be if undeterred by a population whose greater literacy and greater activity (a necessity of modern industrial development) enabled them to at least partially resist.

The idealist rhetoric surrounding the foreign policies of liberal states is only a variant on the historic use of rhetoric by aggressive civilizations in the past: the Greeks had their noble excuses for destroying the people of Melos; the Popes drove Christian armies forward with words of holy purity; the socialist states invent socialist excuses for their assaults. A bit of historical perspective may help us to deal, in our own time, with the missionary-soldiers of other nations, and of ours.

13

Vietnam: the moral equation

When those of us who would make an end to the war speak pas-
sionately of "the moral issue" in Vietnam, only our friends seem
to understand. The government continues to bomb fishing villages, shoot women, disfigure children by fire or explosion, while
its policy brings no outcry of opposition from Hubert Humphrey,
Oscar Handlin, Max Lerner, or millions of others. And we wonder why.

The answer, I suggest, involves the corruption of means, the
confusion of ends, the theory of the lesser evil, and the easy re-
versibility of moral indignation in a species which is aroused to
violence by symbols. To explain all this, however, is to get involved in a discussion of dangerous questions, which many people in the protest movement avoid by talking earnestly and va-
cantly about "morality" in the abstract, or by burrowing energeti-
cally into military realities, legal repartee, negotiating positions,
and the tactics of "broad coalition." Yet it is only by discussing
root questions of means and ends—questions such as violence,
revolution, and alternative social systems—that we can understand what it means to say there is "a moral issue" in Vietnam.

To start with, we ought to recognize the escalation of evil
means during this century—a process in which few of us can
claim innocence. What Hitler did was to extend the already approved doctrine of indiscriminate mass murder (ten million dead
on the battlefields of World War I) to its logical end, and thus
stretch further than ever before the limits of the tolerable. By
killing one-third of the world's Jews, the Nazis diminished the
horror of any atrocity that was separated by two degrees of fiend-
ishness from theirs. (Discussing with one of my students Hoch-
huth's *The Deputy,* I asked if we were not all "deputies" today,

209

watching the bombing of Vietnamese villages; she replied, no, because this is not as bad as what Hitler did).

The Left still dodges the problem of violent means to achieve just ends. (This is not true of Herbert Marcuse and Barrington Moore, Jr., in the book they have done with Robert Paul Wolff: *A Critique of Pure Tolerance*. But it was so true of the Communists in the United States that the government, in the Smith Act trials, had to distort the facts in order to prove that the Communists would go as far as Thomas Jefferson in the use of revolutionary violence.) To ignore this question, both by avoiding controversy about comparative social systems as ends, and foregoing discussion of violence as a means, is to fail to create a rational basis for moral denunciation of our government's actions in Vietnam.

I would start such a discussion from the supposition that it is logically indefensible to hold to an absolutely nonviolent position, because it is at least theoretically conceivable that a small violence might be required to prevent a larger one. Those who are immediately offended by this statement should consider: World War II; the assassination attempt on Hitler; the American, French, Russian, Chinese, Cuban revolutions; possible armed revolt in South Africa; the case of Rhodesia; blacks in America. Keep in mind that many who support the war in Vietnam may do so on grounds which they believe similar to those used in the above cases.

The terrible thing is that once you stray from absolute nonviolence you open the door for the most shocking abuses. It is like distributing scalpels to an eager group, half of whom are surgeons and half butchers. But that is man's constant problem—how to release the truth without being devoured by it.

How can we tell butchers from surgeons, distinguish between a healing and a destructive act of violence? The first requirement is that our starting point must always be nonviolence, and that the burden of proof, therefore, is on the advocate of violence to show, with a high degree of probability, that he is justified. In modern American civilization, we demand unanimity among twelve citizens before we will condemn a single person to death, but we will destroy thousands of people on the most flimsy of political assumptions (like the domino theory of revolutionary contagion).

What proof should be required? I suggest four tests:

1. Self-defense, against outside attackers or a counterrevolutionary force within, using no more violence than is needed to repel the attack, is justified. This covers the Negro housewife who several years ago in a little Georgia town, at home alone with her children, fired through the door at a gang of white men carrying guns and chains, killing one, after which the rest fled. It would sacrifice the Rhineland to Hitler in 1936, and even Austria (for the Austrians apparently preferred not to fight), but demands supporting the Loyalist government in Spain, and defending Czechoslovakia in 1938. And it applies to Vietnamese fighting against American attackers who hold the strings of a puppet government.

2. Revolution is justified, for the purpose of overthrowing a deeply entrenched oppressive regime, unshakable by other means. Outside aid is permissible (because rebels, as in the American Revolution, are almost always at a disadvantage against the holders of power), but with the requirement that the manpower for the revolution be indigenous, for this in itself is a test of how popular the revolution is. This could cover the French, American, Mexican, Russian, Chinese, Cuban, Algerian cases. It would also cover the Vietcong rebellion. And a South African revolt, should it break out.

3. Even if one of the above conditions is met, there is no moral justification for visiting violence on the innocent. Therefore, violence in self-defense or in revolution must be focused on the evildoers, and limited to that required to achieve the goal, resisting all arguments that extra violence might speed victory. This rules out the strategic bombing of German cities in World War II, the atom bombing of Hiroshima and Nagasaki; it rules out terrorism against civilians even in a just revolution. Violence even against the guilty, when undertaken for sheer revenge, is unwarranted, which rules out capital punishment for any crime. The requirement of focused violence makes nonsensical the equating of the killing of village chiefs in South Vietnam by the Vietcong and the bombing of hospitals by American fliers; yet the former is also unjustified if it is merely an act of terror or revenge and not spe-

cifically required for a change in the social conditions of the village.

4. There is an additional factor which the conditions of modern warfare make urgent. Even if all three of the foregoing principles are met, there is a fourth which must be considered if violence is to be undertaken: the costs of self-defense or social change must not be so high, because of the intensity or the prolongation of violence, or because of the risk of proliferation, that the victory is not worth the cost. For the Soviets to defend Cuba from attack—though self-defense was called for—would not have been worth a general war. For China and Soviet Russia to aid the Vietcong with troops, though the Vietcong cause is just, would be wrong if it seriously risked a general war. Under certain conditions, nations should be captive rather than be destroyed, or revolutionaries should bide their time. Indeed, because of the omnipresence of the great military powers—the United States and the USSR (perhaps this is not so true for the countries battling England, France, Holland, Belgium, Portugal)—revolutionary movements may have to devise tactics short of armed revolt to overturn an oppressive regime.

The basic principle I want to get close to is that violence is most clearly justified when those whose own lives are at stake make the decision on whether the prize is worth dying for. Self-defense and guerrilla warfare, by their nature, embody this decision. Conscript armies and unfocused warfare violate it. And no one has a right to decide that someone else is better off dead than Red, or that someone else should die to defend his way of life, or that an individual (like Norman Morrison immolating himself in Washington) should choose to live rather than die.

It would be foolish to pretend that this summary can be either precise or complete. Those involved in self-defense or in a revolution need no intellectual justification; their emotions reflect some inner rationality. It is those outside the direct struggle, deciding whether to support one side or to stay out, who need to think clearly about principles. Americans, therefore, possessing the greatest power and being the furthest removed from the problems of self-defense or revolution, need thoughtful deliberation most.

All we can do in social analysis is to offer rough guides to replace nonthinking, to give the beginnings of some kind of moral calculus.

However, it takes no close measurement to conclude that the American bombings in Vietnam, directed as they are to farming areas, villages, hamlets, fit none of the criteria listed, and so are deeply immoral, whatever else is true about the situation in Southeast Asia or the world. The silence of the government's supporters on this—from Hubert Humphrey to the academic signers of advertisements—is particularly shameful, because it requires no surrender of their other arguments to concede that this is unnecessary bestiality.

Bombings aside, none of the American military activity against the Vietcong could be justified unless it were helping a determined people to defend itself against an outside attacker. That is why the Administration, hoping to confirm by verbal repetition what cannot be verified by fact, continually uses the term "aggression" to describe the Vietnamese guerrilla activities. The expert evidence, however, is overwhelming on this question:

1. Philippe Devillers, the French historian, says "the insurrection existed before the Communists decided to take part. . . . And even among the Communists, the initiative did not originate in Hanoi, but from the grass roots, where the people were literally driven by Diem to take up arms in self-defense."

2. Bernard Fall says "anti-Diem guerrillas were active long before infiltrated North Vietnamese elements joined the fray."

3. The correspondent for *Le Monde,* Jean Lacouture (in *Le Viet Nam entre deux paix*) confirms that local pressure, local conditions led to guerrilla activity.

4. Donald S. Zagoria, a specialist on Asian communism at Columbia University, wrote recently that "it is reasonably clear that we are dealing with an indigenous insurrection in the South, and that this, not Northern assistance, is the main trouble."

One test of "defense against aggression" is the behavior of the official South Vietnamese army—the "defenders" themselves. We find: a high rate of desertions; a need to herd villagers into concentration-camp "strategic hamlets" in order to control them; the use of torture to get information from other South Vietnamese, whom you might expect to be enthusiastic about "defending" their country; and all of this forcing the United States to take over virtually the entire military operation in Vietnam.

The ordinary people of Vietnam show none of the signs of a nation defending itself against "aggression," except in their non-cooperation with the government and the Americans. A hundred thousand Vietnamese farmers were conducting a rebellion with mostly captured weapons (both David Halberstam and Hanson Baldwin affirmed this in *The New York Times,* contradicting quietly what I. F. Stone demolished statistically—the State Department's White Paper on "infiltration"). Then they matched the intrusion of 150,000 American troops with 7,500 North Vietnamese soldiers (in November 1965, American military officials estimated that five regiments of North Vietnamese, with 1,500 in each regiment, were in South Vietnam). Weapons were acquired from Communist countries, but not a single plane to match the horde of American bombers filling the skies over Vietnam. This adds up not to North Vietnamese aggression (if indeed North Vietnamese can be considered outsiders at all) but to American aggression, with a puppet government fronting for American power.

Thus, there is no valid principle on which the United States can defend either its bombing, or its military presence, in Vietnam. It is the factual emptiness of its moral claim which then leads it to seek a one-piece substitute, that comes prefabricated with its own rationale, surrounded by an emotional aura sufficient to ward off inspectors. This transplanted fossil is the Munich analogy, which, speaking with all the passion of Churchill in the Battle of Britain, declares: to surrender in Vietnam is to do what Chamberlain did at Munich; that is why the villagers must die.

The great value of the Munich analogy to the Strangeloves is that it captures so many American liberals, among many others. It backs the Vietnamese expedition with a coalition broad enough to include Barry Goldwater, Lyndon Johnson, George Meany, and John Roche (thus reversing World War II's coalition, which excluded the far Right and included the radical Left). This bloc justifies the carnage in Vietnam with a huge image of invading armies, making only one small change in the subtitle: replacing the word "Fascist" with the word "Communist." Then, the whole savage arsenal of World War II—the means both justified and un-justifiable—supported by that great fund of indignation built against the Nazis, can be turned to the uses of the American Century.

To leave the Munich analogy intact, to fail to discuss communism and fascism, is to leave untouched the major premise which supports the present policy of near genocide in Vietnam. I propose here at least to initiate such a discussion.

Let's refresh our memories on what happened at Munich. Chamberlain of England and Daladier of France met Hitler and Mussolini (this was September 30, 1938) and agreed to surrender the Sudeten part of Czechoslovakia, inhabited by German-speaking people, hoping thus to prevent a general war in Europe. Chamberlain returned to England, claiming he had brought "peace in our time." Six months later, Hitler had gobbled up the rest of Czechoslovakia; then he began presenting ultimatums to Poland and by September 3, 1939, general war had broken out in Europe.

There is strong evidence that if the Sudetenland had not been surrendered at Munich—with it went Czechoslovakia's powerful fortifications, 70 percent of its iron, steel, and electric power, 86 percent of its chemicals, 66 percent of its coal—and had Hitler then gone to war, he would have been defeated quickly, with the aid of Czechoslovakia's thirty-five well-trained divisions. And if he chose, at the sign of resistance, not to go to war, then at least he would have stopped his expansion.

And so, the analogy continues, to let the Communist-dominated National Liberation Front win in South Vietnam (for the real obstacle in the sparring over negotiations is the role of the NLF in a new government) is to encourage more Communist expansion in Southeast Asia and beyond, and perhaps to lead to a war more disastrous than the present one; to stop communism in South Vietnam is to discourage its expansion elsewhere.

We should note, first, some of the important differences between the Munich situation in 1938 and Vietnam today:

1. In 1938, the main force operating against the Czech status quo was an outside force, Hitler's Germany; the supporting force was the Sudeten group inside led by Konrad Henlein. Since 1958

(and traceable back to 1942), the major force operating against the *status quo* in South Vietnam has been an inside force, formed in 1960 into the NLF; the chief supporter is not an outside nation but another part of the same nation, North Vietnam. The largest outside force in Vietnam consists of American troops (who, interestingly, are referred to in West Germany as *Bandenkampfverbande*, Bandit Fighting Units, the name used in World War II by the Waffen-S.S. units to designate the guerrillas whom they specialized in killing). To put it another way, in 1938, the Germans were trying to take over part of another country. Today, the Vietcong are trying to take over part of their own country. In 1938, the outsider was Germany. Today it is the United States.

2. The Czech government, whose interests the West surrendered to Hitler in 1938, was a strong, effective, prosperous, democratic government—the government of Beneš and Masaryk. The South Vietnamese government which we support is a hollow shell of a government, unstable, unpopular, corrupt, a dictatorship of bullies and torturers, disdainful of free elections and representative government (recently they opposed establishing a National Assembly on the ground that it might lead to communism), headed by a long line of tyrants from Bao Dai to Diem to Ky, who no more deserve to be ranked with Beneš and Masaryk than Governor Wallace of Alabama deserves to be compared with Thomas Jefferson. It is a government whose perpetuation is not worth the loss of a single human life.

3. Standing firm in 1938 meant engaging, in order to defeat once and for all, the central threat of that time, Hitler's Germany. Fighting in Vietnam today, even if it brings total victory, does not at all engage what the United States considers the central foes— the Soviet Union and Communist China. Even if international communism *were* a single organism, to annihilate the Vietcong would be merely to remove a toenail from an elephant. To engage what we think is the source of our difficulties (Red China one day, Soviet Russia the next) would require nuclear war, and even Robert Strange McNamara doesn't seem up to that.

4. There is an important difference between the historical context of Munich, 1938 and that of Vietnam, 1966. Munich was

the culmination of a long line of surrenders and refusals to act: when Japan invaded China in 1931, when Mussolini invaded Ethiopia in 1935, when Hitler remilitarized the Rhineland in 1936, when Hitler and Mussolini supported the Franco attack on Republican Spain 1936–39, when Japan attacked China in 1937, when Hitler took Austria in the spring of 1938. The Vietnam crisis, on the other hand, is the culmination of a long series of events in which the West has on occasion held back (as in Czechoslovakia in 1948, or Hungary in 1956), but more often taken firm action, from the Truman Doctrine to the Berlin blockade to the Korean conflict, to the Cuban blockade of 1962. So, withdrawing from Vietnam would not reinforce a pattern in the way that the Munich pact did. It would be another kind of line in that jagged graph which represents recent foreign policy.

5. We have twenty years of cold-war history to test the proposition derived from the Munich analogy—that a firm stand in Vietnam is worth the huge loss of life, because it will persuade the Communists there must be no more uprisings elsewhere. But what effect did our refusal to allow the defeat of South Korea (1950–53), or our aid in suppressing the Huk rebellion in the Philippines (1947–55), or the suppression of guerrillas in Malaya (1948–60), have on the guerrilla warfare in South Vietnam which started around 1958 and became consolidated under the National Liberation Front in 1960? If our use of subversion and arms to overthrow Guatemala in 1954 showed the Communists in Latin America that we meant business, then how did it happen that Castro rebelled and won in 1959? Did our invasion of Cuba in 1961, our blockade in 1962, show other revolutionaries in Latin America that they must desist? Then how explain the Dominican uprising in 1965? And did our dispatch of the Marines to Santo Domingo end the fighting of guerrillas in the mountains of Peru?

One touches the Munich analogy and it falls apart. This suggests something more fundamental: that American policy makers and their supporters simply do not understand either the nature of communism or the nature of the various uprisings that have taken place in the postwar world. They are not able to believe that hunger, homelessness, oppression are sufficient spurs to revolution, without outside instigation, just as Dixie governors could not believe that Negroes marching in the streets were not led by outside agitators.

So, communism and revolution require discussion. They are sensitive questions, which some in the protest movement hesitate to broach for fear of alienating allies. But they are basic to that inversion of morality which enables the United States to surround the dirty war in Vietnam with the righteous glow of war against Hitler.

A key assumption in this inversion is that communism and Nazism are sufficiently identical to be treated alike. However, communism as a set of ideals has attracted good people—not racists, or bullies, or militarists—all over the world. One may argue that in Communist countries citizens had better affirm their allegiance to it, but that doesn't account for the fact that millions, in France, Italy, and Indonesia are Communist party members, that countless others all over the world have been inspired by Marxian ideals. And why should they not? These ideals include peace, brotherhood, racial equality, the classless society, the withering away of the state.

If Communists behave much better out of power than in it, that is a commentary not on their ideals but on weaknesses which they share with non-Communist wielders of power. If, presumably in pursuit of their ideals, they have resorted to brutal tactics, maintained suffocating bureaucracies and rigid dogmas, that makes them about as reprehensible as other nations, other social systems which, while boasting of the Judeo-Christian heritage, have fostered war, exploitation, colonialism, and race hatred. We judge ourselves by our ideals; others by their actions. It is a great convenience.

The ultimate values of the Nazis, let us recall, included racism, elitism, militarism, and war as ends in themselves. Unlike either the Communist nations or the Capitalist democracies, there is here no ground for appeal to higher purposes. The ideological basis for coexistence between Communist and Capitalist nations is the rough consensus of ultimate goals which they share. While war is held off, the citizens on both sides—it is to be hoped and indeed it is beginning to occur—will increasingly insist that their leaders live up to these values.

One of these professed values—which the United States is trying with difficulty to conceal by fragile arguments and feeble analogies—is the self-determination of peoples. Self-determination justifies the overthrow of entrenched oligarchies—whether foreign or domestic—in ways that will not lead to general war. China, Egypt, Indonesia, Algeria, and Cuba are examples. Such revolutions tend to set up dictatorships, but they do so in the name of values which can be used to erode that same dictatorship. They therefore deserve as much general support and specific criticism as did the American revolutionaries, who set up a slave-holding government, but with a commitment to freedom which later led it, *against its wishes,* to abolitionism.

The easy use of the term "totalitarian" to cover both Nazis and Communists, or to equate the South Vietnamese regime with that of Ho Chi Minh, fails to make important distinctions, just as dogmatists of the Left sometimes fail to distinguish between Fascist states and capitalist democracies.

This view is ahistorical on two counts. First, it ignores the fact that, for the swift economic progress needed by new nations today, a Communist-led regime does an effective job (though it is not the only type of new government that can). In doing so, it raises educational and living standards and thus paves the way (as the USSR and Eastern Europe already show) for attacks from within on its own thought-control system. Second, this view forgets that the United States and Western Europe, now haughty in prosperity, with a fair degree of free expression, built their present status on the backs of either slaves or colonial people, and subjected their own laboring populations to several generations of misery before beginning to look like welfare states.

The perspective of history suggests that a united Vietnam under Ho Chi Minh is preferable to the elitist dictatorship of the South, just as Maoist China with all its faults is preferable to the rule of Chiang, and Castro's Cuba to Batista's. We do not have pure choices in the present, although we should never surrender those values which can shape the future. Right now, for Vietnam, a Communist government is probably the best avenue to that whole packet of human values which make up the common morality of mankind today: the preservation of human life, self-determination, economic security, the end of race and class oppression, that freedom of speech which an educated population begins to demand.

This is a conclusion which critics of government policy have hesitated to make. With some, it is because they simply don't believe it, but with others, it is because they don't want to rock the boat of "coalition." Yet the main obstacle to United States withdrawal is a fear that is real—that South Vietnam will then go Communist. If we fail to discuss this honestly. we leave untouched a major plank in the structure that supports U.S. action.

When the jump is made from real fears to false ones, we get something approaching lunacy in American international behavior. Richard Hofstadter, in *The Paranoid Style in American Politics,* writes of "the central preconception of the paranoid style— the existence of a vast, insidious, preternaturally effective, international conspiratorial network designed to perpetuate acts of the most fiendish character."

Once, the center of the conspiracy was Russia. A political scientist doing strategic research for the government told me recently with complete calm that his institute decided not too long ago that they had been completely wrong about the premise which underlay much of American policy in the postwar period—the premise that Russia hoped to take over Western Europe by force. Yet now, with not a tremor of doubt, the whole kit and caboodle of the invading-hordes theory is transferred to China.

Paranoia starts from a base of facts, but then leaps wildly to an absurd conclusion. It is a fact that China is totalitarian in its limitation of free speech, is fierce in its expression of hatred for the United States, that it crushed opposition in Tibet, and fought for a strip of territory on the Indian border. But let's consider India briefly: it crushed an uprising in Hyderabad, took over the state of Kerala, initiated attacks on the China border, took Goa by force, and is fierce in its insistence on Kashmir. Yet we do not accuse it of wanting to take over the world.

Of course, there is a difference. China is emotionally tied to and sometimes aids obstreperous rebellions all over the world. However, China is not the source of these rebellions. The problem is not that China wants to take over the world, but that various peoples want to take over their parts of the world, and without the courtesies that attend normal business transactions. What if the Negroes in Watts really rose up and tried to take over Los Angeles? Would we blame that on Castro?

Not only does paranoia lead the United States to see international conspiracy where there is a diversity of Communist nations based on indigenous Communist movements. It also confuses communism with a much broader movement of this century—the rising of the hungry and harassed people in Asia, Africa, Latin America (and the American South). Hence we try to crush radicalism in one place (Greece, Iran, Guatemala, the Philippines, etc.) and apparently succeed, only to find a revolution—whether Communist or Socialist or nationalist or of indescribable character—springing up somewhere else. We surround the world with our navy, cover the sky with our planes, fling our money to the winds, and then a revolution takes place in Cuba, ninety miles from home. We see every rebellion everywhere as the result of some devilish plot concocted in Moscow or Peking, when what is really happening is that people everywhere want to eat and to be free, and will use desperate means and any one of a number of social systems to achieve their ends.

The other side makes the same mistake. The Russians face a revolt in Hungary or Poznan, and attribute it to bourgeois influence, or to American scheming. Stalin's paranoia led him to send scores of old Bolsheviks before the firing squad. The Chinese seem to be developing obsessions about the United States; but in their case we are doing our best to match their wildest accusations with reality. It would be paranoid for Peking to claim that the United States is surrounding China with military bases, occupying countries on its border, keeping hundreds of thousands of troops within striking distance, contemplating the bombing of its population—if it were not largely true.

A worldwide revolution is taking place, aiming to achieve the very values that all major countries, East and West, claim to uphold: self-determination, economic security, racial equality, freedom. It takes many forms—Castro's, Mao's, Nasser's, Sukarno's, Senghor's, Kenyatta's. That it does not realize all its aims from the start makes it hardly more imperfect than we were in 1776. The road to freedom is stony, but people are going to march along it. What we need to do is improve the road, not blow it up.

The United States Government has tried hard to cover its moral nakedness in Vietnam. But the signs of its failure grow by the day. Facts have a way of coming to light. Also, we have recently had certain experiences which make us less naive about governments while we become more hopeful about people: the civil rights movement, the student revolt, the rise of dissent inside the Communist countries, the emergence of fresh, brave spirits in Africa, Asia, Latin America, and in our own country.

It is not our job, as citizens, to point out the difficulties of our military position (this, when true, is quite evident), or to work out clever bases for negotiating (the negotiators, when they *must,* will find a way), or to dissemble what we know is true in order to build a coalition (coalitions grow naturally from what is common to a heterogeneous group, and require each element to represent its colors as honestly as possible to make the mosaic accurate and strong). As a sign of the strange "progress" the world has made, from now on all moral transgressions take the form of irony, because they are committed against officially proclaimed values. The job of citizens, in any society, any time, is simply to point this out.

14

The prisoners: a bit of contemporary history

Somewhere on the flight between Bangkok and Paris, our tensions beginning to ebb, I confessed to Dan Berrigan (after all, he is a Jesuit priest) that I, despite heroic efforts to match my political science colleagues on the Cynicism Scale, had somehow retained in my bones a granule of naivete about governments, especially my own. And this despite my recent talks to students about Machiavellianism in the contemporary world, and my entranced reading of *The Spy Who Came In From the Cold* (which can be seen as a modern-day version of William Godwin's early anarchist novel, *Caleb Williams,* where a man is viciously hunted by *all* governments). But let me explain.

The State Department had learned from Radio Hanoi that North Vietnam was about to release three captured American fliers, and had read in *The New York Times* (all this is known as Intelligence) that a wire from Hanoi to David Dellinger invited a "responsible representative" to come to Hanoi to receive the fliers. After Dellinger had phoned Father Berrigan at Cornell and me in Boston (What was he thinking—that the two of us might, with strain, comprise one "responsible representative"?), Ambassador-at-large Harriman's office asked for a meeting with the two emissaries before their departure. The next day, a State Department man arrived in New York, while Berrigan and I were talking with Dave Dellinger and Tom Hayden, two veterans of the New York-to-Hanoi peace run. Tom Hayden was also a recent conveyer of three NLF prisoners from Cambodia to the United States.

The man from State had several things on his mind. One: the government would be happy to validate our passports for travel to North Vietnam. (No, thanks, we said; we don't recognize the government's right to approve or disapprove where citizens travel.) Second: if the Vietnamese would like some reciprocal act, perhaps the U.S. could release a few captured North Vietnamese sailors. (If the circumstances of the capture were similar, these would have been picked up at Coney Island; otherwise it was *not* a parallel offer; nevertheless, we absorbed the suggestion.)

Third (this came near the end, almost as an afterthought): we might make clear to the Vietnamese that the United States would negotiate on the basis of the San Antonio formula, and would not require, for a cessation of bombing, that the North stop all supplies to the South: only that it not increase the present flow. (I wondered if henceforth all major international crises were to be settled by formulas made in Texas towns; it seemed to me Geneva, with all its difficulties, was more neutral than San Antonio.)

What was most important to the man from State, however—and quite clearly his main reason for contacting us—was the question: how would we return home with the fliers? by what route? by which aircraft? We really didn't know; all we had to go by was one cablegram from Hanoi. We suggested that we would wait and see what developed in Hanoi. To the proposal that we and the fliers all return to the States from Vientiane by military aircraft, Father Berrigan and I said this would not please us; the man from State then said they could provide a plane which was "as far from the military as you can get"—but he did not mean Mohawk Airlines, only another kind of government plane. Nevertheless, we tentatively agreed that how we went home would be left, as far as possible, up to the pilots themselves.

That Wednesday evening, January 31, we departed from Kennedy Airport. The next twenty-eight hours were spent almost continuously on airplanes, as we dashed halfway around the globe (Copenhagen, Frankfurt, Rome, Teheran, Karachi, Calcutta, Bangkok, Vientiane) in order to intercept the Friday night flight from Vientiane to Hanoi. This was a special plane run by the International Control Commission (a vestige of the Geneva Accords; its members are Indians, Poles, Canadians), six times a month (every Friday, every other Tuesday), which departs from Saigon in the morning, then flies to Pnompenh, to Vientiane, and arrives in Hanoi at night, and back again. We made it to Vientiane on schedule, only to be informed that the NLF offensive in Saigon had closed Tan San Nhut airport, and kept the I.C.C. plane from taking off.

So we spent a week in Vientiane (the next scheduled flight, Tuesday, was also cancelled), waiting until the I.C.C. plane could manage to leave Saigon. In the meantime, we visited the North Vietnamese embassy, which offered tea, sympathy, and visas to Hanoi. We visited the Cambodian embassy (we were beginning to think the I.C.C. plane would never make it) in order to obtain transit visas for Pnompenh, because the only way to get to Hanoi besides the I.C.C. plane is via China, and there is a flight from Pnompenh to Canton. We approached the Chinese embassy for transit visas, but were tersely discouraged at the embassy gate, and turned our hopes to the more substantial Chinese mission in Pnompenh.

We talked with journalists (NBC and CBS crews had flown in from Tokyo and Seoul to record our mission). We talked with young Americans in the International Volunteer Service; these IVS people were the best-informed of all; they spoke Lao or Vietnamese, lived with the villagers rather than in the sprawling American Levittown outside of Vientiane, and harshly criticized United States policy in both Vietnam and Laos. We spent a day with Lao villagers, and also interviewed a Pathet Lao spokesman in Vientiane.

From time to time we met with the folk at the United States Embassy. Earlier an Embassy man had met us on arrival at the airport, to say that the Ambassador would be happy to see us, but considering the "delicacy" of our position, would understand if we did not visit him. They now asked us once again if we wanted our passports validated (the last approach was: "Not even verbally?"), discussed the problem of the canceled I.C.C. flights, and once more showed great concern over how the pilots would come home. Again we agreed: we would leave it to the pilots themselves to decide.

My first reaction to the question of the route home was to consider it rather unimportant. Yet it became evident that the United States Government was much concerned, indeed (and this took me by surprise) apprehensive. Why? Did they want to get the pilots out of the deadly hands of the peace movement (Berrigan and Zinn)? This didn't seem crucial; they offered to take us back on the same plane. Apparently, they did not want the pilots to meet the world press in an unfettered series of interviews—in Bangkok, Paris, New York, and wherever else the commercial airline would stop. Why? Did they think Hanoi radio was accurate in describing the pilots as "repentant"? This did not seem likely. These were not reluctant conscripts but career military men who had gone through intensive training; an Air Force major, an Air Force captain, and a Navy lieutenant. They had been prisoners a short time (all were shot down in October 1967). And judging from the three NLF prisoners released to Tom Hayden, the other side was either not using "repentance" as a condition for release, or had very loose criteria.

What it seemed to come down to (and all this is inference, because the Embassy people never discussed their anxiety explicitly; Father Berrigan and I were hardly seen by them as psychiatric counselors) was worry, not about desertion or denunciation (although this was always an outside chance), but merely about the possibility of embarrassment, perhaps by showing a bit of warmth toward the Vietnamese, or (at worst) an implied criticism of the bombing of the North. We who spent much of our time denouncing governments for their insensitivity to human need cannot really comprehend how delicate are the antennae of governments to any criticism, to any disturbance of the carefully constructed but frail image they hold up to the world. Thus, Dan Berrigan and I, assuming cool rationality on the part of the Leviathan, could not predict that it would remain so fiercely determined to have its way on something as minor as the route home—and even at the risk of hurting (as it turned out) its "own," the fliers.

On Friday, the 9th of February, the I.C.C. plane received special dispensation to take off from harassed Saigon, and arrived at Vientiane, ready to take us and a handful of others (mostly I.C.C. personnel and their families; also an elegantly dressed young British Foreign Service officer) to Hanoi. It was a very old four-engined Boeing craft, of which there had been only six left in the world as of two years ago, we were told. Now there were only three; the others had crashed, including one lost with all aboard on the run from Vientiane to Hanoi (apparently shot down, but it was still a mystery).

The plane flew along a narrow, prearranged corridor, at pre-scribed altitude, at agreed-upon time and airspeed (so that all those anti-aircraft batteries below would hold fire) and had a last-minute check by radio with Hanoi before takeoff to make sure Hanoi was not being bombed. As we crossed the Laos-Vietnam border, the French stewardess handed out flak helmets, but it was an easy flight. Over the Hanoi airfield, a searchlight picked us out, and we were soon on the ground, received warmly by mem-bers of the Democratic Republic of Vietnam Peace Committee, holding out two bouquets of flowers (it is hard to be unmoved when the people who have been bombed for three years by your countrymen extend their hands). Then, an eerie auto trip through the night into Hanoi, past bombed-out buildings, anti-aircraft crews bunched in the darkness, people on foot and on bicycles moving along the road in an endless, thick stream.

In that first get-together with the Peaceniks of Hanoi (it was like visiting friends in San Francisco: "what would you like to see while you're in town, fellows?") we hit it off right away. They were a far cry from the apparatchiks of East or West—a loose bunch—young, dressed in rough jackets, hands in pockets—great guys: Oanh, Hieu, Vann, Phan. Three spoke English. One spoke French. That first night, the airmen were mentioned briefly and then that subject disappeared from the agenda while we explored people and places in Hanoi—a fascinating, intense learning of history, politics, and day-to-day living. This went on for five days, and Berrigan and I were beginning to wonder about the prisoners when, on Wednesday evening, returning from one of our discus-sions-over-tea, we found our friend Oanh waiting for us at the hotel. (A composer, his casual slouch deceptive; he was unerr-ingly efficient.) He said: "Please eat supper quickly. In one hour we will meet the three prisoners."

We drove through dark streets to the prison; it seemed like so many other government buildings, an old French villa adapted to the new exigencies. Inside, there was the usual introductory tea session. The prison commandant read to us his data on the three fliers: Major Norris Overly, thirty-nine, flying out of a base in

South Vietnam, wife and two children in Detroit; Captain John Black, thirty, flying out of Udom airfield in Thailand, wife and three kids in Tennessee; Lieutenant (Junior Grade) David Methany, flying off an aircraft carrier, twenty-four, single.

Then, we were invited into another room, where Berrigan and I were seated at a small table with two of our Peace Committee buddies. Along the wall to our right was a table for the prison commandant and his interpreter. Along the wall to our left, below a photo of Ho Chi Minh, another table, with three empty places. On the tables were tea, cookies, and cigarettes. Hieu whispered to us: when they come in, we will introduce you briefly. He hesitated: "Whether or not you shake hands is up to you."

There was a curtained door to our left, and a very short, very tough-looking soldier came quickly through it, followed by the three fliers, who stood behind their seats, bowed to the commandant, and sat down. Dan and I were introduced. We walked over and shook hands. Then followed an hour of what can only be described as small talk: "You fellows are looking good." (They did; they looked well-fed, indeed more rounded than Dan Berrigan and I, though that is not saying much.) "Where are you from?" "Oh yes, I know that town." "Do you know so-and-so in Des Moines?" And so on. An absurd conversation under the circumstances? Perhaps.

About half an hour through our chat, Major Overly became aware we had left the Vietnamese out of the conversation and turned to the prison commandant with a mild apology for our immersion in American-type subjects. The commandant was gracious. He wore spectacles, and his manner was mild. But he dropped one disturbing statement into the room: "You realize that if Hanoi is bombed before you leave, we may reconsider our decision to release you." Back in the hotel later, Dan and I mused and pondered over the encounter.

Hanoi had not been bombed in our first five days there, although, from the first morning, there were alerts which sent everyone into shelters. After our return to the States, newspapermen kept referring to the "bombing pause" over Hanoi—but on those five days of "the pause" the skies were completely overcast. The day after our first meeting with the fliers, Thursday, was the first day of our stay that the sun shone. And on that day, the bombers came. We crowded into a shelter with several Catholic lay leaders with whom we had been visiting, and heard the bombs exploding in the outer districts of Hanoi, planes droning overhead.

We wondered later about the priorities of the American government. They knew we were in Hanoi to pick up three fliers; did it not occur to them as at least a slim possibility that to bomb Hanoi at exactly that time might endanger the release? Granted that the military objectives of the bombing were more important to the United States than any consideration for the lives of the Vietnamese (with hundreds of schools, hospitals, churches destroyed, with whole villages razed, with anti-personnel bombs dropped in huge quantities, this was clear); were those military objects also more important to the United States Government than the freedom of three American fliers, who themselves had been engaged in that same military action? The insistence that the bombing should go on anyway could be seen as an admirable lack of chauvinism on the part of the United States Government: to it, all people, even Americans, were created equally expendable. It was exactly this equalitarian ruthlessness that would be (yes, *The Spy Who Came in From the Cold*) revealed again when we brought the three airmen back from Hanoi.

We prepared to leave Hanoi on Friday, the next scheduled arrival of the I.C.C. plane. This was two days after our first formal meeting with the airmen, one day after the bombing. As if to provide what scientists call a "control" on the thesis that a bombing "pause" meant bad weather, that Friday the skies were murky, and there was a "pause" over Hanoi.

In the afternoon, we met with Pham Van Dong, the Premier of North Vietnam, a man of high intelligence, oceanic calm, and exuberant personal warmth (altogether, a man of such stature as to make us cringe thinking of the Kys, Chiangs, Parks, Duvaliers, and other leaders of the free world). His grasp of political realities was both firm and subtle: "your leaders make a mistake when they think we are depending on the American peace movement. It is our own efforts, our own determination that we count on. We have no illusions about the power of the peace movement. However, it is a fact that as the war goes on, your own problems at home will intensify, and as the social issues in the United States become more difficult to solve, the war will become an intolerable burden on your society, and your people will demand that the war end, for their own sake."

Several hours before takeoff from Hanoi, we "received" the three airmen for the North Vietnam Peace Committee in a little formal ceremony: Oanh made a brief statement for the Committee; Dan Berrigan made one for us; Lieutenant Methany for the fliers ("We thank the North Vietnamese for their kindness.") Then we went back to the hotel, where the Committee had arranged for me and Father Berrigan to have supper alone with the fliers. (Throughout, the handshake incident being only one example, they treated with sensitivity our relationship with the fliers.) The supper was splendid, served in a room by a battery of waiters (endless bowls of hot potage, cold cuts, chicken, bread, and beer). Methany (the youngest, blonde, only a few years as a Navy flier, and not sure as the other two about a military career) said, in the nearest we got to any discussion about the war: "I hope we get a chance to talk about the war with you fellows. You know, I'm a flag-waver from way back; I believe in fighting to defend my country. But I hope we get to talk."

Over supper, we discussed the route back to the States from Vientiane. We laid out the alternatives carefully: the government would probably have an army plane waiting at Vientiane; it would get the men home faster (perhaps twelve to twenty-four hours faster) than a commercial flight. (Air France could take us from Bangkok to Paris to New York, arriving Sunday noon.) It would also mean no press harassment—although Methany, the youngest, had handled the press quite coolly at the just-finished ceremony, despite a wild scene of flashbulbs, whirring cameras, importunate questioners from the world press. We noted that the U.S. government obviously preferred that the men take a military plane, yet had assured us at least twice that the fliers were free to choose their own route home.

On the side of a commercial flight was only one factor: the North Vietnamese had indicated to Dan Berrigan and me that (without setting it as a condition for the release) they would not be pleased if the fliers were immediately trundled into a military plane and taken to a military base. Somehow, they thought that would violate the spirit of the release. It was not that they had illusions about the men rejecting military life after their arrival in the States; indeed, they had said to Berrigan and me that it was even conceivable that the three would return to bomb North Vietnam again, and this would sadden them. But even if this occurred, they said, they would retain their basic feeling that the American people, even the American fighting men, were not their enemies.

After that brief summary of the alternatives, Major Overly spoke very firmly: "Our first concern must be for the fellow prisoners we left behind, and the possibility of future releases by the North Vietnamese. It's clear that we should go back to the States together by commercial flight." The other two agreed immediately, and there was no more discussion of this.

The flight from Hanoi to Vientiane was smooth; the stewardess served candies and *apéritifs* and we all relaxed. I sat between Major Overly and Captain Black. Father Berrigan sat with Methany. Overly told me about his experiences in captivity. "I was shot down north of the DMZ. The next twenty-eight days—the trek, under military guard, north to Hanoi—were an experience I never want to have again. I was abused, spat on, threatened, beaten. But I could understand exactly why those people would want to kill me. My guard saved my life three times. It was all strange. One moment, someone would want to kill me. The next minute another Vietnamese would act towards me with such compassion that it just staggered me. I had a huge infection on my back and was in great pain. They gave me sulfa, and after a long time it was cured. When I got to the regular prison, the worst was over. We were well treated. I got no indoctrination, just a few books on Vietnamese history. We got plenty to eat, medical care as needed. The Air Force has a rule against men shot down returning to the combat zone; that's fine with me. I've got three years to go before I can retire. I'd like to do something Stateside maybe."

Overly and Black knew I had written some books; they wanted to know about them, wondered how they could get copies. I promised to send them some, took their addresses. Overly said: "Before this trip is over, I'm going to tell you my whole story, in detail. I think we owe that much to you fellows."

That never happened. As we taxied into the Vientiane airfield, the pilot called a message from the tower: "Will the five men connected with the prisoner release please remain aboard the plane while the other passengers descend." We could see a great gathering on the field of newsmen, cameras, lights. The other passengers got off. Four neatly dressed men got on, and introduced themselves. One was the American Ambassador to Laos, William Sullivan. The others were his air attaché, his naval attaché, and his press attaché. Sullivan asked the fliers if they needed medical attention. His whole manner was crisp, neat, and cool toward the three; but perhaps Berrigan and I could not understand the sentiment that lies beneath those official exteriors—did not McNamara choke up saying goodbye to the Pentagon? The pilots said no, they had no urgent medical problems. (One of the statements made later by a navy spokesman was that the men took military planes so they could have medical attention. We have developed the technology of the lie far beyond the crude days of the Ten Commandments.)

Sullivan moved quickly to his most important business: "You men can choose whether you go home by commercial line or by military plane. However, you do understand that you are still members of the armed forces, and it is my duty to report to you that the Department of Defense has expressed the preference that you go home by military aircraft. About a hundred feet away on the airfield is an army jet, waiting and ready to take the three of you to Udorn Airfield in Thailand, and then tomorrow you will fly home. I might add that this decision was made in Washington." He hesitated a moment. "Indeed, it comes from the White House."

There was a bit of silence. Then Major Overly responded. "Sir, I have been in the Air Force seventeen years, and when my government speaks like that, I know what it means. We will go back by military aircraft." Captain Black quickly assented. Lieutenant Methany was obviously upset. He said: "Wait a minute. Let's talk about this." Then followed forty minutes of tense argument in the confines of the old Boeing plane. We agreed on the advantages of the military plane (speed, and less harassment by the press) but asked if it overrode the matter of future prisoner releases by the North Vietnamese. Whether or not the Vietnamese released future prisoners, the Ambassador said, was a cold matter of political calculation with them. In the grade-B movies about the Red Menace, the thickset man with the heavy Russian accent says: "There is no room for sentiment in our considerations, comrades." We have not yet done justice in grade-A movies to the same point made by slim, dapper men, speaking with our own clear tongue.

The Ambassador turned to me: "I didn't know the North Vietnamese were setting conditions for this release." They were not setting conditions, I replied; it was a more subtle problem, one of psychology and spirit. The Ambassador questioned how we knew that this was indeed what the North Vietnamese preferred. Major Overly cut in: "The North Vietnamese told us exactly the same thing." (This was news to me; I had not known they expressed their feelings to the fliers also.)

What advantage of the military plane, we persisted, could be more important than the question of future prisoner releases? Well, the Ambassador countered, it might be hurtful to such releases if the men met the press and said the wrong things. We told about the very first press encounter in Hanoi, where the fliers had handled themselves admirably, with no embarrassment to anyone. Besides, the simple device of a prepared statement could take care of such problems. So: what other objection was there?

The Ambassador could only keep saying: "They have considered all the alternatives in Washington, before making their decision. The best minds in Washington have been involved." (We let this slide; the NLF offensive was still going on, and why rub it in to the "best minds"?) We did suggest that the men in Washington, smart as they were, had not recently been in North Vietnam, had not spoken with North Vietnamese, were not in a position to judge this situation as well as the fliers or we could. Sullivan's reply, aside from being a stunning *non-sequitur,* was a good example of how an intelligent man, trapped in a bureaucratic decision, makes unintelligent statements: "The man in Washington who had much to do with this decision came out of a Japanese prison camp in 1945 weighing ninety-seven pounds." Dan Berrigan said drily: "Look at these three men. None of them weighs ninety-seven pounds. I don't see the analogy."

Berrigan had had enough. "Let's go," he said to me. The fliers were very troubled. Methany was fighting back some indefinable emotion. They shook our hands. "We're sorry," they kept repeating. "Good luck," we said. Overly whispered something to me, quite warm, quite personal. They walked out, talked to the cameras, lights, crowding newsmen, then went to the army jet. They were no longer prisoners, yet not quite free.

As I write this, that argument about the route home seems as it did at the start of our trip, ludicrously trivial—an almost childish dispute on both sides. Three men released from war—how puny a fact was even that, with millions still trapped in the cauldron of death that is Vietnam. Why should these three be released—these, who dutifully bombed villages, roads, people, schools (not deliberately, let's agree—only inevitably)? Why not the three tiny Vietnamese kids we found squatting in the entrance to the air raid shelter one day? Perhaps there was a larger issue involved. Perhaps we move closer to the end of the war whenever even one of the parties shows compassion, in a unilateral act, and toward the most guilty of warriors—the blind bombardiers.

Now don't get sentimental, even my most radical friends insist; there must have been some political motive on the part of the North Vietnamese in this prisoner release. Well, all right. But all decent acts that occur in this world are marred by some selfish motivation; if we let that fact determine how we respond to such acts, the possibility of ending the vicious cycle of reciprocal cruelty is foreclosed. If people and nations can only react on the basis of the most cynical interpretations of the others' conduct, the world doesn't have a chance.

There is something else, too. I asked Oanh that last day (as we sat next to one another at a little goodbye luncheon) if there wasn't *something* we should ask from the United States Government in reciprocity for the release. He shook his head. "You don't understand. We have released these men in the time of our lunar New Year. That is a very important holiday to us, very deep in our tradition. It is the time when, wherever we are, we return to our families for the New Year. So we thought of a small gesture, even in the midst of war, in the spirit of the holiday to release three men to go back to their families." And so they preferred that the fliers be returned directly to their homes, rather than what did take place: the immediate flight of the pilots to the very air base in Thailand from which one of the men (Black) had taken off to bomb North Vietnam.

Against the cynicism of the Ambassador (as well as my own) another fact must be measured: it is canonized in the revolutionary ideology of North Vietnam that enemy soldiers are to be treated with compassion. From the start of the war against the French, Ho Chi Minh insisted on this. In a message (September 26, 1945) meant not for the world, but for his own troops, he said: "I want to recommend to our southern compatriots just one thing: as far as the Frenchmen captured in the war are concerned, we must watch them carefully, but we must also treat them generously. We must show to the world, and to the French people in particular, that we want only independence and freedom, that we are not struggling for the sake of individual enmity and rancor. We must show to the world that we are an intelligent people, more civilized than the homicidal invaders."

The word Ho used was "show," not "tell." If the prisoner release was "propaganda" (as the newspapermen kept saying, before and after our flight to Hanoi) it was propaganda by *deed,* which, if generally adopted, would improve the world overnight. The U.S., if envious, could respond with its own propaganda move: stopping the bombing in the North. Or with the greatest propaganda of all: withdrawing all its bombers, all its guns and troops, from Vietnam.

The pinched, mean reaction to the prisoner release (a "propaganda ploy," *Life* said lifelessly) is an indicator of what has happened to the spirit of generosity we always liked to believe was characteristic of America. Some future generation will catch the irony better: that a tiny country, under daily attack, should deliver back to the Behemoth, three of its marauders. And the Behemoth, meanwhile, has been seeking to imprison those who have not bombed or killed a single soul—but who have spoken the forbidden words to the Behemoth's children: Thou Shalt Not Kill.

Whatever softening possibility came from this small act of the Vietnamese was destroyed by this country's fear. Never in history has a country been so rich, so powerful and so fearful. In this case, it was a fear of something as small as three very straight American airmen saying something slightly embarrassing to Washington—an event so unlikely, and so minor, that only a government almost hysterical in its anxiety would behave as ours did. True, a government so harassed by fact as ours today, so trembling on the brink, fears even the slightest nudge, the smallest breeze from an unexpected direction. It refuses to take even the tiniest risks.

In risk, however, lies the only hope of escape from deep troubles—the risk of humane response to humane acts, or even the risk of unilateral initiatives. This is not possible, however, when a nation has forgotten its professed values and is instead obsessed with political advantage as an ultimate objective, when it has adopted as a universal criterion for all its actions that of Colonel Cathcart in *Catch-22*, who measured everything in the world by a simple test: "will it give me a black eye, or put a feather in my cap?" Our sickness is even worse than that, because our single test is (and we are ready to blow up the world on the results): will it give *them* a black eye, or a feather in their cap?

This obsessive fear, that if the next point is won or lost, the game, the world, and all the galaxies are lost (yes, those deadly dominoes again), leads to disregard not only of the lives of the enemy's children, but of one's own. When the American people discover this—that our government is not only indifferent to whether the Vietnamese live or die, but also to whether Americans live or die—then we will have a great commotion through the land, and the war will come to a screeching halt.

15

Violence: the double standard

The problem of violence, as I write this essay, is pressing pain-fully on us, in the movement of troops to Southeast Asia, in the tensions of every major city and college campus in the United States. I assume, therefore, that practical concerns, based on ethical values, should guide our inquiry into violence.

As social scientists, we worry that the values we hold as human beings should not distort our scholarship. But we must also be careful that a myopic focus on scholarship should not obliterate our values. Perhaps one way of approaching this problem of ob-jectivity is to decide that our values will intrude at certain con-sciously chosen points—not in the midst of empirical data gather-ing (because we don't want to blind ourselves to uncomfortable facts), but before and after: in the questions we pose, and in applying our findings to the world around us.

I am concerned with two values, and the historic fact that a single-minded concentration on one or the other distorts our moral vision. In one simplistic standard, the absence of violence—as it is usually defined—is a supreme objective. (As usually defined, violence is the overt use of physical force against human beings, resulting in biological injury or death, or the risk of either.) However, to refuse to engage in the kind of social action which risks this may mean reconciling oneself to the status quo, or to the kind of glacial evolution toward progress that Herbert Spencer (in *First Principles*) did not want to disturb. And the status quo itself may include a number of evils (forms of violence, really, if we go beyond the usual definition) other than abrupt, overt physical harm.

To absolutize the value of nonviolence is to defer all social change that cannot be accomplished without violence. To absolutize the value of social change, on the other hand, is to be willing to pay extreme costs in human life for puny reforms.

Social change, then, and the avoidance of violence, are twin objectives, which creates the problem of always ascertaining the correct balance between the two. I would suggest that the balance is less difficult if we use a broader definition of violence, to include biological and psychic damage below the level of the overt: malnutrition, disease, alienation, psychological repression, fear, humiliation. This definition still leaves the ethical problem of weighing alternatives in human relations, but without the pretense that overt physical violence is the sole evil.

There is a basic misconception about the United States, I am going to argue, which goes something like this: that the U.S. is a peculiarly nonviolent nation, with a special dispensation for achieving social change through peaceful parliamentary reform. This idea, I believe, is based on two failures of vision: one is a failure to recognize how much overt violence has characterized our behavior toward other nationalities, other races—the outgroups of our society; the other is a failure to recognize the place of violence—both overt and hidden—in whatever important change has occurred in American history.

This failure of perception brings about a double standard: there is, on the one hand, a national tendency to absolutize the value of social change at the expense of human life when the violence required for this change is directed at other nations or other races; and on the other hand, a tendency to absolutize the value of peace (at the expense of social change) within the national frame, within the going system.

With these preliminary statements, I would like to attempt a brief, impressionistic survey of violence and social change in the history of the United States. And then I want to suggest a number of propositions about violence which are important to keep in mind if we care about both peace and change.

Among those few historians and political scientists who, since World War II, have looked up momentarily from specialized scholarly pursuits to make broad judgments about American history, the dominant motif has been the idea of consensus. Richard Hofstadter, in *The American Political Tradition,* stressed the fact that American political thought and behavior, from the Founding Fathers through Franklin D. Roosevelt, stayed within a rather narrow band of agreement; that the rivalries of Hamilton and Jefferson, Jackson and Clay, Lincoln and Douglas, Cleveland and Harrison, Teddy Roosevelt, Woodrow Wilson and William Howard Taft, even FDR and Herbert Hoover, were family quarrels.

Herbert Agar, in *The Price of Union,* saw the remarkable similarity of the two major parties (which Lord Bryce had commented upon in the late nineteenth century) as an essential requirement of American peaceful development. And Louis Hartz, in *The Liberal Tradition in America,* noted the lack of extreme right or extreme left movements in this country and found a fundamental core of belief, based on the ideas of John Locke, acting as a political and ideological gyroscope for this country, constantly bringing it back to dead center.

These major interpretations, largely accepted by their colleagues, and pointing, I must emphasize, to important truths, nevertheless have reinforced what was already an exaggerated emphasis on peace and stability in national development. This "consensus school" of American studies, it should be noted, grew up after World War II, when the internal conflicts of the thirties were fading from memory, and before the civil rights revolution had gotten under way. Its emphasis, I believe, can be very useful in pointing to the limitations of American self-consciousness, but also misleading as a guide to the realities of the American past.

Our first great social upheaval was the expulsion of the British and their local officialdom, in the establishment of an independent nation. A new privileged class was created, based on the overthrow of the royal and proprietary colonial governments and the redistribution of land after the confiscation of royal, proprietary, and Loyalist estates. There were accompanying changes: the diminution of property requirements for political participation in the new state constitutions; the abolition of primogeniture and entail; the disestablishment of the Anglican Church, and the freeing of slaves in the northern states.

This was accomplished by seven years of warfare, in which 25,000 in the Continental Army were killed—about one out of every eight men who served. To judge the extent of this violence, one would have to consider that the same ratio of dead in our present population would amount to a death list of one and a half million.

The next great social change was the pacification of the continent and the creation of a vast common market, from ocean to ocean, 1500 miles deep, through which labor, capital, raw materials, and finished goods, could move freely. This was a vital prerequisite for the development of that industrial colossus which in the twentieth century would produce half the world's goods with 6 percent of the world's people. And the creation of this common market involved a series of violent acts which we have conveniently put out of memory.

The first of these acts was the removal and extermination of the Indians, who at the time of Columbus numbered one million in what is now the United States, and who are about 400,000 today. Violence certainly is frequent *within* groups, but it seems to be invoked most easily when directed at strangers. The outsider is either physically odd, linguistically or culturally distinct, or is invested with strangeness because of distance—or, even in the absence of these, is *declared* an outsider by the manipulation of verbal symbols. Thus he becomes an invisible victim, an object of sorts, toward which enmity can multiply without qualm. In the early nineteenth century, a French traveler noted this in American treatment of the Indian:

> In the heart of this society, so policed, so prudish, so sententiously moral and virtuous, one encounters a complete insensibility, a sort of cold and implacable egoism when it's a question of the American indigines. . . . it's the same pitiless instinct which animates the European race here as everywhere else.

There were six hundred distinct Indian societies at the time the white man arrived in North America, John Collier tells us (he was commissioner of Indian Affairs in the Roosevelt Administration and one of the world's leading authorities on the Indians) and there was not one square mile of the continent unoccupied or unused. "These societies existed in perfect ecological balance with the forest, the plain, the desert, the waters, and the animal life." Their warfare with one another was controlled, moderate, cautious; their ambitions were small.

Then the white man came, and not one white conqueror, as in the area south of the Rio Grande, but various powers: Spanish, Dutch, French, English, battling with one another, and drawing the Indians into their battles. Still, the Indian societies were kept whole, and rule was indirect, as a calculated policy of the competing European powers, and then codified by the new United States as the basic law of Indian relations.

But when the Spanish, Dutch, French, English were gone from the continent, Collier says, ". . . there remained only one expanding empire, race-prejudiced and with a boundless land hunger. The former policies toward Indian societies and Indianhood became reversed; a policy at first implicit and sporadic, then explicit, elaborately rationalized and complexly implemented, of the extermination of Indian societies and of every Indian trait, of the eventual liquidation of the Indians, became the formalized policy, law and practice."

The record is hard to read without flinching, because it is the shadowed underside of the most cherished events in American history. We romanticize the early Virginian adventurers, but they settled on the territory of the Powhatan Confederacy and destroyed its members in bloody warfare. We are proud of the Puritans, but that great Puritan divine, Cotton Mather, a leading intellectual of the colony, when disease decimated the Indians after the *Mayflower* landing, said: "The woods were almost cleared of those pernicious creatures, to make room for a better growth." When the New England settlers burned the wigwams of the Pequots and massacred them as they fled, Cotton Mather recorded it coolly: "It was supposed that no less than six hundred Pequot souls were brought down to hell that day."

After the Civil War, the Plains Indians were hunted down, harassed, killed, the remaining ones squeezed into the Indian Territory of Oklahoma, and finally driven out of there too. The United States Army crushed the Indian in a series of wars and battles: the Chivington Massacre of 1864 in Colorado, the Black Kettle massacre by Custer in 1868 in Texas, the driving of the Cheyennes South in 1878, and the Massacre of Wounded Knee in 1890. There were the Cheyenne-Arapaho War and the Sioux Wars of the 1860's. In the 1870's came the Red River War, the Nez Percé War, the Apache War, and more Sioux Wars.

In the record of violence, we might note a phenomenon different than either the quick destruction of the body, or the slow destruction of the spirit—the elimination of the means of life, land, shelter, clothing, food. For the Plains Indian, this was accomplished by the slaughter of his most essential raw material: the buffalo. First the railroads split the great herds in two parts; then professional hunters with repeating rifles made the plains a slaughterhouse; by 1870 one million a year were being killed. By 1875 the southern herd was practically exterminated, and ten years later, the northern herd.

Collier says: "It was among the Plains Indians that the policy of annihilation of the societies and then of the individual Indian personality was carried to the farthest extreme." This statement is important because it is a recognition of violence beyond the physical: the destruction of culture and personality.

This sounds strangely familiar to us these days, because we have lately become aware that lynching was not the worst thing that happened to the Negro in this country. In Stanley Elkins' comparison (in his book *Slavery*) of the Nazi concentration camps with the American slave plantation, his concern is not the whippings and beatings, but the assaults on the psyche, the warping of the self, the crippling of identity. And of course, this did not end with the outlawing of slavery, because the violence done to the Negro person continues on the southern plantation, in the southern town, and in the northern ghettos. Again and again, the young Negro uses the term "concentration camp" or "prison" to describe the ghetto.

The evacuation of the Indian was one necessary step in the forcible clearing of that national area which would house the most productive economy in world history. Piece by piece, what is now the United States was assembled, at times by clever diplomacy, as with the Louisiana Purchase and the Oregon Territory, at other times by violence, as with East Florida after a campaign of harassment by Andrew Jackson, as with the southwestern states (from New Mexico to California) after the Mexican War.

By the time of the Civil War, the United States extended from ocean to ocean. By 1890, Frederick Jackson Turner could use the Census Bureau's finding that the frontier was gone to start a train of discussion on its meaning. That Turner saw the extension of the frontier as a benign influence on American democracy is still another sign of the national tendency to test our benevolence by how we behave toward one another, and not toward those—whether Indians, Negroes, Mexicans, or Spaniards—beyond the physical or psychological frontier.

The Civil War, with all its complexities, was very much a part of the same process described above, a violent and successful effort on the part of the national government to maintain its control over a great agrarian hinterland whose raw materials and markets were needed for the burst of economic development which would take place in the late nineteenth century. President Lincoln said plainly that the retention of the South in the Union, and not slavery, was his main concern.

My point is that the presumed peaceful constitutional and economic development of this great territory of the United States required a war that took 600,000 lives. Out of a population of 33,000,000, 2,300,000 young men went to fight, and one out of four died. If applied to our present population, it would be as if three and a half million died in war. Edmund Wilson, in his biting introduction to *Patriotic Gore,* takes some of the romantic nonsense not only out of the Civil War Centennials, but out of all adulatory treatments of American territorial growth.

In the course of the war, slavery was abolished. Whether it was the prime cause of the war or not (and we would have to distinguish between its economic-political aspects and its human aspects to discuss that) its abolition was one of the great social changes in American history, and was a consequence of the most ferocious burst of violence this nation has ever experienced. It is hard to see how slavery could have been ended when it was, without either a series of revolts such as those planned by John Brown, or a devastating war waged, ironically, two years later, by the very government that condemned John Brown to death for seeking a *less* costly means of emancipating the slave.

If the position of the Negro in this country is any test of the thesis that our free institutions have developed on the basis of peaceful parliamentary change, that thesis could hardly be advanced with any seriousness. That it can be advanced is testimony to how small a part the Negro plays in the national consciousness. He is always an exception, to be noted, and then shoved aside, so that the state of the nation can be calculated without his troublesome presence. (When one-sixth of the nation consisted of black slaves, this was known as "the peculiar institution.")

Furthermore, the violence done to the Negro in his state of slavery, beyond physical mistreatment—divesting him of property, of wife and children, of education, of African culture, of his own identity as a human being—the process of total alienation—was never properly counted, even by our more humane scholars, who often limited their concern to wondering how many Negroes were really whipped by the plantation owner. And the violence done to the black man's spirit, in contemporary society, is only beginning to enter our consciousness.

With independence from European control secured, with the continent united and pacified (and here, as with the American Revolution there were bonuses: a National Bank, Tariff, Railroad Acts, Homestead Acts, no longer opposed by the South), the next great change was the industrialization and urbanization of an agrarian nation. This can be considered a peaceful development only if violence is construed narrowly as overt, intense physical harm. Those who worked on the railroads, in the mines, in the factories and mills, were subjected to a kind of servitude destructive of both body and spirit. The hours were long, the wages low, and often there was a serf-like incarceration in company towns.

George Fitzhugh, in *Cannibals All,* just before the Civil War, had castigated northerners who criticized slavery while holding on to their industrial system. "You, with the command over labor which your capital gives you, are a slave owner—a master, without the obligations of a master. They who work for you, who create your income, are slaves, without the rights of slaves."

The depressions of the 1870's and the 1890's brought great distress. During the first three months of 1874, for instance, about ninety thousand homeless workers, many of them women, lodged in New York City's police station houses, huddled together on benches. They were turned out at daybreak, hungry, to make room for the next batch. The Granger, Greenback, and Populist Movements rose in response to the distress of farmers in those years.

The depressions eased, and the movements declined, but the point is that the nation's industrial progress was made at great human cost to millions of people, a cost that must be reckoned in any expanded definition of violence. Barrington Moore's *Social Origins of Dictatorship and Democracy* illustrates, in his words, "the contributions of violence to gradualism" in the chapter where he discusses the enclosure movement in England, another country with supposedly peaceful parliamentary development.

Another of the important social changes in American history was the development of what we call the "welfare state," the establishment of acceptable living standards for two-thirds of the nation, limiting poverty and distress to those parts of the population which cannot easily combine (farm and service workers) or which lack a territorial base (migrant workers), or which are set off racially from the rest of the population. The welfare state began slowly in the "Progressive Era" with the legislation of the Wilson administration and reached its height with the New Deal. What is often overlooked is the part played by violence of an overt kind in bringing about what is called "The Age of Reform" that starts in the twentieth century.

The Progressivism of Roosevelt-Taft-Wilson followed a period of the most violent labor struggles any country has ever seen: the railroad strikes of 1877, which brought troops and workers into armed conflict; the Haymarket events of 1886, the Homestead Strike of 1892, the Pullman Strike of 1894, the Lawrence Textile Strike of 1912, the Colorado Coal Strike of 1913–14, culminating in the Ludlow Massacre. This was the period of Big Bill Haywood, Mother Jones, and the Industrial Workers of the World.

As for the New Deal, it was accompanied by violent strikes, sit-down and regular. The mayhem documented in the LaFollette Committee hearings is startling to anyone who thinks that the quiet politicking and the eloquence of FDR tells the story of the New Deal reforms.

The most important social change of recent years is the *de jure,* although not the *de facto,* end of segregation in the South, and the awakening of the nation to the outcry of the Negro, for the first time since Reconstruction. Whatever the inadequacies, the lack of enforcement, of the various Civil Rights Bills passed since 1957, however empty are many of the passionate statements on racial equality from the White House, it seems quite clear that ten years of turbulence in the Negro community, from the Montgomery boycott of 1955 to the Selma March of 1965, had a great deal to do with these small gains.

As we take a quick overview of all these events, we find, I believe, that American society does show a growing consensus over time. What we have, however, is not one long consensus, but a series of steps toward consensus, each accompanied by violence which either destroyed, expelled, or incorporated a dissident group.

Thus, the Revolution established a new consensus based on Independence, expelling the British and their Loyalist supporters. Those not satisfied with the new privileged classes (the Shays Rebels in Massachusetts, the Whiskey Rebels in Pennsylvania) were suppressed by force of arms, to create an outwardly peaceful consensus under the new Constitution. Those left out of the new arrangement—the black people—were repressed with the entire paraphernalia of the slave system. Organized labor, after the 1877–1939 period of violent strikes, was brought into the fold with New Deal legislation. And recently, the middle-class Negro has been pacified with the promise of incorporation into white-middle class life, leaving his militant black brethren (Stokely Carmichael, Eldridge Cleaver) outside the consensus.

More and more elements of American life have been invited into the dominant in-group of American society, usually after overt violence of various kinds. Each accretion solidifies the group, which can then continue, or even increase, the violence directed toward those outside the consensus. (Respectable Negro leaders will become more welcome at the White House, while the police will get more and more brutal in breaking up Negro rebellions in the cities or on college campuses.) The creation of a substantial consensus at home seems to create the possibility of using even greater amounts of violence against out-groups abroad. (I have not spoken of the rapid increase in the means of violence, and the use of violence, by the United States abroad in this century, because this is too well-known; I would single out as dramatic points of significance the fire-bombing of Dresden, the atom-bombing of Hiroshima, and the napalm-bombing of Vietnam.)

Our much-praised constitutional development, I conclude, is based on a system which keeps peace on the national level (the overall fabric of the economy, the political order, the value-system), while violating it on two other levels of human existence. That is, the system permits disturbing the inner peace of millions of Americans who are too poor, or too colored, or too different in one way or another to be treated with respect by government and society. And in the field of foreign policy it permits an absolutism in decision-making, combined with the basic premise of national sovereignty (guarding this in the world as zealously as South Carolina once tried to guard its sovereignty in the nation), which acts against what both Hobbes and Locke recognized as a basic law of human nature—the preservation of life.

This brings me back to my thesis: that we have a double standard for the judgment of violence within and without the national-racial group, in which we place a supreme value on peace within the society that has already incorporated us, and a supreme value on violence where we seek to control those outside the corporation. This accounts, for instance, for the general alarm with which the government and the public have greeted militant blacks' talk of self-defense, or any departure from absolute nonviolence, along with the general willingness of government and public to use the most fearsome weapons of violence in Asia.

Let me try now to state what some of the elements of a single-standard ethic of violence might be:

1. All forms of pain and abuse—whether overt, concentrated, and physical, or psychological, hidden, and attenuated—should be placed on the same scale of destructive actions. This creates great problems in weighing some forms of violence against others, but is preferable to solving problems too easily by assigning *no* weight to types of violence beyond the standard definition. The common ingredients, the molecular elements, of all kinds of violence, need to be isolated.

2. Official violence should be granted no special privileges over private violence. John Brown was hanged for attempting, by

a rather small-scale act of violence, to free the Negro slaves; but the United States Government draws little opprobrium for a war in which 600,000 were killed in the same cause. A police murder, however unjustified, is privileged in a way that a private citizen's act of murder is not.

3. Violence done by others should be weighed equally with violence done by ourselves. We were horrified when Hitler killed about a thousand people by dropping bombs on Rotterdam, but accepted easily the killing of over one hundred thousand people in the bombing of Dresden. We count the Vietcong killing of a village chief as more terrible than the American bombing of the population of the village. Pearl Harbor is infinitely more condemned than Hiroshima. We are more troubled by a rock thrown by a Negro at a white policeman than by the policeman's shooting of another Negro. We would be shocked if blacks decided to bomb the state of Alabama to get rid of its oppressive regime—but in international affairs we accept such reasoning.

4. We should assume that all victims are created equal; that violence done to men of other races or other political beliefs is not thereby given special dispensation; a dead Communist is a dead man, as is a dead anti-Communist. George Orwell, in *Homage to Catalonia,* wrote of holding his fire in the Spanish Civil War when a Fascist soldier, running past, had trouble keeping his pants up. "How can you kill a man," he wrote, "who is having trouble holding up his pants?"

5. Violence to property should not be equated with violence to people. A policeman in Atlanta, when I was living there, shot and killed a Negro teen-ager who was running away from a store where a vending machine had been robbed of two dollars. Such scenes can be multiplied by the hundreds; many of those killed in urban uprisings in recent years were doing nothing but looting stores.

6. We should be constantly aware of our disposition to accept violence on the basis of symbolic arguments; animals commit violence for immediate and visible purposes, but humans can be driven to violence by a word, a slogan, a Pavlovian conditioning process, in which we are so far removed from what the symbol stands for that we cannot rationally weigh the human costs and

gains of our own acts. The word "nigger" or "imperialist" or "Communist" has driven, and still drives, rational judgment from the minds of people trapped in the dominant symbolism of our time.

7. We should be aware of Jeremy Bentham's point, in his utilitarian ethic, about *fecundity:* that not only the immediate results of actions be measured, but that we should consider the proliferating effects—of excessive action in the dispensation of overt violence, and of inaction in the toleration of subsurface violence. Insensitivity in either case may lead to unexpected and terrible consequences.

16

Hiroshima and Royan

History can remind us of what we too easily forget—that great moral crusades, whether carried on by nations or revolutionary movements, often bring atrocities committed by the crusaders.

To this fact, we might respond in several ways. Carefully considering the alternatives, we might conclude that this is unfortunate, but necessary to the success of an objective important enough to warrant the cost. Or, we might conclude that while necessary for success, it is so frightful that either the mission must be postponed or another means sought to achieve it. We might decide that it is unnecessary, but an unavoidable consequence of a useful struggle, which we regret but must accept. Or, that being unnecessary, it can be prevented without affecting the larger moral issue adversely. We might even begin to question the validity of a goal which spawns such monstrous children.

In the two-part essay which follows, I intend only two things: to remind us again of the fact of such atrocities, committed in the name of morality by our own and other nations; to propose that in present and future crusades we think hard about how to act.

Hiroshima, with which I start, has been brought to our attention often, but that episode will never be vivid enough in our minds, and we still have not shown that we understand what it suggests. Royan, with which I conclude, is virtually unknown outside of France. It is a smaller-scale atrocity (although more were killed there than in the much more publicized and condemned instances of German bombing in Coventry and Rotterdam).* But it is worth recalling as an example of the countless "small" acts of cruelty committed in situations of moral righteousness.

* In Rotterdam, 980 were killed in the German raid of May 14, 1940. 380 were killed in Coventry. See David Irving, *The Destruction of Dresden,* Holt, Rinehart & Winston, 1964, Chapter 1.

HIROSHIMA

With Robert Butow's research on the Japanese side, Robert Jungk's exploration of the minds of the atomic scientists concerned, Herbert Feis' study of State Department files, and the old records of the U.S. Strategic Bombing Survey—we can approach from four sides the moral question: should we have dropped the atomic bomb on Japan? More important, perhaps we can pull together the evidence, and draw some conclusions to guide us in this frightening time when hydrogen bombers are ready all over the world.

First, let me describe my four sources:

The U.S. Strategic Bombing Survey was set up in November of 1944 to study the effects of bombing on Germany. On August 15, 1945, Truman asked the Survey to do the same for Japan, and one result was its report, *Japan's Struggle to End the War*. The Survey (Paul Nitze and John Kenneth Galbraith worked on it, among others) interrogated seven hundred Japanese officials, later turned the files over to the CIA.

In 1954, an American scholar named Robert Butow, having gone through the papers of the Japanese Ministry of Foreign Affairs, the records of the International Military Tribunal of the Far East, and the interrogation files of the U.S. Army, personally interviewed many of the Japanese principals, and wrote *Japan's Decision to Surrender*. This is the most detailed study from the Japanese side.

Robert Jungk, in a book first published in German, studied the making and dropping of the bomb from the standpoint of the atomic scientists, and in 1958 the American edition was published: *Brighter Than a Thousand Suns*. This book is based largely on personal interviews with the people who played a leading part in the construction and dropping of the bombs.

In 1961, Herbert Feis, who has had unique access to the files of the State Department and to part of the Department of the Army's records on the Manhattan Project, published *Japan Subdued*, which gives us the view from Washington.

What follows now is a compressed chronology of those events which, speeding along in blind parallel on both sides of the Pacific, culminated on August 6th and August 9th of 1945 in the obliteration by blast and fire of the Japanese cities of Hiroshima and Nagasaki.

As early as the spring of 1944, top Japanese admirals anticipated ultimate defeat and began discussing ways of ending the war. In July, the Tojo government fell. In September, the Navy was ready to call a halt, while the Army stood firm. In February of 1945, the Emperor was told by a group of senior statesmen that defeat was certain and peace should be sought at once, and by March a specific peace overture was under cabinet discussion. That month, Tokyo was hit by American fire bombs, and there were eighty thousand killed.

In April of 1945, American forces landed on Okinawa, within close striking distance of Japan, and often considered the southernmost island in the Japanese chain. The Koiso government was replaced by Suzuki, who took office with the specific idea of ending the war as quickly as possible and who undertook approaches to Russian Ambassador Malik about interceding for peace. In this same month, President Roosevelt died, Truman took office, and Secretary of War Stimson told him about the Manhattan Project. In this month too, within that Project, an Interim Committee of distinguished civilians, with an advisory scientific committee of Oppenheimer, Fermi, Arthur Compton, and E. O. Lawrence, was set up to study use of the bomb.

In June of 1945, Okinawa was taken, the Emperor of Japan told a new Inner War Council to plan to end the war, and the Interim Committee advised Truman to use the bomb as quickly as possible, on a dual civilian-military target and without warning. That same month, the report drawn up by atomic scientists James Franck, Leo Szilard and Eugene Rabinowitch, urging that we not drop the bomb on Japan, was referred by Stimson to the scientific committee of four and was rejected.

On July 13, 1945, the United States intercepted Foreign Minister Togo's secret cable to Ambassador Sato in Moscow asking him to get the Soviets to end the war short of unconditional surrender. On July 16th, the test bomb exploded at Alamogordo, New Mexico, and word was sent to Truman at the Potsdam Conference, which began the next day. The Potsdam Declaration of

July 26th called for unconditional surrender, not mentioning the Emperor, whose status was of primary concern to the Japanese.

The Japanese cabinet was divided on unconditional surrender, and while it continued to discuss this, the bomb was dropped August 6th on Hiroshima. While the Japanese were meeting and moving towards acceptance of the Potsdam terms, the Russians declared war August 8th, and the second bomb was dropped on Nagasaki August 9th. Washington's ambiguity about the Emperor delayed final acceptance by the Japanese, but that came August 14th.

Here are the conclusions reached by our four close students of the affair:

The U.S. Strategic Bombing Survey: "Based on a detailed investigation of all the facts and supported by the testimony of the surviving Japanese leaders involved, it is the Survey's opinion that certainly prior to 31 December 1945, and in all probability prior to 1 November 1945, Japan would have surrendered even if the atomic bombs had not been dropped, even if Russia had not entered the war, and even if no invasion had been planned or contemplated." *

Robert Jungk, referring to our interception of the Japanese cables: "But Truman, instead of exploiting diplomatically these significant indications of Japanese weakness, issued a proclamation on July 26 at the Potsdam Conference, which was bound to make it difficult for the Japanese to capitulate without 'losing face' in the process."

Robert Butow, referring to Prince Konoye, special emissary to Moscow who was working on Russian intercession for peace: "Had the Allies given the Prince a week of grace in which to obtain his Government's support for acceptance of the proposals, the war might have ended toward the latter part of July or the

---

* This conclusion is supported by the statements of virtually every top military leader of that period: Eisenhower, MacArthur, Marshall, Leahy, LeMay, etc. After this essay first appeared, Gar Alperovitz published his brilliant study, *Atomic Diplomacy*. His final chapter summarizes the evidence for the argument that political considerations, not military ones, were paramount in dropping the bomb.

very beginning of the month of August, without the atomic bomb and without Soviet participation in the conflict."

Referring to the intercepted cables, Butow says: "The record of what occurred during the next two weeks . . . indicates that Washington failed to turn this newly won and unquestionably vital intelligence data to active and good account."

And: "The mere fact that the Japanese had approached the Soviet Union with a request for mediation should have suggested the possibility that Japan, for all of her talk about 'death to the last man,' might accept the Allied demand for unconditional surrender if only it were couched in more specific terms than those which Washington was already using to define its meaning." ("Specific," Butow means, in relation to the Emperor, for former Ambassador Joseph Grew had been pounding away at the White House with the idea that this question of the Emperor was supremely important, but to no result.)

Herbert Feis: ". . . the curious mind lingers over the reasons why the American government waited so long before offering the Japanese those various assurances which it did extend later." These reasons, Feis says, are a complex of personal motives and national psychology. Truman was influenced by the desire of the Joint Chiefs of Staff to whip Japan further, by the desire of Secretary of State Byrnes for joint action with our allies, by the desire of Secretary of War Stimson to test the bomb, and by domestic criticism of less than unconditional surrender. Also by "the impetus of the combat effort and plans, the impulse to punish, the inclination to demonstrate how supreme was our power. . . ."

Feis sees two questions: was the bombing essential; and was it justified as a way of bringing early surrender. "The first of these, and by far the easiest to answer, is whether it was essential to use the bomb in order to compel the Japanese to surrender on our terms within a few months. It was not. That ought to have been obvious even at the time of decision, but . . . it does not seem to have been." On the second question, Feis is uncertain. He notes the tremendous desire to end the war as quickly as possible, concern that a demonstration bomb would fail. Yet he thinks it probable that such a demonstration, plus Soviet entry, would have brought victory as soon, or a few weeks later.

After rummaging through this mess of death and documents, I have some random ideas which may be worth thinking about:

1. The question of *blame* should be ignored. I can think of two ways in which blame-saying might be useful: in assessing persons who are still alive and about whom a choice might need to be made in the granting of crucial responsibility (for instance if we were picking a head for the Atomic Energy Commission, we would feel safer with Leo Szilard than with Robert Oppenheimer on the basis of experience with the Manhattan Project); and in puncturing illusions about nations whose behavior has often been idealized, like our own. But in general, our concern should be to see what we can learn for the handling of our present situation, not to settle dead arguments. Also, blame-placing sets up psychological blocks to the creation of rapport with people who have made mistakes in the past.

2. One wonders about our easy generalizations as to the difference in decision-making between "democratic" and "totalitarian" countries when we learn of the incredible number of deliberations and discussions that went on in the Japanese higher councils in days when everything was quite literally crashing around their ears—and when we recall, on the other hand, Truman's quick decisions on Korea, and Kennedy's on Cuba.

3. Making sure our military-minded men do not make top political decisions seems very important after seeing how the military in Japan delayed surrender until the bombs were dropped and how military men played such a large part in our decision to drop the bomb. (General Groves, though not an official member of the crucial Interim Committee, attended all its meetings and played a leading part in its decisions. Truman, too, seemed much influenced by the military.) Yet I believe now, after reading the evidence presented by Gar Alperovitz in *Atomic Diplomacy* that this emphasis on the special guilt of the military men is wrong. High civilian officials—Truman, Stimson, Byrnes—seem to have been the crucial decision-makers on the dropping of the bomb. It is a long chain of responsibility, and we need to concentrate on those links which we can ourselves affect.

4. While a decision-making process may seem to thunder along like a Diesel truck, a firm touch by any one of a number of people

can often send it in a different direction. Truman could certainly have applied that touch. Groves could have. Stimson as head of the Interim Committee could have. James Byrnes, carrying to Potsdam a State Department memo stressing the Emperor question, might have affected the final Declaration in such a way as to bring Japanese response if only he himself had believed in the memo. Oppenheimer or Fermi or Compton (since Lawrence already seemed to have objections to the policy) might have turned the tide by a specific recommendation from the scientific advisors to the Interim Committee. Lower down in the pyramid of power, the probability of any one man changing a crucial decision decreases, but it does not disappear. Szilard and his buried petition *might* have brought results, if joined by others. The point is: no human being inside an organizational apparatus should become overwhelmed by it to the point of immobility. He needs to play the probability statistics coolly, exerting his own pressure to the utmost even in the face of complete uncertainty about what others may be doing at the same time.

5. The impulse to "win the war, and as fast as possible" seems to have dominated everyone's thinking, to the exclusion of rational and humane judgments. The most advanced thinkers in the West, its greatest liberals (and radicals), were more sold on this war than on any in history; never were the moral issues more clear in a great conflict, and the result was simplistic thinking about the war. (I recall August 6, 1945, very clearly. I had served as a bombardier in the Eighth Air Force in Europe, flew back to the States for a thirty-day furlough before a scheduled move to the Pacific, and while on furlough picked up a newspaper telling of the bomb dropped on Hiroshima. I felt only gladness that the end of the war was imminent.)

6. Oppenheimer has said that he did "not know beans about the military situation in Japan" when he and his committee decided to reject the Franck report. General Groves and the atom bomb people did not know about the messages the State Department had intercepted, while the State Department did not know the bombing was imminent. This suggests the importance of the free flow of information. But it would be naive to think that evil

acts are only the result of poor communications. Some people can simply change their minds on the basis of new information; with others, a drastic revision of their sense of right and wrong is needed. If Oppenheimer and Fermi and others had only known how close Japan was to surrender, and known that an invasion was not necessary to defeat Japan, their decision would probably have been different. With others, like Groves—and probably Truman—the question would still remain: can we save *any* American lives (or gain *any* political advantage) by killing 100,000 Japanese? With them, the nationalistic morality which equates one American life with one thousand foreigners' lives seems to have obtained; or more likely, as the Stimson-Byrnes-Truman views disclosed by Alperovitz indicate, it was not even American lives, but national power that was the supreme value. Values have little to do with quantities of data; they are not necessarily changed by the mere increase of information. For some people on the verge of change this may not be true, but for most others it takes something beyond mere information: it takes direct experience, psychological convulsion, or irresistible pressure—a general assault on the emotions.

7. All this has implications for those interested in social change. It indicates, I think, that we need to distinguish, in the tactics of ideological conflict, between different kinds of human obstacles, and concentrate carefully on the type of technique needed to deal with each. For some, this means information. For others, we had better not assume that their value-system will be revolutionized in the short run. Instead, our disappointed recognition of the solidity of peoples' value-systems can urge upon us the realistic tactic of playing values against one another. A particular cherished value is not likely to be destroyed, but it can be shunted aside in favor of another which is even more desired. The supreme value of survival has often been the only bulwark against the almost supreme value of power. In the past, such value-clashes have been accidental. Perhaps men can begin to use them deliberately.

8. People must be willing to make decisions "out of their field." Oppenheimer and the other three scientists on his committee felt that the dropping of the bomb was really out of their province as

scientists. We should lose our awe of the specialists and stop assuming the "expert" knows his stuff. There is a certain incompatibility between specialization and democracy.

9. The effort made to change a decision not-of-one's-own in a particular situation should match the dimensions of the peril involved. Ordinary and routine methods of protest may not be enough today, when the entire human race is at the mercy of a handful of decision-makers. More is required than calm and reasoned action. Or, to be more exact, we need to think calmly and reasonably about taking extreme measures. In C. P. Snow's novel, *The New Men,* British scientists, fearful that the United States will drop the atomic bomb on a helpless city, hold a meeting. They reject the wild and irrational plan advanced by one of them to reveal the entire secret to the public in an effort to stop the bombing. They decide instead to do the sane, sensible thing. They appoint a committee to visit the United States and to impress their ideas on top American officials. The committee departs. The other scientists wait for its return, and while waiting, they hear on the radio that the bomb has been dropped on Hiroshima. So much for their sane, sensible decision.

ROYAN

In mid-April of 1945, a combined air-ground attack completed the destruction of the French seaside resort of Royan, a town of ancient chateaux and lovely beaches (a favorite spot of Picasso), on the Atlantic coast near Bordeaux. It was ten months after D-day, the invasion of Western Europe by Allied Forces—and three weeks before the final surrender of Germany. The official history of the U.S. Army Air Forces in World War II refers briefly to the attack on Royan: [1]

> On 14 through 16 April more than 1,200 American heavies went out each day to drop incendiaries, napalm bombs, and 2000-pound demolition bombs on stubborn German garrisons still holding out around Bordeaux. The bombing was effective, and French forces soon occupied the region.

(A note on the accuracy of bombing. According to the official history those bombs were dropped "on stubborn German garrisons." This is misleading. The bombs were dropped in the general vicinity of Royan, where there were German garrisons [mostly outside the town] and where there were also civilian occupants of the town. It was my participation in this mission, as a bombardier with the 490th Bomb Group, that prompted me, after the war, to inquire into the bombing of Royan. At the time, it seemed just another bombing mission, with a slightly different target, and a slightly different cargo of bombs. We were awakened in the early hours of morning, went to the briefing, where we were told our job was to bomb pockets of German troops remaining in and around Royan, and that in our bomb bays were thirty 100-pound bombs containing "jellied gasoline," a new substance [now known as napalm]. Our bombs were not precisely directed at German installations but were dropped by toggle switch over the Royan area, on seeing the bombs of the lead ship leave the bomb bay—a device good for saturation bombing, not pinpoint bombing [aside from the fact that the Norden bombsight, which we were trained to use, could not be counted on to hit enemy installations and miss nearby civilians from a height of 25,000 feet]. The toggle switch was connected to an intervalometer which automatically dropped the bombs, after the first fell, in a timed sequence. I remember distinctly seeing, from our great height, the bombs explode in the town, flaring like matches struck in fog. I was completely unaware of the human chaos below.

In 1966, I spent some time in Royan, and found in the town library most of the material on which this essay is based.

In the same chapter of the official Air Force history, the sentence following the description of the Royan bombing reads:

"The last attack on an industrial target by the Eighth Air Force occurred on 25 April, when the famous Skoda works at Pilsen, Czechoslovakia, received 500 well-placed tons. Because of a warning sent out ahead of time the workers were able to escape, except for five persons."

I remember flying on that mission, too, as deputy lead bombardier, and that we did not aim specifically at the "Skoda works" [which I would have noted, because it was the one target in Czechoslovakia I had read about] but dropped our bombs, without much precision, on the city of Pilsen. Two Czech citizens who lived in Pilsen at the time told me, recently, that several hundred people were killed in that raid [that is, Czechs]—not five.

The bombing of villages by American planes in the Vietnam war has been accompanied by similar claims, in military accounts, that only military targets are aimed at. But the nature of bombing from high altitudes, saturation style, makes this a lie, whatever the intention of the spokesman. Atrocities in modern warfare need not be deliberate on the part of the fliers or their superiors; they are the inevitable result of warfare itself. This fact does not exculpate the bombardiers; it implicates the political leaders who make the wars in which bombardiers fly, and all the rest of us who tolerate those political leaders.)

A letter from Colonel H. A. Schmidt, of the Office of the Chief of Military History, Department of the Army, responding to my request for information on the bombing of Royan, stated: [2]

> The liberation of the port of Bordeaux required the reduction of the bridgeheads of Royan, la Pointe, de Grave and Oléron. The Royan sector was the principal German garrison holding out in the Bordeaux area, and first priority in the operations. The Eighth U.S. Air Force paved the way of the Allied ground forces by massive bombing.

The quick, casual description of potentially embarrassing episodes is common in histories written by men in government. Winston Churchill, who was Prime Minister when the city of Dresden was indiscriminately saturated with fire-bombs in February 1945, leaving 135,000 dead, and who had approved the general strategy of bombing urban areas, confined himself to this comment in his memoirs: "We made a heavy raid in the latter month on Dresden, then a centre of communications of Germany's Eastern front." *

* David Irving, *The Destruction of Dresden*, Part II, esp. Ch. II, "Thunderclap," which shows the part Churchill played in pushing the massive raids on cities in Eastern Germany; and Part V, Ch. II, where Churchill later seems to be trying to put the blame on the Bomber Command.

Strenuous arguments were made for the bombing attacks on Hiroshima and Dresden on the basis of military necessity, although ultimately the evidence was overwhelmingly against such arguments. In the case of Royan, it was virtually impossible to even launch a defense of the attack on grounds of military need. It was a small town on the Atlantic coast, far from the fighting front. True, it commanded the sea entrance to Bordeaux, a great port. But this was not crucial, either for the local population, or for the general conduct of the war. At first without Bordeaux, and later without its port facilities, the Allies had invaded Normandy, taken Paris, crossed the Rhine, and were now well into Germany. Furthermore, the general air-ground assault on Royan took place three weeks before the end of the war in Europe, at a time when everyone knew it would all soon be over and all one had to do for the surrender of the German garrisons in the area was to wait.*

Nevertheless, on April 14, 1945, the attack on Royan began, reported as follows in a dispatch from London the next day to *The New York Times:*

> The full weight of the United States Eighth Air Force was hurled yesterday against one of Europe's forgotten fronts, the German-held pocket in the Gironde Estuary commanding the great southwestern French port of Bordeaux. The blow by 1,150 Flying Fortresses and Liberators, without fighter escort, preceded a limited land attack by French troops. . . .
>
> Some 30,000 to 40,000 Nazi troops have been holed up in the Gironde Estuary pocket since the tides of war swept around and past them last summer. . . . The striking force was probably the biggest heavy bombing fleet ever sent out from Britain in daylight without escorting fighters. Five of the big planes failed to return.

Was the air raid worth even the loss of only five air crews— forty-five men? That was just the tip of the tragedy, counted in lives lost, homes destroyed, persons wounded and burned. For the next day, April 15, the attack was heavier, and the airplanes had

---

* Also, in a remark I must confine to a footnote as a gesture to the equality of all victims: there was something to distinguish Royan from both Hiroshima and Dresden; its population was, at least officially, friend, not foe.

a new weapon. A front-page dispatch in *The New York Times* from Paris reported "two days of shattering aerial bombardment and savage ground attacks in the drive to open the port of Bordeaux." It went on:

> More than 1300 Flying Fortresses and Liberators of the United States Eighth Air Force prepared the way for today's successful assault by drenching the enemy's positions on both sides of the Gironde controlling the route to Bordeaux with about 460,000 gallons of liquid fire that bathed in flames the German positions and strong points. . . .
>
> It was the first time that the Eighth Air Force had employed its new bomb. The inflammable substance is dropped in tanks that are exploded on impact by detonators that ignite the fuel, splashing the flaming contents of each tank over an area of approximately sixty square yards.

The liquid fire was napalm, used for the first time in warfare. The following day, there was another bombing, with high explosive bombs, and further ground assaults. Altogether, it took three days of bombing and land attacks to bring the Germans in the area to surrender. The French ground forces suffered about two hundred dead; the Germans lost several hundred. There is no accurate count on the civilian dead resulting from those attacks, but *The New York Times* dispatch by a correspondent in the area reported:

> French troops mopped up most of Royan, on the north side of the river's mouth. . . . Royan, a town of 20,000, once was a vacation spot. About 350 civilians, dazed or bruised by two terrific air bombings in forty-eight hours, crawled from the ruins and said the air attacks had been "such hell as we never believed possible."

In a few weeks, the war was over in Europe. The town of Royan, "liberated," was totally in ruins.

That eve-of-victory attack in mid-April 1945 was the second disaster suffered by Royan at the hands of the Allied forces. On January 5, 1945, in the darkness before dawn, two waves of heavy

British bombers, about an hour apart, flew over Royan, which was still inhabited, despite a voluntary evacuation in the preceding months, by about two thousand persons. There was no warning, there were no shelters. The bombs were dropped in the heart of the city (completely missing the German troops, who were outside) within a rectangle marked out by flares dropped by one of the planes. Over a thousand people were killed (some of the estimates are twelve hundred, others fourteen hundred). Several hundred people were wounded. Almost every building in Royan was demolished. The later attack in April, came therefore, on the ruins of buildings and the remnants of families, and made the annihilation of the city complete.

That January bombing has never been adequately explained. One phrase recurs in all the accounts—*"une tragique erreur."* The explanation given by military officials at the time was that the bombers were originally scheduled to bomb in Germany, but because of bad weather there, were rerouted to Royan without a map of the German positions. French planes from nearby Cognac were supposed to mark the positions with flares but this was either not done, or done badly, or the flares were carried away by the wind.*

A dispatch written by a local person soon after that bombing, entitled "La Nuit Tragique," contained this description: **

Under the German occupation. It is night, calm reigns over the sleeping town. Midnight sounds in the Royan church. Then one

* This is repeated as late as 1965 in Dr. J. R. Colle's book, *Royan, son passé, ses environs* (La Rochelle, 1965), who summarizes the incident in his chapter, "La Résistance et La Libération."

** The periodical in which the article appeared is no longer available, but the article, along with many others to which I will refer, was collected in a remarkable little book, produced by a printer in Royan, a former member of the Resistance (Botton, Père et fils) in 1965, entitled: *Royan— Ville Martyre*. The translations are mine. A bitter introductory note by Ulysse Botton speaks of *"la tuerie"* (the slaughter) of January 5, 1945. There is a picture of the rebuilt Royan, modern buildings instead of ancient châteaux. "Our visitors, French and foreign vacationers, should thus learn, if they do not know it, that this new town and this modern architecture proceed from a murder, to this day neither admitted nor penalized. . . ."

o'clock, then two. . . . The Royannais sleep, muffled against the chill. Three, four o'clock. A humming is heard in the distance. Rockets light up the sky. The inhabitants are not afraid; they are tranquil, because they know that Allied airplanes, if these are such, will aim at the German fortifications, and besides, is this not the evening when German supply planes come in? The clock sounds five. Then follows the catastrophe, brutal, horrible, implacable. A deluge of steel and fire descends on Royan; a wave of 350 planes lets go 800 tons of bombs on the town. Some seconds later, the survivors are calling for aid to the wounded. Cries, death rattles. . . . A woman appeals for help, her head appears alone, her body crushed under an enormous beam. . . . A whole family is imprisoned in a cave, the water mounts. The rescuers lift their heads—this humming, yet, it is another wave of planes. This achieves the complete destruction of Royan and its inhabitants. Royan has gone down with the civilized world, by the error, the bestiality, the folly of man. [*Royan a sombré en même temps que le monde civilisé, par l'erreur, la bêtise et la folie des hommes.*]

Eight days after the attack, an article appeared in *La Libération* appealing for help: "American friends, you whose Florida beaches have never known such hours, take charge of the reconstruction of Royan!" [3]

In 1948, General de Larminat, who was in charge of French forces in the West (that is, the Bordeaux region) for the last six months of the war, broke a long silence to reply to bitter criticism of both the January and April bombings by local leaders. He exonerated the French military command at Cognac, saying they were not responsible for directing the English planes to Royan. It was, rather, a "tragic error" by the Allied Command; the whole episode was one of the unfortunate consequences of war: *

> Will we draw from this an excuse to attack our Allies, who gave countless lives to liberate our country? That would be pro-

* Botton collection. This is, of course, a widely held view: "c'est la guerre"—a resigned, unhappy surrender to inevitability. We find it again in *Le Pays d'Ouest*, a postwar periodical, now defunct, which published an article, "Le Siège et Attaque de Royan," saying: "Whatever the reason, the bombardment of Royan, on January 5, 1945, must be considered among the regrettable errors that unfortunately it is hard to avoid in the course of the extremely complicated operations of modern war."

foundly unjust. All wars carry these painful errors. Where is the infantryman of 1914–18, and of this war, who has not received friendly shells, badly aimed? How many French towns, how many combat units, have suffered bombings by mistake at the hands of allied planes? This is the painful ransom, the inevitable ransom of war, against which it is vain to protest, about which it is vain to quarrel. We pay homage to those who died in the war, we help the survivors and repair the ruins; but we do not linger on the causes of these unfortunate events because, in truth, there is only a single cause: War, and the only ones truly responsible are those who wanted war.

(Compare this with the explanation of the Dresden bombing given by Air Marshal Sir Robert Saundby: [4]

It was one of those terrible things that sometimes happen in wartime, brought about by an unfortunate combination of circumstances. Those who approved it were neither wicked nor cruel, though it may well be that they were too remote from the harsh realities of war to understand fully the appalling destructive power of air bombardment in the spring of 1945. . . .

It is not so much this or the other means of making war that is immoral or inhumane. What is immoral is war itself. Once full-scale war has broken out it can never be humanized or civilized, and if one side attempted to do so it would be most likely to be defeated. So long as we resort to war to settle differences between nations, so long will we have to endure the horrors, the barbarities and excesses that war brings with it. That, to me, is the lesson of Dresden.)

Some important evidence on the January bombing appeared in 1966 with the publication of the memoirs of Admiral Hubert Meyer,[5] French commander in the Rochefort-La Rochelle area (the two Atlantic ports just north of Royan). Meyer, in September and October 1944, when the Germans, having fled west from the Allied invasion in northern France, were consolidating their pockets on the Atlantic coast, had begun negotiating with the German commander of La Rochelle-Rochefort, Admiral Schirlitz. In effect, they agreed that the Germans would not blow up the port installations, and in return the French would not attack the Germans. Then the Germans evacuated Rochefort, moving north into the La Rochelle area, to lines both sides agreed on.

In late December 1944, Meyer was asked to travel south along the coast from Rochefort to Royan, where the second German coastal pocket was under the command of Admiral Michahelles, to negotiate a prisoner exchange. In the course of these talks, he was told that the German admiral was disposed to sign an agreement to hold the military *status quo* around Royan, as had been done by Schirlitz at Rochefort-La Rochelle. Meyer pointed out that Royan was different, that the Allies might have to attack the Germans there because Royan commanded Bordeaux, where free passage of goods was needed to supply the Southwest. The Germans, to Meyer's surprise, replied that they might agree to open Bordeaux to all but military supplies.

Conveying this offer to the French military headquarters at Saintes and Cognac, Meyer received a cool response. The French generals could not give a sound military reason for insisting on an attack, but pointed to *"l'aspect moral."* It would be hard, said General d'Anselme, "to frustrate an ardent desire for battle—a battle where victory was certain—by the army of the Southwest, which had been champing at the bit for months." * Meyer said the morale of the troops was not worth the sacrifice of a town and hundreds of lives for a limited objective, when the war was virtually won, that they did not have the right to kill a single man when the adversary had offered a truce.** Further discussion, he was

* This is Meyer's recollection of the conversation, in his chapter, "Royan, Ville Détruite par erreur." Meyer tends to glorify his own activities in this book, but his account fits the other evidence.

** Three other pieces of evidence support Meyer's claim of German readiness to surrender:

A. A dispatch in *Samedi-Soir* in May, 1948 (reproduced in part in the Botton collection) tells a strange story which goes even further than Meyer. It reports, on the basis of a document it claims to have found in the Ministry of the Armed Forces, that a British agent, with the code name of "Aristede," parachuted into France to join the Resistance, reported later to his government in London that the Germans in the Royan area had offered to surrender if they would be given the honors of war, but that the French General Bertin said a surrender to the British would create a "diplomatic incident." This was, allegedly, September 8, 1944.

told, would have to await the return of General de Larminat, who was away.

Meyer left that meeting with the distinct impression that the die was cast for the attack (*"l'impression très nette que les jeux étaient faits, que Royan serait attaquée"*). This was January 2nd. Three days later, sleeping at Rochefort, he was awakened by the sound of airplanes flying south toward Royan. Those were the British Lancasters, three hundred and fifty of them, each carrying seven tons of bombs.

Meyer adds another piece of information: that about a month before the January 5th bombing an American General, Commander of the Ninth Tactical Air Force, came to Cognac to offer the Southwest forces powerful bombing support, and suggested softening the Atlantic pockets by massive aerial bombardment. He proposed that since the Germans did not have aerial defenses for Royan, here were good targets for bomber-crew trainees in England. The French agreed, but insisted the targets be at two points which formed clear enclaves on the ocean, easily distinguishable from the city itself. No more was heard from the Americans, however, until the bombing itself.* As it turned out, not trainees, but experienced pilots, did the bombing, and Meyer concludes that

B. An open letter to General de Larminat by Dr. Veyssière Pierre, a former leader of the Royan Resistance (reproduced in the Botton collection) says: "Now we are sure that in August and September, 1944, the German high command—the commander of the fortress of Royan—made proposals of surrender that, if they had come about, would have prevented the worst; we know that on two occasions, he had made contact with Colonel Cominetti, called Charly, commander of the Médoc groups; we know also that these attempts at negotiations were purely and simply repulsed by the French headquarters at Bordeaux, in order, no doubt, to add to the grandeur of military prestige."

C. The article of Paul Métadier (reprinted in a pamphlet available in the library of Royan) in *La Lettre Médicale,* February 1948, gives Sir Samuel Hoare, former British Ambassador to France, as a source of the fact that the French military command had opposed the surrender of the German General to the British.

* This story appears also in Robert Aron's *Histoire de la Libération de La France, June, 1944–May, 1945* (Librairie Arthème Fayard, 1959). Aron adds the point that the American general spent some time on this visit with an FFI (French Forces of the Interior) journalist who called the inhabitants of Royan "collaborators."

even the American general (sent back to the U.S. after this, as a scapegoat, Meyer suggests) was not completely responsible.

Some blame devolved, he says, on the British Bomber Command, and some on the French generals, for not insisting on a point DeGaulle had made when he visited the area in September— that aerial attacks should only be undertaken here in coordination with ground assaults. Meyer concludes, however, that the real responsibility did not rest with the local military commanders. "To wipe out such a city is beyond military decision. It is a serious political act. It is impossible that the Supreme Command [he refers to Eisenhower and his staff] had not been at least consulted." In the event, he says, that the Allies are shocked by his accusations, they should open their military dossiers and, for the first time, reveal the truth.

If by January 1945 (despite von Rundstedt's Christmas counteroffensive in the Ardennes) it seemed clear that the Allies, well into France, and the Russians, having the Germans on the run, were on the way toward victory—then by April 1945 there was little doubt that the war was near its end. The Berlin radio announced on April 15 that the Russians and Americans were about to join forces around the Elbe, and that two zones were being set up for a Germany cut in two.[6] Nevertheless, a major land-air operation was launched April 14th against the Royan pocket, with over a thousand planes dropping bombs on a German force of 5,500 men, on a town containing at the time probably less than a thousand people.*

An article written in the summer of 1946 by a local writer commented on the mid-April assault: [7]

These last acts left a great bitterness in the hearts of the Royannais, because the Armistice followed soon after, an Armistice foreseen by all. For the Royannais, this liberation by force was useless since Royan would have been, like La Rochelle, liberated normally some days later, without new damage, without new deaths, without

---

* Colle, *Royan, son passé, ses environs.* He reports the Germans, under Admiral Michahelles had 5,500 men, 150 cannon, 4 anti-aircraft batteries. They were well entrenched in concrete bunkers and surrounded by fields of land mines.

new ruins. Only those who have visited Royan can give an account of
the disaster. No report, no picture or drawing can convey it.

Another local person wrote: *

> Surely the destruction of Royan, on January 5, 1945, was
> an error and a crime; but what put the finishing touches on this folly
> was the final air raid on the ruins, on the buildings partially damaged,
> and on others remarkably spared on the periphery, with that infernal
> cargo of incendiary bombs. Thus was accomplished a deadly work of
> obvious uselessness, and thus was revealed to the world the powerful
> destructiveness of napalm.

The evidence seems overwhelming that factors of pride, military
ambition, glory, honor were powerful motives in producing an
unnecessary military operation. One of the local commanders
wrote later: "It would have been more logical to wait for the surrender of Germany and thus to avoid new human and material
losses" but one could not "ignore important factors of morale"
(*"faire abstraction de facteurs essentiels d'ordre moral"*).**

In 1947, a delegation of five leaders of Royan met with General de Larminat. After the war, the citizens of Royan had barred
de Larminat from the town, in anger at the military operations
under his command which had destroyed it, and at the widespread
looting of the Royan homes by French soldiers after "liberation."
He hoped now to persuade the Royannais that they had made a
mistake. The meeting is described by Dr. Veyssière Pierre, former

---

* "Les Préparatifs de l'Attaque" in Botton collection. The same writer
claims (on the basis of a historical work by J. Mortin, *Au carrefour de
l'Histoire*) that the formula for napalm was found in the eighteenth century by a Grenoblois goldsmith, who demonstrated it to the minister of
war, after which Louis XV was so horrified he ordered the documents
burned, saying that such a terrifying force must remain unknown for the
good of man.

** *Revue Historique de l'armée,* January, 1946. An article in a regional journal after the war commented on those engaged in the April attacks: "Thanks to them, one could not say that the French army remained
impotent before the German redoubts on the Atlantic wall." *Le Pays
d'Ouest,* copy in the library at Royan.

leader of the Resistance in Royan, and a holder of the Croix de Guerre, who says he hoped to get an explanation of the "useless sacrifice" of the population of the town, but "my self-deception was total, absolute." He quotes de Larminat saying the French military did not want the enemy "to surrender of his own accord; that would give the impression the Germans were unconquered." *

Another member of the French delegation, Dr. Domecq, a former Mayor and Resistance leader, responded to General de Larminat also: [8]

> Royan was destroyed by mistake, you say, my general. . . . Those responsible have been punished, the order to attack, a few days before liberation, could not be questioned by the military. . . . The Germans had to feel our power! Permit me, my general, to tell you, once and for all, in the name of those who paid the cost: "La Victoire de Royan" does not exist, except for you.

General de Larminat responded to the criticism in a letter addressed to Paul Métadier.** Pride and military ambition, he pointed out, were not sufficient explanations for such a huge operation; one had to seek a larger source: "This pride, this ambition, did not have the power to manufacture the shells which were used, to create the units which were sent, to divert the important aerial and naval forces that participated." De Larminat said that he had prepared the necessary plans for liquidating *"les poches d'Atlantique"* but that he did not judge the date. The date was fixed for him, and he executed the plans.

He ended his reply with an appeal to patriotism: "Must we therefore, throw opprobrium on old combatants because some isolated ones committed acts, unhappily inevitable in wartime? This is how it has been in all the wars of all time. No one ever, that I know, used this as a pretext to reduce the glory and the

* Open letter to General de Larminat, caustically addressing him as "Liberateur" de Royan. Reproduced in Botton collection.

** The exchange between Métadier and de Larminat is in a pamphlet in the possession of the library in Royan. The original Royan library was destroyed during the bombings, and in 1957, after twelve years, a new library was built.

valour of the sacrifices made by the combatants." He spoke of the "simple, brave people" who will put "glory and national independence" before "material losses" and give "the respect due to those who fell, and for which many sacrificed their lives, to a patriotic ideal that the malcontents (*"les attentistes"*) have always ignored."

Admiral Meyer, who is more sympathetic to de Larminat than most of the general's critics, had watched the attack on Royan from the heights of Medis, and described the scene:

> The weather was clear, the warmth oppressive. Under a fantastic concentration of fire, the enemy positions, the woods, and the ruins of Royan flamed. The countryside and the sky were thick with powder and yellow smoke. One could with difficulty distinguish the mutilated silhouette of the clock of Saint-Pierre, which burned like a torch. I knew that the allied planes were using for the first time, a new kind of incendiary explosive, a kind of jellied gasoline, known as napalm.

Larminat, he said, had good days and bad days. And this was one of his bad days, for in the evening after Royan was taken, and Meyer went to see the General: "He was visibly satisfied with having achieved this brilliant revenge. . . . Without saying that he was intoxicated with success, the General seemed to me however to have his appetite stimulated. . . ."

That exultation was felt at all levels. A press correspondent on the scene described the very heavy artillery bombardment which prepared the attack on the Royan area: 27,000 shells. Then the first aerial bombing on Saturday, April 14th, with high explosives. Then the bombing all Sunday morning with napalm. By seven that evening they were in Royan. It was a blazing furnace. (*"La ville est un brasier."*) The next morning, they could still hear the clatter of machine guns in the woods nearby. Royan was still burning (*"Royan brûle encore"*). The dispatch ends: "It is a beautiful spring." [9]

With Royan taken, they decided to attack the island of Oléron, opposite Rochefort. As Meyer says:

The new victory had inflamed the passions of our soldiers, giving them the idea that nothing could resist them. News from the German front forecast a quick end to the war. Each one wanted a last moment to distinguish himself and get a bit of glory; moderation was scorned, prudence was seen as cowardice.

Meyer did not believe the attack on Oléron was necessary. But he participated assiduously in planning and executing it, happy to be once again involved in a naval operation, and convinced that his duty was only to carry out orders from above.[10]

The attack on Oléron was disputable from the point of view of general strategy. It was a costly luxury, a conquest without military value, on the eve of the war's end. But this was not for me to judge. My duty was limited to doing my best in making those military decisions which would fulfill my orders.

Meyer blames the political leaders above. Yet *blame* seems the wrong word, because Meyer believes it honorable to follow orders, whatever they are, against whatever adversary is chosen for him: *"Quant au soldat, depuis des millénaires, ce n'est plus lui qui forge ses armes et qui choisit son adversaire. Il n'a que le devoir d'obéir dans la pleine mesure de sa foi, de son courage, de sa résistance."* *

One can see in the destruction of Royan that infinite chain of causes, that infinite dispersion of responsibility, which can give infinite work to historical scholarship and sociological speculation, and bring an infinitely pleasurable paralysis of the will. What a complex of motives! In the Supreme Allied Command, the simple momentum of the war, the pull of prior commitments and prepara-

* At one point, Meyer quotes Bismarck, who made German students write: "Man was not put in the world to be happy, but to do his duty!" In another frightening glimpse of what a well-trained military man of our century can believe, Meyer talks fondly of that special bond of the sea (*"une commune maîtresse: la mer"*) which unites sailors of different nations in their patriotic duty, and points, as an example of such laudable unity in action, to the landing of European troops in China in 1900 to crush the Boxer uprising.

tions, the need to fill out the circle, to pile up the victories as high as possible. At the local military level, the ambitions, petty and large, the tug of glory, the ardent need to participate in a grand communal effort by soldiers of all ranks. On the part of the American Air Force, the urge to try out a newly developed weapon. (Paul Métadier wrote: "In effect, the operation was above all characterized by the dropping of new incendiary bombs which the Air Force had just been supplied with. According to the famous formulation of one general: 'They were marvelous!' ") And among all participants, high and low, French and American, the most powerful motive of all: the habit of obedience, the universal teaching of all cultures, not to get out of line, not even to think about that which one has not been assigned to think about, the negative motive of not having either a reason or a will to intercede.

Everyone can point, rightly, to someone else as being responsible. In that remarkable film *King and Country,* a simple-minded British country boy in the trenches of World War I, walks away one day from the slaughter and is condemned to death in a two-step process where no one thinks he really should be executed but the officers in each step can blame those in the other. The original court sentences him to death thinking to make a strong point and then have the appeals tribunal overturn the verdict. The appeals board, upholding the verdict, can argue that the execution was not its decision. The man is shot. That procedure, one recalls, goes back to the Inquisition, when the church only conducted the trial, and the state carried out the execution, thus confusing both God and the people about the source of the decision.

More and more in our time, the mass production of massive evil requires an enormously complicated division of labor. No one is positively responsible for the horror that ensues. But everyone is negatively responsible, because *anyone* can throw a wrench into the machinery. Not quite, of course—because only a few people have wrenches. The rest have only their hands and feet. That is, the power to interfere with the terrible progression is distributed unevenly, and therefore the sacrifice required varies, according to one's means. In that odd perversion of the natural which we call society (that is, nature seems to equip each species for its special needs) the greater one's capability for interference, the less urgent is the need to interfere.

It is the immediate victims—or tomorrow's—who have the greatest need, and the fewest wrenches. They must use their bodies (which may explain why rebellion is a rare phenomenon). This may suggest to those of us who have a bit more than our bare hands, and at least a small interest in stopping the machine, that we might play a peculiar role in breaking the social stalemate.

This may require resisting a false crusade—or refusing one or another expedition in a true one. But always, it means refusing to be transfixed by the actions of other people, the truths of other times. It means acting on what we feel and think, here, now, for human flesh and sense, against the abstractions of duty and obedience.

PART THREE

17

Freedom and responsibility

There are two ways in which history has a "meaning." The actual past has affected the present situation in which we find ourselves; this kind of meaning is out of our hands—it has already been determined. But also, our recapitulation of the past affects what we do about this situation; this is in our hands. And because there are many ways in which we can tell about the past, we can give it various meanings. It is in this sense that Karl Popper says: ". . . although history has no meaning, we can give it a meaning." [1]

The historian is thus free to give one meaning or another to past events. I can choose, by the way I tell the story, to make World War I seem a glorious battle between good and evil, or I can make it seem a senseless massacre. There is no inherently true story of World War I if some absolute, objective past is sought—there is only the question of which version is true to which present purpose. There is only the meaning created by the historian—a meaning represented by the effect on those who listen to the story.

Factual accounts of the past—since they involve selection and emphasis, turn out on inspection to be interpretations of the past. (Nietzsche: "There are no facts, only interpretations.") Thus, what we call "interpretations" of history would show the same characteristics I have thus attributed to "straight" renditions of past events. That is, there can be no inherent "meaning" of any interpretation—its meaning would consist of its effect on the actions of those who read it. And if so, we would have to go beyond the ostensible meaning of the words of that interpretation, because the effect on the reader is not created only by those words, but by the total setting of those words—who the author is, the context in which he writes, the emotive as well as rational emanations of the writing, the particular condition of the reader as he receives the message. The meaning of any writing then is in the total interaction between the writer, the reader, and the setting in which the reading takes place. This makes the meaning of any historical account dynamic, subjective, fluid, relational. It also creates the possibility that the total effect of a historical interpretation might be different than the literal message of the words on the page—in the way that continued screams of "Silence!" would have a meaning utterly different than the literal meaning of the word "silence." There would be a difference between the surface content of a historical statement (what the words seem to say), and the existential content (what effect the words have on the real world).*

Let us, for instance, take the "meaning" of various interpretations of history which seem to say that man is not free, that the history of man is shaped by impersonal, irresistible forces. The Greeks ascribed enormous power to their pagan deities. From Augustine in the fifth century to Bishop Bossuet in the seventeenth century, it was the Providential hand of the Christian God that moved history. In the post-Enlightenment atmosphere of Western Europe, mystical forces were replaced by secular ones. Condorcet preached the certainty and power of Progress. Marx spoke of the inevitability of Socialism. Freud pointed to the inescapable psychological heritage of Eros, rooted in the biological makeup of man and in the "totem and taboo" of early societies.

Yet, when one looks beyond their words, these stern spokesmen for "inevitability" in history behaved quite strangely. That is, they behaved as if nothing was inevitable, as if a great deal depended on their actions. The Greeks were so reluctant to leave

* This may be comparable to Susan Sontag's critique of interpretation as "the revenge of the intellect upon the world," when she says, "To interpret is to impoverish, to deplete the world in order to set up a shadow world of 'meanings.'" Susan Sontag, *Against Interpretation,* Delta edition, 1966, p. 7. But the ability to impoverish is also the ability to enrich.

things to their Gods that they created the most dynamic civilization of their time. The church fathers of Christianity, apparently not trusting to the workings of Providence, organized an enormous bureaucracy, waged wars, and ruled empires. The Calvinist believers in predestination were among the most active of doers, combining piety and viciousness, but seldom relaxing.

And similarly with the secularists. Condorcet, for all his faith in the inevitable progress of mankind, took such an active hand in the French Revolution that he died in prison. Marx, while insisting on the power of impersonal forces in determining consciousness, was a tireless participant in the revolutionary movements of his time. And Freud, refusing to surrender his patients to the drives and conflicts he himself had identified, fathered a school of resourceful and energetic therapists.

What are we to make of this odd disparity between these thinkers' reputed subservience to "laws of history" and their incorrigible activity? Part of the explanation is that we tend to misread when we have a point to prove (when we ourselves are more concerned with dead analysis than with action). That is, the so-called inevitabilists often showed, in various asides, that they understood the limits of determinism and the power of man. Condorcet, for instance, does say the perfectibility of man is "from now onwards independent of any power that might wish to halt it." But he also says that his observations about man "will instruct us about the means we should employ to make certain and rapid the further progress that his nature allows him still to hope for."

So with Augustine, who believed that "God's dealing in history is beyond our disposal, and his providence . . . overrules the intentions of man," also argues in *The City of God* against the pagans' idea of the cyclical recurrence of joy and grief, not by proving they are wrong, but by saying it will make us miserable to believe that: "Who, I say, can listen to such things? . . . Were they true, it were not only more prudent to keep silence regarding them, but even . . . it were the part of wisdom not to know them." Augustine here is not concerned with scholarly disputation, but with the *effect* of his words on people's behavior.

But more important, the disparity between quoted words and the actions—both of the writer and his followers—suggests that

we cannot talk about the "meaning" of words as they appear, isolated, on the printed page. The meaning of words is found in the
interaction between the words themselves, and the reader whom
they affect. Ambiguity in language is resolved in the definiteness
of action.

Thus, the meaning of Hegel's words, reduced to literal translation, leave him a spokesman for conservatism, God, and the Prus-
sian state. But the meanings of Hegel, in the existential sense, are
various, depending on who acts upon his ideas and to what effect.
Some in Germany have given an absolutist meaning to him. Others have taken his dialectical notion of social change ("World history is the progress of the consciousness of freedom") [2] and have
become revolutionaries. Herbert Marcuse gives us both meanings
of Hegel. He talks of Hegel's dialectics as liberating us from "the
self-assurance and self-contentment of common sense" but also
says: "Dialectical thought has not hindered Hegel from developing his philosophy into a neat and comprehensive system which, in
the end, accentuates the positive emphatically." (To Marcuse, it
is *negative* thinking which we desperately need to break through
the present.[3]

Probably the clearest example of how the "meaning" read into
words by scholars (and others) is refuted by the consequences of
those words can be found in Karl Marx. There has been a barrage
of academic criticism of Marx, based on the notion that his writings show man as bound by iron laws of history, determined by
economic necessities, etc. "Marx speaks as if he thought his laws
were fully as deterministic as certain laws of natural science," says
Morton White.[4] Clinton Rossiter says: "Both Engels and Marx
used the words 'inevitable' and 'necessary' so often in describing
the influence of the mode of production on the course of history
that they ought to be treated as men who meant what they said." [5]
Karl Popper criticized Marx as "a prophet," a finder of "inexorable laws." Popper agrees that Marx, if faced with a choice "would
have decided to be a maker and not merely a prophet." But these
"activist tendencies," he finds, are "counteracted" by Marx's desire to predict the future on the basis of "laws" in history.[6]

But—going beyond scholarly exegesis—does it really matter
that Marx's activist statements, expressed in his *Theses on Feuer-*

bach are outnumbered by his lengthy discussion of the "laws" of capitalist development, if, in fact, his total body of writings led, not to passivism, but to the most powerful revolutionary movement of modern times? Indeed, the activist element in Marx, always powerful, is receiving especially strong emphasis today.* The wave of Existentialist-Marxist thought coming out of both Western and Eastern Europe these days emphasizes the concept of praxis in Marxian thought, the freedom of man to act. Gajo Petrovic, for instance, the Yugoslav philosopher, writes, *"Ce qui constitue l'essence de l'historique, c'est justement le transcendement du naturel, le dépassement de l'opposition entre la nécessité et le hasard aveugle par l'activité consciente libre."* [7]

We see thus, with Marx, how the "meaning" of a writer, when reduced to his words alone, is empty, scholarly, academic, and how the writer as an actor in history takes on the only meaning which relates to our lives. My point in all this is not to engage in still another discussion about what Augustine, Condorcet, Hegel, Marx "really meant," but to escape the whole scene of scholarly discussion by drawing attention to the consequences *in action* of historical writing. The meaning, then, of a writer will be found not just in what he intends to say, or what he does literally say, but in the effect of his writing on living beings.**

This irony in "meaning," which comes out of the clash between the literal and the existential, shows itself again when we turn from the so-called determinists to their critics, who deride the "big theory" and the "iron law" in history. In recent years, immediately irritated perhaps by Arnold Toynbee's suggestion of a grand historical pattern in the birth and death of civilizations, but with

* In George Lichtheim's interpretation, Marx's emphasis on freedom of action was crippled by Engels' mechanistic approach. George Lichtheim, *Marxism: An Historical and Critical Study,* Praeger, 1962, pp. 152, 236–43.

** One meaning of Frederick Jackson Turner, beyond his own idea of the relationship between democracy and the frontier, comes from the fact that he wrote into a time of social-Darwinism, imperialism, nativism, and national pride. Thus, Walter Webb, building on Turner in *The Great Plains,* Blaisdell, 1959, tells us that Europe owed its freedom, prosperity, dynamism to its own frontier in America. This was in 1931, just before Hitler rose to dominate Europe.

grievances still felt against Marx, Spengler, and others, many philosophers and historians have rebelled at the idea that men are
ruled by "laws" or "patterns" of historical development. Appealing to modern confidence in man's potency, they have decried the
idea of "inevitability." Presumably, they are freeing us from iron
necessity.

But when we turn from words to their consequences, we find
that what these scholars have given us in their emphasis on "critical history" versus "speculative history" * is a decade of meticulous inspection of the historian's intra-academic problems as a
professional craftsman. The words of these scholars stress freedom, but they have created a closed circle of scholastic argument
which produces no waves of energy in the society outside, and little effect on practicing historians.**

The issue then, of whether man is free to move in history or is
bound by historical laws cannot be answered by restricting our
search to what thinkers say. They may say man is bound, and the
manner in which they say this may be invigorating for human freedom; they may say man is free, and by the nature of their discussion immobilize us all inside a scholarly argument.

This suggests that we must move away from scholastic notions
of "meaning" to see that meaning is not given by the writer alone
but by the interaction between him and his reader, in the specific
situation in which it is received. An idea fulfills its meaning at the
moment when, by its effect on others, it becomes an act.*** By
writing history, we are engaging in an act which (through the
reader) has consequences, large or small, on behalf of humane
values or in opposition to them. We then begin to answer the question "Is man free?" in the way that two people discussing the

* The formulation is that of W. H. Walsh, the Oxford philosopher, in
Philosophy of History: An Introduction, Harper & Row (Torchbook edition), 1960.

** See, as the major forums for this kind of writing, the pages of *History and Theory* since the founding of that journal in 1960.

*** Ernst Cassirer makes a point somewhat like this about language:
"The receiver does not take the gift as one accepts a stamped coin. For he
cannot receive it except by using it, and to make use of it is to give it a
new stamp . . . Every living linguistic usage undergoes a continual change
in meaning." *The Logic of Humanities,* Yale University, 1961, p. 198.

question, "Should we have a conversation?" have already given the answer.

When the historian decides that *he* will henceforth be free, that is, when he will begin to tell history in such a way as to consciously create meanings for present action, he faces one obstacle inherent in the subject. That is: for those who unearth the data on the past, as well as those to whom they present it, the sheer weight of the past is oppressive. Events that have already taken place develop the look of having been necessary; indeed they were, but only at the instant they occurred, when further interference was impossible. The necessariness of the past tends to carry over into our thinking about the future, and weigh down our disposition to action. Man, wounded by his history already, then tends to be transfixed by it.*

History can have another effect, however. Like memory, it can liberate us when the present seems an irrevocable fact of nature. Memory can remind us of possibilities that we have forgotten, and history can suggest to us alternatives that we would never otherwise consider. It can both warn and inspire. It can warn us that it is *possible* for a whole nation to be brainwashed, for "enlightened" and "educated" people to commit genocide, for a "democratic" country to maintain slavery, for oppressed to turn into oppressors, for "socialism" to be tyrannical and "liberalism" to be imperialist, for whole peoples to be led to war like sheep. It can also show us that apparently powerless underlings can defeat their rulers, that men (for at least moments of time) can live like brothers, that man can make incredible sacrifices on behalf of a cause.

Our historical experience is limited, however, and while it suggests some of the things that are possible, it has not even begun to

---

* Arnold Toynbee (perplexing those constant critics who harp on his "laws") keeps trying to escape the weight of his own ten volumes. He writes that "a civilization is not like an animal organism, condemned by an inexorable destiny to die after traversing a predetermined life-course. Even if all other civilizations that have come into existence so far were to prove in fact to have followed this path, there is no known law of historical determinism that compels us to leap out of the intolerable frying-pan of our time of troubles into the slow and steady fire of a universal state where we shall in due course be reduced to dust and ashes." Somerville abridgment of Vols. I–VI of *A Study of History*.

exhaust the total range of possibility. Because of the limits of our imagination, tyrannized as we are by the past, we find it hard to accept that there is a universe of tricks still to be played that has barely been touched in all of human history. In other words, the past suggests what can be, not what must be. It shows not all of what is necessary, but some of what is possible. The more we understand the limitations of history, the more it can be liberating rather than oppressive.

This is surely not to say that all possibilities are present all the time, that we are completely free at every moment. There is a world of hard fact which assails us at every turn, every decision. But because these facts are *here,* they exert a disproportionate influence on our actions. Nietzsche wrote: "People think nothing but this troublesome reality of ours is possible." He spoke of the "historically educated fanatic of the world-process" who "has nothing to do but to live on as he has lived, love what he has loved, hate what he has hated, and read the newspapers he has always read. The only sin is for him to live otherwise than he has lived." [8]

The only way to compensate for the bullying nature of history is to behave *as if* we are freer than our "rational" calculations tell us we are. We can never—because the present is harsh and the future obscure—weigh accurately how free we really are, what our possibilities are at any moment. Because of this uncertainty, knowing our tendency is to overestimate the present, there is good reason for acting on the supposition of freedom.*

Hans Reichenbach, a philosopher of the Vienna Circle of logical positivism, recognizing that we are continuously faced with uncertainty, suggested that the answer is not to be immobilized, but to act on the basis of probability, or what he called "the approximate posit":

> If anything can be achieved at all, we shall reach our aim by applying the method of approximate posit; otherwise, we shall not attain anything. . . . We are often confronted by similar situations

---

* William James in *The Dilemma of Determinism,* an address to Harvard Divinity students published in the *Unitarian Review,* September 1884, makes a similar point. Reprinted in William James, *Essays in Pragmatism,* Hafner, 1954.

in daily life. We want to reach a certain aim and we know of a necessary step, which we shall have to take in order to attain this aim, but we do not know whether this step is sufficient. He who wants to reach the aim will have to take the step, even if it is uncertain whether he will reach his aim in this way.[9]

A Yugoslav philosopher, trained both in Marxism and logical positivism, goes even further in his emphasis on taking risks. Mihailo Markovic writes that "historical laws should be conceived as tendencies and not inevitabilities." He criticizes "those Marxists who . . . fail to see that in our era history is becoming an increasingly open process, with more and more possibilities and more and more freedom." When people reach a certain "critical awareness of themselves and their times" then "the historical process will not lead to what seemed most probable according to existing laws" but to achievements "on the very margin" of possibility. Markovic points to the Yugoslav Revolution (he himself was involved as a Partisan) as an example of men acting in the face of the probable.[10]

There is increasing support for this emphasis on man's freedom in recent psychological theory which emphasizes capacities. Since Freud, psychologists have come to have greater faith in man's ability to change his life, despite the force of early circumstance. Erik Erikson speaks about psychologists being often surprised by the strength of people, which seems to come, he says, from "unexpected encounters . . . and from opportunities beyond our theoretical anticipations." [11]

Acting as if we are free is a way of resolving the paradox of determinism and freedom, of overcoming the tension between past and future.* It is risky, and yet (unless one is content with things

* Isaiah Berlin, in his essay "Historical Inevitability," makes a bit too rigid a connection between freedom and responsibility as against the notion of determinism. We don't have to make a clear choice between determinism and freedom; all we need to do is declare our *uncertainty* about the extent to which we are blocked and the extent to which we are free, in order to assert our responsibility. Indeed, Berlin himself does say as much, in talking about it as a pragmatic problem. "Hence the ancient controversy between free will and determinism, while it remains a genuine issue for the theologians and philosophers, need not trouble the thoughts of those whose

as they are) it is just as risky to act as if we are bound, and there is far less chance of reward. The leaps that man has made in social evolution came from those who acted *as if:* the four Negro youngsters in North Carolina who walked into Woolworth's in 1960 and asked for a cup of coffee acted as if they would have some effect; Garrison, Phillips, and Douglass, against all visible common sense, acted as if they would arouse a cold nation against slavery; England in 1940 acted as if it could deter a German invasion; Castro and his tiny group in the hills behaved as if they could take over Cuba.

The Existentialist emphasis on man's freedom leads others to accuse them of a blind refusal to recognize the limits set by the world around them. They say that Jean-Paul Sartre, trying to reconcile the freedom of the Existentialists with the historical "laws" of Marxism, is attempting the impossible.* But surely, Sartre does not fail to see the far-flung armies, the crowded prisons, the blind judges, the dead rulers, the passive masses. He talks the language of total Freedom because he knows that acting as if we are free is the only way to break the bind.

Freedom brings Responsibility. The Existentialist call for action is a demand that man exercise responsibility for changing the world about him, rather than passively accepting that world as it is. But the notion of Responsibility, like Freedom, can remain abstract. It takes on meaning only when the historian recognizes that his writing of history is an act, thrust into the world, for which he is responsible.

Here, too, as with Freedom, there is a curious deception, where the usual idea of "responsibility" for the historian turns out to have different meanings on the printed page and in the real world. This shows up in the matter of moral judgment. The customary division among historians is between those who declare (as Her-

concern is with empirical matters—the actual lives of human beings in the space and time of normal experience. For historians determinism is not a serious issue. . . ." Isaiah Berlin, *Four Essays on Liberty,* Oxford University Press, 1969.

* See the critique by George Lukacs in *Existentialism or Marxism?* and that by Roger Garaudy, *Literature of the Graveyard,* reprinted in George Novack, ed., *Existentialism vs. Marxism,* Delta (paper edition), 1966.

bert Butterfield) that the historian must avoid moral judgments, and those (Geoffrey Barraclough) who deplore the loss of moral absolutes and the surrender to "historicism" and "relativism," (that is, to the idea that all moral judgments are tentative and relative depending on the historical period and situation).* The irony is that the moral judgments usually called for deal with the dead past, and often in a way that weakens moral responsibility in the living world.

Moral indignation against Nazism illustrates the point. It can become focused on an individual of the past, and in that case it buries itself with that person and sticks to no one else. Thus, Germans who obeyed orders during the war may now weep at a showing of *The Diary of Anne Frank,* blaming the whole thing on Adolf Hitler. (How often these days in Germany does one hear "If not for Adolf Hitler . . ."?) It is this *ad hominem* assignment of responsibility, this searching the wrong place for blame in a kind of moral astigmatism, which Hannah Arendt tried to bring to world attention in her dissection of the Eichmann case.[12]

But is it any better to widen responsibility from the individual to the group? Suppose we blame "the Nazis." Now that the Nazi Party does not exist, now that anti-Semitism appears in other groups, now that militarism is the property of the "democratic" government of West Germany as well as the "socialist" government of East Germany, doesn't that kind of assignment merely deflect attention from the problems of today? And if we simply widen it to include Germans and Germany, what effect does this have except to infinitesimally decrease the sale of Volkswagens, and to permit every other country in the world but Germany to commit mayhem in a softer glow?

What we normally do then, in making moral judgments, is assign responsibility to a group which in some specific historic instance was guilty, instead of selecting the elements of wrong, out of time and place (except for dramatic effect) so that they can be applicable to everyone, including ourselves. (Is this not why Brecht, Kafka, Orwell are so powerful?) It is racism, nationalism,

* The statements by Butterfield and Barraclough are reprinted in Hans Meyerhoff, ed., *The Philosophy of History in Our Time,* Doubleday (Anchor edition), 1959.

militarism (among other elements) which we find reprehensible in Nazism. To put it that way is alarming, because those elements are discoverable not just in the past, but right now, and not just in Germany, but in all the great powers.

I am suggesting that "responsibility" in history can only have meaning in immediate activity. It is an old and useless game among historians to decide today whether Caesar was good or bad, Napoleon progressive or reactionary, Roosevelt a reformer or a revolutionist.* In a recounting of past crimes, it is senseless to ask: Who was guilty then? unless it leads directly to: What is our responsibility now? **

Erik Erikson has written of Freud's concern because his patient Dora had confronted her family with some of their misdeeds. "Freud considered this forced confrontation an act of revenge not compatible with the kind of insight which he had tried to convey to the patient. If she now knew that those events had caused her to fall ill, it was her responsibility to gain health, not revenge, from her insight." [13] What makes this story even more interesting is that there is a suggestion that Freud may himself have been guilty of the same thing, by being annoyed with what his patient had done, and discontinuing her treatment.

It is this irony in moral judgment which explains why George Kennan, starting from a certain set of values, can oppose a "moralistic" approach to other countries.[14] This approach, he says, is based on past misdeeds; it looks backward rather than forward. It leads to fixed enmities and fixed friendships, both based on past conditions; it prohibits a flexibility directed to the future.

All sides engage in this. When the Soviet Union defines imperialism as a characteristic of capitalist nations, it is limiting the abil-

---

* Certain of these questions, when based on a present problem, are pertinent. For instance, was Socrates right or not in submitting to the death penalty?

** Isaiah Berlin weakens his argument for "responsibility" by his dwelling on past, dead responsibility, urging us to "make out the best, most plausible cases for persons and ages remote or unsympathetic" and to judge an "individual in history . . . innocent or guilty." From his essay, "Historical Inevitability," reprinted in Isaiah Berlin, *Four Essays on Liberty,* Oxford (Galaxy edition), 1969, pp. 103–4.

ity of its people to criticize undue influence exerted over another country by a socialist nation. When it defines corruption as a manifestation of "bourgeois" culture, it makes it more difficult to deal with a phenomenon in its own society. When the United States defines the Soviet sphere as "totalitarian" and the West as "free" it makes it difficult for Americans to see totalitarian elements in our society, and liberal elements in Soviet society. Such moralizing can permit the United States to condemn the Russians in Hungary and absolve itself in Vietnam.

To define an evil in terms of a specific group, where such an evil is not inherent in the group but capable of springing up anywhere, is to remove responsibility from ourselves. It is what we have always done in criminal law, which is based on revenge for past acts, rather than a desire to make constructive social changes. (Capital punishment notably, but also *all* imprisonment, illustrates this.) It is often said that the French were always prepared for the *last* war. In the modern world, we are always ready to identify those responsible for the *last* act of evil.

On this, the artist is usually more perceptive than the historian, knowing that the crucial thing is to reveal the relationship between evil and ourselves. But both can instruct us. Thus, for present purposes, it is enormously useful to show (as Hannah Arendt did) how genocide could result from the piling up of mundane bureaucratic decisions by ordinary men. Or to show (as in *Lord of the Flies*) how innocent children can become monsters, or (as in Bergmann's film *The Virgin Spring*) how a loving father can become a vengeful murderer, or (as in *Who's Afraid of Virginia Woolf?*) how an "ordinary" man and wife can become vultures. To respond to an act already consummated, by punishing the specific ones who *were* guilty is to leave us free to act, unnoticed, in the same way, until the day of judgment—always one disaster behind.

A work like *The Deputy* (an amalgam of history and art) succeeds, when people, instead of asking: Why did the Pope remain silent? ask instead: Why do people everywhere, at all times, and *now,* remain silent? When such a question is asked, the play itself has broken the silence of the stage. Those of us who are deputies of that Muse, history, now need to break ours.

18

The historians

Even in the sixties, when students, blacks, anti-war protesters were creating commotions, those historians and philosophers who philosophized about history remained, with few exceptions, impeccably academic. One need only consult the pages of *History and Theory* in those years, or *The American Historical Review,* or the *Doctoral Dissertations Published in American Universities,* to corroborate this.*

To find leading scholars in the fields of philosophy and history who urge that the writing of history should serve the large needs of society, we have to turn to earlier periods. (This, surely, is one of the uses of history; we can reach in and pluck from it some inspirational and intellectual support when we are in need.) Thus, we find in Alfred North Whitehead's *The Aims of Education:* [1] "The understanding which we want is an understanding of an insistent present. The only use of a knowledge of the past is to equip us for the present. . . . The present contains all that there is."

Carl Becker, of that same generation, wrote: [2]

During the hundred years that passed between 1814 and 1914 an unprecedented and incredible amount of research was carried on, research into every field of history—minute, critical, exhaustive (and exhausting!) research. Our libraries are filled with this stored-up knowledge of the past; and never before has there been at the disposal

* Undoubtedly, the race question was the most vital, the most troublesome domestic issue. From 1960–66, inclusive, of 3265 dissertations in modern history, eighteen dealt with this problem (less than one percent). See *Doctoral Dissertations Published in American Universities.* Of 446 articles in *The American Historical Review* from 1945 to 1968, five dealt with the Negro question (about one percent).

of society so much reliable knowledge of human experience. What influence has all this expert research had upon the social life of our time? Has it done anything to restrain the foolishness of politicians or to enhance the wisdom of statesmen? Has it done anything to enlighten the mass of the people, or to enable them to act with greater wisdom or in response to a more reasoned purpose? Very little surely, if anything. . . .

To dig even deeper into the past, there is Francis Bacon: [3]

> Upon these intellectualists . . . Heraclitus gave a just censure, saying, "Men sought truth in their own little worlds and not in the great and common world.". . . But the greatest error of all the rest is the mistaking or misplacing of the last or furthest end of knowledge. For men have entered into a desire of learning and knowledge, sometimes upon a natural curiosity and inquisitive appetite; sometimes to entertain their minds with variety and delight; sometimes for ornament and reputation; and sometimes to victory of wit and contradiction; and most times for lucre and profession; and seldom sincerely to give a true account of their gift of reason, to the benefit and use of men. . . .

We who think about history need to decide from the start whether history should be written and studied primarily "for the benefit and use of men," rather than primarily "for lucre and profession." Indeed, the first question to be asked by anyone philosophizing about any activity is: What is it for? Without knowing our goal, how can we judge whether one kind of historical work is preferable to another?

All this could be waved aside with the rejoinder that everyone knows the purpose of studying the past is to *help*. Well, if everyone knows it, they do not show it. Those historians and philosophers who comment on history philosophically, theoretically, seem to be speaking "in their own little worlds" as Heraclitus put it. There is a vast universe of discourse about history far removed from the urgent concerns of "the great and common world." What Carl Becker said about World War I can be applied to World War I and to the Vietnam War. How long will we suffer such embarrassment?

My aim in the next few chapters is to look at what the academic historians and philosophers do when they deal with the "philosophy of history." I will argue that they seem to have lost their way without realizing it, because they have forgotten the humanistic goals of historical work. If they are not lost, it is because they are content to wander aimlessly so long as it is "interesting" or in respectable company. (I put "interesting" in quotations because we have weakened the word by neglecting its denotation as some *interest* to be gained or lost, beyond mere curiosity.)

Let us first look at what the historians have been saying. A good starting point is *History,* published by Princeton University Press in 1965, and written by Higham, Krieger, and Gilbert. This is an important book because it represents the professional historians' considered summary of the state of historical writing in the U.S. at that time. It is also, I would claim, an inadvertent summary of the formalism and academic detachment that mark much of American historiography today.*

A close examination of the concluding chapter in the "Theory" section of the book, entitled "The Renewal of History," shows a mood of satisfaction with the position of historiography since the mid-1950's. This mood seems to be based on the improvement of the historian's professional position rather than on any notable contribution made by historians to American society. John Higham, who writes this chapter, speaks of "a revival of confidence in historical knowledge," and notes that "the historian's morale and his position in American culture" had "hearteningly improved." He sees "signs of quickening vitality" in the profession and cites as one of these signs a "reinvigorated American Historical Association" that was "growing prodigiously in membership and activities." [4]

What does all this mean? To speak of an improvement of the

---

* I am not alone in my reaction. Jurgen Herbst, reviewing the same book in *History and Theory,* Vol. V, No. 1, 1966, fears that the great preoccupation of American historians seems to be with methodology rather than with values. "Does the study of history have no purposes and goals which define its means? The authors bypass these questions." Herbst criticizes the authors of the book for not saying what he thinks they mean. "They could have told us that we have failed to live up to our greatest challenge: to speak to the conditions of our time."

historian's "position in American culture" does not tell us very much about the *substance* of the historian's position; whether we should be happy with Higham's statement depends on our estimate of the state of American culture. If American culture shows, in these past few decades, an increasing specialization among professionals, a growing dedication to money, grants, funding, an intoxication with quantitative criteria of success, if *how much* is produced is more important than what and for whom, then should we be happy that the historian's position in such a culture is improved? The *culture* makes it appropriate to point to the growth in membership of the A.H.A. and to the quantity of its activities. But a much more pertinent question (not from the standpoint of the going American culture, but from the transcendental purpose suggested by Bacon, Whitehead, Becker) would be: In what way have the activities of the American Historical Association and its members focused historical knowledge on the solution of the problems pressing in on America and the world in the 1950's and 1960's? (I have noted in a previous chapter the approval with which the leading officer of the American Historical Association described the dismissal of the issue of Vietnam from the agenda of an international conference of historians.)

Higham, viewing the recent tendencies of American historiography, seems to accept as a favorable development the rejection of the "presentism" of Progressive and New Deal days represented by men like Beard and Becker. "The label present-minded," he writes about the period since World War II, "now loomed up as an epithet," and "the fixed point that everyone grasped was the simple axiom that history is basically an effort to tell the truth about the past." *

* A good example of this mood is Cushing Strout's *The Pragmatic Revolt in American History: Becker and Beard,* Cornell (paper edition), 1966. Strout's concern is with "the crucial idea of the disinterested historical imagination" (p. 47), and while sympathetic to Becker and Beard, he floats in and out of grasping and ultimately misunderstanding their position. Clearly Strout cannot totally embrace a "disinterested" history because near the end of his book he says: "Yet the involvement of the historians in actual history, though it generates his interest in certain problems, need not, any more than the scientist's involvement in nature, stifle his objectivity in assessing the evidence according to the highest critical

That "axiom" is far from simple, however. The "truth" about the past cannot be everything that happened because that is both impossible to know, and confusing if known. If it is an event about which very little is known, like the trial of Socrates, or the death of Christ, or the rebellion of Nat Turner, we are stuck with what may be a very unrepresentative or distorted picture of what happened there. If it is an event with a huge number of known details, like the American Civil War, we are forced to select, and the principle of selection (unless we stick pins blindfolded into the volumes of *The War of Rebellion: Official Records*) will depend on a present interest, whether we acknowledge it or not.*

standards of his profession." Despite this statement, he assumes that Becker's "emphasis on present social needs and hopes" is tied to a "seeming mockery of any kind of historical truth or objectivity." (The word "seeming" is important, of course.) Further, Strout misunderstands the position of the presentist when he says: "The historian, from this point of view, becomes the rationalizer of the collective social consciousness of the day, fabricating a useful past" (p. 42). He forgets that the present has *conflicting* interests, and that a presentist historian may either represent the dominant social consciousness of his day or the rebellious consciousness of his day.

* John Dewey wrote: "If the fact of selection is acknowledged to be primary and basic, we are committed to the conclusion that all history is necessarily written from the standpoint of the present, and is, in an inescapable sense, the history not only of the present but of that which is contemporaneously judged to be important in the present." *Logic: The Theory of Inquiry,* Holt, 1938, p. 236. When historians do deal with the philosophy of history, they often do so in impatient criticism of those who ask more of the historian than the profession wants to give. For instance, Burleigh Taylor Wilkins ("Pragmatism as a Theory of Historical Knowledge: John Dewey on the Nature of Historical Inquiry," in *The American Historical Review,* July, 1959, interprets Dewey's emphasis on *present* concerns in the selection from the historical past to mean that Dewey is not concerned with historical *accuracy*. He counters Dewey's claim that culture-bound judgments affect the historian's selection with: "But is not the disinterested love of truth a value as well, perhaps an eternal one that survives from culture to culture?" The real argument, however, is not between cultural relativism and trans-temporal truths, but rather between one or another value within any culture, between one or another transtemporal value. Thus, a persistent concern for the underdog in a world of injustice (represented *within* each era by a different *specific* concern) crosses all historical periods so far, and may affect the historian's selection of a problem to work on (without affecting his accuracy in presenting the

Higham's apparent satisfaction with the movement away from presentism is a sad bow to orthodoxy (and therefore to that special present interest represented by a scrupulous unconcern with current problems) by someone whose own historical writing (notably his *Strangers in the Land*) has been attuned to important problems.

Higham emphasizes the turn from presentism by noting that "liberal and even progressive" scholars (like J. H. Hexter, the Yale historian) were part of that movement: [5]

> Hexter and other disengaged spirits now argued that the relativists wrongly equated knowledge with certainty and truth with completeness: knowledge is always open to doubt, and all truths are partial. The historian's "frame of reference" includes present values, to be sure; but it also includes a large and growing mass of data about the past. The past is just as real, and just as capable of making itself felt in the formulation of historical generalizations, as is the present.

This is a misconception of what the relativists were saying. They knew very well that all knowledge was open to doubt and all truths partial. What they were asking is that the historian, acknowledging this as a fact, should deliberately seek to focus knowledge, not by random choice of past facts, or from simple curiosity, or with a desire to show the glories of America, but through the prism of a present urgency, whether it be starvation or war or race prejudice or something else.*

Surely Robinson and Beard did not have to be told that a "large and growing mass of data about the past" was important; most of their lives were devoted to digging up such data. But to talk about *both* past data and present values as in the "frame of reference" is to attempt a poor compromise between past-minded-

---

facts pertinent to that problem); and this, I would argue, is preferable as a guide to such selection over the "disinterested love of truth" which answers the technical problem of historical accuracy but not the larger problem of human relevance.

* This deliberate focusing is what Karl Mannheim calls *relationism* to distinguish it from an unconscious relativism. *Ideology and Utopia*, Harcourt, Brace (paper edition), 1957.

ness and present-mindedness which does justice to neither. While our body of facts must come from both past and present, the "frame of reference" through which we view those facts is a frame of *present* values.*

The New Historian (Robinson, Beard, Becker) was "defending his participation in the forward thrust of life," Higham says, and this is certainly true. But he then goes on to a *non-sequitur*— that this way of thinking "received a decisive check when the course of history failed to vindicate progressive values." [6] Higham seems to think that because the New Historians "looked to the present and future direction of history for criteria of what is important and desirable" this meant they were tied to an idea of inevitable progress, and if the century then filled up with catastrophes this must explode their presentism. But progressive values need not be vindicated by history—they need not be shown to be winning—in order to be kept alive. The holding of certain values by the historian does not require that history move toward those values, only that the historian try his best to move that way, *whatever* the actual flow of events. To use present humane concerns as a starting point for historical inquiry does not commit one to pessimism or optimism.

The coming of World War II, Higham says, contributed to this attack on presentism. It "freed historians not from dependence on the present, but from an overdeveloped commitment to it." But how can one have an "overdeveloped" commitment to the present if, as Whitehead tells us, "the present is all that there is." What else is there to be committed to but present and future, with life

---

* Both Marxism and pragmatism (or rather, "early" Marxism and "early" pragmatism) assert this. For instance, in his essay, "Karl Marx and the Classical Definition of Truth" (*Towards a Marxist Humanism,* Grove, 1968), the Polish philosopher, Lesjek Kolakowski notes the similarity (though he denies the identity) of the Jamesian pragmatic view of what is historically "true," and the Marxian view: "If, then, the countless different pictures of the same collection of facts co-exist and if all are approximately compatible with accepted technical rules of scholarly work, then the choice among them is defined by a more general choice, one of a certain view of the world, which constitutes an integral part of historical interpretation. . . . It is a choice of positions and not of theoretical theses; practical, not speculative" (p. 62).

itself the highest value? The past is dead. Surely, it is useful, as a cadaver is useful to an anatomist, and interesting, as souvenirs and photos are, but we cannot be "committed" to it in any sense and still call history a humanistic rather than a necrophilic endeavor.

As I have indicated above, "past-mindedness" is impossible; it is always a present concern that moves the historian. I suspect that the historian who stresses "past-mindedness" is really telling us that *his* present value is the appreciation of history as a profession, that his concerns are academic rather than social, that the "discipline" of history is competing with other disciplines, rather than joining them to solve social problems. This is the mood I find in Higham when he tells us (with what seems like satisfaction) that after World War II the historian declared some independence from the social sciences and this "reconstituted the historian's autonomous identity." [7] He talks of history getting rid of its "inferiority complex," now considering the social sciences as "contributory to history" rather than vice versa, so that historians can maintain "their own unspecialized identity." When historians become concerned with their own identity crisis, introspection has replaced social concern.

Describing historians' current views Higham says: "The task of historiography would always require the utmost divestment of bias and the penetration of a realm beyond the immediate self and its immediate society." [8] Once again, we find the failure to distinguish between two kinds of bias. One makes the historian lean to certain humanistic goals (peace, health, liberty) and may require that he ask certain questions of the data, but not that he falsify any of the answers he finds. The other bias is on behalf of certain instruments (party, nation, race, etc.) which easily leads to dishonesty in ascertaining facts, and incongruity with ultimate goals.* To go "beyond the immediate self and its immediate society" is to go nowhere, except possibly toward a metaphysical past, a deistic future.

Let us see how this "divestment of bias" applies to a current

* Lesjek Kolakowski makes a distinction somewhat like mine in his essay, "Karl Marx and the Classical Definition of Truth," *Towards a Marxist Humanism,* Grove, 1968, p. 63.

work. Thomas F. Gossett ends the preface of his book, *Race: The History of an Idea in America* with the sentence: "Finally my hope is that this book may help readers understand the cruelty and the absurdity of racism." [9] He was expressing bias. The very selection of his topic reflected this bias. But once his topic was selected—the history of race doctrine and bigotry in America— he could give a representative sample of such doctrines without distortion of the facts. Was this bias of Gossett's something he should subject to the "utmost divestment"?

Or another example, not so recent. Back in the forties, A. K. Weinberg wrote *Manifest Destiny,* a history of expansionist doc- trine in the United States, as Gossett's book is a history of racial doctrine. A certain bias seemed to motivate Weinberg to pick *this* topic out of so many others: the desire to show the illogic, the inconsistency, the absurdity of all the rationale for American ex- pansionism. He did this by presenting a straight, factual account of the reasons given by various Americans for the acquisitions of Florida, Texas, California, Puerto Rico, etc. Should he divest him- self of such bias?

Higham gives antiquarianism a more sophisticated guise in his book. "Accordingly, the historian can and should make use of his present in the very act of transcending it. . . . Standing at the in- tersection between past and present, the historian can reject the pragmatic doctrine of his subservience to present purposes while welcoming the incentives and general awareness of the present in discovering new vistas of the past." [10] The present, Higham seems to be saying, should be around somewhere in the consciousness, but it is *instrumental,* for the purpose of history is to discover "new vistas of the past." I would suggest that Higham's statement be rewritten to say the historian "can and should make use of his *past* in the very act of transcending it" in order to help mankind toward "new vistas of the *future.*"

That his concern for the past is really a concern for profession- alism in the present is shown once again in Higham's discussion of "the humanistic implications" of history today. One might think that phrase refers to the uses of history in furthering human needs. But no, the discussion is all about the link between history and literature and philosophy, without asking how *these* other disciplines are themselves linked with humanistic problems. Once more, we have become obsessed with *instruments* which came to be called "humanistic disciplines," so we begin to think that when we discuss those instruments we are doing something "humanistic."

As a sign of increasing humanistic concern, Higham notes that in 1931 the American Historical Association listed "just ten works in the philosophy of history" and in 1961 "fifty-nine titles, almost all published in recent decades." But what does this mean if we don't know the content of those works—if we are not sure that the philosophy of history is concerned with humanistic ends? Indeed, as Hexter has pointed out, and as we shall see in the following chapter, its main concern has been methodology.

Past-minded historians criticize that subjectivity which leads some historians to study the past from the standpoint of a bias for certain human needs. They are not so critical, however, of another kind of subjectivity.[11]

Perhaps the most fundamental methodological proposition that has come out of this latest encounter with European thought is the necessity for historians to participate subjectively in whatever past they wish to understand. No amount of scientific analysis or synthesis can take the place of that crucial act of human empathy by which the historian identifies himself with another time and place, reenacting the thoughts and reliving the experience of people remote from himself.

Why is this proposition unaccompanied by the suggestion that the historian should seek empathy with people *today* in other places, rather than in other times (the blacks, the Chinese, the poor of Appalachia, the soldiers in the field)? Would this not be far more important as a starting point for historical writing than empathy with the dead? Such an act of *present* empathy would guide the most important decision a historian must make—about what sort of problem he will undertake to study.

Of course, if a historian is studying the clash of ideas on the morality of slavery it would be useful to identify sufficiently with John Fitzhugh so as to present accurately his defense of slavery, as with Frederick Douglass to present the viewpoint of the slave. But it would take a *present* interest in racism today, and a conjecture that presenting the Fitzhugh-Douglass views might have a good effect on today's thinking, to make the historian decide to study *that,* rather than the question of who fired the first shot at Fort Sumter, or what was Grant's strategy at Vicksburg.*

Higham himself sums up (perhaps with a trace of criticism here, though one must strain to detect it) the value-free state of American historiography today: [12]

> Most historians today seem to accept the responsibility of taking their stand at no one place, either inside or outside the scene of action. Instead, they move about, viewing a situation from within and from above, blending subjective identification with objective analysis, uniting art with science, recognizing the complementarity of perspectives and the multiplicity of relationships by which the historian—and he alone—undertakes to grasp a transition in human affairs in its full contextual significance.

The historian become Superman is what this passage describes. Except that the comic book Superman *does* know what side he is on. Is it an acceptance of "responsibility" to stand "at no one

---

* There is a persistent misunderstanding of the problem of moral judgment in historical writing, which insists that a historian must set aside his present moral concerns in order to understand and therefore record accurately an opposing morality in the past. Cushing Strout says of the historian in *The Pragmatic Revolt in American History:* "If he is to understand why the Puritans hanged witches, he must set aside the ordinary conventions of his own world in order to recreate a life in which hanging witches made sense." Of course, the historian's anti-witchhunt bias should not prevent him from truthfully recreating those events, but it is probably *exactly* that bias which leads him to explore these events in the first place. What is crucial is to understand that the accurate recreation of the past is not the ultimate aim of the historian (which one is led to infer from Strout's emphasis) but rather that this (yes, *accurate*) recreation is an instrument for furthering a present bias. Furthermore, it is not a matter of disjunction between past and present scales of morality, since there are contesting moral views in every epoch. Do we not in our own time need to *understand* racist thinking while seeking to use the data of this time for anti-racist purposes?

place"? Certainly not to the huge numbers of people who have problems needing whatever help history can offer. But perhaps to the "reinvigorated American Historical Association . . . growing prodigiously in membership and activities" and heartened by Higham's phrase "and he alone," which solves the identity problem of the historian at last.

If all this is not Higham's viewpoint but he is merely *describing* how historians in fact do think, we have here a fine example of how a supposed objective description, by focusing on *part* of a reality, reinforces that part of it. It conveys to people in the field that *this* is the going orthodoxy of the profession; it influences younger historians seeking approval, and older ones wanting to stay in line. It is a perfect instance of how selection (because although it is the dominant view, it is not the *only* one) supports *some* present concern, and whether Higham means to or not, his selection supports a disguised brand of antiquarianism.

If we chose to select from the work of historians with a view to encouraging a presentist purpose, we could take note of the opinion of Carl Degler, another American historian, in a review [13] of Samuel Eliot Morison's *The Oxford History of the American People,* probably the largest selling single-volume history of the United States since Beard's *Rise of American Civilization.* Degler notes that Morison's comprehensive history gives just one paragraph to Henry David Thoreau, and comments: "If, as Morison suggests in his preface, the purpose is to tell us how people behaved in the past, then Thoreau does not deserve a place in his story. . . . Thoreau simply had no impact on his times. . . ." Clearly, if the *present* were the key to selection, then Thoreau needs much more attention than Morison gives him.

Degler says: "What gives historical events significance or meaning? Certainly it is not the events themselves, as antiquarians aver, for, of the thousands of events that a chronicler of a single year would record, only a handful reach the pages of the historian. The criterion of meaning is subsequent events."

I would amend Degler's statement to replace "subsequent events" with "contemporary problems." To support his statement he notes that the 1832 Nullification movement in South Carolina is important because there was a subsequent secession movement in 1860, whereas the New England secession movements of 1804 and 1814 are not important because there was no subsequent event to give them importance. What Degler overlooks is that it is not the 1860 secession movement that makes the 1832 Nullification movement important, but various problems of today (race, politics, separatism, federalism) which make that 1860 secession important. Thus, if we had a *present* issue of "states' rights," then it might be very valuable to bring up the 1804 and 1814 secession movements in New England to prove (as Arthur Schlesinger, Sr., did in *New Viewpoints in American History*) that "states' rights" have usually been a mask for *other* purposes. So, it is not merely subsequent but *present* events that determine what is important to study in the past.

When historians refuse to let their deepest values (rather than their professional ones) guide their work, the result is often a set of empty arguments about methodology, a spurious "theorizing" which races around in the academic stratosphere with no particular destination. Francis Bacon put it this way:[14]

> These pronouncements have no other sense or purpose than to promote a deliberate and artificial despair both as regards the acquisition of knowledge and the possibility of action. They are a shameful device for safeguarding the honor and glory of their art. To this end the Academics made a cult of the incomprehensibility of nature and condemned man to eternal darkness. The same end was served by the doctrine that Forms (that is, the true differences of things) are indiscoverable. The intention was to keep men walking up and down for ever in nature's forecourt without ever paving a way into her palace.

For instance, we find a persistent debate among those historians who insist their primary job is *narration,* and those who insist their main job is *interpretation.* The distinction is put this way by an eminent historian, Louis Gottschalk, in his preface to *Generalization in the Writing of History:* * "Historians . . . are said to

* Gottschalk was chairman of a committee set up by the Social Science Research Council to report on "historical analysis," to see if historians could derive useful concepts from their work. The book is the committee's published report. Gottschalk, *Generalization in the Writing of History,* University of Chicago, 1963, p. v.

fall into two groups. One may be called 'descriptive historians'; they attempt to give an account of the event or situation under consideration in its own unique setting. The other may be called 'theoretical historians'; they try to find in their subject matter a basis for comparison, classification, interpretation, or generalization."

Of course, most historians do both; yet some histories are clearly more narrative, while others are more interpretive. For instance, Max Farrand's *The Framing of the Constitution* is mainly a narrative of the Convention, while Charles Beard's *An Economic Interpretation of the Constitution* is primarily an attempt to generalize from the data. What concerns us here is that historians will argue over one method rather than the other as the more desirable one, or the more important one, or the one more appropriate to the historian; what I want to show is that this argument is pointless or value-less.

A leading advocate of "narrative history" over "theoretical history" is J. D. Hexter of Yale. Hexter's most powerful polemic is directed not against fellow historians who theorize, but against philosophers who see the main job of historians as "causal explanation." This angle of attack, however, seems to come from some unspoken nonaggression pact between Hexter and the theory-seeking historians against the common enemy (philosophers) rather than from a genuine commonality of interest.*

What Hexter is mainly arguing for is the role of the historian as the skillful teller of stories about the past (Garrett Mattingly's evocative history of *The Armada,* for instance). In his article "The Rhetoric of History," [15] he makes an important point, that the writing of history itself is an act which superimposes a mean-

---

* David Potter, striving for theory in Gottschalk, *Generalization in the Writing of History,* quotes a Hexter paragraph as proof that Hexter endorses theorizing in history. But a careful reading of that paragraph discloses that Hexter is doing there what he usually does, defending narrative as against theoretical history. He does this by pointing out that narrative history, while more than a list of factual statements, is not nearly a complete list of statements about an event; yet, it may tell us "something"— and this is valuable. To do that limited but useful job, Hexter tells us, is "the working conviction of historians as contrasted with their inept excursions into theory."

ing on the bare facts. The trouble with Hexter's point is that he sees the purpose of this act by the historian as the traditional antiquarian one, to recreate history, so far as possible, as it actually was. He holds to this purpose stubbornly—and eloquently—against all the good sense that argues this is impossible, and against the presentist belief that it is insufficient. He talks of the "essential function" of history as "its capacity to convey knowledge of the past as it actually was."

I would claim that the historian, even when he is trying to tell the details of an event as close to the original reality as possible, should have a purpose beyond the mere telling of something interesting—and this purpose decides for him *what,* among the infinite number of past events, he decides to tell about. His rhetoric is useful, yes, when history is an art-form, a story. But if history is to be more than that—and I am arguing that in our times it must be more—that rhetoric should be used to enhance a set of humane values connected with the present urgent problems of man. This demands more than does Hexter when he says: "But the historian's goal in his response to the data is to render the best account he can of the past as it really was."

Hexter says historians "allege that when a piece of historical work is well done and properly set down, readers will know more about the past after they have read it than before." But this is a puny aim, too easy to fulfill, and blesses too generously so much of the wasted intellectual effort filling the library shelves with "more about the past," period.

In a review of two books by philosophers on the philosophy of history (Morton White, *The Foundations of Historical Knowledge;* Arthur C. Danto, *Analytical Philosophy of History*) [16] Hexter scores neatly against those philosophers who can't bear with the historian just telling a story, who insist that he must always be "explaining" something, utilizing the scientific method in some way (that is, utilizing "general laws" in his explanation). Of course he is right. Unless explanation is for some purpose, it is explanation for its own sake, which is hardly superior to narrative for its own sake. And if explanation can serve some good purpose (to help us understand, let us say, why nationalist ideology plays a role in fomenting war), then it is conceivable that narratives, too, dealing with certain events which people do not know, may add to their information so as to give them a different view of things. A simple narrative of the Spanish-American War may tell as much about the absurdity of certain international adventures as any sophisticated "explanation" of that event. Some things simply don't have to be explained to people. They explain themselves.

The trouble is, Hexter is not making just this point. He is not arguing for narrative on the ground that it can serve humane values as well as "explanatory" stories; he is arguing for it because it leads us to "knowing more about the past." If we start from the idea that history is knowledge, and knowledge for its own sake is all we seek, then Hexter is right. If we start from the idea that the "scientific method" is important, for its own sake, then the "scientific," theoretical historian is doing fine. But if our starting point is: How can history serve man today? then it doesn't matter if the method is narrative or explanatory. Then the question becomes: A narration of what? Explanation of what? Narrative can be socially useless or enormously revealing (of some present puzzlement). Explanation can be meaningless or instructive.

That the generalizing historian is prone to what Hexter calls "inept" excursions into theory is due not to some methodological lack but to the same ethical failure which leads to empty narratives—the failure to start historical inquiry with a social rather than a private or professional motive. It may be worth taking a look at some of these excursions.

It is understandable that historians—either prodded by the analytic philosophers or by their own consciences—might begin to question the adequacy of their attempts to generalize from the facts they dig up. For instance, Samuel Eliot Morison, in his book *The Founding of Harvard College,*[17] says of the Puritans in early New England: "They were a free and happy people." I would not counter this generalization with another: "The Puritans were a repressed and unhappy people." But there is as much evidence (or more) for the second statement as for the first, and so Morison's generalizing deserves a critique.

All sloppy generalizations require criticism, because they inculcate what might be dangerous habits; but some generalizations are immediately of more social concern than others. Morison's is not as bad as the assertion found in some textbooks about the happy slaves, singing in the fields, which is not only dubious as a generalization, but also detracts from the white American's understanding today of why the black person might have a historic basis for his bitterness. But his generalization does contribute to the common glorification of this country's early years; it feeds arrogance and dulls the critical faculties we need so much today.

Nevertheless, the avoidance of such crude generalizations as Morison's, the attention to reasonable accuracy, does not guarantee that whatever generalizing is done is *useful*. Let's take a statement introducing the essays in *The Reconstruction of American History,* referring to the fact that New England produced many historians: "Clearly the New England intellect distrusted the rational abstractions of political theory and the relaxing temptations and fabrications of the novel." How "clear" this conclusion is from the fact that New England did produce a number of fine historians is dubious. But even if true, of what use is such a generalization? One might say: "How interesting!" Or, "How droll!" But it is as if two lovers are sitting on a hillside in a critical moment of their relationship when matters need to be resolved, and one of them says: "I've been thinking: every time we've met, it was a Tuesday."

Historians sometimes seem to think that generalizing about *anything* is somehow a step beyond simple narrative toward "interpretation," and therefore, presumably toward some higher, more theoretical, level of history. That generalizations *can* be important for the present is shown from one in Woodward's *The Strange Career of Jim Crow.* After noting that not long after the end of slavery, there were many instances in which whites and blacks in the South used the same facilities, like railroad trains, whereas later segregation laws pretended to be founded on an unbreakable tradition, Woodward comments: "State ways can change folkways." That is, the government's attitude, expressed in its laws, can change people's behavior despite "tradition."

As an example of a generalization which, because it is deceptive, *is* important, take the statement by Ernest R. May in his essay "America As a World Power," [18] where he says about the Spanish-American War: "American public opinion had frenziedly demanded war." Now unless one realizes that in 1898 there were no ways of testing general public opinion, and that the frenzy was mostly the fulminating of a few very important newspapers (and even if one grants that the press had a strong influence on those who read it), one might well be led into another generalization: "Wars come because people demand them." Such a generalization obscures the way decisions for war are made by a handful of men at the top, and the way public opinion is manipulated just before and after the decision, to build support for it.*

American history has its favorite generalizations, passed on from one era of historians to the next. For instance, there has been, in American historiography, an enormous amount written on Puritanism as being fundamentally ingrained in "the American character." Yet, as one historian of that period has noted: [19] "It is very difficult, however, to be sure what these traces are."

Richard Schlatter, in his essay on Puritanism [20] points to those elements which modern historians have considered as carried over from Puritanism into contemporary America: morality and religion, education and literature, democracy and limited government, the Puritan ethic in business life, and "a sense of mission." As against this, Schlatter says bluntly that "The founders of New England were not democrats." But he too succumbs when he says that in defying the Fugitive Slave Law, Emerson's "Puritan conscience was at work." What of the Puritan conscience of Daniel Webster, who played such a large part in getting Congress to pass the Fugitive Slave Law? As for the Puritan ethic in business, where, Schlatter says, "there is general agreement that some connection can be traced between Puritanism and a later American business ethic," how would he account for the fact that this same ethic became manifest in all the leading capitalist countries of the West, Puritan or not, as well as in Shintoist Japan?

Schlatter himself provides enough argument to question the traditional talk about the importance of the "Puritan heritage," and to point up the methodological weakness of such generalizations. But—and this is my main point—even if one could find a valid generalization about the connection, why is this important?

* Elsewhere, May does refine his statement. But in this essay it is not qualified.

Of what use is it to any really important question before American society today? Schlatter concludes that "we will not be able to identify with precision the elements of the Puritan tradition in modern America until we have patiently and carefully studied the whole record. Until we do know the story in detail, talk about the Puritan tradition in America will be mostly speculation." We can foresee fifty more doctoral dissertations on the subject, and the shelves of Puritanism expanding. But how will more details known about the Puritans solve the complex problem of the connection between Puritan behavior and contemporary America, or lead away from empty "speculation"? If we could know everything about the Puritans, what will that do for us? *

There may well be historical data from the Puritan period that could have some effect on life today. But if so, it would have to be drawn out carefully in response to a significant question. To the question: What are the elements in building up the hysteria of a community either for an evangelical religion or against those who become its scapegoats? one might well look deeply into the sermons of Jonathan Edwards or the witchcraft episodes.** The witchcraft trials illustrate how a dramatic narrative can have in itself enormous significance today, without any pretentious conceptualizing or theorizing. Where *facts* about the past obviously connect in some way with facts in the present, the conceptualizing

---

* Carl Becker in the *Philosophical Review* (1940): "If we had all the data of all the events and a mind capable of grasping the data in their actual relations, everything would be immediately understood and immediately pardoned. In this timeless existence there would be no occasion for 'views,' no occasion for distinction between facts and non-facts, facts and interpretations, meaning and non-meaning, good and bad, being and becoming: everything would simply be, the entire blest *wie es eigentlich gewesen sei* would just be there and nothing to write home about. We would have the Truth, and the Truth would make us free, free to do nothing—except sit and contemplate the Truth." Quoted in Cushing Strout, *The Pragmatic Revolt in American History: Becker and Beard,* Cornell University Press (paper edition), 1966, p. 38.

** Thus, Perry Miller's work on Jonathan Edwards would clearly be useful for the first part of the question, and for the second, Marian Starkey's *The Devil in Massachusetts* or Arthur Miller's imaginative reconstruction in *The Crucible.*

is done in the mind of the reader, and generalizing intercession by the historian becomes superfluous.

Where generalization is useful, it does not depend on how recent or ancient is its data. A piece of research about the distant past may be more pertinent for today than a piece of research about the present, if it aims from the outset to answer an important question. In an article in the *American Political Science Review,* Arthur S. Goldburg [21] presents five graphic models of various factors influencing voting, none of which leads to a current live issue. (The substantive *issues* in voting are absent.) Furthermore, the author concludes simply that it is not yet time to conclude,* that more research is necessary; this is a common plea by social scientists, where research is not *designed* to lead to action, or to change, no matter how much research is done. On the other hand, historian Lee Benson, in *The Concept of Jacksonian Democracy: New York as a Test Case* sets out to ask a question which is very relevant to the persistent two-party system in America: How much real difference is there in the two major parties? He finds that in that time the leadership sources, voting support, campaign slogans, and terminology were the same for both parties.

The advantage of "theoretical" work over "empirical" work should be that it has gone a step beyond fact-gathering, and has generalized from dead data for the purpose of illuminating living data. Those who forget this original aim of theory become entranced with the instrument itself, and make a fetish of "theory," reify the process of conceptualization itself.

Take the German historian, Gerhard Ritter, who pleads for a scientific, theoretical history.[22] "In order to affect life, history must first and above all be real science," he says, thus putting forward to some indefinite time in the future (for if history is not "real science" now, when will it ever be?) history's connection with the living. Unless that connection is found now, and is maintained all through the attempt to become more scientifically rigorous, history

* "In concluding the present analysis, it is important to bear in mind that we are as yet far from concluding the inquiry into causality in voting behavior." Arthur S. Goldburg, "Discerning a Causal Pattern Among Data on Voting Behavior," *American Political Science Review,* December 1966.

moves farther and farther away from life.* And indeed, Ritter's
essay itself shows the danger, because his idolization of "scientific history" moves him in the space of one essay from the intention "to affect life" to a confession that this is illusionary: [23]

> But admittedly this process of clarification and consolidation
> of historical knowledge advances exceedingly slowly, with endless de-
> bates and many reverses. And so at the end of this general considera-
> tion one will impatiently ask what practical contribution this kind of
> uncertain knowledge . . . can make to resolving the troubles of our
> time. We would in fact be well advised to maintain no illusions about
> it. A contemplative mode of thought like the historian's, aiming at
> retrospective understanding and cautious judgment, seems neither
> adapted to penetrating the deep darkness of the future nor useful in
> those bold schemes and ventures without which high politics would
> simply not take place. Not without justice has the historian been called
> a prophet facing backwards who, as it were, advances backwards into
> the future.

What I am criticizing here is not the modesty which scholars
might justifiably have about the impact of their work, but the
idea that such impact should not be their purpose. Ritter's talk
about the aim "to affect life" turns out to be the conventional talk
of the historian, inserted to maintain his audience, but soon
dropped. Ritter talks of "the pride of the historian (as of all gen-

---

* Ritter says: "We are familiar with Friedrich Nietzsche's passionate
protest against the excess of historical culture in his century. . . . But
Nietzsche's thesis—that strict justice and accuracy in particular matters
much less than the life-giving efficacy of history—having done so much
mischief in the European world of letters, still persists in its influence."
"Scientific History, Contemporary History, and Political Science," *History
and Theory,* Vol. I, 1961. Ritter is distorting Nietzsche here. Nietzsche
would say (as in his *The Use and Abuse of History*) that everything matters less than life-giving efficacy, but he did not couple this with tolerance
of inaccuracy. More important, what has done more "mischief" in Europe,
inattention to "accuracy" (who were more meticulous than the European
historians?) or betrayal of their society by inattention to the tyrannies
growing around them as they pored over their "particular matters"?
Nietzsche's *The Use and Abuse of History* remains a brilliant corrective
to stultifying historical exhumation.

uine scholarship) to pursue his science purely as an end in itself, exclusively for the sake of determining the truth." He is begging the question here, because that is the root of the difficulty—the conception of what is "truth." We would need to recall Polonius to adapt his banal old speech for the "scientific" historian: "to thine own age be true, and then it must follow as the night the day, thou canst not be false to any age."

Ritter deserves quoting because his view shows up repeatedly in one form or another as the traditional response of the historian when begged by harassed people for help: I am adding to your stock of knowledge about the world. My job is not to help you act. But take comfort. The sheer increase in knowledge of the past will *somehow* help you. If, however, the historian cannot tell the citizen how his data will help, how can he expect the citizen to make use of it? Ritter says: [24]

> . . . if we ask what historical science can contribute toward coping with the needs of our time, the answer can only be that it will teach us to see reality more clearly, that it will help to disseminate a dispassionate understanding: taking positions and making decisions are primarily the concern of the actors, not of the spectators. The historian's gaze is directed toward the past; that of the actor, necessarily toward the future.

That the highest levels of theory do not necessarily lead to a higher wisdom but may in fact be convoluted and pretentious exercises is revealed by historian Othmar F. Anderle's essay "A Plea for Theoretical History." [25] He is disturbed by the rise of what he calls "the Historiographical Opposition" with its pragmatic emphasis, and urges that historians start with a "solid, empirical foundation" and with "rational and logical principles" to move toward "the synopsis which our time requires." A grand synopsis— a theory of theories about history—this is what Anderle seeks, and he describes its goals this way: [26]

> . . . the conception, verification and systematization of theories on the essence, interrelation, and meaning of historical phenomena, the building of heuristic hypotheses, the discovery and derivation

of types of facts and processes, laws and regularities, the discovery, through abstraction, of useful schematas and patterns, the formation of general concepts, advantageous to investigation and organization of historical study, the organization and interpretation of the facts discovered by specialized field study, and ultimately, the synthesis of these factors into a historical world-picture.

This has the grandeur of a Hegelian onward-upward to the end of historiography. But there are two flaws in this magnificent prospectus. The first is fatal even from Anderle's standpoint: it is the assumption that historical knowledge is cumulative and progressive, that if we can only "know more" about a subject, wisdom will follow (even the kind of "wisdom" Anderle is concerned with, which is a kind of academic knowledge, not necessarily related to social issues). Let me cite three examples:

1. Fifty years after the end of World War I, with the mountains of research continuing to grow, we are still debating the same issues that were debated at the time.*

On the specific question of American intervention in the First World War, we might note Richard W. Leopold's "The Problem of American Intervention, 1917: An Historical Retrospect." [27] Leopold surveys the historical literature, which quite clearly reveals a basic clash in interpretation between opponents and supporters of American intervention, continuing even while the monographs and documents piled up. Somehow, Leopold manages to ignore the obvious "presentist" conclusion from this: that regardless of the bulk of sheer data, present views of foreign policy seem to determine the historian's attitude. Hence, he concludes his article in orthodox fashion, listing soberly all the work remaining to be done by historians, with phrases like "a second untilled area" (more monographs dealing with state and sectional sentiment), ". . . a third somewhat neglected aspect. . . . No one has really read the Congressional Record for 1914–17. . . . There is a crying need for scholarly biographies of. . . . Perhaps the records of

---

* For instance, Fritz Fischer's monumental *Germany's Aims in the First World War.* And see the argument in the pages of *The New York Times Book Review,* Dec. 8, 1968, between Gordon Craig and D. F. Fleming on Fleming's *The Origins and Legacies of World War I.*

other diplomats will be helpful. . . ." And: "Nor should it be assumed that the last word has been said on Bryan."

Indeed, it is quite clear from Leopold's article what *his* present value is: "It is imperative that future historians treat American intervention in 1917 as but a single step, albeit an important one, in the transition of the United States from a role of relative indifference to world affairs to one of active participation. Perhaps when that point is grasped, they will be more tolerant than their predecessors of the hesitations, inconsistencies and even mistakes of those who steered the ship of state in 1914."

Leopold's present concern (1950: the middle of the Cold War) is that people look rather warmly at America's new role of "active participation" in the world. To those heads of state in the world who benefited from American postwar activity, this is welcome. To those nameless people (Asian and Latin-American peasants, mainly) who suffered as a result of American "active participation"—America's entrance into World War I might seem less noble. And after all, it is too late to do anything about American participation in World War I; it is not too late to decide for or against similar bloody engagements "for liberty" in the present and future. No additional data on World War I can decide the moral question of what would be better, for a moral question can only be a present question, to be answered by present needs.

2. With regard to Charles Beard's thesis on the American Constitution, we find a Princeton historian writing: [28]

> Where Beard's hypotheses are concerned there is something peculiar in the fact that a half-century after his book appeared we still cannot answer satisfactorily the question whether the various political factions involved in the struggle over the Constitution were economic in origin or representative of man's "propensity" to quarrel heatedly over "frivolous and fanciful distinctions."

3. To take an even longer time-span, the almost two hundred years since the American Revolution, we find a historian examining various interpretations of the Revolution and concluding: [29]

> On the basis of this brief survey of interpretations of the Revolution, it would be very difficult to demonstrate clear and consistent

progress in the interpretation of historical events as the result of the longer time-perspective of successive historians. Neither do we find that the opening up of untapped archives and the discovery of new documents (beyond a certain point, of course) results in notably improved or (in any final sense) more acceptable interpretations.

The more serious objection to Anderle's vision of a long development of historical theory, leading to "ultimately, the synthesis of these factors into a historical world-picture" is not that it is impossible, but that it is pointless. Indeed, its impossibility is connected with its pointlessness, because the very setting of a metaphysical goal, divorced from immediate need, precludes the possibility of a solution. The only achievable objective of such a vast enterprise as Anderle describes is professional gratification. He tells us, in fact, that his aim is to restore the purposes of the classical historian. And: "The classical historian considered his discipline as an end in itself." [30]

We find a similar approach expressed not long ago in the official hierarchy of American historians. The Committee on Historiography of the American Historical Association, in its Bulletin 64, designed to discuss the relationship between history and the social sciences, said: ". . . the conscientious historian, even when engaged upon monographic research, never permits himself to forget the final goal, namely, comprehensive synthesis." [31]

There can be no "comprehensive" synthesis however, in an ongoing, infinite development out of a past slightly known. Should there not be a more modest yet (in another sense) larger aim: that each level of historiography, however incomplete, whether empirical or theoretical, should serve some special purpose? For this, there is no waiting until some great day of historical reckoning. For this, a relevant theoretical point can be made at any moment of time, because it is not so sweeping in its ambition; it aims to connect some fact of the past, through the medium of a theoretical statement, with some fact of the present, and thereby illuminate that present in a way that can help us make our own future.

For instance, whatever the emendations that diligent research might add to Beard's thesis on the Constitution over the years, affecting details of his thesis, his *fundamental* point has been a useful one in every period of American history since he expressed it: that constitutions (and therefore governments) are more than what they appear on their face, a collection of legal propositions; that they represent in some way important to understanding (and whatever the details or the indirectness of this representation) the clash of economic interests in the larger society. Thus, Staughton Lynd, examining the latest critiques of Beard, finds that the Constitution represented not a conflict of capitalist versus landed interests, but a coalition of all wealthy interests. But, he says, "Beard's fundamental plea for a 'removal of the Constitution from the realm of pure political ethics and its establishment in the dusty way of earthly strife and common economic endeavor' remains valid." [32]

It may be instructive to inspect a discussion among historians in the work edited by Louis Gottschalk, *Generalization in the Writing of History*.[33] This Committee is a direct descendant of that which produced Bulletin 64, quoted above on the "final goal . . . comprehensive synthesis." The collection of essays is in itself a striking illustration of the accuracy of at least one generalization: that historians (with few exceptions) do not have as a major concern whether their generalizations will be useful to help solve the problems of our time. When we search in the Foreword to the report, written by the editor Louis Gottschalk, for some clue to what all this generalization is *for,* we never really find out. He says at one point, speaking of the historian, that "his ultimate purpose is not alone the dispassionate study of historical vestiges but also a reconstruction of mankind's past, of past beings and doings, of the course of human events." But this is almost exactly the antiquarian's purpose—to reconstruct the past, as a task in itself, for itself.

At one point Gottschalk does say that the historian "needs to have some conscious, if only ad hoc, philosophy or theory of purposes, causes, and ends." [34] But that philosophy or theory is not intended to aim the work of the historian to any social purpose: it is only so that he can more effectively fill in the gaps about the past. When one looks at Gottschalk's own "purposes . . . ends," we cannot find anything but reconstructing the past for its own sake, and generalizing about the past for its own sake.

The report of the Gottschalk committee follows very much the style of the analytic philosophers (whom we will discuss in our next chapter). Instead of testing both the validity and the *usefulness* of generalizations, it sets out to answer the very limited question "of what the historian in fact has done" when he has generalized. It poses the methodological question of "whether the historian could make substantive generalizations that were more than truisms," without asking about the relevance of generalizations, whether justifiable by empirical evidence or not. It is the validity, and not the usefulness of generalizations, which concerns the Committee. Indeed, Gottschalk reports that ultimately the Committee asked the essayists for the volume "to write essays which, after sampling the concepts and generalizations in that literature, would undertake to indicate which in their judgment were wholly valid, partly valid, partly invalid, or wholly invalid, and in each case why." [35] I am not arguing against the need to check the validity of generalizations, only that this methodological test should be second to the substantive one, checking the relevance of valid generalizations.

The strongest clue to Gottschalk's rejection of ethical values as a touchstone for historical investigation comes in his own essay "Categories of Historiographical Generalization." Here he lists six different kinds of historical generalizers, but says about the sixth group (the "cosmic philosophers" like Augustine, Joachim of Floris, Condorcet, Hegel, Marx, Spengler, Toynbee): [36]

> I deliberately choose to deal with it only in passing on the ground that its practitioners are more or less consciously special pleaders, belonging to the disciplines of theology, philosophy, or political speculation rather than to that of history as a branch of learning, *no matter how well they use historical knowledge and no matter how much more important they may be to the world than academic historians.* The tests of their hypotheses are not conformance with historical evidence and plausibility or probability *alone;* they require other standards than, or *in addition to,* the canons of historical investigation and other kinds of convictions than those derived from historical research and tight inference from testimony [my emphasis].

What are the "other standards" of the "special pleaders," the cosmic philosophers? Their present concerns, their values. This,

Gottschalk believes, is enough to disqualify them from serious attention "no matter how well they use historical knowledge and no matter how much more important they may be to the world than academic historians." What should be more vital to the historian than using his data "well," and being "important" to the world? If those are not the paramount twin concerns of the academic historian, as Gottschalk suggests, my theme follows: that the academic historian is the blind scholastic of our time, hardly deserving of emulation by young people entering the field of history, if those young people care about the world. (Note that Gottschalk is not accusing the "special pleaders" of ignoring "historical evidence and plausibility or probability," but of not using them "alone," of requiring "other standards." He has drawn the issue perfectly.)

And what does Gottschalk conclude from the work of the essayists writing in his book on historical generalization. They "all agree that the historian willy-nilly uses generalizations at different levels and of different kinds. They all agree, too, that some good purpose is served when he does so, if only to present a thesis for debate." [37] Is that a sufficieny good purpose for the enormous amount of work done by historians in generalizing, "to present a thesis for debate"? *

True, historians when actually at work (including Gottschalk himself) [38] often present generalizations that are useful for the present. But because this has been largely a random event, there has been great scholarly waste.

For instance, Chester G. Starr, in his "Reflections upon the Problem of Generalization," [39] discusses two generalizations. One comes from the work of a Harvard psychologist, David C. McClelland, and a student of his named David E. Berlew. It uses studies of Greek literature to conclude that the Achievement Motive

---

* Again, let Bacon speak: "But to quarrel over every detail is to conclude nothing but sow forever the seeds of fresh dispute. . . . The aim of your philosophy is not in the course of time to kill those doubts, which are the enemy, and to press on into new spheres of knowledge, but to suffer those everlasting 'problems,' which are our Carthage, to keep us always in trim for a fresh debate." "The Refutation of Philosophies," in a recent translation by Benjamin Farrington, *The Philosophy of Francis Bacon,* University of Chicago, 1964.

(what McClelland calls *n* Achievement), reflected in Greek literature, was important in stimulating the growth of Greek civilization. The other comes from an essay by Hermann Strasburger
(*Historische Zeitschrift,* CLXXVII, 1954) and concludes that, as
Starr puts it, "the Greek felt no strong sense of political unity in
an ideal community; on the contrary, he considered himself an individual in a rural, personal environment."

Noting that the first generalization uses mathematics and the
second is more subjective in its method, Starr says he prefers the
second because it is more "stimulating for further thought." Exactly how it is more stimulating for further thought, and what that
further thought would then be, he does not specify. He says only
that "the most desirable generalizations are those which place the
facts in a new light and lead to further generalizations based upon
these facts." [40] In another place he says generalizations are "stimulating for further thought" when they are in opposition to the
common opinion on a subject. But if generalizations are useful
because they lead to other generalizations, or just because they are
odd and so lead to a continuing debate—what is the goal of those
other generalizations or that continuing debate? We find ourselves, with such generalizations, in the realm of pure academic
history, unless, and this Starr does not show us, those generalizations can lead to putting under a new light, not the facts of the
past, but the facts of the present.

As an illustration of a generalization drawn from ancient Greek
history which seems to me important because it is pertinent to
contemporary issues, I would suggest the following: when one
takes Pericles' funeral oration and analyzes it in detail as a pane-
gyric of Athenian society, and when one then studies the behavior
of the Athenians, toward the Melians as to others, in the Pelopon-
nesian War, as reported by Thucydides, one might reasonably generalize as follows: "The existence of a relatively humane, cul-
tured, democratic society in the domestic sphere does not at all
guarantee that the same qualities will carry over into affairs beyond the borders of that society."

Now this is a generalization about societies made on the basis
of observation of one society; but it is stimulated by a problem in
the present: the tendency of national states (whether socialist or

capitalist) to claim that their special social systems at home create a special dispensation to benign action abroad. This is one of the most useful kinds of generalizations for two related reasons: it is a *negative* generalization in that it aims only to cast doubt on another generalization currently in use which may be harmful (in this case that which obfuscates the external cruelty of a nation by appealing to its citizens' satisfaction with their own conditions); and because it aims at disproof rather than proof it can rest on one important piece of evidence—one society, in this case.*

True, this generalization doesn't close out the issue; the case may be an exception. More debate is stimulated. But it is debate around a crucial issue of our time, utilizing historical evidence from the past as well as present. As the classicist M. I. Finley says: "The issues in one historical period are not essentially different from those in another." [41] The generalization I have suggested would lead to skepticism at Soviet claims that a socialist society by its internal nature cannot be imperialist or unjust to other nations, as well as at the claims of the United States that its liberalism implies beneficence in its dealing with foreign nations. The idea could be supported by many pieces of data in history, drawn from the actions of liberal Western nations toward Africa and Asia in the nineteenth and twentieth centuries; it has been overlooked precisely because it is pointed at our deepest prejudices and hence needs a historical instance, far removed from us, to awaken our thought.

In one of the essays in the Gottschalk volume, there is a deliberate attempt to generalize in a useful way. Robert R. Palmer says that in his book, *The Age of the Democratic Revolution,* he began with "certain general ideas" which had among their aims, "to suggest relevancy and significance, which seem in the end to mean a relationship between these eighteenth-century events and persons now living." Palmer says: "I am aware that my whole book, though I hope not in an obvious or naive way, is pro-revolutionary. . . ." [42]

* Karl Popper has made the point, in his writings on the philosophy of science, that we cannot possibly prove "laws" of society, but we can disprove them. *The Logic of Scientific Discovery,* Hutchinson (London), 1959.

Palmer discusses the revolutionary movements not only in England, France, and America, but in Holland, Belgium, Sweden, and Switzerland. He concludes that this general movement "became democratic . . . when in various ways in various countries certain dissatisfied persons, not content merely to liberate the constituted bodies from a superior authority, wished to reconstitute or open up these bodies themselves, make them more truly representative or elective, and subordinate them to the 'people.' " This is a vital problem for today, when once again we face the fact that the mere existence of representative bodies, whether in socialist or capitalist countries, "totalitarian" or "democratic" countries, more and more beclouds the inability of these bodies to represent the needs of the population. Similarly, the Estates General for eighteenth-century France, the colonial Councils for America, Parliament for the British people, the Swedish Diet for the Swedish people (also instituted as gestures toward democracy) were inadequate and required not merely more authority against the monarch but a reconstitution of their own character.

In Thomas C. Cochran's essay "The Historian's Use of Social Role" he suggests that the concept of "social role," much in use among sociologists, might be useful for historians. The concept refers to the observable fact that the behavior of a person depends to a large extent on the expectations of his culture, or some group within that culture, about how a person in his situation should behave. Hence, a policeman may use his club because he is expected to use his club, a politician may speak platitudinous nonsense because the culture has defined this as the way a politician speaks, and the churchgoing person sitting at the reception desk will lie that "Mr. Stokes is not in" because in our business culture the *role* of the receptionist in a business firm is so much more potent than the Commandments of the Bible.

To trace the operation of *role* historically might indeed be useful, because it is suggestive of how to change society today. It makes a difference even in our determination to effect change if we understand certain kinds of behavior are not hopelessly rooted in man's "nature" but are the results of role-conditioning and can be changed once society creates a new set of expectations.

David Potter's essay in the Gottschalk report reminds us that the historian, even if he claims to be an empirical gatherer of facts, or abjures generalizing on the ground that it would be subjective, nevertheless inevitably theorizes. Thus "the real choice is between the conscious application of reasoned and stated assumptions and the unconscious application of unreasoned and unrecognized assumptions." [43]

Is it not one of the unrecognized assumptions of historians today that written history remain, as Anderle described it, "an end in itself"? Does not the historian unconsciously play a role of keeping the present political fabric intact by generalizing merely, as Gottschalk said, "to present a thesis for debate"? How can we escape the assumptions and roles pressed on us by our own culture? Perhaps, plunging deep into history, we can remind ourselves through Francis Bacon, that "the furthest end of knowledge" is "the benefit and use of men."

19

The philosophers

What might we expect from philosophers who think about history? Given my fundamental premise—that the past should be studied in such a way as to help us move towards certain obviously desirable goals—there are a number of valuable jobs that philosophers might do. As ethicists they could help clarify the historians' thinking about values (the problem of multiple values, value hierarchies, etc.). As logicians, they might check the work of the historian in proceeding from premise to conclusion (for instance, in analyzing certain syllogistic constructions that could be inferred from traditional historical analyses: the American press clamored for war with Spain; therefore public opinion was responsible for the Spanish-American war; therefore it is popular lust for war which brings about war). As analysts of language they might help the historian express more clearly and accurately both factual and theoretical statements, and identify metaphysical ones (like Morison's about the Puritans as "a free and happy people"). But in any case, it seems to me the aim of the philosopher of history should be to do what philosophers are gifted at: to criticize the work of the specialists from a larger standpoint in order to proceed toward certain human goals which historians, philosophers, and everyone else presumably care about.*

* This would be an application to history of the Baconian exhortation in *The Great Instauration* to seek knowledge "not either for pleasure of the mind, or for contention, or for superiority to others . . . but for the benefit and use of life," as opposed to the Aristotelian and Thomist view of knowledge for contemplative purposes. Francis Bacon, *The New Organon and Other Writings,* Bobbs-Merrill (Liberal Arts Press), 1960, p. 15. There is an excellent argument on this whole point in Hans Jones, "The Practical Uses of Theory," *Social Research* (Summer 1959, pp.

With no such guide as I have just suggested, philosophers of history may demand our respectful attention just because they discuss "interesting" things; where the interest is purely academic, or narrowly professional. Using the kind of criterion I propose, we would have to conclude that much of the discussion of philosophy of history that has taken place in the United States in the past decade has been trivial, pretentious, tangential.

Let us take up first the continuous debate over "explanation" in history which has dominated much of the published work in philosophy of history this past ten years. That debate has preempted the pages of *History and Theory,* the leading publication in the philosophy of history in this country; it was one of the chief themes in the symposium on the philosophy of history which took place in 1962 at New York University; it takes up about one-fourth of the space in such a recent attempt at a comprehensive survey of the philosophy of history as Patrick Gardiner's *Theories of History.* It is not an exaggeration to say that this is the single most-discussed topic in the philosophy of history in the United States since the end of World War II.

What I will try to argue is that this entire discussion falls within the realm of Tolstoy's definition of history as "a deaf man replying to questions which nobody puts to him." [1] If the deaf man is a collectivity—that is, an association of scholars, then the fact that *society* (with which presumably scholars in history and the hu-

---

127–66) reprinted in Maurice Natanson, *Philosophy of the Social Sciences* (Random House, 1963).

But it should be noted that the Athenian heritage is not uniform on this question nor is Aristotle unambiguous on the "Aristotelian" mode. In *The Meaning of History* (Braziller, 1964, p. 36), Erich Kahler says:

> The Greeks did not yet seek knowledge for knowledge's sake, nor essentially for technological and economic advantage. They were not concerned with that aimless amassing of facts, such as is practiced in our historical and social sciences, with that theoretical pragmatism, collecting data for future use, which, even should they be called for, could hardly be reached in the endless files of incoherent material. Greek historical research was pragmatic in a way utterly different from ours: the Greeks wanted to know in order to achieve an orientation in their world, in order to live in the right way; knowledge was closely connected with action, it was indeed part of action.

manities are ultimately concerned) has not asked such questions
is disguised by the fact that the scholars ask the question of one
another repeatedly, and thus maintain the appearance of being
importuned.

The source of the argument seems to be the inconsolable desire
by some historians to think of history as a science, and the passionate urge of some philosophers to assure them that this is true.
This in turn has led other historians and other philosophers to dig
delightedly for the holes in such an assumption, and to find another kind of standing for history, not according it the status of a
science, but nevertheless assigning it a vital function in modern
culture. And so the discussion has gone on and on—based on an
original question in which those beleaguered by the real problems
of society could have no interest unless it was going to lead to
some insight, some action on their behalf. This latter aim seems
to have been lost completely on the participants in the discussion,
so immersed are they in the pleasure of academic combat. Academic controversies, however aimless the original question, have
a tendency to burgeon in size, like a football pileup at the bottom
of which there is really no football, but which attracts more bodies
simply by its presence.

The current debate seems to have begun with Carl Hempel's
article, "The Function of General Laws in History," which appeared in the *Journal of Philosophy* in 1942, and which has led
to a long list of attacks and defenses. Hempel insisted that general
laws (or "universal hypotheses"—he used these terms inter-
changeably) were common to both history and the natural sciences and "form an indispensable instrument of historical research." A universal hypothesis, Hempel said, asserts this regularity: "In every case where an event of a specified kind C occurs
at a certain place and time, an event of a specified kind E will
occur at a time and place which is related in a specified manner to
the place and time of the occurrence of the first event." C and E
refer to Cause and Effect, so Hempel is telling us that there are
causal explanations in history based on general regularities, as in
the natural sciences.

Hempel now gets more specific in describing the elements of
this cause-effect generalization. A scientific explanation of an

event, he says, either in nature or history, has the same two elements:

1. "the determining conditions for the event to be explained" (if it is the cracking of an auto engine's radiator which is to be explained—this is Hempel's illustration—then the determining conditions would be all the specific circumstances of the event: that the car was left in the street all night, that the radiator had not been drained of water, that the temperature fell to below freezing levels).

2. "the general laws on which the explanation is based" (in this case, the general law is that water will freeze to ice at 32 degrees Fahrenheit under normal atmospheric pressure).

Applying this to history, Hempel gives two examples of general laws in explaining history. One is that of the Dust Bowl migration of Oklahoma farmers to California, which he says, can be explained by some general law about people tending to migrate towards places where living conditions are better. The other is that of revolutions, which might be explained by the general law that where a large part of the population becomes discontented, revolution is likely. He is aware that these are weak "general laws" (in the case of revolution, for instance) because "we are hardly in a position to state just what extent and what specific form the discontent has to assume, and what the environmental conditions will have to be, to bring about a revolution." And of course, there are obviously many other factors necessary before migration takes place.

Because a hard and fast causal explanation (where *every* time C occurred, E occurred) seems unlikely in history, Hempel suggests that we might talk about "probability hypotheses" instead of "universal hypotheses." This does not mark history as radically different from other sciences, he says; in medical science, if a person who has never had measles stays with someone who has it, a doctor would then advance the *probability* that the person would catch it. Hempel also suggests that especially in historical explanation, where so much is unknown in the event to be explained, we might have an "explanation sketch" rather than a full-fledged explanation. But this still has scientific standing, he notes, because at least it is potentially capable of being filled out, as opposed to some mystical, irrational explanation (by race, or palmistry, or whatever) which has no such potential.

Hempel noted that historians use general laws whether they mean to or not, even if they are just writing simple narratives. For instance, "Russia's cruel winter drove Napoleon's armies into retreat," he would say, involved meteorological laws. He objects to the claim of historians (he is clearly talking here about the British philosopher Collingwood) that they can "explain" the past by putting themselves in the mental position of historical figures and empathizing with them to understand their actions. This, he says, involves general laws of psychology; you can "explain" a madman's actions by knowing the laws of abnormal psychology even if you can't put yourself mentally in his place.

Hempel's view of explanation is called, in the language of the philosophy of science, "the deductive model" or "the covering law" model because it deduces the explanation of some event from a general law covering such events plus the specific conditions surrounding this event. To get a bit more technical, the process of explanation is considered by Hempel to have two elements, the *explanandum* (the event to be explained, like the Okies migrating to California), and the *explanans* (the covering law plus antecedent conditions: that troubled people go to better surroundings; that the Okies were troubled).

The aim of Hempel's essay is to show "the methodological unity of empirical science"—whether physics, biology, history, or whatever. All of these disciplines, he is saying, work with generalizations which serve as the basis for explaining particular phenomena.

Let us first grant what is reasonable in Hempel's argument—the idea that historical explanation involves generalization to a degree less exact than "a law" (which implies universal validity) and yet is valid enough to be useful. If I say: "Lincoln signed the Emancipation Proclamation not so much because of anti-slavery feelings but because of abolitionist pressure, military utility, and the need to retain popular support," I am invoking at least these generalizations: that the pressure of vocal minorities has some effect on American presidents; that moral concern is less a factor than political gain in motivating a political leader. These generalizations will not infallibly explain every other presidential action in American history or every other act of every political leader in all history. But they are true enough for past actions (a fact derived from studying many other acts of statesmen in the past) and predictable enough for future actions, to reduce somewhat the naivete of a beginning observer of politics about the effect of moral motives on the decisions of political leaders, and to suggest the possible effects of his own action as pressure. What this particular explanation does is form a link in a chain connecting similar events apprehended before and after this one; it *uses* the generalization to help in the explanation at hand; and it *adds* to the strength of the generalization as it will be used to explain other events in the future. It is not infallible as a guide; but it is suggestive. To make the mildest claim for it, it is true *enough* to be more useful than approaching a problem from scratch.

What I have done here is to make a claim for Hempel's "covering law" theory which is weaker than that implied by his own rigorous methodological presentation; this fends off—I hope—those of his critics who turn away from his theory completely because as they say—rightly—social science has not found any *universal* laws. And yet I make a claim for it strong enough to show that the events of history are not merely unique—they are also possessed of enough common characteristics to be of some help to us. If we see from studying the pattern of black uprisings in American cities 1965–68 that many of them were provoked by actions of white policemen against black people in the ghetto areas, a conclusion that both urban stability and racial justice require a change in police practice seems reasonable—even if the proposition "white police brutality provokes angry black responses" is not a *universal* law.

Hempel's critics, anxious to show that history is different than science, sometimes seem to forget that the sciences, more and more, recognize their truths as probabilistic rather than universal. Ernest Nagel distinguishes between science and common sense by the fact that in science "a significant proportion of conclusions supported by similarly structured evidence remains in good agreement with additional factual data when fresh data are obtained." [2] His expression, "a significant proportion of conclusions," hardly warrants making more rigorous demands on history. I am not denying here that the degree of probability will be much higher in the natural sciences than in the social sciences; I only claim that we should not confuse "scientific knowledge" with certain or universal or absolute knowledge.

Pierre Duhem writes, "A law of physics is, properly speaking, neither true nor false but approximate." [3] What is crucial in Duhem's point is that how true the law is depends on the uses to which it is put. Some general statements will be true enough to be used for certain purposes, but not nearly accurate enough for other purposes. It is with this *pragmatic* view in mind that generalization in history should be considered as adequate or not, true or not, rather than by some abstract consideration of whether it constitutes a "law"—irrespective of the use to which the "law" is to be put.

This statement buttresses the usefulness of Hempel's covering-law doctrine, if one doesn't demand so much of it. But it also reveals the weakness of Hempel's thinking, in that his notion of "the covering law" is abstracted from any *purpose* of the historian, and so is stripped of whatever meaning it might have. To "explain" a historical event is meaningless unless we know what the explanation is for.* Hempel talks of "explanation" as an abstract occupation unconnected with purpose (is there an assumed purpose which he thinks he need not discuss with us?).

Hempel's finding of common ground between history and science is useful in showing the degree of generalization in history. This is profoundly important, because if we only know each event as unique, not linked to others across time, historical investigation adds only to our knowledge of the dead past, and not to our capacity to act in the present and future. The historian's claim that history is "different" because historical events are peculiarly unique is greatly exaggerated; events in nature are also unique.

---

* John Passmore ("Explanation in Everyday Life, in Science and in History," *History and Theory,* 1962, Vol. 2, pp. 105–23), makes a useful point in listing nine different means of "explanation" and suggesting that explanations have different requirements depending on their *purpose.* This fits my basic point on the difference between an academically contemplative purpose and one involving action *in* history.

While there is a "law" covering falling objects in general, every explanation of every different falling object in history is different in some degree because, beyond the general rules applicable to all falling objects, there are always unique circumstances affecting the fall of each particular object. A theoretical physicist, Mario Bunge, writes: *

> The unique, unrepeatable, specific character of socio-historical events is hardly disputable. The question is whether this uniqueness or *Einmaligkeit* is peculiar to human affairs or is a part of *all* concrete objects—though admittedly to a lesser extent on levels lower than that of society or culture . . . no thoughtful physicist believes now that there are in the real world (in contrast to theoretical schemes) two bits of matter (whether endowed with mass or not) in *exactly* the same state and interacting with *exactly* the same fields. No two macroscopic events can be strictly identical.

There is a crucial difference between the kind of explaining done by scientists and that done most often by historians. The scientist is not intent on explaining the unique past event for its own sake. The unique qualities of the event are by definition unrepeatable and thus have no value beyond intellectual curiosity. It is the generalizable qualities of the event that concern the scientist because they are applicable to other phenomena; *they* are the live residue of the dead past event, transferable to the living universe in some way. The historian who concentrates on explaining *the* event of the past is concentrating on its uniqueness, that is, on a corpse.

Hempel, however, does not discuss the purpose or the function of explanation: This leaves us in the position of seeing all generalizable historical facts as equal—that is, they are equal in being subject to the methodology (covering laws) Hempel is telling us

---

* Mario Bunge, *Causality: The Place of the Causal Principle in Modern Science,* Meridian, 1963, pp. 265–66. And: "Besides complexity, a further factor tends to obscure historical lawfulness, namely, the usually forgotten fact that single scientific laws, of whatever kind, do not hold in concrete, specific, individual instances; *scientific laws hold only for classes of facts. . . .*" (his emphasis) p. 270.

about. But by sticking to methodology and ignoring the human aims of explanation—which would then lead to discriminating among various explanations not just in terms of their methodological validity but in terms of their significance—Hempel strips historical explanation of its human meaning. (Perhaps this is understandable, because the physical scientist *assumes* some sort of human ends in his work, and Hempel transfers this pre-methodological objective automatically to the writing of history, where, unfortunately, there is *not* that universal acceptance by historians of such aims.)

Even in terms of "science," this is a cramped approach. As Marx Wartofsky says of the "reification" of science, it "comes to be taken as some transhuman or superhuman essence, as an entity in itself, or a 'thing' apart from the matrix of human conditions, needs, and interests in which it originates and develops. There is a danger which lies in this reification of science. The continuity of science with common sense, of scientific activity with fundamental human activities, of scientific understanding with the common understanding is broken. . . . The definition of science as 'an organized and systematic body of knowledge' characterizes science from the point of view of its structure. But science is also an activity, an ongoing process of inquiry, whose description in structural terms alone is inadequate. In this latter sense we need also to characterize the functions, the modes of activity, the typical procedures of science with respect to the ends or purposes they serve." [4]

Other philosophers seeing Hempel's "scientific" approach as coldly methodological, seek to restore history as a "humanistic" discipline by describing its work differently. These critics of Hempel, however, make the same twin mistakes: they concentrate on methodology, ignoring the human purposes of historical writing; and they limit their work to passively describing how the historian in fact works, rather than critically analyzing historical writing in order to make suggestions to the historian.

The statements of various critics of the "covering law" approach might be summarized roughly in the following package: that historians do not in fact use generalizations the way Hempel claims they do, even unconsciously; that no "laws" of society can be found, really, to serve as such generalizations; that history has a status different though no less noble than physics and biology, as a humanistic endeavor giving us either "explanations" or "interpretations" or "understanding" of the past, but without the rigorous ambition of "scientific" explanation with which Hempel saddles the historian.

The anti-Hempelians, however, do not find some truly *human* aim for the historian which his methods might serve, but rather still another kind of professional niche for historical research. They also fail to ask: What is this all for? Suppose we "explain" the battle of Marathon, whether in Hempelian terms or in theirs: where does that leave us? For instance, one of these philosopher critics of Hempel, Marvin Levich, deriding Hempel's standard by saying it has enabled no one to give a valid explanation of anything in history, suggests "rational understanding" and "interpretation" as less ambitious and more accurate descriptions of what historians do. He then lists three problems: [5]

1. Whether a stone inscription discovered by Prof. M. H. Jameson will require revising a history of the Persian Wars, especially the campaign of 480.
2. What did Marvell think of Cromwell when he wrote "The Horatian Ode"?
3. To what extent was fifth-century Athens a democracy?

Levich's third question is potentially productive as a question which might throw light on contemporary democracies. But what of the first two, beyond esthetic interest? Are they important problems? Does their "interpretation" or "rational understanding" *matter?* Seeing the three questions listed in apparent equality we are impressed once again with the aimless character of all this thinking about history, the indiscriminate coupling of inconsequential questions with consequential ones. Would we not have enough trouble figuring out how to study fifth-century Athens in a way relevant to current problems of democracy without expending our limited intellectual resources on what Marvell thought of Cromwell when he wrote "The Horatian Ode"?

The foremost of Hempel's critics is William Dray, who (in his book *Laws and Explanation in History,* and in various articles) suggests historians behave differently than Hempel claims; they do not use "covering laws." Rather than explaining *why* something happened, Dray says, the historian might explain *what* happened —and perhaps name it, as by calling something "social revolution." Dray says: "The historian's problem is to discover *what it really was* that happened. And he deals with it by offering an explanation of the form 'It was a so-and-so.' " [6]

The point Dray makes is both incontestable and trivial. Yes, historians *do* such things; yes, this might be called the use of a "general concept" rather than Hempel's "general law." But what is the importance of this observation? It does not answer the question of *what for?* Is the "general concept" more useful than the "general law"? If so, how, and to what purpose?

Why does Dray not explore the effect of using one general concept or another on the consciousness of those people being addressed by the historian? To call the New Deal a "social revolution" may have a soothing effect on an American public. When we consider that in the 1960's widespread poverty was discovered in America, perhaps we should conclude that a soothed public was not cognizant enough of the severe limitations of that "social revolution." Dray says that this summing up in general concepts as "Age of Enlightenment," "Renaissance," etc., allows the historian "to bring a wide range of facts into a system or pattern." For what purpose? The concept may lead or mislead, may contribute to a particular value or diminish it. Calling the period which included the heaviest lynching of Negroes "The Progressive Period" has what effect on generations of students?

Dray ignores this crucial issue of the *emotive* character of the general concept. To point out that the historian uses concepts like "it was a so-and-so" is surely a puny job for philosophers. How useful a role might they play if—as analysts of language—they pointed out how the term "Radical Reconstruction" would have an effect on the American public; or how calling a Negro outbreak a "riot" or a "rebellion" would be significant. Dray of course would protest that this—having an effect on the public—is not what he has set out to do; all he aims for is to describe what the historian does. But surely others need not limit themselves to describing *what Dray does* if their suppositions are different—if they believe the role of the scholar is not only to describe but to evaluate.*

Dray objects to the covering law doctrine because it "sets up a kind of conceptual barrier to a humanistically oriented historiography." [7] And: "What drives us to the study of history, as much as anything else, is a humane curiosity: an interest in discovering and imaginatively reconstructing the life of people at other times and places." Of course, "curiosity" is a human attribute, worth satisfying, but is *that* what we think of as "humanistically oriented" scholarship?—to simply discover and reconstruct the past? As an esthetic goal for individuals at given times, who can argue against the satisfaction of curiosity? But is it the main concern of historical inquiry in a time of great troubles?

While Hempel is interested in what links a historical event to others through some "covering law," Dray is concerned with the uniqueness of the event. And those qualities of it which are unique cannot of course be explained by any covering law. [8]

> It is my contention that the historian, when he sets out to explain the French Revolution is just *not interested* in explaining it as *a* revolution—as an astronomer might be interested in explaining a certain eclipse as an instance of eclipses; he is almost invariably concerned with it as *different* from other members of its class. . . . As long as the historian sticks to the problem he has set himself, he cannot appeal to a covering generalization derived from general knowledge of revolutions.

He then goes on to quote the British philosopher Michael Oakeshott to the effect that a *presupposition* of historical inquiry is its concern with the unique, that historical inquiry is different from

* The process that Dray talks about, of pulling a set of events together under a name, is called by another writer on the philosophy of history, W. H. Walsh (in his book *Philosophy of History,* Harper [Torchbook edition], 1960), "colligation under appropriate conception." But this does not do very much for us: indeed, it is in itself the "naming" of a historical procedure which has the effect of making us feel something important has been done, while perpetuating our scholarly passivity.

scientific inquiry in this regard. "The moment historical facts are regarded as instances of general laws, history is dismissed." *

When Dray says this "is the *characteristic* approach of historians to their subject-matter" [9] he is happy to have discovered their approach; he is unconcerned with criticizing it. Of course, he has discovered accurately: the main concern of many historians has been to deal with the past as dead events; they have left it to others, more concerned with life, to find the connections between these dead events and those live ones going on around us. But the unique in any historical event is dead; for history to see its job as focusing on this is to make of the historian a coroner.

This is not to deny that the unique qualities of historical events are fascinating, esthetically, and that these qualities give a historical investigation its dramatic excitement. However, inside the uniqueness are those common cores of human concern which touch us because they are still alive. It is the study of these which makes history vital. If we limit our function to immediate esthetic pleasure, to personal interest, there is no need to go beyond the unique. But as soon as we talk of "explanation," we have gone beyond immediate perception to an inquiry based on general human needs. It is what the French Revolution can tell us about revolutions today, about the behavior of people today, which makes it important as a field for historical inquiry.**

---

* William Dray, *Laws and Explanation in History,* Oxford University, 1957, pp. 47–48. Again, it must be noted that the philosophers of science do not make such grandiose claims for the "covering" of physical events. A "general law" is not a universal law. Bunge says the word "exception" is not an unscientific word. ". . . exceptions are just the least frequent alternatives in a collection of facts." *Causality,* p. 266. Similarly, Hans Reichenbach has made the point that "laws" in both nature and society are probabilistic, not universal. "The Logical Foundations of Probability" in *Readings in the Philosophy of Science,* edited by Feigl and Brodbeck, Appleton-Century-Crofts, 1953.

** The point just made answers philosopher Alan Donagan, who comes down heavily on the side of Dray against Hempel, in his article "Historical Explanation: The Popper-Hempel Theory Reconsidered" (*History and Theory,* 1964, Vol. 4, pp. 3–26), saying Hempel's notion of "probability" in general laws in history enables one to explain "mass-events" but not the specific one. The distinction is important in showing the difference between the contemplative historian and the active one. If your idea is to do some-

There is a difference between explanation for the purpose of just knowing, and explanation for the purpose of doing. Dray in his book uses his car's engine stoppage as an example: "Suppose that the garage mechanic says to me: 'It's due to a leak in the oil reservoir.' Is this an explanation of the seizure? To me, who am ignorant of what goes on under the bonnet, it is no explanation at all . . . If I am to understand the seizure, I shall need to be told something about the functioning of an auto engine, and the essential role in it of the lubricating system . . . I need to be told, for instance, that what makes the engine go is the movement of the piston in the cylinder; that if no oil arrives the piston will not move because the walls are dry . . ." But Dray completely misses the point of Pierre Duhem that explanations suffice or do not suffice depending on what is needed at the time, not by any abstract standard.

How can Dray *really* understand the engine stoppage unless he goes even further than he has said, and understands *why* the dryness of the cylinder walls prevents the piston movement? Every scientific explanation runs to a point where there is something left unexplained; but that doesn't matter if the explanation goes far enough to satisfy the purpose of the questioner. If he has a practical need, then the explanation must go far enough to solve that need; if his purpose is to *"know"* in the abstract, there is no explanation which will be sufficient to get him to fix the leak. If he were a student of auto mechanics, requiring to know more about the situation, "It's due to a leak in the oil reservoir" would not be enough. But if he has no specific purpose beyond *knowing,* then the explanation he goes into is still not enough, nor will *any* ever be enough.*

So long as Hempel and Dray have different purposes in mind— Hempel to use and find connections between historical events, in

---

thing in the future, the specific event is irrelevant; it is the nonspecific qualities you seek to learn from. When Donagan concludes that "Hempel's inductive-statistical model throws no light on causal explanations of individual events" we have to agree, with the stress on the word *individual.*

* Robert MacIver, in *Social Causation* (Harper [Torchbook edition], 1964), shows how limitless is causal inquiry even when a particular aim gives focus to the inquiry. When there is no aim but *knowing,* the depths of investigation have no bottom.

order to explain the *kind* of an event it is; Dray to explain exactly *this* event and no other—they will remain at odds. If history is to have a use in connecting past to present, it must go beyond the uniqueness of events to their similarities. Thus, Hempel, if not too much is demanded of his "laws," at least points us toward the social uses of history even if he seems to ignore what that pointing is for. Dray, concerned for a "humanistic" use of history, is attuned to that aspect of human need which derives esthetic pleasure from apprehending the particular qualities of an event; but he ignores the more pressing humanistic need today for a history which can mediate between past and present to affect the future.

Another philosopher, Maurice Mandelbaum, helps clarify the dispute between Hempel and Dray.[10] He supports the idea of a covering-law but recognizes that a law cannot account for any one event in its totality, because in its totality it is unique. However, if the event is broken up into sub-events, each can fit some generalization. The Civil War for instance, cannot be explained in its totality by any "law" because it is unique—but if you abstract from it the effect of economics on politics; the tendency of nations to reject partition; the drive of cultural segments of nations for autonomy; the polarization of positions by ideological conflict, etc., you are dealing with qualities of the Civil War which it shares with other historical phenomena, and for which some sorts of probabilistic generalizations may be invoked.*

Thus, the historian still needs to learn from the scientist, who understands that the unique events of the past are dead, and that explanations of them in their unique totality are useless. The scientist is not concerned to explain the exact path traversed by a falling leaf, except to the extent it throws light on the motion of matter through space. Mandelbaum himself, however, is still the academic philosopher, seeing these generalizations mainly for contemplative reasons. He is interested enough in the purpose of all this investigation into history to say that the task of history and all the social sciences is to "attain a body of knowledge on the basis of which the actions of human beings as members of a so-

---

* As Mario Bunge puts it, "Concrete, hence, unique objects, such as historical events, may be viewed as intersections of a large (perhaps infinite) number of laws." *Causality,* p. 27.

ciety can be understood." [11] But he is timorous about declaring that this understanding is to further even the most generally accepted goals. This aim he says, "does not rule out the possibility" that this understanding "may be instrumental to some further aim, such as that of attaining the means of controlling human behavior, or for promoting human welfare. (Nor of course does it affirm that is the case.)" So long as philosophers and social scientists are rather indifferent to the goal of "human welfare," their emphasis on questions which further that welfare becomes, as it has been thus far in the work of historians, a matter of chance.

Alan Donagan follows Dray's example in pointing to kinds of historical explanations that he claims do not follow Hempel's model.[12] These are "rational explanations" of actions by people in history where the historian "explains" the action by understanding (in Dray's words) "the reasonableness of a man's doing what this agent did, given the beliefs and purposes referred to," in which case his action is "appropriate." But this is subject to the same arguments we have made. If the action and its reasons are unique, what is the *use* of the explanation? And if it has some linkage with similar actions and reasons in the present, then it *does* involve generalizations of a probabilistic nature.

Again, the concern of almost all these philosophers seems to be to *describe* what the historian does rather than to criticize and prescribe. And so both Hempel and his critics insist they are accurately depicting what the historian in fact does. Donagan at one point says the difference between him and Dray on one hand and Popper-Hempel on the other (Karl Popper has argued for the Hempel idea) is that he and Dray "respect the scientific status of historiography *as it is*" (my emphasis). What historiography needs from philosophers, however, is not humility and respect but sharp constructive criticism.

The notion of "rational explanation" of Donagan and Dray follows the work of the British philosopher R. G. Collingwood, who also saw the historian as seeking an empathetic understanding of persons in the past who made decisions. But, unlike them, Collingwood is not concerned just with explaining the past decision in its uniqueness. Like them, he wants to dissociate history from science but he accepts the association at the point where it is most important—the common need to generalize. Collingwood says: ". . . it is just the universality of an event or character that makes it a proper and possible object of historical study . . . something that oversteps the limits of merely local and temporal existence and possesses a significance valid for all men at all times." [13]

Nevertheless, Collingwood is vague on the most important social function of history. What is history for, he asks? "My answer is that history is 'for' human self-knowledge . . . knowing . . . his nature as man . . . Knowing yourself means knowing what you can do, and since nobody knows what he can do until he tries, the only clue to what man can do is what man has done. The value of history, then, is that it teaches us what man has done and thus what man is." [14]

Collingwood does see a social use in history. This distinguishes him from those whose interest is the specificity of past events. The esthetic quality of those specific events is valuable for that minority which so far in history has had the leisure for esthetic observation; and will be valuable some day for the majority, when it has that leisure. But at this moment history (without losing its esthetic vitality) is desperately needed to help us get to "some day."

The activist element in Collingwood's formulation is in his view that this self-knowledge gained through history teaches us "what man can do." But this becomes passive because Collingwood's view of "what man can do" must remain constricted if "the only clue to what man can do is what man has done." Nietzsche has warned us against this.[15]

This may be a conservative interpretation of Collingwood's view. It is possible to interpret him in another way, which would make his "self-knowledge" future-oriented and innovative—by saying that *despite* the burden of the past we can find in its crevices signs and hints of human possibilities never really exercised: spurts of cooperation even in the competitive jungle, acts of nobility from time to time, glints and glimmers of a better life.

There is one additional troublesome point in both Dray and Collingwood. They believe history is the study of past acts undertaken with some idea in mind. As Collingwood says, history studies "acts which we do on purpose, and these are the only acts which can become the subject-matter of history." [16] What of that great number of acts in history which are undertaken through compulsion or necessity or habit? Both Dray and Collingwood believe the historian must somehow reenact in his mind the actors' reasons for doing what he did in the past. Collingwood writes:

> When an historian asks "Why did Brutus stab Caesar" he means "What did Brutus think, which made him decide to stab Caesar?" . . . All history is the history of thought. But how does the historian discern the thoughts which he is trying to discover? There is only one way in which it can be done: by re-thinking them in his own mind . . . [17]

Does this not limit historical work in two ways: by the fact that the largest quantity of historical evidence concerns the thinking of the most powerful and articulate men of the past—so that we are more likely to try to think with John Calhoun than with Nat Turner? And, because historians are themselves part of a privileged class in society, will they not be *better* at understanding Calhoun than Turner, better at empathizing with the elite than with the mass?

Let us turn to another philosopher, writing about history. W. H. Walsh of Oxford, says, "it is the business of historians to construct not just a plain narrative of what occurred in the past, but what I call a *significant narrative*." [18] There is ambiguity in "it is the business of"; it could mean Walsh is describing what the historian does; it could mean he is suggesting what the historian's proper business ought to be. The very uncertainty of this phrase indicates how closely in the mind of Walsh and so many of the contemporary philosophical analysts of history the *ought* touches the *is*. These philosophers, intimidated by what the historians *do* at present, thus illustrate in their own work how a historian (in their case, the philosopher as a historian of historical writing), by his overwhelming concern with the past, allows that past to dominate his beliefs (and by transference those of his readers) about what ought to be.

By his phrase "significant narrative," Walsh says he means "a narrative which is, in a sense, self-explanatory; which makes us see not only the order of the events but also their connections. . . . A narrative of this kind is indispensable, if we are to answer the questions which teachers of history put to their pupils and independent students of the subject to themselves; such questions as 'What difference did it make to the policies of Gladstone that he was a high churchman?' and 'What was the significance of the career of Stresemann?' "

When you ask trivial questions, you will get trivial answers. Walsh does not bother to ask if the questions put all these years by teachers of history to their pupils "and independent students of the subject to themselves" *should* be answered. Why not ask the question: Why are these questions significant? If philosophers could set as a job for themselves analyzing the questions historians ask and trying to assess *what these questions are good for*—they would be making a valuable contribution to the philosophy of history. Wouldn't a truly "independent" student of history forsake his dependence on the traditional questions and try to find questions that "matter"? *

The historian's aim (and Walsh's, since he accepts uncritically what the historian *does*) is a "connected story." He calls this "colligation . . . kind of surface rationality: the fact that this, that and the other event can be grouped together as parts of a single policy or general movement": "the Renaissance," the Enlightenment," etc.[19] But the question is: Connected to what?

Walsh thinks "periodization is an essential part of historical work" but how significant in itself is the fact that events are connected together by time or place? Isn't the important connection the one between the past events and our own time? This is a connection we deliberately draw (but no more arbitrarily than we assemble facts by time and place) in order to affect our lives. Does the connection between Winstanley and Cromwell have any important meaning packaged as "the Puritan Revolution" unless that is related to another package: John F. Kennedy and Martin Luther King, for instance?

Walsh is inhibited continually by his need to *describe* what the historian does, and so he places a great deal of emphasis on the

* The word *matter* is central to philosopher Peter Caws, who in his book *Science and Human Values* criticizes the emptiness of much contemporary philosophy.

fact that "historians study the past for its own sake." [20] He feels compelled to add, however: "But the matter is perhaps not quite so simple as this suggests . . . Surely it is not absurd to maintain that we study the past because we think the study will illuminate the present, and should not do so if we had no such belief."

Later in his book, Walsh breaks out of the entrapment, saying the "irreducibly subjective" quality of the historian's thought will not trouble us so much if we simply see the function of history in a different way.[21] "Instead of saying, as we have earlier in this book, that the primary aim of the historian is to discover truth about the past for its own sake, we must now lay stress on history's serving a practical purpose. History, we shall argue, is not so much a branch of science as a practical activity." (He finds that Collingwood, whom he admires, "at least toyed" with the idea of such a function for history.) Walsh says rightly that while this view could lead to distorting the past, it need not—that people with varying practical aims can write different kinds of history while sticking to the basic "rules" of the craft, like the rules of evidence for what happened.

This would lead to different "perspectives" in history, all of which would be correct in the light of the different practical aims. We could even avoid so much difference, Walsh says, if we went beyond the positivist search for a general law of human nature, to a general ethic—"not merely standard knowledge of how people *do* behave in a variety of situations, but further a standard conception of how they *ought* to behave." [22]

To Walsh's credit, he does not accept readily the argument that this is impossible. He says only that "the achieving of it is clearly not going to be accomplished in the immediate future." But is it not true that we already have among a good part of mankind, and among perhaps a majority of historians, an agreement on certain fundamental values? Does not *most* of the scholarly world agree— on the need to abolish war, race hatred, poverty, destructive competition? The problem is not to attain unanimity; when we get unanimity, it will be too late to use it. The problem is that historians have not yet *decided* to consciously dedicate their historical work toward the achievement of those values on which they fundamentally agree. They are held back by traditional conceptions of the true aims of the historian, by the false notion that commitment to values requires distortion of the evidence, by professional pressures, by the fact that economy and psychological security lie in neutrality. It is indeed toward such a deliberate decision among scholars (especially the young ones) that this book is pointed.

How common among philosophers is the contemplative view of scholarship is shown by the way Ernest Nagel defends the "objectivity" of the historian.[23] Nagel says that while of course the historian deals with "value-impregnated subject matter or with occurrences manifesting various passions, it by no means follows that he must himself share or judge those values or passions." This is like defending a man against the charges of rape by claiming he is a eunuch. Surely it is not necessary to violate the facts (hide them, or manufacture them) in order to focus on those which advance a vital human value. The distinction between instrumental and ultimate values in affecting accuracy, which I spoke of earlier in this book, is important here. Neither the medical researcher working on curing disease nor the researcher working for some government on bacteriological warfare needs to distort the evidence (indeed, he had better not) to pursue his aim. The historian simply has not made up his mind that his primary aim is a therapeutic one.

Thus, Nagel, commenting on the Hempel-Dray issue of "laws," misses the point. We should distinguish he says, between the medical diagnostician, who, like the historian, *uses* laws, and the physiologist, who, unlike the historian, searches for *new* laws. The distinction between using and finding is important, but the medical diagnostician uses laws for a specific purpose which guides all his activity—to cure sick people; the historian has not yet acknowledged this is his guiding aim.

Even Bertrand Russell has on occasion overestimated the logical connection between "explanation" and action. "The Socialism of earlier days (before Marx and Engels) certainly criticized the existing capitalist mode of production and its consequences. But it could not explain them, and therefore could not get the mastery of them." Is there such a necessary connection between explanation and "mastery"? Surely the working classes of the industrialized Western European countries had more theoretical mastery of their societies in the form of Marxist explanation than either the Chinese or the Cuban peasants—but the latter mastered their societies while the others are still "explaining."

Russell (in the same book) gives us the ground for doubting his own faith in "explanation" as such, when he quotes Marx's second point in *Theses on Feuerbach* that: "The contest as to the reality or nonreality of a thought which is isolated from practice is a purely scholastic question." He notes that Dewey and James held basically the same view that *knowledge* means something only when it is connected with purposive action.*

Morton White's *The Foundations of Historical Knowledge*,[24] is a good illustration of the impotence characteristic of recent work in the philosophy of history. White is one of the foremost Americans in the field. His work is representative, not wholly in the answers he gives, but certainly in the questions he deals with.

White starts off by observing with satisfaction that the era of "grand speculation about the development of society," with its "pretentious volumes" and "futile debates"—he mentions Hegel, Marx, Vico, Spengler, Toynbee—is over. Now, "philosophers—especially British and American philosophers—came to focus so much of their attention on the logic of language, the method of science, and the analysis of concepts." Thus: "instead of seeking to chart the development of epochs, cultures, and civilizations, the contemporary philosopher of history is more interested in analyzing historical thought and language . . ." He is "more anxious to elucidate the terms that are commonly employed by his-

---

* From *Freedom and Organization, 1814–1914*, Ch. XVIII, reprinted in Gardiner, *Theories of History*. There is (besides Marx, James, Dewey) some support for what I have been saying about active versus contemplative scholarship in Jean-Paul Sartre's attempt to join Existentialism and Marxism. Sartre believes "meaning" is grasped by people who are acting. ("I know because I act," to combine Descartes and Sartre.) In Sartre's own terminology, the historian needs to move from the "practico-inert" (a person or a scholar as a passive victim—or even a passive reporter of events) to *praxis* (consciousness-action). (Jean-Paul Sartre, *Search For A Method*, Knopf, 1963.) John Dewey wrote: "Intelligent understanding of past history is to some extent a lever for moving the present into a certain kind of future." (*Logic: The Theory of Inquiry*, Holt, Rinehart and Winston, 1938, p. 239.)

torians and historically minded thinkers, and eager to advance toward a clearer understanding of the chief intellectual activities of the historian." He is "theoretically oriented, primarily interested in analyzing the parts played by factual statements, lawful generalizations, and value judgments in historical investigation and writing." *

White is thus telling us that his main concern is with historians, not with history, with language and not with life, with a description of what historians do, not a set of critical judgments about whether they are doing the world any good, or how they might start doing such good. Such an aim can hardly be called "pretentious"; it pretends to very little, and indeed can accomplish very little. It is what Peter Caws calls "secondary activity," of which he says (quoting C. D. Broad) it is "quite good fun for those people who like that sort of thing." [25]

The grand speculators of history (Marx, Spengler, Toynbee, etc.) are vulnerable to criticism for their interpretations of the past, for their attempts to extract "laws" of historical development out of the small historical experience of man on this planet. But they are potent; the ideological children they have produced may be imperfect, but they have had an effect on the world, and still do. The celibate philosopher of language has given no overambitious interpretations of the world for us to criticize; but his work never ventures outside that small circle of academics who dispute about "what the historian does." The limited historian confines himself to telling the past "as it actually was" rather than consciously narrating and/or interpreting in such a way as to have an

* Morton White, *The Foundations of Historical Knowledge*, Harper & Row, 1965, pp. 2–3. Peter Winch, in *The Idea of a Social Science and Its Relation to Philosophy* cites the "under-labourer" idea (from Locke's *Essay Concerning Human Understanding*), where Locke says, Let's not hope to be Boyles and Newtons: "It is ambition enough to be employed as an underlaborer in clearing the ground a little, in removing some of the rubbish that lies in the way to knowledge." This, Winch says, is characteristic of the "let's clarify the language" school of philosophers (which A. J. Ayer refers to as the work of "journeymen" as opposed to "pontiffs"). But Winch's criticism stems from a different viewpoint than my own. He wants the philosopher to deal with larger metaphysical and epistemological problems; I want the philosopher to define his role not by "small" or "large" questions, but by questions relevant to problems on which we must act.

effect on history himself. The limited philosopher of history confines himself to telling about historians "as they actually are," rather than leading them in directions which have meaning.

The Communist Manifesto of Marx and Engels, with its brief, powerful interpretation of historical development, has energized or supported countless people in their revolutionary activity. If the theory is wrong, let us have criticism of it; let the philosophers suggest how it is illogical, how it misfits the facts, how it is ethically unsound—so that we may construct a historical theory which may lead to *more* appropriate action in the world. But it has already proven its *truth* in the only way truth has meaning for human beings, in how it affects the way they live.

If by "a clearer understanding of the chief intellectual activities of the historian" White meant a critique of the historian's work on the basis of certain humanist values, we would have something. But White himself does not start with such values; he is willing to try to describe how the historian may be involved with values; but he does not seem to want to be involved himself. Whatever criticism he makes of the historian starts from no fixed ethical point in space; it can therefore proceed toward no ethical goal. It can only go round and round in ever tinier academic circles.

What Peter Caws says about philosophers of ethical theory can be applied to philosophers of historical theory: [26]

> Scholarly disengagement is once more a convenient excuse: descriptive ethics exhibits the principles that men have in fact adhered to at various times and in various places, but it need not pass judgement on them; the analysis of ethical language uncovers implicit presuppositions, but is more concerned about their logical relations to the rest of the system than about their truth.

The preoccupation with language of philosophers in the English-speaking world, which White is pleased to now apply to the philosophy of history, is described by Caws as making philosophy "virtually irrelevant to anything happening on the plane of daily human involvement."

White goes to great lengths to argue, in his first few chapters, for the Hempelian "regularity" theory of explanation—that there are "covering laws" involved in historical explanation. He admits, in the face of all the criticism of the "covering law" theory, that in order to cover a concrete, complex historical event, the "law" may become so complicated as to apply only to *that* event. But he blithely dismisses this by saying he sees "no reason to think" this need "always" be so—a rather weak defense, especially since he gives us no example of where it is *not* so. Indeed, his main defense of the "covering law" theory is to weaken it sufficiently so he can embrace it, by admitting: "Historical explanations are, in general, more tenuously constructed, more debatable, more subject to doubt than the explanations of natural scientists."

This is certainly true, but it gets White into difficulty, because he has just put himself on record as knocking down the "speculative" philosophers of history on the ground that their "laws" are not very reliable. Indeed, he goes on to criticize the Marxian "law" of class struggle in society by talking of "the paucity of examples." Even a "paucity" is larger than one—which is all White can give us in illustrating regularity theory. His example is Holland: "Whenever a nation is subjected to the challenge of the sea, has excellent soil, is assisted by its neighbors, and has an excellent maritime situation, it will rise to great heights of success."

"Explanation" is less important, I would argue, for the universality of its application than for its energizing power as a *suggestion* about what people ought to do. Thus the Marxian notion of class struggle is far more *true* (to a given set of values) than any of White's generalizations based on "covering laws." It is also more of a "true" explanation even by White's own standard of "covering" more situations.

White is so anxious to put down the speculative theorists that he forgets he has set easy standards for his covering laws, and demands the certainty of laws of physics in dealing with Marxian statements. Referring to the Marxian concept of a relationship between the economics of any epoch and its ideology, White says: "But surely this way of speaking is not to be compared in clarity with that of the physicist . . ." * White had just finished telling

---

* White, *The Foundations of Historical Knowledge*, p. 42. Yet it is a theoretical physicist (Mario Bunge, *Causality*, p. 269) who gives the status of a "by now quite obvious, sociohistorical law statement" to the idea that

us that we mustn't discard the covering law of Hempel despite its weakness because "we all know that historical explanations are, generally speaking, less strongly supported than those in natural science." He then goes on (again switching his posture, as he moves from attacking the "speculators" to defending the "regularists") to say: "The main point I wish to make is that regularism, as I conceive it, does not require its advocates to hold that the general laws offered in support of singular explanatory statements 'apply to all times and places.' "

Engels' letter to Bloch on historical materialism makes the same kind of defense against an attempt to erect Marxian theory into an absolute.[27] The difference is that the Marxian probabilistic statements are socially potent; White's are either trivial or academic (he gives us dead historical statements as about Holland in the seventeenth century, or examples from everyday life, like getting a rash from eating spinach).

Ironically, White's criticism of the Marxian theory of history, if analyzed from a Marxian perspective, suggests something about the philosopher of history in the United States in the 1960's: Is it not plausible that the affluence of the academic philosopher in America has a strong effect on his tendency to stay in the realm of academic discourse, as if there were no urgent problems of material deprivation on which historians and philosophers might work? It is not a Marxist, but a rather proper American historian (Arthur Mann, of the University of Chicago) who wrote: [28]

> By 1950 even intellectuals who had made a cult of alienation were happy to call America home. There was much to be happy about: a rising standard of living, increasing opportunities for scholars, cultural pluralism, the welfare state, and a healthy balance of power between big business, big labor, and big government. Living in such a going concern, few scholars acquired the kind of compassion, resentments, and hopes for a more egalitarian society that had enabled a previous generation to identify itself with economic and political reform.

"deep changes in the mode of production such as the renewal or reorganization of technical equipment, in the long run, elicit the renewal of social structure . . ."

In his entire discussion of "explanatory arguments," White does not come up with one statement about history for which he can declare as much plausibility or as much significance as the Marxian statement he dismisses (that ideology is to an important degree a reflection of material circumstance).

My point here is not to argue for the "laws" of the speculative historians, but rather to note that the new generation of philosophical analysts, instead of subjecting these "laws" to criticism from standards of value that might lead us to more potent statements about history, have retreated from them into sterile, valueless academic discussion.

Marx's theory of the relationship between economics, ideology, politics, and law is not workable as a formula. But it *is* profoundly important as a way of suggesting to us that we must look behind ideology, beneath laws and constitutions, to the less visible but nevertheless vital aspects of existence. This is why Beard's work on the Constitution, however wrong he may have been on details, is still a powerful instrument for understanding our society; we still need, in the 1960's to look behind legal forms to the *interests* involved. Indeed, political scientists, without paying homage to Marx, have pointed more and more to interests behind political alignments, to pressure groups behind legal encounters.

To take a current case: someone respectful of Marxian analysis (without being dogmatic about it) might have been suspicious of the euphoria that surrounded the civil rights "victories" of the early 1960's, since these victories were represented mostly by civil rights *laws*. A perceptive Marxist (or any perceptive observer) might have said: Yes, but what are the material conditions of the black person in America, even with all these laws? That penetration beneath the surface of the culture might have led many people—even before the urban outbreaks in Watts, Chicago, Detroit, etc., took place—to understand that much more was needed than laws to solve the problem of racial conflict in America.

White's test for "truth" in theorizing about history is unrelated to the future, or to action—it is a formal test. He wants Marxists to be able to "determine the values of their variable 'p,' 'r,' and 'a' " (standing for philosophy, religion, art; this is the academician's pretentious way of keeping the non-elite out of the discussion).[29] That is, he wants the Marxian theory to meet a quantitative test which he cannot meet with his own "regularity" theory. But the only meaningful test for a theory is life itself; does that theory enhance our understanding, improve our actions, so as to move us closer to a humane world?

A theory's correspondence with known facts of the past is only the first step toward truth; the most important test is its correspondence with the present. Since the theory must help us make a transition from past to future, to create *new* situations, it can only be partly true for the past, crudely true for the future. It may leave much open. It may only push us in a generally desirable direction. If it does that, it is "true" in the way a good navigator, even with an imperfect reading of the going winds, gives the pilot a "true" heading. The navigator's heading, if it even *helps* steer the craft towards home, has more "truth" than a map made by a mole of a cartographer who seeks to reproduce the terrain exactly as it is (an impossible job), ignoring the need of the pilot for even imperfect instructions. Neither the imperfect navigator nor the mole of a cartographer can claim scientific neutrality, because they are in a plane that is aloft and going *somewhere,* whatever they do. So the historian.*

At another point in his book, White says: [30] "The historian is not primarily a moral judge. With Spinoza he may say after much of his work, 'I have labored carefully, not to mock, lament, or execrate, but to understand human actions.' " White is confusing mock-lament-execrate-moralize (which is pointless) with action on behalf of moral goals, which has a point. Spinoza, according to David Bidney's study, "accepts the Platonic doctrine that virtue is knowledge but interprets knowledge in the Baconian sense of efficient power." [31]

---

* Later, in his chapter on "Explanatory Statements" (p. 75) White admits he can't really distinguish between a law and an "explanatory law" although he insists on the distinction. But. he says: "Philosophy, like science, moves in a piecemeal way toward the truth, and there is no reason to spurn part of the truth because we do not possess all of it. . . ." He is much more generous to his own piecemeal truths than to those of the Marxists. Later he defends what he suspects might be an "inconsistency" (p. 103), by saying the Marxists claim laws, whereas he only claims "regularity."

White's enslavement to "the linguistic habits of the historian" forces him to discard reasonable solutions for problems he has posed because they turn out to contradict the way historians work. In his chapter on "Historical Narration" he catalogues various ways of deciding which chronicle or which narrative of a given body of events is preferable. He takes up what he calls "pragmatic essentialism," that is, William James' view that what is essential in any body of facts depends on the practical concerns of the questioner.*

White cannot abide James' approach. "However tempting such a view may be, we are immediately struck by one difficulty in it. James' view may be plausible . . . But what about the typical subject of the historian, the dead and buried individual or the extinct civilization. Surely we have no immediate practical interest in such entities . . . So a teleological view which is narrowly pragmatic seems incapable of sustaining an analysis of the superior basis for a chronicle of a thing which is in the distant past." Instead of using James' test as a way of deciding what kind of narratives are significant, he uses the present production of narratives to determine whether James' test is adequate. Again, the surrender to what *is,* the forsaking of judgment, the abnegation of critical philosophy. If White is serious about searching for tests to evaluate narratives, isn't their usefulness for the present an important test? Is it too horrible to contemplate that the critic-philosopher might say to historians working on "The Shield Signal at Marathon": Your narrative is not as important to a troubled world as Thucydides' narrative of the Athenian treatment of the Melians because yours leads us nowhere but into antiquity, whereas Thucydides is suggestive for international relations today?

Again, all that White can summon up against an evaluative-pragmatic approach is that it isn't done: "Some basic statements are included in chronicles without any intention to facilitate practical action of any kind. . . . One may try to construct a chronicle which is based exclusively on this pragmatic principle of selection. . . . But such principles of selection are not used in all of the histories that historians write, and it is unlikely that they

---

* This is the counterpart, in choosing chronicles or narratives, of operability in choosing causes, which I will discuss in the next chapter.

will permit them to construct causally coherent narratives." This begs the question, because if our notion of "causal coherence" is itself based on pragmatism, it doesn't matter if it does not have such coherence by White's standard.

As a result of his lack of *present* concerns, White can only find "that there is no one simple criterion on the basis of which we select the main facts in a chronicle." Since historians in fact use various bases for constructing their chronicles, White is "against a monistic theory of what happened" and for "a pluralistic view of admissibility to the set of basic statements about what happened in the career of the central subject, and to the chronicle as a whole." The historian "may choose what is conspicuous, interesting, useful, fascinating, frightening, instructive, or beautiful, so long as he constructs a coherent narrative . . ."

Again, the question is begged; exactly what is a "coherent" narrative must be decided by some test, and he has given us no such test. The implication is that a narrative constructed on the basis of what is "beautiful" in a situation may give coherence to it. Thus, Margaret Mitchell's picture of plantation life in the Old South may have a marvelous coherence, which we would be disrupting if we suggested that its *practical* effect is to persuade Americans that the Negro might well be better off under slavery.

A historian can construct his narrative on any basis he chooses, White says. "We may allow the historian to choose his facts with eyes on all kinds of considerations, so long as he writes true and connected narrative." The very prescription of "true and connected" is advice to historians rather than mere description of what they do; this drifting back and forth from normative to cognitive is typical of White's approach. But again: what is a "true and connected" narrative? True to *what* is exactly the question we are trying to answer. Connected with *what?* White has no standard to judge truth or connection.

Now White moves clearly to the question of what should the historian do in a narrative. "And if we are seeking a definition of the notion of what features should be recorded by a professional historian, I do not think that any useful one can be supplied. At best we may say that what should be recorded are those features of the central subject which colligate the data and/or those which

record items of interest and value to the historian." The closest
White can get to criteria is "interest and value" but this is left
empty, in a world full of problems.*

In his final chapter, White manages to discuss "point of view"
at length without ever declaring his own point of view about the
world, about history, about *life*. Oddly enough it is Marx, bela-
bored so confidently by the "scientific" philosopher Morton
White, who, whatever his failings, omissions, false predictions,
gives us a clue to White's neutralism in history. I am quoting
George Lichtheim's statement that to Marx, " 'science' itself represents an 'ideological' manner of thinking which of its nature
cannot yield an adequate report of the world." **

Lichtheim's statement about philosophy in general seems to

---

* White jabs sharply (pp. 259–60) at E. H. Carr, who proposes in *What
Is History?* (Knopf, 1962) that we should approach history with a view
toward making a better world. "That is why it is so strange that E. H. Carr
should think that he has extracted the essence of history 'properly so-
called' when he suggests that the test of historical importance is relevance
to the future triumph of the masses in Asia and Africa. He is of course
entitled to think that only such facts are worth recording, but not to think
that he is delivering the essential truth about history as a discipline." White's
footnote reference to the Asia-Africa passage is to page 176 in the 1962
edition of E. H. Carr's *What Is History?* But a check of page 176 shows
that there is *nothing* on Africa and Asia on that page, and nothing close
to what White claims Carr says. Indeed, I can find no statement in Carr's
book which suggests that "the test of historical importance is relevance to
the future triumph of the masses in Asia and Africa." Carr does speak of
Asia and Africa on page 198, but there he only criticizes "the tendency of
dominant groups in this country—and perhaps elsewhere—to turn a blind
or uncomprehending eye" to "the march of progress in Asia and Africa."
White's mistake is puzzling.

** George Lichtheim, "The Concept of Ideology," *History and Theory,*
Vol. 4, pp. 164–95, 1965.

Another way of describing the culture-bound limitations of science, and
indeed all knowledge, is that of Werner Heisenberg, *From Plato to Planck,*
where he says "in science we are not dealing with nature itself but with
the science of nature—that is, with nature which has been thought through
and described by man." Quoted in Paul Mattick, "Marxism and the New
Physics," *Philosophy of Science,* October 1962, p. 360.

It is against this that a philosopher like Herbert Marcuse urges "negative thinking," to escape the past, to create a different world than the one
we have known in that narrow corridor of experience we call history.

have special pertinence to the linguistic philosophers pretending to philosophize about history. "Philosophy does not change the world: it interprets it and thus reconciles the world to itself." This (whatever benign intentions he may have) is the meaning of White's glaring attention to what historians actually do, his interpretation of how they speak about the past, his scrupulous unconcern, in an entire book on the philosophy of history, for any *live* human problem.

What the German poet Gottfried Benn once said can be applied to all those philosophers who insist on writing "about" culture rather than "living it," who want to record and interpret rather than change, and who therefore only embed us all more deeply in what *is:* [32]

I am struck by the thought that it might be more revolutionary and worthier of a vigorous and active man to teach his fellow man this simple truth: You are what you are and you will never be any different; this is, was, and always will be your life. He who has money, lives long; he who has authority, can do no wrong; he who has might, establishes right. Such is history! *Ecce historia!* Here is the present; take of its body, eat, and die.

20

Philosophers, historians, and causation

It may be helpful to illustrate with one problem—causation—
how both philosophers and historians tend to deal with theoretical
questions of history, to the advantage of dead scholarship and the
disadvantage of living people. Morton White's *The Foundations
of Historical Knowledge* is once again a good starting point. And
then we shall turn to the historians.*

When White begins to discuss cause (not "contributory" cause,
which is only one of a chain of causes, but *the* "decisive" cause)
he again shows his inclination to merely describe how historians
deal with cause rather than to analyze in any constructive, critical
way, how the notion of cause might be useful: [1]

* Cause is very much involved in most discussions of historical explanation which I have dealt with in the previous chapter. I am assuming
that causality is a special case of explanations, both deserving of special
treatment, and useful for illustration, because it is more focused than explanation in general. I would not restrict the definition of cause as tightly
as Mario Bunge, who says socio-historical events are "eminently non-
causal" because they are "at the same time strongly *self-determined* (in-
ternally determined by the structure of the social group itself), definitely
dialectical (consisting in or brought about by struggles of human groups),
partly teleological (striving, though mostly unconsciously, toward the at-
tainment of definite goals), and typically *statistical* (the collective result
of different individual actions largely independent of one another). . . ."
Mario Bunge, *Causality,* Meridian, 1963, p. 274.

Bunge limits causality to the unusual instance where "if C happens then
(and only then) E is always produced by it," so that both 1:1 correspondence between C and E, and *production* (as distinct from a weaker connection between C and E) is stressed. For my instrumental and pragmatic
use of "cause," it may be useful many times to seek potent factors in social
change even where the potency is limited, or when the C at hand is not
the only possible producer of the effect.

352

. . . I shall in this chapter critically examine a number of defective theories of *the* cause and also defend what I think is a satisfactory theory. Briefly stated, that theory is that *on most occasions when historians assert* [my emphasis] that a contributory cause is the (decisive) cause, (a) that cause is the abnormal contributory cause, (b) it is sometimes selected from a point of view which another investigator may not share, and (c) we cannot always establish on absolute grounds that one of these points of view is superior to others. Because of its stress on the abnormality of the selected contributory cause I shall call this doctrine "abnormalism."

It is odd, we might note in passing, that White who has just finished supporting the "regularity" theory of explanation, insisting on the existence of "explanatory laws" which hold for more than one situation, now will support a causal explanation which cannot possibly apply to more than one situation, because it depends on that factor which is unique to the situation being explained.

More important, however, than White's inconsistency here, is that his theory about the causes of past events is irrelevant to events of the present and the future—that is, to the living rather than to the dead. The two examples he uses to illustrate his point also illustrate mine. One is the "Pirenne thesis" about the collapse of Mediterranean civilization after the eighth century being due to that abnormal precipitating event: the Moslem invasion. The other is the case of a man getting indigestion from eating parsnips. Again, the parsnips were the abnormal intruder into his body.

If there is anything important in studying the causes of that collapse of Mediterranean civilization, however, it is in what it may tell us about the collapse of *other* civilizations. Toynbee's theory about the decay of civilizations, whether right or wrong, is at least aiming to learn something about today; he has something vital to suggest to us about the West *now;* singling out the Moslem invasion is useless for that. Similarly with the indigestion; if it is to be useful to the rest of us, it is not the parsnips but something about the parsnips—possibly showing up in many other foods—which might cause indigestion. White's focus on abnormal cause insures that his interest is in a past event, not in the world around us.

Let me illustrate with an actual event how White's "abnormal cause" might be used. In Cambridge, Maryland, on July 24, 1967, blacks roamed through the streets destroying property, "rebelling" (according to black militants) or "rioting" (according to city officials). It was one of forty-one "major" or "serious" disorders studied by the National Advisory Commission on Civil Disorders for that year.[2] Of twenty-four disorders studied closely by the Commission: [3]

> We found a common social process operating in all 24 disorders in certain critical respects. These events developed similarly, over a period of time and out of an accumulation of grievances and increasing tension in the Negro community . . . The specific content of the expressed grievances varied somewhat from city to city. But in general, grievances among Negroes in all the cities related to prejudice, discrimination, severely disadvantaged living conditions and a general sense of frustration about their inability to change those conditions.

What if a historian were determining "the cause" of the uprising in Cambridge, Maryland? Cambridge shared that "common social process" with other American cities having large numbers of black people living in miserable conditions. But to find the cause of the *Cambridge* uprising, one would have to find a factor unique to Cambridge, the "abnormal cause." There was one such factor, much-publicized: The angry young black leader Rap Brown had made a speech in Cambridge in which he reportedly said: "Don't be trying to love that honky to death—shoot him to death." Police Chief Kinnamon of Cambridge said that that "was the sole reason for our riot." [4] By the "abnormal cause" theory, Kinnamon would seem correct. As for getting at the root of Negro unrest, it was a dangerously misleading analysis.

There is, however, a way in which the "abnormal cause" idea could lead to a socially useful policy: if we took the common conditions of *black* communities (discrimination plus poverty) as abnormal to communities in general. This might lead us to action against those conditions. The "abnormal cause" principle in itself does not allow us to distinguish between the first use of it, which is socially harmful, and the second, which is useful—because White is not looking for a social policy but an academic tool.

White is puzzled about making a decision when we can find more than one abnormalism in a chain of causation. ". . . I must say that I see no way of supporting the conclusion that one is absolutely superior to the other, i.e., *no way that reflects our actual mode of speech on these matters."* (I have emphasized that part of White's sentence which once again shows his enslavement to reporting how historians describe their own work, rather than to creative criticism.) For instance, where a man with ulcers eats parsnips and suffers, White says "I know no basis on which one can say" that the doctor's diagnosis (stressing ulcers as the cause) is superior to the wife's (stressing parsnips as the cause). "It may be said, of course, that the diagnosis of ulcers might lead to the removal of ulcers; but then the diagnosis of parsnips might lead to the elimination of parsnips from the man's diet. The point is that there are basic differences of interest, basic differences in concern and curiosity, which may lead historians to ask different questions; and in answer to these different questions they will call different things the cause of a given event."

White has given us the clue to the missing "basis" for selection; it is just that he is reluctant to accept the aim of *action*. Clearly, *if* one accepts the goal of health, then one can distinguish among causes by the extent to which they can be worked on to create a better situation. For each individual, it can be decided whether maintaining a better diet, or having his ulcers removed, is preferable—thus making either the ulcers or his food *the* cause. For other individuals beyond this one, similar decisions can be made. Whether you are a doctor or a wife tells you which of several operable causes is *the* cause for you.

For White, no one can say what is *the* cause, because he refuses to declare an interest, a set of values. All he wants to do is recognize that different people have "basic differences of interest, basic differences in concern and curiosity" (he gives equal rank to concern and curiosity). In the world of history, can we not agree on a set of values: elimination of war, of poverty, of racism, of oppression—and discuss causes from the standpoint of their operability for the removal of those evils? If we pretend to remain aloof from values, we "know no basis," of course, for making distinctions.

I have argued that to talk of cause as a general, abstract, theoretical problem can lead us nowhere. We must start from values which we want to achieve; then we can pick out that link in the causal chain which, if operated on, can move us toward those values. Morton White, in his general attack on all other notions of cause but his own, gives four pages to what he calls a "technological or pragmatic concept of causation." These are his terms for what I call *operable cause.**

White's arguments against this are weak. He criticizes the idea of "manipulability" because then "we also introduce relativity." That is, when the light goes out because someone has turned the switch off, the manipulable cause for someone who wants the light on is the switch, which he can turn on to restore the light. But for the engineer at the power station, the manipulable cause is *his* main switch, which can also control the situation. Well, this "relativity" is exactly pertinent and necessary to the notion of operable cause; only an academic discussion of cause can ignore the question of who we are and what capacity we have to change things. If we are concerned with action, then *the* cause becomes whatever I (whether I am the man in the apartment or the engineer at the power station; whether *I* am the physician of the man with ulcers, or the wife preparing his meals) can work on. This is "relative" only if one wants a disinterested view of the situation from the outside. It is absolute if each of us sees cause as *his* problem of action.**

* My approach is similar to the one E. H. Carr defends in his book, *What Is History?* Knopf, 1962. R. G. Collingwood has also suggested this (*An Essay on Metaphysics*). Stephen Toulmin notes that for scientists, causation becomes important when there is a practical purpose in mind; hence the word occurs frequently in medical journals, but not so much in general works on physics. "Developments which we are interested in producing, preventing, or counteracting—these are the typical sorts of thing about whose causes we ask. Correspondingly, to discover the cause of one of these developments is to find out what it is that needs to be altered, if we are to produce, prevent, or counteract it." *The Philosophy of Science,* Harper (Torchbook edition), 1960, pp. 119–22.

** Incidentally, White uses the "relativity" of operable cause against it; but earlier he accepted relativity as an inevitable fact in his "abnormalism"

The "main difficulty" with the pragmatic approach, White says, is that it approaches cause "too narrowly" because it insists on causes that are "producible or preventable by the person who says that it is the cause." True, in one sense, this is "narrower" than an attempt to deal with cause from some academic, disinterested point of view (in the same sense that any focused approach is "narrower" than any general one). But it is the academic approach that is ultimately narrow, because it is like a widemouthed funnel which takes in everything but is closed at its exit and thus cannot lead anything anywhere. The pragmatic approach, because it is discriminating, is narrow on the receiving end, but it leads to large possibilities for action.

White says the pragmatic theory "would rule out as faulty or false many historical explanations in which a natural disaster like an earthquake is said to be the cause of a certain event." No, not as "faulty or false," just not worth discussing as much as the flimsy construction of houses, which determined that the earthquake took a thousand lives instead of ten, and which, unlike an earth tremor, *is* operable.

White also (predictably) argues against the "pragmatic" notion of operable cause on the ground that some or many historians don't use it. "Some historians call standing conditions of a kind that *they* are not able to manipulate the cause of an event . . ." He talks of the pragmatic approach as not being true to "the linguistic habits of the historians"—as if the job of philosophers should not be precisely to criticize what historians are doing rather than recording what they say. What he has been trying to do, White says, is "to describe the language of ordinary historians." [5] But (to judge him for a moment by his own claim of describing the factual conditions) he has not given us evidence that most historians view cause from the standpoint of "abnormalism": that is rather, his preference, which he defends not by data that it is customary, but by arguments that it is *good* (broad, let us say, as opposed to the "narrow" approach of the pragmatist).

Actually, the use of "cause" by historians is so varied (and so unaccompanied by hard thought *about* causation, we might add)

theory of cause, where there might be several abnormal causes and White could find no way of choosing among them.

that White's selection of abnormalism is quite arbitrary. It is a selection which ignores the use of causal analysis as a guide to action in history; it is a foil for passive speculation. In this sense, the term "speculative" which White applies to Spengler, Marx, Toynbee, etc., is more aptly applied (in the literal sense of the word) to himself; he is a spectator, theorizing, conjecturing, at some distance from the world of strife.

Let us turn now to several historians who theorize about the problem of causation. To strengthen his call for a *conscious* use of generalizations, David Potter points to the unconscious and constant reference to causes of historical events.[6] He asks that causation be consciously and deliberately treated, and quotes E. H. Carr that "the study of history is inescapably the study of causes." He notes Carr's point that since any causal chain is infinitely long, for the historian "his only criterion of selection, as Carr observes, must be the significance of the points which we choose to emphasize. *But we have no yardsticks for measuring significance.*"[7] (My emphasis.) Potter is ignoring here that yardstick which Carr himself suggests: our own need to act on the basis of what we have learned from history. Here is what Carr says:[8]

> The faculty of reason is normally exercised for some purpose. Intellectuals may sometimes reason, or think that they reason, for fun. But, broadly speaking, human beings reason to an end. And when we recognized certain explanations as rational, and other explanations as not rational, we were, I suggest, distinguishing between explanations which served some end and explanations which did not.

Earlier, Carr has said: "The historian distills from the experience of the past . . . and from it draws conclusions which may serve as a guide to action." Ignoring this, Potter is left only with "sagacity and applied experience" as a guide, in other words, with effectiveness in method rather than the quality of one's beliefs about right and wrong, without which "sagacity" has no substance.*

* Social scientists seem more inclined than historians to look at cause pragmatically. For instance, Robert M. MacIver, in *Social Causation* (Har-

For instance, in the chain of causation leading to the Supreme Court decision on desegregation in 1954, we might include among other causes: the suits brought by Negroes, the composition of the Supreme Court, the new atmosphere created by the emergence of independent African states, the effect of the defeat of Nazi racism in World War II, the growth in Negro consciousness as shown in Negro poetry and literature and organization, even the money contributed by whites to the NAACP enabling it to pay for lawsuits.

To arbitrarily pick out one of those causes as *the* cause would be simplistic and pointless. To list all the causes we can think of is more intellectually formidable but leaves us still in the academy and not at any point of action. To emphasize that cause about which we can do something in similar future cases is full of meaning, if historical *meaning* is, as I am postulating, not a directionless academic one, but connected to *us* and what we *do*, and how we shape the future. Thus, to a Supreme Court justice, the role of the Court in affecting that change would be an operable cause; to a white person, support of the Legal Defense Fund of the NAACP; to a Negro writer, continuing the consciousness-expanding work of Countee Cullen, Langston Hughes, Richard Wright, James Baldwin, WEB Dubois; to a President of the United States, thinking carefully about his next appointment to the Court. On the other hand, to single out World War II would meet some abstract criterion of "truths" but it leads nowhere; it ignores the larger truth, the human meaning, that comes from singling out an operable cause.

Carr himself gives the example of a man who goes out in his automobile to get cigarettes; he has been drinking; he drives a car with faulty brakes; he goes around a blind corner, and has an accident. To say that he was killed, because, among other reasons, he was a smoker, gives us the least meaningful truth about his ac-

---

per [Torchbook edition], 1964, p. xiii) discusses the causes of delinquency, and concludes that there are many factors, and many unknowns "but our knowledge of causation is already reasonably sufficient as a guide to the strategy necessary for the control and reduction of delinquency, whether in low-delinquency of high-delinquency areas." Yet, the failure to deliberately specify the policy objective of a search for cause has the danger of filling the net with scads of inedible fish.

cident because it is the least operable. To the city fathers, the point about the blind corner would be meaningful; to purchasers of cars concerned with mechanical safety standards, the faulty brakes. Thus, operable cause discards theoretically "true" causes in the chain which give no guide to action, and singles out those elements on which *we* can work in some future case.

Let us look at the causes of the American Civil War. The literature on this is overwhelming; we have not only actual historical works attempting to explain the Civil War, but other works compiling or explaining the various explanations.* The student going through all this literature will soon notice, though he may hesitate to say it, that the problem of "What Caused the Civil War" seems as far from a solution as before, even though the quantity of paper on it is mountainous. He might say: "Well, this is the way of science, to acquire more and more information, while the solution seems just as far away, and then suddenly, one day . . ." But when he looks at other problems in history (the causes of the American Revolution, the causes of World War I, the causes of the decline of the Roman Empire) he finds the same pattern of quantitative but not qualitative accumulation. This might lead him to suspect that there is something *fundamentally* wrong with the inquiry. To put it another way: if, in an infinite number of instances, the answer to a type of problem seems just as far away after a century of research as it did after a year of research, one might gently inquire: is there something wrong with our question?

I think so. To ask "what caused the Civil War?" as a general question leads us nowhere. It is meaningless because it is infinite in its meanings. It is like being given a detailed map of Europe, and being asked: What is the use of this map? Well, it has an infinite number of uses, depending on what you need to do. If you define your objective: "I need to know how to get from Rome to Utrecht," then one can show specifically how the map is useful. With no starting point, with no destination, the "meanings" of the

* See, for instance, Howard K. Beale's essay, "What Historians Have Said About the Causes of the Civil War," in *Theory and Practice in Historical Study: A Report of the Committee on Historiography,* Social Science Research Council, 1946. See also Thomas J. Pressly's book, *Americans Interpret Their Civil War,* Princeton, 1954, and *The Causes of the American Civil War,* edited by Edwin Rozwenc, D. C. Heath, 1961.

map are unlimited in number, which is close to saying the map is "meaningless."

In 1956, a session of the American Historical Association was devoted to the question: "Can Differences in Interpretations of the Causes of the American Civil War Be Resolved Objectively?" A long paper on this topic was presented by Lee Benson and Thomas J. Pressly. The authors analyzed at length five interpretations of the causes of the Civil War:

1. Charles W. Ramsdell, in "The Natural Limits of Slavery Expansion" (*Mississippi Valley Historical Review,* September 1929), argued that the war was caused by an unnecessarily heated squabble between North and South over whether the western lands acquired from the Mexican War would be slave or free. Ramsdell's argument was that slavery had pretty well reached its natural limits of both territorial expansion and profitability and would have died a natural death if hotheads north and south had not created the false issue about slavery's expansion and thus brought on the Civil War.

2. Arthur C. Cole's *The Irrepressible Conflict, 1850–1865,* Macmillan, 1934, saw the war as coming, despite the desire of moderate men representing propertied interests for stability and compromise, out of the fierce self-consciousness of two different cultures: "the slave-plantation culture of the South and the industrial and small-farm culture of the North."

3. Louis M. Hacker, *The Triumph of American Capitalism,* Simon and Schuster, 1940, ascribed the war to the need of the growing industrial capitalist class of the North for political control of the Nation (for tariffs, a bank, free land, internal improvements, railways, etc.) which the Republican victory in 1860 represented, leading to the Southern reaction of secession and war.

4. David M. Potter, *Lincoln and His Party in the Secession Crisis,* Yale University, 1942, argued that the war came despite popular sentiment for compromise in both North and South because Lincoln and the other Republican leaders did not offer a compromise, especially on the western lands, that would enable the Unionist sentiment of the South to hold off against the fire-eaters.

5. Allan Nevins, *Ordeal of the Union,* Charles Scribner's Sons,

4 vols., 1947–50, saw the war coming as a result of a failure of leadership North and South, in not really trying to find a solution for the problem of "race-adjustment" of which slavery was one aspect.

After examining these five interpretations in detail, Benson and Pressly conclude that: ". . . at present we know of no set of procedures by which the overall or total differences between the five interpretations, as they are now formulated, can be effectively resolved." However, they do find specific statements, or "sub-interpretations" which might be capable of objective resolution, that is, could be decided by empirical evidence. And so they take one such sub-interpretation, the question of agitation for the reopening of the African slave trade. They find that while Ramsdell and Hacker both agree that the Southern slave system was coming into hard times, Ramsdell thinks the movement for the reopening of the slave trade was weak, while Hacker thinks it was strong. Furthermore, they could see no way of finding "direct" evidence to support one view or the other (and indeed found none in their examination of secondary sources), but did see a possibility that if "objective indexes" could be constructed (to measure opinion for and against reopening of the trade) that might be done.

Here, after seventy-three pages of careful work, is the conclusion of Benson and Pressly:

> . . . the authors of this paper do not assume or maintain that through the use of "objective indexes" all differences between all sub-interpretations can be resolved objectively, but that method seems to us the most promising one to try; nor do the authors assume or maintain that the objective resolution of differences between sub-interpretations will necessarily lead to the objective resolution of differences between total or overall interpretations. We do not know whether differences in interpretations of the causes of the American Civil War can ever be resolved objectively, but we think that the most effective way to attempt that task is to try first to resolve the differences between sub-interpretations.

One can see why Benson and Pressly are modest in their claims. Even if one could conclude (with Ramsdell) that support for the slave trade reopening was weak and that therefore slavery could not expand in *that* direction (which in itself makes the unwarranted assumption that popular opinion is always crucial in determining what happens) where does this really leave us in deciding the larger question, when there is an infinity of other problems to consider?

The whole question of "What Caused the Civil War?" is one of those delightful academic questions which can keep generations of historians going round and round, piling up the doctoral dissertations, the books, the symposia at the American Historical Association, and 1) not reaching any clear conclusion, 2) not reaching any conclusion which would be useful in answering E. H. Carr's question "whither?" * Indeed, we may begin to suspect now that the first point is related to the second: that a question so unfocused as to make an answer impossible is also a question that is meaningless.

Five years after that symposium, Lee Benson wrote an article on "Causation and the American Civil War" [9] in which he brings the issue closer, in my opinion, to meaningful inquiry. He says that when the historian tries to find out why certain events occurred, "His ultimate goal is to uncover and illuminate the moves of human beings acting in particular situations, and, thus, help men to understand themselves." Benson has given us a present, pertinent problem. Surely, it will help decide what we must do if we understand more about what causes people to act the way they do. But that is a different kind of question from "what caused the Civil War." It is the kind of question we might address to any human event, large or small.**

Such a question, however, would have to be clearly focused. We might ask: Was Lincoln, in his actions toward the South, more

* "Good historians, I suspect, whether they think about it or not, have the future in their bones. Besides the question: Why? the historian also asks the question: Whither?" E. H. Carr, *What Is History?*, p. 143.

** For such an objective, we might learn as much from a relatively small action in the past (let us say, studying why Harry Truman decided to set up a Civil Rights Committee in 1948) as from a large action. Our tendency is to study large and glamorous historical actions, but it is our *present* concern that should be large, even if the historical event that illuminates it is small.

moved by humanitarian considerations on slavery, or by political considerations on the power of the Republican Party over a unified national state? The answer to such a question, combined with answers to similar questions addressed to other leaders in other situations, might help us assess more realistically the motives of our political leaders today. It affects our capacity to act as citizens upon our government—and the manner in which we act—if we assume our government will act on the basis of political self-interest.

There are questions about the past whose answers are useful only to the past. "Why did the Civil War come?" is such a question, because the Civil War is a unique, unrepeatable event, and to know why that particular war of 1861–65 came about is to tell us nothing useful today. The only way we can discuss *that* war is by including factors that were only operable for that time (like the question of Western expansion of slavery, the quality of soil in the cotton states, the African slave trade). But if we ask questions which are important today, then we can focus on evidence from other events, which might help us. In that case we would need to find elements in the event of the past, abstracted from the specifics of that event, which relate to our time. That is a different kind of inquiry than that engaged in by historians who ask: "What caused the Civil War?"

Benson finds that while different historians have emphasized different factors in causing the Civil War (the clash of economies, of political interests, of cultures), all have given importance to "public opinion." This, he points out, is a very complex problem. "Civil War historians must estimate the extent to which Northerners' opinions on the expansion of slavery were influenced by economic, political, moral, or other objectives." It does not take much reflection to see how this is an endless quest: Which Northerners? Which organs of public opinion? Which of their many opinions? At what exact time?, etc., etc. Yet, Benson says, this study of public opinon is "the most effective way to begin an attack upon the overall problem of Civil War causation." Imagine the strength of the less effective attacks when one considers the difficulty of estimating how much *Uncle Tom's Cabin* influenced Northern opinion as weighed against a thousand other factors?

Instead of suspecting his initial question, his basic direction,

Benson goes on and on to find more for historians to do in that same direction: "Unfortunately, at present, historians are poorly equipped to demonstrate the state of public opinion on any issue . . ." Presumably, then, the equipment must be developed. And as for the influence of literature on public opinion: ". . . no set of systematic propositions have yet been developed to define the relationships between literature and life . . ." We must begin to develop a set of "systematic propositions." The situation might seem to be rather desperate, but Benson concludes that progress might be made if we could begin to narrow the range of "potentially verifiable explanations." But, we need "more powerful conceptual and methodological tools with which to reconstruct the behavior of men in society over time."

Again, we have a quick rerun, in one article, of the historians' dispensation to start out to "help men understand themselves"—a present motive—and then to get lost in the galaxies of academic disputation, searching in vain for new methods of navigating through the universe when one does not have a destination. If our values, our concerns, our present needs do not precede our methodology, there will be only madness to our method.

The futility of much academic inquiry into "causation" is seen quite clearly by Cushing Strout: [10] "A specter haunts American historians—the concept of causality. After nearly a hundred years of passionate and dispassionate inquiry into 'the causes of the Civil War' the debate is still inconclusive." Strout points out that one can generalize about a phenomenon like voting behavior because there is recurring evidence, but not about civil wars, because there was only one. This should give a clue: that there is no point looking for the cause of a unique event—it will have a unique cause, or rather, a unique combination of causes. But if one looks for the cause of this *kind* of event, the aim being to be able to understand and act on similar events in the future, that is another matter.

However, Strout does not conclude that causal inquiry should be addressed to some pertinent problem of today. He falls back, rather, to the argument that the historian should be content with "descriptive analysis," which is closer to his traditional job of "narration," and that the historian wants "the dramatic logic" of a situation "which demands to be humanly understood rather than scientifically explained." That would be fine if by "humanly" understanding a situation Strout means learning from it in a way to aid human progress in our time.

Strout supports narration as "a form of explanation, which aims not at logical rigor of implication but at a dramatic comprehensibility, appropriate to the untidy, passionate, and value-charged activities of men." This is laudable, if then Strout would go further and suggest what passions should guide us, what values we should be charged with, and how we can use these values and those passions as guides to the narrative work we do as historians. Instead he seems to be taking part again in that empty argument between the "narrative" people and the "theory" people, which has become an argument about method, devoid of human content. Whether we have narrative or causal explanation or "descriptive analysis," our logical rigor, and factual accuracy will be wasted unless we start with a vital question.

We are more likely to find causal inquiry focused on "operable cause" in the work of political scientists than historians. This is because the artificial separation of those disciplines from one another has led to an illogical division of labor in which the political scientist is permitted to aim at policy formation, while the historian sticks to narrative or "interpretation." This deprives the political scientist of much historical evidence, and the historian of a focus. Unfortunately, the aim on which political scientists focus is too often set by the national government.*

In his article "On the Etiology of Internal Wars," [11] Harry Eckstein discusses the causes of revolution from the standpoint of doing something about them, because for political scientists, it *is* considered professionally okay to aim at policy. Thus, Eckstein describes internal wars:

> All involve the use of violence to achieve purposes which can also be achieved without violence. All indicate a breakdown of some dimension in legitimate political order . . . All tend to scar societies

* See Hans Morgenthau's sharp criticism of the profession in Monograph Six, The American Academy of Political and Social Science. *A Design for Political Science: Scope, Objectives, and Methods,* 1966.

deeply and to prevent the formation of consensus indefinitely. There is, consequently, at least a possibility that general theories about internal war may be discovered—general theories which may also help to solve problems posed by specific instances.

He notes the limitations of historical inquiry into causation, pointing out the enormous number of theories advanced to explain the causes of the French Revolution, with no conclusiveness. Nevertheless, on the basis of various comparative studies of revolution he finds that certain factors tend toward internal war in roughly this order of importance: the efficacy of elites, disorienting social processes, subversion, the facilities of the rebels. Certain factors tend toward preventing the revolution, roughly in this order of importance: effective repression, conciliation, diversion, facilities of incumbents.

One can go through those lists, and, depending on whether one is a rebel or a supporter of the incumbent regime, find those causes which are to some extent operable. I would not swear by Eckstein's list of causes; my aim in reporting them is to indicate that a causal inquiry aimed at policy is at least a start toward meaningful scholarly work.

There is one conclusion of Eckstein's which should be especially interesting for intellectuals:

> . . . revolutions are invariably preceded by the "transfer of allegiance" of a society's intellectuals and the development by them of a new political "myth." If intellectuals have any obvious social "functions" . . . they are surely these: to socialize the members of a society outside of the domestic context, in schools and adult learning situations; to reinforce and rationalize attitudes acquired in all social contexts; and to provide meaning to life and guidelines to behavior by means of conscious doctrines where events have robbed men of their less conscious bearings. Intellectuals are particularly important in the education of adolescents and young people, and it has been shown quite definitely that political socialization occurs (or fails) mainly in the years between early childhood and full maturity. It could also be shown that among revolutionaries the young tend to predominate, sometimes quite remarkably. Together these points go far to explain

why the alienation of intellectuals is, in Edwards' language, a "master-symptom" of revolution: a condition that makes revolutionary momentum irreversible.

For historians in particular, for scholars generally, this is a meaningful causal statement, because for them it is eminently operable.

It may be, as one suspects from Eckstein's language in his initial definition of "internal war," that his main concern is to prevent revolution, that he is probably more sympathetic with "legitimate political order" and "consensus" than with social change. But the factor he describes can work both ways.

So here is something for us to do: we can begin the withdrawal of allegiance from the state and its machines of war, from business and its ferocious drive for profit, from all states, all bullying authorities, all dogmas. We can begin to suggest, and to act out, alternative ways of living with one another. It is possible, barely possible, that we can be a *cause* of change, that coming generations will have a new history.

Notes

CHAPTER 2   *History as Private Enterprise*

1. Edward N. Saveth, ed., "Conceptualization of American History," *American History and the Social Sciences,* Free Press, 1964.

2. *Ibid.,* p. 8.

3. Benedetto Croce, quoted in Hans Meyerhoff, ed., *The Philosophy of History in Our Time,* Doubleday (Anchor edition), 1959.

4. James Harvey Robinson, *The New History,* Free Press (paper edition), 1965, p. 24.

5. Irwin Unger, "The 'New Left' and American History," *American Historical Review,* July 1967.

6. Morton White, *Social Thought in America,* Beacon (paper edition), 1947, pp. 227–228.

7. Clipping from New York *Graphic* in *LaGuardia Papers,* New York Public Library.

8. Barrington Moore, Jr., *Political Power and Social Theory,* Harvard University, 1958.

9. David Potter, "Explicit Data and Implicit Assumptions in Historical Study," Louis Gottschalk, ed., *Generalization in the Writing of History,* University of Chicago, 1963.

10. Arthur Mann, "The Progressive Tradition," John Higham, ed., *Reconstruction of American History,* Harper (Torchbook edition), 1962.

CHAPTER 3   *What Is Radical History?*

1. Barbara Tuchman, *The Guns of August,* Macmillan, 1962, p. 72.

2. Herbert Aptheker, *A Documentary History of the Negro People,* Citadel, 1951, p. 2.

3. New York *Daily News,* February 6, 1928.

4. Jesse Lemisch, "The American Revolution from the Bottom Up," Barton Bernstein, ed., *Towards a New Past,* Pantheon, 1968.

5. *Report of the National Advisory Commission on Civil Disorders,* Bantam, 1968, p. 483.

6. Richard Pfeffer, ed., *No More Vietnams,* Harper & Row, 1968, pp. 7, 8.

7. Marilyn Young, *The Rhetoric of Empire,* Harvard University. 1968, p. 231.

8. "Twilight of Idols," *The Seven Arts,* October 1917, reprinted in Randolph S. Bourne, *War and the Intellectuals,* Harper (Torchbook edition), 1964, p. 60.

9. Staughton Lynd, *Intellectual Origins of American Radicalism,* Pantheon, 1968, p. vi.

10. *New York Review of Books,* September 26, 1968.

11. Herbert Aptheker, *A Documentary History of the Negro People.* Citadel, 1951.

12. Robert Michels, *Political Parties,* Free Press (Collier edition), 1962, p. 154.

CHAPTER 4   Inequality

1. Jacques Barzun, *God's Country and Mine,* Little, Brown, 1954.

2. Quoted in Carl Russell Fish, *The Rise of the Common Man,* Macmillan, 1927.

3. "A True Narrative of the Late Rebellion in Virginia, by the Royal Commissioners, 1677," in Charles M. Andrews, ed., *Narratives of the Insurrections, 1675–1690,* Scribners, 1915, pp. 110–11.

4. "Thomas Mathew's Narrative," *Ibid.,* p. 24.

5. See Appendix I, in Cheesman A. Herrick, *White Servitude in Pennsylvania,* John J. McVey, 1927, p. 287.

6. See Abbot Smith, *Colonists in Bondage,* for general information on indentured servitude.

7. Elizabeth Sprigs to John Sprigs, to London from Maryland, September 22, 1756, in Isabel M. Calder, *Colonial Captivities, Marches and Journeys,* Macmillan, 1935, pp. 151–52.

8. Carl Bridenbaugh, *Cities in the Wilderness,* Ronald, 1938, p. 96.

9. *Ibid.,* pp. 96–97.

10. *Statistical Abstract of the U.S., 1969,* p. 326.

11. *Ibid.*

12. *Ibid.,* p. 329.

13. George T. Altman, "The Tax-Cut Mirage," *The Nation,* February 16, 1963.

14. *New York Times,* September 12, 1966.

15. Philip M. Stern, "The Tax Deviates," *The New Republic,* February 1, 1964.

16. John L. Hess, in *The Reporter,* April 1959.

17. See *I. F. Stone's Weekly,* December 14, 1959. Also Vol. 2 of the Tax Revision Compendium, published by the House Ways and Means Committee.

18. Oscar Gass, writing in *Commentary,* October 1965.

CHAPTER 5 The Ludlow Massacre

1. Selig Perlman and Philip Taft, *Labor Movements* (Vol. IV of *History of Labor in the United States,* edited by John R. Commons), Macmillan, 1935.

2. Colorado Fuel and Iron Corporation, *Medical and Sociological Report,* 1914.

3. *Harper's,* May 23, 1914, p. 11.

4. *The New York Times,* February 10, 1914.

5. *United Mine Workers Journal,* August 28, 1913.

6. West, *Report on the Colorado Strike,* Government Printing Office, 1915.

7. House Mines and Mining Committee, *Conditions in the Coal Mines of Colorado,* pp. 2540–63.

8. *Ibid.,* pp. 2631–34.

9. *International Socialist Review,* December 1913.

10. House Mines and Mining Committee, *Conditions in the Coal Mines of Colorado,* p. 2918.

11. *Ibid.,* p. 1659.

12. *International Socialist Review,* December 1913.

13. *The New York Times,* October 27, 1913.

14. Commission on Industrial Relations, *Report and Testimony,* p. 8607.

15. *United Mine Workers Journal,* November 1, 1913.

16. William Brewster, *Militarism in Colorado,* Denver, 1914.

17. *International Socialist Review,* March 1914.

18. Edward Boughton, *Report to the Governor,* Denver, 1914, p. 2.

19. Frank Didano, quoted in *International Socialist Review,* June 1914.

20. Godfrey Irwin, quoted in the New York *World,* April 23, 1914.

21. Commission on Industrial Relations, *Report and Testimony,* p. 7100.

22. New York *World,* April 23, 1914.

23. *The New York Times,* April 22, 1914.

24. *Ibid.*

25. *Ibid.,* April 23, 1914.

26. *Ibid.*

27. *The New York Times,* April 20, 1914.

28. *Ibid.,* April 21, 1914.

29. *Ibid.*

30. *The New York Times,* April 24, 1969.

31. *Ibid.,* April 27, 1969.

32. *International Socialist Review,* August 1914.

33. *The New York Times,* April 22, 1914.

34. *Ibid.,* April 23, 1914.

35. *Ibid.,* April 25, 1914.

36. *Ibid.,* April 28, 1914.

37. United States, *Presidents' Messages and Papers,* Government Printing Office, Supplement, 1913–17.

38. Perlman and Taft, *Labor Movements,* p. 338.

39. House Mines and Mining Committee, *Conditions in the Coal Mines of Colorado,* Vol. II, Appendix.

CHAPTER 6   LaGuardia in the Jazz Age

1. George Soule, *Prosperity Decade,* Rinehart and Co., 1947, p. 5.

2. Paul H. Douglas, *Real Wages in the United States, 1890–1926,* Kelley, 1930, p. 391.

3. Soule, *op. cit.*

4. Frederick C. Mills, *Economic Tendencies in the United States,* National Bureau of Economic Research, 1932, p. 555.

5. Robert S. and Helen M. Lynd, *Middletown, A Study in American Culture,* Harcourt, Brace, 1929, pp. 23, 53, 85.

6. Merle Curti, *The Growth of American Thought,* Harper, 1933, pp. 692–3.

7. *Congressional Record,* April 28, 1924, pp. 7391–7392.

8. *Ibid.,* May 23, 1924, pp. 9351–9352.

9. *Ibid.*

10. *Ibid.,* January 30, 1926, pp. 3052–3053.

11. *The New York Times,* September 21, 1926.

12. *Ibid.,* July 16, 1927.

13. New York *Evening Journal,* May 4, 1925.

14. Washington *News,* March 20, 1928.

15. New York *Evening Graphic,* December 2, 1925.

16. Pittsburgh *Sun Telegraph,* February 4, 1928.

17. William Allen White, *A Puritan in Babylon.*

18. Harvey O'Connor, *Mellon's Millions,* John Day, 1933, pp. xi–xv.

19. *Ibid.,* pp. 126–128.

20. LaGuardia to Miss Clara Artus, February 18, 1924, *Ogden Mills Papers,* Library of Congress.

21. *Butler Papers,* April 14, 1924, Columbia University.

22. *The New York Times,* May 31, 1924.

23. *Ibid.,* May 13, 1928.

24. *LaGuardia Papers,* New York Public Library.

25. New York *American,* January 1, 1929.

26. William A. Williams, "The Legend of Isolationism in the 1920's," *Science and Society,* Winter 1954.

27. Herbert Feis, *The Diplomacy of the Dollar, 1919–1932,* Norton (paper edition), 1966, pp. 4–25.

28. Foster Rhea Dulles, *America's Rise to World Power,* Harper, 1954, p. 134.

29. Thomas A. Bailey, *A Diplomatic History of the American People,* Appleton-Century-Crofts, 1958, p. 711.

30. Council on Foreign Relations, *Survey of American Foreign Relations, 1929,* p. 192.

31. *Relations Between the United States and Nicaragua,* Government Printing Office, 1928.

32. *LaGuardia Papers,* January 13, 1927.

33. *Ibid.*

34. *Coolidge Papers,* Library of Congress, Washington, D.C.

35. *Congressional Record,* March 23, 1928, pp. 5251–5252.

36. Henry L. Stimson, *American Policy in Nicaragua,* Scribner, 1927, pp. 116–127.

CHAPTER 7 The Limits of the New Deal

1. Richard Hofstadter, *The Age of Reform,* Knopf, 1955, p. 317.

2. Thurman Arnold, *The Symbols of Government,* Yale University, 1935, pp. 270–71.

3. Harry Hopkins, "The Future of Relief," *The New Republic,* 1937, p. 8.

4. James MacGregor Burns, *Roosevelt: The Lion and the Fox,* Harcourt, Brace & World, 1956, p. 376.

5. "Rooseveltian Liberalism," *The Nation,* June 21, 1933, pp. 702–03.

6. Joseph Ratner, ed., *Intelligence in the Modern World: John Dewey's Philosophy,* Modern Library, 1939, p. 423.

7. Reprinted in *Liberalism and Social Action,* Capricorn Books, 1963, p. 54.

8. *Ibid.,* p. 62.

9. *Ibid.,* p. 88.

10. Arthur M. Schlesinger, Jr., *The Politics of Upheaval,* Houghton Mifflin, 1960, pp. 176, 647.

11. "The Myth of the Marxian Dialectic," *Partisan Review,* 1939, pp. 66–81.

12. Reinhold Niebuhr, *Reflections on the End of an Era,* Charles Scribner's Sons, 1934, p. 158.

13. "The Age of Distribution," *The Nation,* July 25, 1934, pp. 93–96.

14. "The Future of Liberalism," *The Journal of Philosophy,* No. 9, 1935, pp. 230–47.

15. Upton Sinclair, *The Way Out,* Farrar & Rinehart, 1933, p. 57.

16. Robert MacIver, "Social Philosophy," in *Social Change and the New Deal,* ed. William F. Ogburn, University of Chicago, 1934, pp. 107–13.

17. Rexford Guy Tugwell, "The Principle of Planning and the Institution of Laissez-Faire," *American Economic Review,* Supplement, March 1932, pp. 75–92.

18. Raymond Moley, *After Seven Years,* Harper & Brothers, 1939, pp. 370–71.

19. David Lilienthal, *T.V.A.: Democracy on the March,* Pocket Books, 1944, Chapter 18, "Planning and Planners," pp. 206–13.

20. William O. Douglas, "Protecting the Investor," *The Yale Review,* Spring 1934, pp. 521–33.

21. William E. Leuchtenberg, *Franklin D. Roosevelt and the New Deal,* Harper & Row, 1963, p. 259.

22. James MacGregor Burns, *Roosevelt: The Lion and the Fox,* Harcourt, Brace & World, 1956, p. 322.

23. Max Lerner, "Propaganda's Golden Age," *The Nation,* November 11, 1939, pp. 523–24.

24. Abraham Epstein, " 'Social Security' Under the New Deal," *The Nation,* September 4, 1935, pp. 261–63.

25. Congressman Henry Ellenbogen of Pennsylvania, *Congressional Record,* August 19, 1935, pp. 13675–13677.

26. Henry E. Sigerist, "Socialized Medicine," *The Yale Review,* Spring, 1938, pp. 463–81.

CHAPTER 10   Liberalism and Racism

1. See Staughton Lynd, *Class Conflict, Slavery, and the U.S. Constitution,* Bobbs-Merrill, 1967, pp. 153–213.

2. John Hope Franklin, *From Slavery to Freedom,* Knopf, 1956, p. 153.

3. Arthur M. Schlesinger, Jr., *The Age of Jackson,* Little, Brown, 1946, p. 522.

4. rf. James MacPherson, *The Struggle for Equality,* Princeton University, 1964.

5. C. Vann Woodward, *Reunion and Reaction,* Doubleday Anchor, 1956.

6. Willie Lee Rose, *Rehearsal for Reconstruction,* Bobbs-Merrill, 1964, pp. 385–89.

7. rf. Elliot M. Rudwick, *Race Riot at East St. Louis July 2, 1917,* Southern Illinois University Press, 1964.

8. Frank Freidel, *F.D.R. and the South,* Louisiana State University, 1965, p. 73.

9. Walter White, *The Crisis,* October 1935.

CHAPTER 12   Aggressive Liberalism

1. *New York Review of Books,* March 14, 1968.

2. *Ibid.,* May 23, 1968.

3. From *Winston S. Churchill: Young Statesman 1901–1914,* edited by Randolph Churchill, quoted by D. A. N. Jones, *New York Review of Books,* May 23, 1968.

4. *American Historical Review,* July 1966.

5. Thomas A. Bailey, *A Diplomatic History of the American People,* Appleton-Century-Crofts, 1950.

6. *Ibid.*

CHAPTER 16   Hiroshima and Royan

1. Wesley Craven and James Cate, *The Army Air Forces in World War II,* Vol. III, p. 783.

2. Letter of November 9, 1967.

3. Reprinted in the Botton collection.

4. David Irving, *The Destruction of Dresden,* Holt, Rinehart & Winston, 1964, pp. 9–10.

5. Admiral Meyer, *Entre matins: Rochefort, La Rochelle, Royan* (1944–1945), published by Robert Laffont, Paris.

6. *New York Times,* April 16, 1945.

7. M. Dasseux, in the Botton collection.

8. Botton collection.

9. M. François Jean Armorin, "L'Attaque de Royan" in Botton collection.

10. Meyer, *Entre matins.*

CHAPTER 17   Freedom and Responsibility

1. Karl Popper, *The Open Society and Its Enemies,* Princeton, 1950, p. 461.

2. GWF, Hegel, *Reason in History,* Bobbs-Merrill (Library of Liberal Arts edition), 1953, p. 24.

3. Herbert Marcuse, *Reason and Revolution,* Preface to the 1960 edition, Beacon.

4. Morton White, *Foundations of Historical Knowledge,* Harper & Row, 1965, pp. 32, 33.

5. Clinton Rossiter, *Marxism: The View from America,* Harcourt, Brace (paper edition), 1960, p. 45.

6. Popper, *The Open Society and Its Enemies,* pp. 387–88.

7. Gajo Petrovic, "Histoire et Nature," *Praxis,* 1966, p. 71.

8. Friedrich Nietzsche, *The Use and Abuse of History,* Bobbs-Merrill, (Library of Liberal Arts edition), 1949.

9. Hans Reichenbach, "The Logical Foundations of Probability," in Feigl and Brodbeck, *Readings in the Philosophy of Science,* Appleton-Century-Crofts, 1953.

10. Mihailo Markovic, "Cause and Goal in History," *Praxis,* 1966.

11. Erik Erikson, *Insight and Responsibility,* Norton, 1964, p. 162.

12. Hannah Arendt, *Eichmann in Jerusalem,* Viking, 1963.

13. Erik Erikson, "Psychological Reality and Historical Actuality," in *Insight and Responsibility,* Norton, 1964, pp. 167–168.

14. George Kennan, *American Diplomacy,* New American Library (Mentor edition), 1962.

CHAPTER 18   *The Historians*

1. Alfred North Whitehead, *The Aims of Education,* Mentor edition, 1956, p. 14.

2. Carl Becker, "What Are the Historical Facts," *The Western Political Quarterly,* September 1955. Quoted in Hans Meyerhoff, ed., *The Philosophy of History in Our Time,* Doubleday (Anchor edition), 1959, pp. 136–37.

3. Francis Bacon, *Advancement of Learning,* Oxford, 1900, Book I, Chapter V.

4. John Higham, "Theory," Higham, ed., *History,* Prentice-Hall, 1965.

5. *Ibid.,* p. 133.

6. *Ibid.,* p. 134.

7. *Ibid.,* p. 135.

8. *Ibid.,* p. 136.

9. Thomas F. Gossett, *Race: the History of an Idea in America,* Southern Methodist University, 1963, p. viii.

10. John Higham, *History,* p. 136.

11. *Ibid.,* p. 143.

12. *Ibid.,* pp. 143–44.

13. *Tri Quarterly,* Northwestern University, 1967.

14. Benjamin Farrington, "The Refutation of Philosophers," *The Philosophy of Francis Bacon,* Liverpool University, 1964, p. 127.

15. J. D. Hexter, "The Rhetoric of History," *History and Theory,* Vol. VI, No. 1, 1967.

16. *New York Review of Books,* February 9, 1967.

17. Quoted in Richard Schlatter, "The Puritan Strain," John Higham, ed., *The Reconstruction of American History,* Harper (Torchbook edition), 1962.

18. Ernest May, "America As a World Power," *ibid.,* p. 183.

19. Kenneth Murdock, *Literature and Theology in Colonial New England,* quoted in Richard Schlatter, "The Puritan Strain," *ibid.*

20. *Ibid.*

21. Arthur S. Goldburg, "Discerning a Causal Pattern Among Data on Voting Behavior," *American Political Science Review,* December 1966.

22. Gerhard Ritter, "Scientific History, Contemporary History, and Political Science," *History and Theory,* Vol. I, 1961, pp. 261–79.

23. *Ibid.*

24. *Ibid.*

25. *History and Theory,* Vol. IV, 1964, pp. 27–56.

26. *Ibid.*

27. *World Politics,* April 1950.

28. Burleigh Wilkins, reviewing Lee Benson's *Turner and Beard: American Historical Writing Reconsidered, History and Theory,* Vol. III, 1963, p. 261.

29. Page Smith, *The Historian and History,* Knopf, 1960, p. 197.

30. Othmar F. Anderle, "A Plea for Theoretical History," *History and Theory,* Vol. IV, 1964.

31. *Social Sciences in Historical Studies,* Social Science Research Council, 1954.

32. Staughton Lynd, *Class Conflict, Slavery, and the U.S. Constitution,* Bobbs-Merrill, 1967, p. 20.

33. Report of the Committee on Historical Analysis, Social Science Research Council, University of Chicago, 1963.

34. Louis Gottschalk, ed., *Generalization in the Writing of History,* University of Chicago, 1963, pp. v–vi.

35. *Ibid.,* p. ix.

36. *Ibid.,* p. 124.

37. *Ibid.,* p. 208.

38. rf. Gottschalk, "Causes of Revolution," *American Journal of Sociology,* 1944.

39. Chester G. Starr, "Reflections upon the Problem of Generalizations," Gottschalk, ed., *Generalization in the Writing of History.*

40. *Ibid.*

41. M. I. Finley, "Generalization in Ancient History," *ibid.*

42. Robert R. Palmer, "Generalization About Revolution: A Case Study," *ibid.*

43. David Potter, "Explicit Data and Implicit Assumptions," *ibid.*

CHAPTER 19   The Philosophers

1. Tolstoy, *War and Peace,* Epilogue.

2. Ernest Nagel, *The Structure of Science,* Harcourt, Brace & World, 1961, p. 13.

3. Pierre Duhem, *The Aim and Structure of Physical Theory* (a section of which is reprinted in Danto and Morgenbesser's *Philosophy of Science,* Meridian, 1960).

4. Marx Wartofsky, *Conceptual Foundations of Scientific Thought,* Macmillan, 1968, p. 24.

5. Marvin Levich, reviewing Sidney Hook, ed., *Philosophy and History* in *History and Theory,* Vol. IV, No. 3, 1965.

6. William Dray, " 'Explaining What' in History," in *Theories of History,* edited by Patrick Gardiner, Free Press, 1959.

7. Dray, "The Historical Explanation of Actions Reconsidered" in Hook, ed., *Philosophy and History,* New York University, 1963.

8. Dray, *Laws and Explanation in History,* Oxford University, 1957, pp. 47–48.

9. *Ibid.,* p. 50.

10. Maurice Mandelbaum, "Historical Explanation: The Problem of 'Covering Laws,'" *History and Theory,* Vol. I, 1961, pp. 229–42.

11. Mandelbaum, "Societal Facts," an article from *British Journal of Sociology,* 1955, reprinted in Gardiner, ed., *Theories of History.*

12. Alan Donagan, "Historical Explanation: The Popper-Hempel Theory Reconsidered," in *History and Theory,* Vol. 4, 1964, p. 326.

13. R. G. Collingwood, *The Idea of History,* Oxford University, 1956 (paper edition), p. 303.

14. *Ibid.,* p. 10.

15. Nietzsche, *The Use and Abuse of History,* Liberal Arts Press, 1957 (paper edition), p. 58.

16. Collingwood, *The Idea of History.*

17. *Ibid.,* pp. 214–15.

18. W. H. Walsh, "Meaning in History" in Gardiner, *Theories of History.*

19. W. H. Walsh, *Philosophy of History,* Harper Torchbook, 1960, pp. 59–64.

20. *Ibid.,* p. 40.

21. *Ibid.,* pp. 110–11.

22. *Ibid.,* p. 118.

23. Ernest Nagel, "Some Issues in the Logic of Historical Analysis," *Scientific Monthly,* 1952, reprinted in Gardiner, *Theories of History.*

24. Morton White, *The Foundations of Historical Knowledge,* Harper & Row, 1965.

25. Peter Caws, *Science and the Theory of Value,* Random House (paper edition), 1967, p. 6.

26. *Ibid.,* p. 8.

27. *Selected Correspondence of Marx and Engels,* September 21–22, 1890, Foreign Language Publishing House, Moscow, 1955, p. 417.

28. Arthur Mann, "The Progressive Tradition" in Higham, ed., *The Reconstruction of American History,* Harper (Torchbook edition), 1962.

29. Morton White, *The Foundations of Historical Knowledge,* p. 42.

30. *Ibid.,* p. 194.

31. Robert McShea, *The Political Theory of Spinoza,* Columbia University, 1968, p. 53.

32. Quoted by Hayden White, "The Burden of History," *History and Theory,* Vol. V, 1966, pp. 111–34.

CHAPTER 20 *Philosophers, Historians, and Causation*

1. Morton White, *The Foundations of Historical Knowledge,* Harper & Row, 1965, p. 107.

2. *Report of the National Advisory Commission on Civil Disorders,* Bantam edition, 1968, p. 113.

3. *Ibid.,* p. 117.

4. Quoted in *Newsweek,* August 14, 1967.

5. Morton White, *The Foundations of Historical Knowledge,* p. 181.

6. David Potter, "Explicit Data and Implicit Assumptions," Gottschalk, ed., *Generalization in the Writing of History,* University of Chicago, 1963.

7. *Ibid.,* p. 194.

8. E. H. Carr, *What Is History?,* Knopf, 1962, p. 140.

9. Lee Benson, "Causation and the Civil War," *History and Theory,* Vol. I, 1961, pp. 163–85.

10. Cushing Strout, "Causation and the American Civil War," *History and Theory,* Vol. I, 1961, pp. 163–85.

11. Harry Eckstein, "On the Etiology of Internal Wars," *History and Theory,* Vol. IV, 1965, pp. 133–63.

Index